UNDERSTANDING DANCE

UNDERSTANDING DANCE

Graham McFee

ROUTLEDGE

London and New York

First published 1992
by Routledge
11 New Fetter Lane, London EC4P 4EE

Simultaneously published in the USA and Canada
by Routledge
a division of Routledge, Chapman and Hall, Inc.
29 West 35th Street, New York, NY 10001

Typeset in 10/12 Palatino by
Mathematical Composition Setters Ltd, Wiltshire
Printed and bound in Great Britain by
Biddles Ltd, Guildford.

British Library Cataloguing in Publication Data
McFee, Graham
Understanding dance.
I. Title
793.301

Library of Congress Cataloging in Publication Data
A catalog record for this book is
available on request

ISBN 0–415–07809–1
ISBN 0–415–07810–5 (paper)

Contents

CONTENTS

CONTENTS

Introduction

Dance is an art form which has a powerful impact and a deep importance for me. Such great enthusiasm for dance – indeed, for the arts
more generally – generates the central problem of this book: in what
ways is dance *valuable*? How do the arts contribute to human life? Committed to the value of dance, either from personal feelings or professional obligations (say, as student), one must seek to *understand* that
value. This book was written to fill such a need within dance studies,
especially for those working at an introductory level, but it does not tell
the reader how to understand dance, or what to look for in dances. Still
less does it set up criteria by which dances can be understood or valued.
It is an investigation of the understanding of dance; it describes and discusses *what it is* to understand dance, the nature of that understanding
of dance. The tools used to investigate the understanding of dance are
drawn from philosophy. My belief in the need for such a text is based
on a number of assumptions, which this book aims to make good. The
most fundamental of these are, first, the importance (as a topic for
study) of the understanding of dance, and, second, the need for rigour
in dance studies. Both require further elaboration, given later in this
Introduction.

As a contribution to the philosophical discussion of dance, this book
concerns aesthetic judgements that are made about dances. In this
context the word 'aesthetic' has two distinct uses. *Aesthetics* is a branch
of philosophy concerned with the analysis of reasoning about art, about
criticism and the like.[1] But one of its topics is those judgements we
make when we appreciate the grace, line, elegance, beauty and so on
(or the opposite) of an object or event: aesthetic judgements. So the
topic of this book is reflection (in aesthetics) on aesthetic judgements
made about dance. Hence it concentrates on those forms of dance
which are (also) art forms. The arguments apply to all dance forms for
which this is true, although the examples here are from classical ballet
and modern dance. And the use of the word 'judgement' does not
require that dances are appraised, judged or evaluated. Rather, the
word judgement is just intended as a general term for all the comments, remarks and so on that are made about dances, some of which
will involve gesture as well as words, and only a few of which will be
judgemental or evaluative.

1

The project

The text is in five parts. Part One (comprising Chapter 1) introduces three key ideas of philosophical aesthetics: the role of definition; the question of the subjectivity of judgements of dance; the distinction between artistic and aesthetic judgement. Discussion of these concepts provides some grounding in philosophical enquiry.

The introduction to the theory of understanding, in Part Two, has the form of answering four questions about the nature of dance. Chapter 2 urges that, in order to be understood, dance must be seen as *human action*: that what marks out an activity as dance (rather than, say, gymnastics) is the context within which it is performed. The focus is on how to understand behaviour as human activity, and hence as dance. Since our concern is with dance as an art form, Chapter 3 addresses the nature of art. It presents a broadly institutional account of art, and (partially) defends it. This chapter also includes some (difficult) asides on general aesthetic or philosophical matters. Chapter 4 focuses on a key fact about performing arts such as dance: that they are both transitory (because one can only confront them *while* they are being performed) and yet permanent, since the same dance (for example *Swan Lake*) can be performed on numerous occasions. Chapter 5 explores the idea that dance is a fit object of understanding by considering the extent to which it is possible to see understanding dance as *like* understanding language. This account depends on Ludwig Wittgenstein's insight into the nature of understanding:[2] that one's understanding of something appears in the *explanations* of that 'something' one would give (in appropriate contexts), together with those one would accept if someone else gave them. This idea, first introduced in Chapter 5, is expanded, applied to dance, and its implications explored in Chapters 6 and 7. These chapters present a picture of dance criticism which locates a central role for such criticism by stressing the connection between *understanding dance* and *explaining (the meaning of) dances*. This leads directly into the heart of the book, Part Three.

The central idea of the book is the theory of the understanding of dance. In a sense, Part Three is the most important section, and the others are designed to introduce it and to expand its conclusions. Making the theory of understanding the centre of our account of dance presents dance criticism as crucial rather than peripheral to the study of dance; and that means both one's own criticism and the criticism of experts, such as Marcia Siegel. But it does so by showing the criticism as internally related to the dance itself. Such a theory therefore offers a reorientation of dance studies away from the dancer and towards the dance. But the value or importance of dance, and hence the justification for engaging in dance study, might still remain unclear. Certainly that whole matter of the financial value of art works is not the issue. But the exact nature of artistic value is problematic. This is of special importance for those with an interest in the use of dance in (formal) education. So Part Three concludes, in Chapter 8, with a consideration of the connection between art (especially dance) and the rest of our lives.

Part Four discusses four concepts which might, with justice, be thought to have a key role in the analysis of dance: these are *style* (Chapter 9, where its connection with technique is discussed); *imagination* and (choreographer's) *intention*, explored in Chapters 10 and 11 respectively; and *expression*, considered in Chapter 12. Such discussions fill out the central analysis, as well as providing a polemic against certain misconceptions. In Part Five the theory thus far is applied to the concept of dance education (Chapter 13 and Conclusion) and to the connection between understanding art (especially dance) and understanding society (Chapter 14); and its implications explored by considering widespread misconceptions concerning aesthetic education (Chapter 13).

Style, structure and audience

The audience for this book is anyone with an interest in the understanding of dance, and in the understanding of philosophical questions thereby generated. Though it should include art critics, philosophers, art historians, art theorists and so on, the primary category here, as identified earlier, must be students of the aesthetics of dance. Their needs modify the book in five important ways.

- First, the philosophical complexity is kept to an absolute minimum. Yet one cannot reduce that level of complexity too far, or one ceases to do philosophy at all (see Rhees, 1969: pp. 169–72), so a balance is struck between simplification and the demands of philosophical rigour.
- Second, there is a certain amount of repetition. This illustrates the interconnectedness of issues, and I have endeavoured to flag it whenever it occurs. The repetitions also mean that one can, to some extent, dip into and out of the work, and hence use it as a textbook, to raise questions, rather than simply reading it from cover to cover.
- Third, and relatedly, although it offers answers to many questions concerned with the nature of the understanding of dance, the questions asked are more important than the answers given. The aim of

the book is that those questions be raised as clearly as possible; others may then offer different answers if the ones found here are not convincing.

- Fourth, I have given a great deal of time to the exposition of views that, I argue, are false. If we are not clear what they amount to, we can neither judge their worth nor attack them with confidence. The reader must, therefore, be alert to the difference between the exposition of views I reject, and the presentation of my own position. But anyone who considers whole chapters cannot fail to do this.

- Fifth, quotations are kept to a minimum in the text, especially early on. This results in a larger number of references than stylistic considerations would lead one to prefer. These, and the notes, provide places where fuller arguments on key topics can be found (the notes in particular introduce peripheral and/or more complex issues). Finally, each chapter ends with a list of recommended reading.

Certainly the chapters are not all of equal complexity, or of equal centrality to the general picture of dance. For example, giving up the institutional account of art described in Chapter 3 would not require giving up the account of criticism in Chapter 6. But the picture is cumulative. Readers who fail to follow one passage may well benefit from reading on. Summaries of arguments are frequent. In the end a full understanding is possible only by tackling *all* of the book.

The examples throughout the book are just that, examples. As such, they betray *my* prejudices as to appropriate objects for aesthetic consideration. These have a tendency towards the abstract, or the 'minimal': that is to say, against the romantic, sentimental and so on. But such examples do not record commitments of mine in any philosophically interesting sense. Rather, they represent examples which I find plausible, and other examples might easily be supplied if mine seem unconvincing to the reader. I have largely chosen to comment on dances I have seen, although I have not hesitated to allow film and television to refresh my memory. My selection has also been influenced by the availability of an appropriate critical literature, since this opens the discussions to those who have not seen the works themselves. In fact, I have been guided throughout by two thoughts about evidence for my claims about dance: (a) that I should depend, as far as possible, on my own experiences and reactions to dances; (b) that I should depend on critical writings which made sense to me, which made sense of my experience – again, as far as possible. This partly explains the preponderance of quotations from the writings of Marcia Siegel, who is not merely a major contemporary dance critic (and hence provides a good

4

example of dance criticism), but whose views strike a sympathetic chord with my experiences of all those dances that I have seen and about which she has also written. Yet the *kinds* of point I find in her work could also be located in other major dance critics and writers on dance: for example, Arlene Croce or Don McDonagh.

The next three sections provide more about the assumptions on which this work is based.

Autonomy for dance studies?

As noted initially, my belief in the aesthetics of dance as a contribution to dance studies is founded on a view of the importance of the understanding of dance as a topic of study. My quest for such understanding is constrained by two fundamental principles (see Baker, 1977: p. 24). The first is the autonomy of aesthetic enquiry: that the concepts and statements used in our discussion of the arts are not logically equivalent[3] to any non-artistic concepts or statements. Without such an assumption, aesthetic enquiry is simply subsumed within (reduced to) some *other* enquiry, whether of the biology of dancers, or the economics of arts activity, or the sociology of the 'consumption' of dances, or some such. By the end of the text, a guarded justification of this principle should be possible.

The second principle is the reality of aesthetic enquiry: that it is possible to give genuine explanations of the concepts and statements used in discussion of (in our case) dance. This principle provides a practical justification for our study, for it implies that the key terms used in discussion of dance stand (in that context) for 'something extraordinary' (Baker, 1977: p. 24). That is to say, without these concepts we cannot understand what is going on in dance – that using other concepts would, in some sense, be missing the point. Again, by the end, some reason for commitment to this principle should be clear.

For the moment, I simply state both principles as being required if the aesthetics of dance is to progress. Certainly if our understanding of dance works were necessarily mysterious or ineffable (if the second principle were denied), we could have no dance *study* worthy of the name. To deny the first principle may be to guarantee the possibility of study at the expense of its being the study *of dance*. To illustrate such a point, Richard Wollheim recounted a comedy act which opened with a man walking around in a pool of light cast by a street lamp. The protagonist was then joined by a stranger who asked him what he was doing. Told that he was looking for a coin, the stranger agreed to help, and both walked around in the pool of light, looking down. Eventually, having found nothing, the stranger asked the protagonist if he were *sure* that this was where the coin was lost. 'Oh, no', the protagonist replied, pointing into the surrounding darkness, 'I lost the coin way over there, but I am searching here because this is where the light is'. The danger for dance studies – and other investigations too – is exactly that: of looking where the light is, rather than attending to what one really wanted to investigate.

Moreover, the task is 'the increase of understanding, not of knowledge; the generation of new insight, not the discovery of new facts' (Baker, 1977: p. 24). This might be expected, for the investigation concerns the concepts used in understanding dance. That is not to say that nothing can be changed, for insight into understanding dance may modify (as well as clarify) what is done by way of dance criticism, dance appreciation – or even dance making!

Rigour

The need for rigour, for a rigorous philosophical investigation, was another of the key assumptions identified initially. Four related ideas are at work here. First, the method of the book is philosophical; second, it aims to prove its claims; third, it aims at truth – although this point is not obvious; finally, its method of enquiry is argument. All of these need amplification, so let us take the last two in reverse order. When we think about dance, very often the method of enquiry simply involves protagonists stating their opinions, views, or (worse) their feelings. To do any of these things is to talk about oneself, not about the dance: this procedure will not advance the cause of knowledge. In whatever way we motivate for ourselves a difficulty we wish to consider (and in the aesthetics of dance we will often do this by appeal to our feelings or reactions), our method of dealing with those difficulties can only be a rational one. The British philosopher McTaggart (1934: p. 15) puts this point with great force and clarity:

> I don't think it's any good appealing . . . to the heart on questions of truth. After all, there is only one way of getting at the truth and that is by proving it. All that talk about the heart only comes to saying "It must be true because we want it to be". Which is both false and rather cowardly.

In the book I have endeavoured to stick to McTaggart's high standards

6

as closely as possible, and at least to give reasons to *suggest* any claims that I cannot prove.

We seek truths; this is worth saying only because it has often been denied. There is a chorus of those who think that in respect of dance (or the arts more generally) one can only have opinions, or views, or claims, and never truth. I have no truck with such subjectivism. This book is written as an attack on that view, not least because such a view denigrates the role of art. If all opinions are of equal worth, then none are worth much. One would not expect to claim that any opinion in physics is as good as any other.

I conclude, therefore, that our dance study must involve learning about proof and about philosophy, *as well as* about the aesthetics of dance. Indeed, this is as much a book about philosophy for those with an interest in dance as it is a book about dance for those with an interest in philosophy. Throughout, attention is given to the nature of argument: in particular, to an understanding of rigour in argument. But when we think about *rigour* in argument, we will typically have to recognize that to be rigorous will be to go fairly slowly. However, this is worthwhile if it helps us understand (and implement) such rigour in our own arguments. The focus on rigour means that throughout, and especially initially, where these ideas are being introduced, space is given to laying out arguments, and considering possible lines of counter-argument. Of course, this procedure is useful in itself, for it takes us towards a revised position. But it is sometimes undertaken to allow the reader insight into argumentative structures.

Throughout, it is acknowledged that arguments are required for one's claims, and that, once an argument is in place, it must be met by those who wish to deny its conclusions. Further, that finding one's opponent's *arguments* insubstantial does not of itself prove the opponent wrong. Conclusions might be right, even if the arguments for them are not sound – although, in the absence of a good argument, we will have no reason to accept any conclusion. Thus some attention must be paid to the plausibility of conclusions as well as to the soundness of arguments. These comments on the space taken for rigorous argumentation (especially for teaching it) have particular application if one looks at the great deal of time spent in this text working through the complexities of arguments, response, counter-response and rebuttal which are characteristic of philosophy. Of course, its outcomes about dance are of importance, but so are these insights into philosophical technique. This work is conceived of as centrally the kind of book which could profitably be worked through by students, not (just) for its *bon mots*, but for a sustained and rigorous discussion, with a clean line of argument.

7

Philosophy

One central misconception about the nature of philosophy is implicit in a request regularly made to those with a training in academic philosophy: the request that we clarify the terms used by practitioners in a certain field. Or, more generally, that those with philosophical training produce a dictionary or a lexicon of the correct ways of talking about – in our case – dance. Worse still is the thought that philosophy is 'just about words'. The motivation behind this request lies in a desire to avoid unclarity and confusion by speaking in a way which doesn't invite unclarities and confusions. This is, of course, a respectable enough desire in itself, but becomes problematic when we ask ourselves where the unclarity and confusion typically lie. A group of American writers in the 1960s claimed 'the terms of ordinary language are notoriously ambiguous and vague' (Feigl and Maxwell; see Bouwsma, 1965: pp. 203–9). If you believed that, you'd be inclined to locate the unclarity or confusion within language as such, and think that somehow a tidying-up of language was what was required. And indeed words are important, for using one particular word instead of another brings with it consequences: as when we described a death as murder rather than manslaughter. Moreover, there are places where such a tidying-up might be advantageous (examples later); and finally, people do often speak as though key problems for, for example, discussions of dance involved confusions about the meanings of terms – confusions based on ambiguity or vagueness.

One can easily see how this works by considering a straightforward case of an ambiguous word. If I say that I am going to the bank, you may be puzzled as to whether I'm going to collect some cash or stand by the river. Theorists of a certain kind claim that what is required here is *disambiguation*: that is to say, tidying up, so that we use the word 'bank' only for one thing, and invent another word for the other. Such a proposal does have some appeal in respect of dance, as of physical education. Indeed, one way of treating many of the discussions in David Best's excellent book *Philosophy and Human Movement* (1978a) is to see it as offering a set of verbal suggestions. For example, for so-called 'non-verbal communication', Best proposes that we cease to use the word 'communication' in those cases where we have what he calls 'percomm', reserving the word 'communication' for the cases he calls 'lingcomm' (Best, 1978a: pp. 138–9). The most important feature here is not whether communication is verbal or non-verbal but whether it is of a 'lingcomm' sort (which may be verbal or non-verbal) or of a 'percomm' sort (and hence not really *communication* at all: see Chapter 12 for

8

clarification). These can sound, then, like verbal recommendations about distinctions we should draw, or clarifications of distinctions we do draw.

Some people, even some professionals, view the task of philosophy in this way. This so-called 'under-labourer' conception of philosophy was very popular in the 1950s, particularly in the philosophy of education (see, for example, Hirst and Peters, 1970: pp. 2–4). The idea was that philosophy somehow tidied up conceptual tools. And if one's job turned on the tidying-up of things conceptual, then one could finish this task, have plenty of clean sharp tools for the investigation or analysis of whatever one wished to examine: to do so would generate some kind of perfect lexicon.

This way of conceiving of philosophy and (associatedly) of understanding and language, is entirely mistaken (Winch, 1958: pp. 3–15). Of course philosophy can and does offer conceptual clarification. But only very infrequently should this be thought of as offering recommendations about how words should be used or clarifications about how they are used. So we should see, for example, David Best's remarks about non-verbal communication not as a suggestion to use certain words, but rather as the requirement that we mark certain distinctions – with the rather surprising rider that we can mark those distinctions in whatever words we like.

That remark sounds unduly paradoxical. The point is not that words don't matter, but that words are often far less confusing than they are supposed to be – once, that is, we consider them in the appropriate context. Utterances typically function as answers to questions, questions arising in the context of a particular debate or discussion. If I ask how long a certain table is, and you reply 'about three feet', your answer (considered in the abstract) may seem ambiguous or vague. It might seem that you should be more precise – '3.1265 feet'. But the standard by which we decide what is a complete, adequate or satisfactory answer to such questions cannot be a standard 'from the outside', or 'in the abstract', but arises from our context. So that if the issue is whether the table will fit though a 3'6" doorway, then the answer 'about 3 feet' is a perfectly adequate answer. And then introducing a string of decimal places is at the least silly, and at the worst positively wrong.

That example shows that *what* we mean *when*, in asking a certain question or giving a certain answer or making a certain utterance, is not something that depends on the words only; and since it doesn't depend on the words only, no lexicon can straighten it out for us, unless that lexicon specified not only words but also contexts. As our contexts

change, this becomes increasingly important, and increasingly impossible. Such examples illustrate the impossibility of making a philosophical lexicon. For, approaching groups of distinctions, one finds
them marked in the same words or in different words. But it is the distinctions alone that matter. An example fairly close to home: a typical
reaction of a group of students asked to distinguish between sport and
physical education and recreation is to huddle in three groups, one
trying to sort out physical education, or worse, to define the term
'physical education'; another trying to do the same thing for 'sport' and
a third trying to do it for 'recreation'. They are importing the assumption that these words have some kind of fixed meaning – either now,
or in the future – which is discoverable. The contrary view that I am
offering is that the issues should be 'What's the difference between
physical education and recreation?', 'What's the difference between
sport and physical education?', and so on (and probably we should say
'differences'). And that what we say about physical education, distinguishing it from recreation, might have little or nothing to do with what
we say about physical education when distinguishing it from sport.

Where does this leave us? It is important to emphasize that we are still
seeking clarity. We are still trying to make speakers aware of what they
are saying, what they are implying, and so forth. But we will not adopt
a lexicon-style approach. It obviously is not true that one can mean just
what one likes by a string of words, but equally the distinctions one
draws in a particular discussion or a particular debate can be clear to
one's audience, even though in some different context those very same
forms of words would be unclear. For example, when I speak to a group
of students about dance, the context of our discussion means that I do
not have to begin by saying what dance is, except perhaps very broadly.
We know what we mean by the term 'dance' – we know the kind of
dance it is, we know the kinds of things which, though also dance,
don't concern us, and no doubt we know that one or two borderline
cases sometimes provide interesting discussion. With a quite different
audience I might have to spend more time on this topic, but I only
spend as much time as is needed. If I speak at the Royal Ballet School
I may have to say that I mean more than just ballet, as they conceive
it, but I don't have to elaborate a great deal. The whole idea is to answer
the perplexity or puzzlement that one's audience has over the issue,
rather than trying to find some mythical 'right answer' to, for example,
what dance is.

So, the business of philosophy *is* clarity: but one should not confuse
the *appearance* of clarity with the real thing. And looking for clarification
is accepting the power of philosophy, and hence the need for rigour!

Notice how an investigation of this sort will be, as we might say, a *second order* investigation: it will begin from the kinds of remarks (often in dance criticism) in which the understanding of dance is manifest. Such remarks are its primary topic (Baker, 1986: pp. 52–5). That explains why this book will not tell us how to understand dance. Rather, on the basis that dance is understood, it will try to articulate that understanding. As such, it will tend to 'leave everything as it is' (Wittgenstein, 1953: Section 124; Baker and Hacker, 1980: pp. 478–9). The aim then is, by and large, that while the judgements we make of particular dances may remain as they were, our understanding of them (and hence our self-understanding) is modified. Again, if this investigation is to have any outcomes, we cannot expect this 'neutral' conception to work at every point. Rather, some judgements will be revised in the light of our investigations. Or, anyway, the basis on which we make those judgements will be modified.

Acknowledgements

This text is the result of many years of thinking about the nature of dance, and of teaching the aesthetics of dance. My first lectures, and some of my earliest writings, prefigure topics and treatments here. Inevitably, such a long duration has built up too many intellectual debts to repay them all in detail here, especially to generations of students and colleagues and to those who have commented on my work at conferences and the like. I hope all those in this category are aware of my sincere gratitude.

The major debts to my friends are as follows: to Gordon Baker, for encouragement, and help with Wittgenstein and more generally; to David Carr, for help 'in the Large and in the Small' and especially for those of his suggestions which have made the text less labyrinthine; to Terry Diffey, for his vigorous support in this and other endeavours; to Bob Goldman, for stimulating discussions over the years of development of this material; to my wife, Myrene McFee, for (in addition to the usual and expected forbearance with the writer) typing the many drafts of this text, and for interventions at every level in its composition. Few (if any) of the pages have not benefited from the exercise of her lively intelligence; to Richard Wollheim, as friend, supporter, sometime supervisor and stalking-horse.

I should also like to thank the Editorial Director for Social Sciences of HarperCollinsAcademic, Sarah Dann, for her support and guidance, and the staff at Routledge for continuing that support.

Some of the material here has been previously published, although it has all been redrafted for this presentation. I thank the editors and publishers for permission to re-use the material which first appeared in their publications, as follows: in Chapter 3 'Wollheim and the Institutional Theory of Art', *The Philosophical Quarterly*, vol. 35, no. 139 (April 1985) pp. 179–85; in Chapter 4 'Dance is a Performing Art' in R. Woodfield (ed.), *Proceedings of the XIth International Conference, Nottingham 1988*, Nottingham Polytechnic Press (1990) pp. 131–5; in Chapter 6 'Criticism and Perception', *British Journal of Aesthetics*, vol. 26, no. 1 (Winter 1986) pp. 26–38; in Chapter 7 'Criticism and the Understanding of Dance', in *Dance: the Study of Dance and the Place of Dance in Society* (Proceedings of the VIII Commonwealth and International Conference on Sport, P.E., Dance, Recreation and Health) E. & F.N. Spon (1986) pp. 271–86; in Chapter 8 'Art, Education and Life-Issues', *Journal of Aesthetic Education*, vol. 22, no. 3 (Fall 1988) pp. 37–48; in Chapter 9 'Daughter of "Understanding Dance"', *Carnegie Research Papers* (1981) pp. 13–20; in Chapter 12 'Expression in Dance', *Laban Centre Working Papers in Dance Studies*, vol. 2 (1989) pp. 44–64; in Chapter 13: 'On the Very Idea of a Kinaesthetic Sense', *Southern Dance Teachers Association Magazine* (1983) pp. 20–31.

Recommended reading

The best brief introduction to general ideas in aesthetics is Ground, 1989. Also of key relevance throughout this text are the books of David Best (Best 1974; Best, 1978a; Best 1985). The only sustained philosophical contribution to dance studies is Sparshott, 1988; but that is a difficult text. Brief introductions to philosophy more generally are Nagel, 1987; and Danto, 1968. Although the second is by a famous aesthetician, neither has explicit discussion of art.

PART I

Groundwork

1
Basic Concepts for Aesthetics

As stated in the introduction, the topic of this book is the aesthetics of dance, and particularly our understanding of the idea of understanding dance. But it is not exclusively about dance. First, throughout the work examples from the other arts are used to make clearer how certain points apply to dance: that is to say, parallels with the other arts offer clarity. But second, general philosophical points are presupposed. In this chapter I shall provide some argument and some elucidation of three such points, as follows:

- the demand for 'definiteness' – in particular, for a definition of, for example, 'dance' – is to be rejected. It is neither helpful nor possible.
- judgements of art – in our case, of dance – are not bound to be subjective judgements. That is to say, it is a mistake to regard such judgements as necessarily subjective. A proper understanding of objectivity makes it plain that, in any interesting sense, such aesthetic judgements can be perfectly objective, at least if they are 'done' properly.
- there is an important distinction to be drawn between the judgements that we make about works of art – what might be called 'artistic judgement and appreciation' – and the other aesthetic judgements that we make, for example those of natural beauty, graceful movement, elegance in man-made devices and so on. This distinction between what has been called artistic judgement and (merely) aesthetic judgement (Best, 1978a, pp. 113–16; Best, 1985, pp. 153–8) is fundamental because our interest in understanding dance lies in understanding dance *viewed as art*: that is, in the making of artistic judgements of dance.

Anyone who is happy to accept these three points or, better, who is familiar with the philosophical arguments which support them, can pursue the dance interest by turning to Chapter 2. For the rest, my aim lies in giving at least some reason for believing each of these three claims.

Definition and 'definiteness'

Faced with questions about the nature of dance and about the nature of our understanding of dance, many writers – especially students – often begin their efforts by attempting to define key terms. So they search set texts for accounts of what dance is, or what understanding is. Again, a typical response to the question 'What is the difference between dance and gymnastics?' would have one group of people trying to say what dance was/is, another trying to sort out gymnastics in the same way – the thought being that putting together these accounts would answer the question. Both of these procedures are based on two assumptions: first, that definitions of such terms are possible; second, that these definitions are helpful – that having a definition of a term shows that you understand that term and, more importantly, that *not* having the definition implies that you do not understand. I shall urge that both of these assumptions are unjustified.

In the sections below I shall explain three points against the need for and possibility of definitions, and produce an argument for them. First, though, it is useful to say something about what a definition is, for the word 'definition' is used in English in a number of different ways. What I shall mean here by a definition of a particular term is an explanation which has 'exact fit' on that term. Moreover, it must be something fairly brief. So one might say that a definition is a concise yet comprehensive characterization of a term, having an exact fit on that term. To explain with a simple example, consider the term 'triangle'. A triangle is (i) a plane figure, (ii) with three straight sides, and (iii) completely bounded by those sides. This explanation, in terms of conditions i, ii and iii, has an exact fit on the notion 'triangle'. We can see this by noting two things. First, anything which fulfils these three conditions is bound to be a triangle. We might say that these three conditions combined are sufficient to guarantee that any figure which satisfies them will be a triangle. And no more conditions are necessary. Suppose we add a fourth condition: (iv) has three sides of equal length. Now, anything which satisfies all four conditions will be an equilateral triangle. So adding the fourth condition means our explanation no longer has exact fit on 'triangle' – for some triangles will then be excluded – for example, right-angle triangles. Second, any figure which fails to fulfil any one of the conditions (i), (ii) and (iii) is not a triangle. For example, a figure which satisfied (i) and (iii) but not (ii) might be a square or a rectangle or a pentagon. Or, a figure which satisfied (i) and (ii) but not (iii) might be some sort of open box shape, for example. So we might say that each of the three conditions individually was necessary. This discussion of a simple example illustrates what I mean by exact fit. A definition of a term will be an explanation with exact fit.

At this point, it might be objected that when, say, students offer definitions at the beginnings of essays, they are not looking for definitions such as these. They are looking for something less than exact fit. My reply is that *by their own lights* they should be searching for an exact fit definition. That is to say, in both the cases described initially they are looking for an explanation which covers all cases, not just some. If all that was wanted were some helpful hints as to what dance was, these might be got without drawing any contrast with, say, gymnastics. And notice, too, that if we mean our definitions to have exact fit, then they can be right (if they have exact fit) or wrong (if they don't). By contrast, if the intention were only to give a helpful hint, then it can only be judged on whether or not it actually is helpful. The point is that such helpfulness could not be determined independently of what was then done with the 'definition'. The so-called definition would not provide a neutral starting point for the essay, but would be judged in terms of what followed. This seems the exact opposite of what the writers or students in question desired. So I conclude that it is reasonable to expect definitions to have exact fit.

Definitions are not required for understanding

The first point is that we can understand terms perfectly well without being able to define those terms. For example, we understand time – we are able to tell the time, to recognize when we are on time for lectures and when we are not, and perhaps to explain the International Date Line – but we cannot define 'time'. This example makes plain that one can understand something quite well without being able to define it: and that means that one can know or understand things without (*always*) being able to *say* what one knows. The fact that one knows or understands is really quite plain in one's behaviour. Nor is time an isolated example here. Most of the words we use in everyday life we do not, as a matter of fact, need to define in order to understand them. It seems clear, then, that definitions are not required for understanding.

17

Definitions do not really aid understanding

The second point to be recognized here is that a definition itself must be understood. Suppose, to take a simple example, I don't know what bachelors are. Now, if I am not to just take your word for it, I have to check up on whatever you tell me. For you might be mistaken and tell me that bachelors are married men. To know that you are wrong, I must know what bachelors are. And that means know it *before* getting a definition.

One must understand what is being defined in order that one judge for oneself the accuracy of a definition. Moreover, the definition itself must be understood – I must know what the words 'unmarried', 'married' mean, if I am to understand what is being said when you claim that a bachelor is an unmarried man. But if I know that much about marriage, then I know what a bachelor is. At best, I just don't know the word 'bachelor'.

This example explains the illusion that definitions are helpful. For sometimes all one lacks is a particular word, and then going to a dictionary, for example, may supply the word into that 'gap'. But notice two things: first, dictionaries do not in general offer definitions, for they do not offer exact fit explanations. Rather, they give a kind of helpful hint. Second, the dictionary explanation of a particular word fits into the matrix of what one already understands, so it is really no major contribution to one's understanding.

The points raised in this section and the previous one support the two claims that (a) one can understand terms perfectly well without being able to define them, and (b) that having a definition is not in general an aid to understanding. Notice that the argument has worked through examples. Against those who would claim that a definition is required for understanding, I offered an example of understanding without definition. Against those who urge that definitions aid understanding, I presented two examples where the central elements of understanding were there prior to the definition and, indeed, were required in order to make sense of the definitions.

To approach the final point I will adopt a different style of argument. One cannot demonstrate the impossibility of defining non-technical terms of sufficient complexity to be interesting. Rather, I shall offer the challenge, by asserting that it is impossible. To make good that challenge, I shall offer reasons why such definitions are not possible, after explaining what I intend to exclude. First, the point of restricting the claim to non-technical terms is obvious: technical terms, like 'triangle', *can* be defined. Second, the restriction to 'sufficient complexity to be

18

interesting' is there to put aside terms like 'bachelor'. Perhaps they can be defined, but the ones that puzzle us – dance, understanding, knowledge, education, skill – are certainly not straightforward in this way. That is what makes them topics for discussion and debate.

Definition (of interesting terms) is impossible

To make good my challenge, consider ways in which a so-called definition of a non-technical term might go wrong. Let us take a simplified example: that of someone claiming to define art in terms of beauty (the Oxford English Dictionary might be seen as doing this). Now, to show that this definition is false, we need only produce a counter-example: an example of a work of art which is *not* beautiful. And that will show that the definition is false, because it will show that it lacks exact fit on the notion of art. There are plenty of examples in the canon of works which cannot reasonably be doubted to be art: Goya's painting *Saturn Eating His Children*, for example, or Shakespeare's play *Titus Andronicus*. These are art, but not beautiful. And even *one* such example will show that the putative definition is wrong. So here we see how anything offered as a definition will be susceptible to counter-examples. Notice too that the counter-example does indeed establish that the claim – for example, the Oxford English Dictionary's claim – is *false*, for the dictionary could be seen as saying that all examples of art were beautiful, and the counter-example as showing that this was not so. This is important, in so far as objectors might claim that all that was being urged was that some cases were like this. But of course, to be urging that would no longer involve offering an exact fit definition.

Someone who still liked the idea of seeing art as somehow connected to beauty might take one of two lines. First, and sensibly, he might give up the definition and content himself with saying that *most* art (or even *some* art) is beautiful. Or, second, he might insist on the definition, and say instead that by the word 'beauty' in this context was not meant what is usually meant by that term. So far, so good. But now he must explain what *is* meant by 'beauty'. And the worry here is that he will explain it as a special art-type beauty: that is, he will explain art in terms of a special sort of beauty, and the special sort of beauty in terms of art. This is no sort of explanation at all. He has made his definition depend on the sort of things it is supposed to explain. So the definition is empty, or vacuous. Thus, this second route, the one which preserves the definition, is seen to be foolhardy.

These, then, are the two ways in which definitions can go wrong. They can be shown to be false by counter-examples, or they can be found to be empty, because they are explained 'in a circle', as it were. My claim, then, is that *all* the so-called definitions of interesting terms will go wrong in one or other of these ways, and hence not be definitions at all, because they will lack exact fit. One might think of the first sort of going wrong – via counter-examples – as a case where the definition has an exact fit on *something*, but not on the term it was supposed to define. And then the second sort of going wrong – vacuousness – would be where the definition is too 'baggy' to have an exact fit on anything.

I have argued that definitions are not necessary for understanding, and that they do not really aid understanding. Moreover, I have offered a challenge by claiming that all definitions of non-technical terms would go wrong either by being shown false via counter-examples, or by being vacuous because explained in a circular fashion. I have not *proved* that this is so, but I have given some reason for thinking that it is so.

Contrasts and examples do *contribute to understanding*

If the points urged above were accepted, does this mean that clarification of key ideas is pointless? Clearly any such clarification should not proceed through the offering of definitions, but does that mean it should not proceed at all? Since the answer to this is no, we must look for some other means of making clarifications.

One procedure is to give clear examples – examples of what one does mean, or of what one is talking about, and also examples of what one is not talking about. In this way, one utilizes the sort of knowledge and understanding that the reader brings to the piece of writing or discussion: in fact, the sorts of things needed to assess any attempted definition. The second method, building on the first, is to clarify what the term at issue is to be compared or contrasted with. Consider, for example, the term 'real' (see Austin, 1970: pp. 86–9). One might have thought of defining 'real', but clearly the word 'real' amounts to different things in different contexts. For example, the real colour of a shirt might be contrasted with the colour after it was dyed, or the colour it looks under ultraviolet light; a real duck might be contrasted with a decoy duck, or with Donald Duck. (So that if I said I was not interested in real ducks, you would not know if my concern was dummies, or cartoons – or geese!) The point here is that one explains words and ideas with such contrasts and comparisons.

To apply, if asked the difference between dance and gymnastics, a good idea might be to think of specific differences in a particular context. That is to say, not to consider the question 'What is dance?' and

'What is gymnastics?', but instead to look at the question 'When is gymnastics contrasted with dance?'. And this might also direct one's attention to, for example, the context of one's discussion. What are we asking the question *for*? We will see, particularly in Chapter 2, that this is a crucial idea.

To conclude, then, I have argued against the need for definitions, and against the possibility of giving them.

The objectivity of appreciation

This is the second general philosophical point noted initially in this chapter: that judgements of dance are not bound to be subjective judgements. So one might expect this section to be about subjectivity. However, I have chosen to draw attention to the correlative notion, objectivity, to emphasize the commitment throughout this work to the idea of judgements, appraisals, evaluations and the like made within the domain of art as being *objective* judgements; and that this is so even though the judgements are made, not on the basis of some measurement (as they really never can be), but on the basis of observations by some informed person.

The problem before us – that concerning the objectivity of aesthetic judgement – appears in many forms and in many places. It arises whenever aesthetic judgements are made. And one reason here is that the possibility of aesthetic value (of a non-monetary sort) is often associated (for reasons we will come to) with the possibility of aesthetic judgements being objective. However, the problem is perhaps most easily seen in questions concerned with aesthetic education (for example Best, 1987). All art-critical judgements raise the question of objectivity/subjectivity. But those concerned with aesthetic education, and especially the assessment of success with respect to aesthetic education, bring the question into the open, since the value dimension is explicit there. There are two apparently contradictory tensions. The first is the need for objective assessment. In *some* sense, anything in education requires an objective assessment: a need to discern or assess that the pupil has understood, learned. Without some such procedure the claims of educators must seem wayward. Moreover, as we shall see, if objective assessment is, in principle, impossible, there is reason to believe that the notion of learning can get no grip. So this is one side of our tension: for discussing an area or a kind of judgement as *subjective* is typically denying accountability in that area or for that kind of judgement.

The other side of the tension is provided by the fact that feeling, individuality, imagination, creativity are crucial to the arts in general and to the arts in education in particular. We know that the arts deal with the feelings, that they are manifestations of creativity, that they depend on the individuality of persons both as creators and as responders. To deny these things is surely to misunderstand the nature of art. But these ideas *seem* inimical to objective assessment. Of course, I shall argue that the tension is only apparent, and hence that it is perfectly possible to provide objective assessment in the arts in general and in education. Moreover, there is something inherently right about a quest of this sort (Best, 1985: p. 13); the tension must be resolvable because the arts *are* concerned with feelings, and the arts *are* taught successfully. That is to say, there must be some resolution here, but the question is how? Centrally, I shall urge that the problems turn around oversimplifications of the idea of objective assessment and of the idea of feeling and so on.

The nature of subjectivity

I begin by saying something about the term 'subjective' and its correlative 'objective'. For clearly, the word subjective has a great many different uses in English. I shall mention just four (see also Nagel, 1979: pp. 166–70; Wollheim, 1984: pp. 38–42). First, subjective might mean private or inner; it might mean idiosyncratic; it might mean biased or prejudiced; or it might simply mean personal, based on feelings or personal involvement. If we look at these four uses, it seems right to divide them so that the first three – private, idiosyncratic and biased – fit together. They represent, I shall say, a pejorative use of the term 'subjective', under which to be subjective is to be somehow bad, wrong, offkey. It is with these three that I shall be chiefly concerned here. For if the term 'subjective' lacks this pejorative force, it will not matter if we end up concluding that aesthetic judgement is *necessarily* subjective.

The use of the word 'necessarily' is important, for if it were concerned simply with the practical possibility, in any situation, of making an objective judgement, we would have to consider a variety of factors, any or all of which might be relevant: for example, the knowledge and experience of the person making the judgement, the likelihood of his having an interest towards judging in one direction rather than another, his commitment to making the decision, his vantage point on the issue, the number of times he had confronted it, and so on. But this is not our concern. When I speak of judgements as necessarily or irreducibly subjective, I intend that however well these judgements are made, however carefully and in whatever distanced and reasonable way, still they will be subjective judgements: as one might put it, that judgements of that kind are, of their very nature, subjective. And the question then arises whether or not this is true of judgements of art.

Earlier I mentioned four uses of the term 'subjective' in English, highlighting three as pejorative uses of the term, and also as the topic of our discussion. But, once we consider these three uses of the word 'subjective', it becomes clear that only one of them really points to a cause for concern for aesthetic judgement. If the word 'subjective' means either biased or idiosyncratic, then it refers to a remediable condition. If I am biased against you, then my bias could be removed, say, if I knew you better. Or, at least, some other person could judge you in an unbiased way. The bias is essentially a personal quirk of mine. If my judgement is idiosyncratic, then perhaps you could convince me to modify it by pointing out its idiosyncracy. Again, and at the least, some other person could judge the matter at hand fairly and reasonably, for idiosyncracy too represents a personal quirk. My point here is that the possibility of a biased judgement, or the possibility of an idiosyncratic judgement presupposes the possibility of a judgement which is not biased or not idiosyncratic. If the word 'subjective' (and its cognates) is used in either of these ways, no problem is generated, in principle, for aesthetic judgement. No doubt, in practice, many examples of aesthetic judgement do betray bias or display idiosyncracy. But this cannot be a necessary feature of such judgements. Rather, the possibility of aesthetic judgement going wrong in either of these ways presupposes the possibility of its being done right, or correctly.

The one remaining pejorative sense of the term 'subjective' is well caught by the idea that 'anything goes'. Earlier, I spoke of this use as involving the claim that subjective judgements were private; but, by itself, such a claim has no clear meaning. If we wish to be clear, we must specify in what sense these judgements are private. My suggestion is as follows: that calling a judgement I make subjective in this sense is claiming I cannot be wrong about it, that my view is necessarily right. Further, that if you claim the opposite, your view too is necessarily right. This point is sometimes made by urging that any opinion is as good as any other. In what follows I shall use the term 'subjective' in this way only (with the exception of one passage which I will clearly identify).

Now two questions remain over the supposed subjectivity of aesthetic judgements. First, are they subjective in the sense just picked out? Second, does that sense of the term 'subjective' really yield the unacceptable consequences implicit in a pejorative use of the term? The second question is the more straightforward, and should be addressed

23

first (without commiting ourselves to its application to aesthetic judgement). Reflection will show that it does indeed generate just those conclusions. For if your opinion is as good as mine (and neither can be wrong) then it makes no sense to speak of your knowing something here that I do not, for our opinions are of equal value. Further, it makes no sense to speak of you teaching me anything in this area, or of my learning anything, for these 'judgements' offered prior to your efforts are of equal weight to those offered afterwards. If aesthetic judgements were subjective this would mean, in the practical situation, that a child, say, cannot in principle be taught dance appreciation, since the judgements he would make before the 'teaching' would be equally as correct, equally as valuable, as those he would make afterwards. Similarly, he cannot be corrected as to what to do next in a particular dance sequence of his own composition, for his opinion carries as much weight as that of the teacher. This means that the ideas of knowledge, teaching and learning simply have no application in any area which is subjective in the sense under discussion. And the consequences would indeed be those outlined above.

At this point an objector might claim that he does not actually mean by the word 'subjective' what I have been urging here; that it is not a matter of 'anything goes'. Yet he still wants to insist on the pejorative force of the term. My reply here is that either he does mean this (but has not acknowledged it) or, if he means something else, he must explain how his new sense of the word both avoids the consequences of my view, and maintains the pejorative force. And clearly this cannot be done. For any argument which shows that the judgements in an area are necessarily subjective in some pejorative way also allows that such notions as teaching, learning, knowledge etc. do not apply. In that sense, he must mean roughly the use of the term 'subjective' which is under discussion. If he chooses to give up the pejorative sense of the term, he will be accepting that there is no accusation in speaking of judgements as subjective; and this is one way of putting my position.

Again, the objector might press here, urging that the accusation amounts to the claim that the judgements in question are not objective. But this is clearly no answer. Our quest here is to understand the terms 'objective', 'subjective'; and that can only be done by getting a purchase on at least one of them, not by assuming a clear understanding of it. I have begun by thinking about subjectivity, and will be turning to objectivity shortly.

Two bad arguments

Earlier I posed two important questions. The second (Does 'subjective' imply unacceptable consequences?) has been answered. To find an area of judgement subjective is indeed to find it an area where key concepts – learning, knowledge – do not apply. I turn now to the first question: Are aesthetic judgements subjective? And treat this in two parts. First I shall consider two bad arguments for the subjectivity of aesthetic judgement – arguments which, while unconvincing, have something to teach us. Further they are commonly employed arguments. Second, I shall offer a reason for doubting that aesthetic judgements are subjective, and this will lead to a discussion of objectivity.

But first we must acknowledge an important constraint on any discussion of subjectivity and objectivity: that it cannot result in our analysing *all* judgements as subjective. For if it turned out that all judgements were subjective, we would still need to accommodate roughly the differences of objectivity/subjectivity acknowledged. We could, in the language of mathematics, *cancel through* by the term 'subjective' in that wide sense. We would still be contrasting the objectivity of judgements of kind X with the subjectivity of kind Y – the feature which applied to all would be, as it were, *super-subjectivity*. Typically, discussions here have contrasted the subjectivity of aesthetic judgement with the objectivity of judgements in science. And, while this is far from obviously correct (Kuhn, 1977: pp. 340–51), the thought that some such distinction must be maintained is an important one.

Let us now consider the first of the 'bad arguments' (see Best, 1985: p. 14) for the subjectivity of aesthetic judgements. It runs roughly as follows: What I see, hence what I can judge, in respect of the aesthetic, depends on *my* sense impressions, my perceptions, what *I* see. But my impressions are *my* impressions, coming through *my* senses. And no one else has them. So the judgements I make cannot be made by any other person. Hence I cannot be wrong about them. (Anything goes!)

This kind of argument is widely heard in discussions of the subjectivity of aesthetic judgement: but even more widely it is simply taken for granted, as something obviously true. This makes it all the more pernicious, for in fact it is obviously false. And two lines of reflection prove that for us. First, and most important here, this argument does no justice to the constraint just referred to. If accepted, it would make all (human) judgement subjective. For even if we choose, as an example, a judgement which a defender of this view might take to be uncontentiously objective – say, that the temperature of a certain beaker of water was 94°C – we find that it too is based on my sense

25

impressions. For how do I know the water temperature? Well, I read the thermometer (or whatever). So it involves a perceptual interaction of mine. (If anyone doubts this, let him try thinking what we would know if we were blind, deaf and anaesthetized since birth. The clear answer is: not much – and that highlights the crucial role of the perceptual.) So if the inclusion of perceptual material automatically imports subjectivity, then all judgements would turn out to be subjective: even the cherished judgements, for example, of science. And this is the best that argument could prove. As we have seen, it makes no sense to claim that all judgements are necessarily subjective. So this line of argument must be rejected.

Less central but ultimately of equal importance is a second comment. Thus far I have tried to say that we should not go along with this line of argument because even if its claims were true it could not prove what it sets out to do. But are its claims true? Does it make any sense to claim that we might, or do, all see things differently? In fact this suggestion makes no sense. The argument to demonstrate this – Wittgenstein's so-called private language argument (Hacker, 1986: pp. 245–75) – is long and complex (we will consider it later). For now, it should suffice to remember how we do treat perceptual cases in practice. We do not doubt, for example, the existence of a phenomenon we call colour-blindness. But what exactly is this phenomenon? How is it to be described? Surely central to any answer will be the idea that, while most of us see red objects as red – and hence distinguish them from, for example, green objects – the colour-blind cannot recognize this difference. Hence they see red and green objects as the same colour, and are mistaken so to do. No doubt we would need to expand this account to accommodate the way such people place colours on a spectrum of hue, shade, intensity and so on, but this is merely a complication of the original idea (Hacker, 1976: pp. 23–31). Now, if that account of colour-blindness is to make any sense, the colour-blind must be seeing things (systematically) differently from the rest of us. But this, in turn, presupposes that there is some way in common that the rest of us see things. And hence, we individually cannot in general and systematically see things differently!

For the two reasons elaborated above, I conclude that the argument under discussion is based on a false premise. But, more importantly, even if accepted, it could not prove what it claims. Yet there is an insight implicit in it, for it reminds us of the *centrality* of the human being in many of the judgements we make. And if, as I will argue, we shall need to accept that the person's role may differ on different occasions, still that role is *there* – and it is important. Any account of human

26

judgement that ignores it is ignoring something central to human experience. And so this involvement of the person does not, of itself, import subjectivity.

Let us turn now to the other bad, but informative, argument sometimes put forward for the subjectivity of aesthetic judgement. It begins from a supposed fact about subjective judgements: that they cannot lead to agreement. And one can see why: for if 'anything goes' then I cannot rationally compel you to accept my conclusion; yours is just as good! So this lack of agreement is taken as an index of subjectivity (Bambrough, 1979: pp. 18–19, 26–34). The argument then claims that there is no agreement possible among aesthetic judgements, and that such lack of agreement is indicative of an area of subjective judgement. So it follows that aesthetic judgements are subjective.

To show the errors in this argument we must concentrate on its claim that the lack of (possible) resolution of disagreement is indeed an index of subjectivity. I begin with some general comments before turning to the specific counter-argument. Of course, implicit in such a claim about subjectivity is the contrary claim that, when an area is objective (such as science) disputes can always be resolved. This is not obviously true. Here it is important to compare like with like (Bambrough, 1979: p. 18). If we take a relatively simple scientific claim – for example, that water boils at 100°C in normal atmospheric conditions – and compare it with a very complex aesthetic claim, we are not really making our point. Let us take two conflicting judgements of a dance by Twyla Tharp as our example of a complex aesthetic phenomenon. And let us agree for the moment that the conflict between these judgements could never be resolved. You continue to say one thing about the Tharp dance, and I continue to say another. Is this any more problematic than some disputes in theoretical physics – for example, as to how many elementary particles there are? I suggest that it is not: both are questions to which different parties offer different reasons, different arguments; neither can guarantee to win over its opponents. But if instead we take a judgement of any acknowledged masterpiece – for example *L'Après-midi d'un Faun* (1912) or the *Spectre de la Rose* (1911) –we would find areas of agreement comparable to those of the simple scientific judgement. Those who disagreed would be wrong, just as, say, the Flat Earth Society is, one might think, just plain wrong.

Two further comments are apposite, before we turn to the central counter-argument. The first concerns the notion of agreement. For, as we shall see (Chapter 3) there is some reason to think that this notion is less crucial than is sometimes supposed by contemporary theorists: that we could, in some circumstances, all be mistaken, as perhaps

27

pre-Copernican man was mistaken about the movement (or otherwise) of the sun and the earth. The second comment builds on the first. A confusing notion typically introduced at this point is the notion of 'a fact'. Of course our debate is about what are and what are not facts, about the sort of things facts are. Hence it is a huge mistake to appeal to this idea for some clarification.

Finally, I turn to the major counter-argument against the view that irreconcilable disputes are an index of subjectivity. The cases I have in mind are any of the 'multiple' figures from psychology, the duck/rabbit (Wittgenstein, 1953: p. 194), for example. We are told of one group who see the figure as a picture of a duck and another who see it as a picture of a rabbit; while a third group see it as the duck/rabbit design. Each can produce a defence of their view, for example, by saying that a certain line depicts the ears of the rabbit, and this defence can be countered by those who see that the line in question is instead the beak of the duck. Here we have our unresolvable dispute. Now, is the interpretation of this figure a subjective matter?

At first glance, one might think that it was. But fuller reflection makes it plain that this is not the situation where 'anything goes'. For any interpretation offered must be answerable to the perceptible features of the design: as, for example, when one group says (pointing to the design), 'This is the ears'. And any interpretation which is not in this way answerable to the perceptible features of the design is plain wrong. In making this point, David Best (see Best, 1985: p. 19) remarked that one could not see the design as just *anything*, for one's view of it had to be answerable to the perceptible features of that design. One could not, he said, see the design as, for example, a clock. A wiseacre in the audience responded that he could, and that it was 3:15! Although this undermined Best's example, it made his point. For to see the design as a clock was again to refer to features of that design as hands of a clock. The clock could not (if it had an ordinary analogue face) be seen as being at 6 o'clock; it was at 3:15 because of the features of the design. (There is a great deal more to be said here; some of it is in Chapter 6.)

What I wish to conclude (with Best) is that the interpretation of the duck/rabbit design is not a matter where 'anything goes'. One can be wrong about it, and hence it is not a subjective matter. Yet it is a matter over which there can be insoluble dispute. So the possibility of an insoluble dispute is *not* an index of subjectivity. Further, if it is not an index of subjectivity, it could not be used to prove that aesthetic judgements are subjective, even if it were conceded that such judgements can lead to insoluble disputes.

One further complication before we leave this topic: it is very difficult to say with certainty how even the duck/rabbit design cannot be seen. It is hugely more difficult to make the corresponding claims about any work of art. For if I assure you that the duck/rabbit design cannot possibly be seen in a certain way, I in effect invite you to try to do just that. And perhaps you can tell a story with some plausibility for any case I make up.[1] One reason is that perhaps I am not being inventive or complex enough. But this practical difficulty does not actually matter, for if the bare possibility of being wrong is conceded, we have demonstrated that this is not an area where 'anything goes'.

I conclude, then, that this too is a bad argument for the subjectivity of aesthetic judgement. But, like the other, it makes a point for us. For it shows us that one can have areas which are *not* subjective, without it being true that there is only one 'right' answer to questions about them. The interpretation of the duck/rabbit is not a subjective matter, because it is not true that 'anything goes' in respect of it, and yet disputes about it may be irreducible.

Objectivity and interpretation

In a sense, much of what has already been said bears on the notion of objectivity, and it is to that notion that I now turn. Like the word 'subjective', the word 'objective' has many uses in English. But it has one which, I shall urge, is both pervasive and misguided. And once this use is clearly identified, and its implicit error made manifest, we will be in a position to diagnose what exactly gives rise to the issues picked out in this section. And this takes us into the most difficult aspect of this topic.

Three main uses[2] of the term 'objective' are: (1) as indicative of the right or uncontentious answer; (2) as distanced or detached; and (3) as answerable to the claims of reasoning and rationality. Notice that the second and third of these are perfectly compatible with the idea that the judgements in question are personal, or based on one's feelings. That is, these uses are perfectly compatible with the fourth use of the term 'subjective' identified earlier (see pp. 22–3). Notice too that the second really identifies a way of carrying out one's judgements: it recommends a distancing of one's judgement on any matter from one's immediate personal concerns about that matter. Yet in this sense, aesthetic judgement could certainly be objective. Indeed, some aestheticians have thought that just such a kind of detachment – disinterested awareness (see Dickie, 1974: pp. 113–34) – was a characteristic of all aesthetic judgement. And even if they are not right, at least the possibility of such detachment is emphasized.

29

Our chief topic for discussion must be the first of the uses of the term 'objective' identified: that indicative of the right or uncontentious answer. For some writers,[3] it is obvious that one's judgements can only be objective if their truth precludes the truth of any other judgements of the same issue: my being right about X means that you can be right about X only by reaching the same conclusion as mine. And the basis for this view is typically twofold: first, it is based on a model drawn from (a view of) science; second, it trades on a view of facts or of a 'real world' (an objective world). Neither of these elements is typically advanced in the form of an argument. Rather, they are used, either separately or together, to offer a picture or model of objectivity. Let us look briefly at each in turn.

Science, for this view, is seen as a search for 'The Truth', which is essentially cumulative, with each new generation of scientists refining and improving the work of previous generations. Thus science, it is thought, works forward, towards the whole truth. We now know more than previous generations, and if there are some topics on which we remain ignorant, this is merely a practical difficulty. On such a view, the method of science will lead us forward, and that method does not centrally depend on theorizing. It is observational and involves the piecemeal accumulation of facts or truths. And all the better if they can be expressed using the 'pure' language of mathematics! If this is how objective judgements are made, then any judgements which are not cumulative in this way cannot reasonably be thought objective. Or so this view goes.

This view of science is typically combined with a pervasive picture of the nature of reality. The thought is that there is some 'way the world is' or some 'facts of the matter' which exist independently of human thoughts, desires, feelings or theories. To put that point more formally, the world could be described *as it is*, rather than as someone, or some group, sees it. And such a description would be completely true. (Indeed, on the model of the previous paragraph, the goal of science is just such a description of the world.) Now, the view concedes, it may well be true that this sort of description is forever beyond human powers, but that does not matter, for that is a practical difficulty. We can, on this view, imagine a being of superior powers who could take this view of the world:[4] it is, one might say, a 'God's-eye-view'. Thus any judgement will be objective just in so far as it conforms to the God's-eye-view. Yet it seems hard to imagine aesthetic judgements doing this. They are inextricably bound up with human feelings and with human values (as noted earlier). They do not seem amenable to the taking of a God's-eye-view. There does not seem to be only one *right way* to understand a particular painting or dance. Additionally, it seems surprising that art should continue to interest humans, since it does not contribute to this generalized 'truth'.

If these conceptions represent the right way to look at science and the world, and, further, if the judgements of science provide the correct model for objective judgement, aesthetic judgements are likely to be discussed as not objective. For they do not seem piecemeal or cumulative – twentieth-century man does not *obviously* understand art better than did Michelangelo (and perhaps obviously does not), and it does not seem that only one right answer is possible.

Luckily for aesthetics, both the conceptions which hold in place the 'one right answer' view of objectivity are deeply flawed. Science does not work like that (Feyerabend, 1978: pp. 16–40), and the view of the world or of facts is misleading generally – and sometimes downright false! As recent work on the philosophy of science has shown (Kuhn, 1977: pp. 270–7), it is a profound mistake to think of science as beginning from a kind of theory-neutral observation. Rather, science is saturated with theory, so that the most realistic way to see the transition from one view of, say, gravity to another is as the replacement of one battery of theoretical concepts by another (what Kuhn [1969: pp. 176–91] calls a 'paradigm shift'). What distinguished the work of Lavoisier (Kuhn, 1969: pp. 56–7), who discovered oxygen, from that of Priestly was not what they did, for they performed the same experiments. It was the theories that they brought to bear on their experiments. To anticipate a phrase from later in this chapter, their observations were 'concept-mediated', and the concepts in question came from their theories.

So science is not the piecemeal accumulation of facts; rather, it is a struggle between competing theories. And it is just not true that science arrives at one right answer. Of course, elementary science may give this impression. There does seem to be one right answer about, say, the boiling point of water. But science is, to a large degree, a seamless web; the theory which holds in place claims about the boiling point of water is ultimately a theory for all physics. And when we reach the frontiers of theoretical physics, we find not one right answer but apparently irreconcilable disputes. To repeat an example mentioned earlier in the chapter, theoretical physicists cannot agree on the number of fundamental (or elementary) particles of which the universe is constructed. However, they can agree that further observation will be irrelevant to their reaching this decision/conclusion. As they see it, they already have all the relevant data. Their task now is to make sense of it – and this involves extensive theorizing about that data.

The upshot of this (too brief) discussion is that the picture of science which holds in place certain conceptions of objectivity is a flawed picture. So that even if it were right to take scientific judgement as our model of objective judgement, this would not be the correct view of science.

Where have we arrived? We have shown that the picture that holds in place the idea of an objective judgement as one yielding a 'right answer' is mistaken. It does not do to assume that what is objective is therefore exclusive. And if this point is accepted, we have three tasks. First, we must explain why objectivity was misconceived in this way. Second, and more important, we must say a little more about the positive conception of objectivity thus developed. Third, we will discuss the outcome of all these remarks for the aesthetics of dance.

The first of these tasks is relatively straightforward. For when we are taught, for example, science, we typically learn a series of (seeming) facts. And, at a rudimentary level, these do represent the 'right answer': they will not be changed by later events. Thus, for example, when Newtonian physics is superseded by the physics of Einstein, we will still need to predict the falling of apples (which Newton did well) and we *may* still need to refer to some force or power in operation here. If we do, we will almost certainly continue to call it the force of gravity. But behind these continuities, we should be aware that much has changed. In particular, the interpretation of key terms will be quite different, even if the terms themselves do not change.

On the second task, we must consider what it means to regard objective judgements as those open to the claim of reason and rationality. We have already seen that it *does not* mean that there will always be one right answer, although in some cases there may be. Rather, it means that any answer which is given must be public, shareable, the sort of thing which we can (collectively) attempt to prove and disprove. And the reasons must be appropriate to the sort of question asked or method used. Here we see a way in which the judgements of science differ from aesthetic judgements: the reasons employed will be what, for brevity, we can call 'scientific' reasons, the sorts of things that practising scientists would recognize and accept. In contrast, judgements of the arts will be based on artistic reasons, and debate about these too will take place in ways which are recognizable to their practitioners. In this requirement for publicly available reasons, one finds the answers to the worries voiced earlier about the accountability of one's judgements. And if such matters are *arguable*, then one may reach a resolution, or equally one may not. But in both cases the judgement will be objective. Thus, although the judgements of science may typically be expected to differ from aesthetic judgements, the differences will not be a question of their objectivity (Best, 1983: pp. 156–7).

It is now appropriate to remind ourselves of something learned from the two bad arguments discussed earlier in this chapter (see pp. 25–9). We saw, first, that any account of subjectivity must allow, in principle, that some judgements are objective, and others are not. Our position does that: those that are public, arguable, amenable to reasoning, are objective; judgements that are not in this way answerable to the claims of rationality are not objective. Further, we have seen that aesthetic judgements imply some role for the person who makes them: they necessarily involve his perceptual system. This too fits in neatly with the conception of objectivity developed here, for just those sorts of observations are crucial to the reasons given in approaching works of art. Finally, we recognize that, while more than one answer was possible, it was not a case of 'anything goes', for any account of a work of art had to be answerable to the perceptible features of that work. And this point too was neatly accommodated, for any comments which fail this test cannot serve as reasons supporting artistic judgements.

Objective and subjective

We have now outlined a sense of the word 'objective' on which it makes perfectly good sense to say that aesthetic judgement is objective. And this is the relevant sense in which other judgements, those of science for example, are objective. But where does subjectivity stand? Earlier, I distinguished four uses of the term 'subjective' (and its cognates), and showed how two of them did not generate worries about the accountability of judgement, while the arguments traditionally used to apply the other pejorative use to aesthetic judgements – the 'anything goes' version – were found wanting. And while this fact does not of itself rule out the conclusion that aesthetic judgements are subjective in this sense, it may prompt us to look elsewhere. So what about the fourth use of the term 'subjective', the one which implies personal involvement, so that the judgement becomes subjective if it necessarily draws on the powers (say, the perceptual or recognitional powers) of human beings? What must be seen is that a judgement could be subjective in *this* sense and also *objective* in the sense that we have been developing objectivity, and that seems contradictory. How is one to proceed?

The answer lies in recognizing that we have only two *words* (subjective and objective) but, as it were, at least three *conditions* to describe.

An example from colour perception may make this point clearly and, for ease of exposition, I will put the point in terms of language, although it is not merely a verbal point. Rather, it turns on the nature of our experience of colour. A traditional but mistaken view might (correctly) regard the sentence 'It is red' as a means of stating something objective; and then it would take both the sentence 'It looks red' and the sentence 'It looks red to me' as stating something subjective. Yet these are clearly different. By our test for subjectivity – that it should be 'anything goes' – only the last of these represents a subjective judgement. When the colour-blind person says 'It looks red to me', and you reply 'Well, it looks green to me', neither of you is contradicting the other. You are both, as it were, describing your own condition. But you *will* be saying something different if you respond 'Well, it looks green', for you will not be telling him how it looks to you, but rather be describing the (public) look of the thing. We can therefore imagine beginning (Hacker, 1976: pp. 30–5; 1987: pp. 125–6) from a claim to actually know how some object is: 'It is red'. If, instead, we choose to say simply that the object *looked red*, we would typically be voicing some doubt on our part as to whether or not it was red. Perhaps it was in the far distance. Or perhaps even denying that it was red: 'It looks red, but that's just in this light'. Of course, putting the matter in this way can be confusing, since I can certainly be saying 'It looks red, and by golly it *is* red!'. Still, the point is fairly clear. For what we are introducing here is a perfectly public, shareable condition. The white object looks red because it is under a red light, or because of the way the sun is setting. However, when I move on to the claim that something looks red *to me*, I am implicitly contrasting it with how that thing *looks*, so that perhaps I have a peculiar colour-blindness brought on, say, by a disease or by drugs. In any case, I say that it looks red to me because I doubt that it looks red, as it were, generally – given the drugs I've taken – or because I know that it doesn't look red, given the disease I've got. The condition here is personal to me.

I take this discussion to illustrate that we have three distinct kinds of case here, picked out roughly by the expressions:

(1) It is red.
(2) It looks red.
(3) It looks red to me.

I will not take the time to show that one could construct similar categories for aesthetic judgements, for these judgements are as complex as the colour judgements are simple. But certainly the second category ('It looks red') is a plausible model for aesthetic judgement, since both imply the use of human perceptual systems. So I propose to apply this schema directly to aesthetic judgement. Let us now ask into which of our two categories (subjective and objective) each of the three judgements falls. Let it be granted throughout that judgement 1 ('It is red') is an objective judgement, and that judgement 3 ('It looks red to me') is a subjective judgement. Certainly this will follow *whatever* account of the subjective we offer. But what about judgement 2 ('It looks red')? Clearly, it is public, answerable to reasons and the like, and I can be wrong about it. So if by the term 'objective' I mean 'public' and so on, then it is objective. And if by 'subjective' I mean that 'anything goes', then that is *not the case* in respect of this judgement. The colour-blind man may think he is describing the look of the thing, but he will be wrong. He is merely describing its look to him. So, by this test, judgements like sentence 2 are certainly not subjective; hence are objective.

However, if we choose instead to explain the term 'subjective' as necessarily involving human perceptual powers or human feelings, judgements of category 2 will turn out to be subjective. So our preferred account of objectivity makes them objective, and the only non-pejorative account of subjectivity makes them subjective! How is this paradox to be dissolved? One strategy would be to invent a new word for category 2 judgements. Peter Hacker (1976: p. 28) suggests calling them 'anthropocentric judgements', but this expression hardly trips off the tongue, and I cannot see it catching on. The only other answer is to be careful when we encounter these words in the writing or thought of others – for how are they using these words? – and to be even more careful in our own case. Indeed, it may be good advice to simply excise the words 'subjective' and 'objective' from one's philosophical vocabulary. But if one chooses not to do so, the moral to remember is this: that there is no *pejorative* sense of the term 'subjective' under which aesthetic judgements are subjective, and if this means that they are objective, all to the good. Certainly there is no general or abstract reason why aestheticians, artists, aesthetic educators should worry on this point.

To conclude this section, let me point out one consequence for aesthetic education of adopting the picture of subjectivity offered here: educators need no longer debase their subjects by arguing for curriculum time for them simply as a *contrast* to 'objective' studies such as science and mathematics, as 'the other side of the coin'. For, while they offer something different, it is not (as I am arguing) something less objective, of less worth, or less concerned with knowledge and understanding.

35

Feeling and reason

Earlier (see pp. 21–2) I claimed that the confusion surrounding the objectivity (or subjectivity) of artistic judgement – in particular, the tension between the demand for accountability and the need for an involvement of the feelings – resulted not only from a misconception about the nature of subjectivity and objectivity, but also from an oversimple view of the feelings. To clarify this point, we might imagine an objector to our position saying that, at most, our account of objectivity has shown the place of *reason*, of reasoning and rationality, within aesthetic judgement. But this, he might urge, is just as inimical to the contribution of feelings, emotions, imagination, creativity, as was the other conception of objectivity.

To reply, we must recognize three things. (All are topics for later discussion, and so are here presented briefly and dogmatically.) First are the considerations brought together as Wittgenstein's so-called private language argument. They amount to a proof that a traditional picture of the feelings, which makes my feelings a kind of private object which only I can look at, is a confused or mistaken picture. There is no logical bar to knowing the thoughts and feelings of another person, only the practical problems of getting to know a person well, of recognizing lying and self-deception and so on (Dilman, 1975: p. 211). Once this point is accepted, we see that it is a mistake to regard *my* feelings as a sort of thing about which *you* cannot offer helpful remarks, comments, explanations. (In fact, we often behave in just this way in practice, telling our friends what they are feeling.) But if my feelings are thus in the public domain, there can be no objection *in principle* to their serving as reasons for judgements. Further, they can themselves sometimes be explained, giving reasons (Best, 1985: pp. 24–33).

The second point to remember is that thought and feeling are vast categories in our psychology, rather than isolated instances. So that the traditional contrast between matters of feeling and matters of reason is a mistaken one. Certainly there are some cases where there is an opposition between the rational and the emotional. But this does not show that there is always such an opposition. Indeed, one might cite the arts as proof that this is not always so. But if a less contentious example were required, we need only turn to the practice of philosophy. For, while argument is essentially a rational activity, it is nevertheless one about which one can feel very strongly: indeed, the etymological basis of the idea of the philosopher – as a LOVER of wisdom – picks up this very point.

The third consideration concerns the role of reasons in explaining

36

one's feelings or reactions. As such, it brings together the two raised above. For when I make a judgement of a work of art, you can typically ask me why I think that, and those who understand art understand the sorts of things which might be said in answer to such questions. It will not do, for example, to simply say that one feels it. That is a retreat into personal taste in the arts, which it would not be in, say, the case of one's enjoyment of food (see Chapter 7 [see Cavell, 1969: pp. 91–3]). Of course, the problem may just be that you do not know what to say. But then I can show you, for example, the writings of critics. Is any of their explanations the one you want? And if not, why not? In this way, we can begin to discuss the reasons for your judgement. If a person repeatedly refuses to enter into this kind of discussion, we may feel that he does not really appreciate *art* at all, but rather is just enjoying a sequence of attractive movements, pleasing sounds or pretty colours (this is the topic for the next section of this chapter). What I am suggesting, then, is that it makes perfectly good sense, at least in the arts, to discuss one's feelings and to use them – and other things -- as reasons for one's aesthetic judgements.

It is worth recording one further point (Best, 1985: pp. 10–11): that one might take *all* reasoning as, in the end, depending on human reaction to certain things. To put that another way: that humans *just do* feel certain ways and that it is a mistake to try to explain this fact. But this does not, of course, mean that we do not offer reasons for our specific judgements. Nor does it mean that such reasons are mere rationalizations. This is a complex topic, but briefly the point is this: the reasons offered in support of aesthetic judgements are genuine reasons. They do explain those judgements. Yet if asked *why* those things count as reasons, we could try, first, to talk generally about aesthetic judgement (see the next section and Chapters 6 and 7); eventually we might concede that people simply do see things in certain ways. When I recognize that a certain conclusion follows from some other claims – when I recognize a point of logic – that recognition is a human capacity, something people simply do. To characterize this situation, Lewis Carroll ([1894] 1973: pp. 1104–8) imagines a debate between Achilles and a tortoise, in which the tortoise constantly requires a reason to take him from the truth of the premises to the truth of the conclusion. When Achilles offers such a reason, the tortoise accepts *it* in turn as a premise, but now requires a reason to get from the truth of the new premise to the conclusion. If Achilles offers one, the tortoise again accommodates it *as a premise*, but this gets him no further towards the conclusion. Achilles insists that, having accepted the premises and their reasons, the tortoise *must* accept the conclusion. If not, he says, 'Logic would take you by the throat, and *force* you to do it' (Carroll, 1973: p. 1107). But we know better. What leads one forward in argument is not some other reason; rather, it is one's ability to recognize reasons as compelling. And just such a recognition is fundamental in the case of aesthetic judgement. What this means, of course, is that feeling has a greater role in rationality than is generally recognized. It follows that acknowledging the role of feeling in one's reasons (although not in one's conclusion) is *not* tantamount to accepting subjectivity. And nowhere is this more true than for aesthetic judgement.

Now, I certainly have not proved that aesthetic judgements are not subjective, in the 'anything goes' sense. For I have not refuted *all* arguments which might establish that they were. Rather, I have refuted two *key* arguments, so that they at least cannot be used to reach this conclusion. Further, I have offered an alternative picture of subjectivity and objectivity, one which allows us to see what it would mean to say that aesthetic judgement is perfectly objective. And this picture coheres with the (acknowledged) fact that teaching and learning does take place in respect of aesthetic matters, a fact which a subjectivist position would find inexplicable.

The artistic and the (merely) aesthetic

We need, in this discussion, to make two major kinds of points. The first is to articulate the contrast (drawn by David Best,[5] among others) between our judgements of works of art and our judgements of other 'objects' in which we take an aesthetic interest. But additionally we need to notice some features which distinguish both those categories (that is to say, both artistic and aesthetic judgements) from very many of the other judgements that we make – from what, for the purposes of this discussion, I shall call 'functional' or 'purposive' judgement and appreciation. And we should remind ourselves of a point made in the Introduction: that the term 'judgement' here does not imply anything necessarily judgemental or evaluative. Rather, it functions as a catch-all term for the various different kinds of comments or remarks made about art works. It is also worth bringing out that these distinctions should be seen as colouring our experiences. And it is to that point that we turn first.

Experience as concept-mediated

We can anticipate this point fairly succinctly, for it simply amounts to the claim that all experience takes place under concepts. And hence different concepts imply different experiences. When I look out of the window I see (undifferentiatedly) a row of trees; you, with your greater botanical knowledge, see oaks, ashes, beeches and so on. And it seems right to describe these as differences in what we see. We experience the situation differently. The following example brings out this point. A child might use the word 'dog' of all four-legged animals, both in reality and in pictures. Does this child have the concept 'dog'? The answer seems to be 'no', because the concept 'dog' would implicitly contrast dogs with other creatures such as horses, elephants, cats. The child's application of the word 'dog' does not differentiate between dogs and horses, so it seems right to say that the child does not have the concept 'dog' at all. Does the child *see* dogs? Well, there is a clear sense, it seems to me, in which the answer again is no; for what the child sees are (undifferentiatedly) horses, dogs, elephants and cats. Notice that I am not saying that the child does not see horses and elephants as different but, rather, as with my viewing of trees, he does not see the differences as important, or relevant.

The point is that all our experience depends on the concepts we have: that there is no non-conceptual or preconceptual experience. Of course, the relationship between concepts and experience is a reciprocal one, since one acquires concepts in experience. There is a major difficulty here: namely, how one begins this procedure, how one ever acquires any concepts. But this is a large and vexed question. If one tries to imagine the beginnings of language, exactly the same difficulty applies. Until one has words, one cannot learn words (Baker and Hacker, 1984a: pp. 386–8).

If we have suggested that all experience is concept-mediated, it will follow that experiencing objects under different concepts is experiencing them differently. The remainder of this chapter argues that we experience works of art differently from the other things that we experience aesthetically, and that we do so because we experience them under different concepts.

Aesthetic versus purposive: the 'large' notion of the aesthetic

Because the word 'aesthetic' has a variety of different uses in English, it is important for us to draw a few distinctions between aesthetic judgements in the widest sense and the other judgements that we might make of objects. For example, we take an aesthetic interest in the beauty of the sunset: we talk about the pleasing changes in the character of the light and about reflections and so on. But we could take another interest in the sunset. We could, for instance, be taking some meteorological interest, using a folk saying such as 'red sky at night, shepherds delight'. Equally, we take an aesthetic interest (or, as we shall go on to say, an artistic interest) in a painting or a play. But, again, we might easily take some other kind of interest here. For instance, we might consider a painting solely in terms of its ability to cover up a nasty stain on our wallpaper. Here, we would not be considering the qualities of the painting, beyond perhaps its size. Or we might take an *economic* interest in a play if, say, we were its producers. Our interest would be exhausted by the extent to which this play attracted a large audience.

Of course (following on from the previous section), each of these different *ways of seeing* works of art, each of these different kinds of interest we take in the work of art, depends on the underlying concepts under which the works are perceived. So that, for example, taking an economic interest in a dance amounts to bringing economic concepts to bear on that dance, or to perceiving it under economic concepts. But, of all the different kinds of concepts which might be brought to bear, only one sort (or, as we will see, really two sorts) is of relevance to our topic: aesthetic concepts. And we come to understand them more clearly through a contrast.

We have shown that one may take various other kinds of interest in objects in which one also, and perhaps typically, takes an aesthetic interest; so it is important to broadly draw a distinction between aesthetic interest and these other kinds of interest. I shall characterize the other kinds of interest as 'purposive' or 'functional', although neither word is perfect for my concern. By a purposive judgement, I shall mean one which operates in terms of the *means* to an otherwise specifiable *end*: that is to say, we specify end or outcome on one hand, and the means of achieving that outcome on the other. Implicit in this conception is that the means can be considered independently of the end, and that typically there will be a number of means to that very same end. So here are two features (independence of end, variety of means) which characterize purposive judgements. As we shall see, these are not characteristic of aesthetic judgements in the widest sense. When we are concerned with aesthetic matters, we are concerned with the beauty of *this* (that is, of a particular novel, dance or whatever). To speak of 'another means' to the same end in such a context would be nonsense (Beardsmore, 1971: pp. 11–19). If we think about a novel, for example, in which we take an aesthetic interest, we will speak about its form and its characters and so on. If we change it, it is no longer *that* novel; the form and characters would be different. Contrast, for example, a report of a car accident. Two newspapers might report the accident in different terms, but which amount fundamentally to the same thing. Either of those forms of words are adequate as a means to describe the car accident. Nothing similar could be said about the novel. So it makes no sense to speak of the novel as one means, among many, to an end; we would not get precisely that object of interest distinct from, roughly, that sequence of words. Second, in the case of purposive judgements, we can specify the means independently of the end. Can this be done in the case of the novel? What that novel amounts to, its author's 'end', is not something he could say completely except by pointing to the novel, for *that* is the end, the outcome. There may be some broad generalizations he could make, 'I mean to expose social conditions in nineteenth century England' for example, but such general ends do not specify this novel rather than some other. To specify the end of this novel we must speak about ends realized in a certain way. And that means that one cannot specify the end independently of the means, for there is no 'otherwise specifiable end'.

A useful case here may be provided, at least roughly, through a discussion of sport. For some sports – for example, soccer, rugby, hockey – we can specify the end of the game broadly independently of the means of satisfying that end. So in soccer, the end is to score goals, within the rules of soccer. And the means by which those goals are scored, as long as they are within the rules of soccer, is not crucial; any goal is equally one goal in the team's total. So here we typically take a purposive interest in these sports. We are typically concerned about who wins, independently of how they win. Of course we can take an aesthetic interest in the elegance of goals or moves, or even of particular players, but this is not fundamental to the nature of soccer. By contrast, some sports do require some degree of aesthetic interest. For example, in competitive gymnastics, the aim is not merely to, say, get over a box, but to do it in such and such a fashion. That is to say, we cannot specify what is to be done independently of how it is done. For such sports, we typically are required to take an aesthetic interest. For this reason, David Best (1978a: p. 104) has distinguished between purposive sports such as soccer and aesthetic sports such as gymnastics. We can take an aesthetic interest in the purposive sports, but it is not fundamental to the nature of the sport. I mention this example because it may help to clarify the sense in which taking an aesthetic interest implies concentrating on something other than a means to an otherwise specifiable end.

Thus I have suggested that there is a distinction to be drawn between purposive or functional consideration, judgement, appraisal on the one

41

hand and, on the other, aesthetic consideration, judgement and appraisal. One use of the word 'aesthetic' which incorporates many differences simply refers to the kind of interest with grace and beauty and the like which we have been discussing here, and which we would contrast with purposive or functional interest. However, for our purposes, there is more to be said, and it is to that which we now turn.

The artistic and the aesthetic

The aim here is to draw a distinction within what, in the previous section, we called 'aesthetic' judgement, that is, to distinguish *within* the category of the aesthetic in the largest sense. The basic distinction (from Best, 1978a: pp. 113–16; Best, 1985: pp. 153–4) is between our appreciation for, judgement of, interest in works of art on the one hand and, on the other, our judgement of, appreciation for other aesthetic objects: sunsets, mountains, birdsong, fountains and firework displays for example. That is, our appreciation of works of art (artistic) is contrasted with our appreciation of other aesthetic objects ('merely' aesthetic). And these distinctions are drawn within the category of concepts discussed in the last section (see pp. 39–42). As we saw there, to subsume an object before us under one batch of categories is to perceive it in a particular way, because such perception is concept-mediated. And this means that it makes a difference whether we see the object before us under concepts appropriate to art (that is, make an artistic judgement about it) or under concepts appropriate to the merely aesthetic. The clearest way to articulate this distinction sharply is to consider a case where a spectator confronts a work of art but, through lack of knowledge or understanding, brings to bear on it merely aesthetic concepts. And this means that the spectator is not able to bring to bear on that object the concepts appropriate to the appreciation of art; concepts such as form, style, meaning. Typically, listening to music involves bringing to bear just these notions: form, tonal structure and, perhaps, a sense of content. Additionally, we typically see the music as the product of some artist. By contrast, our appreciation of the beauty of birdsong is simply 'aesthetic appreciation'. The concepts previously mentioned do not typically apply. And certainly the crucial idea of a *category* of art (Walton, 1978) – in the case, say, of 'serial music' – has no application. Now, in this case, the spectator has failed to hear the 'object' before him as serial music, and thus has misperceived it. If, for example, that listener knows nothing of serial music, he may be attending to a particular piece (say Webern's *Symphonie Opus 21*) as though it were a pleasing succession of natural sounds, birdsong, for example. And this

42

might be a highly enjoyable experience, but it is not an experience of art. So it seems right to say that this listener would not be hearing *music* at all. He would be unable to engage in the kinds of discussion which might typically accompany the attention to music, for example, critical discussions. Because he lacks the kind of understanding necessary to perceive the work within acceptable ranges (and to avoid misperceiving it), this listener is not really confronting the work of art at all, for he is not confronting it *as* a work of art.

I have articulated this example in terms of our judgement or appreciation of music. But it could equally well be applied in the case of the other arts. For example, I cannot appreciate a poem in French unless I understand the sounds as French words, that is, unless I have at least some grasp of French. Thus, while I may be able to appreciate a plash of sound as such, lacking the grasp of the language I am unable to appreciate the poem, and hence not the art work. Here, as in the music case, we are pointing to a difference between our 'merely aesthetic' appreciation of sounds, and our appreciation where the sounds constitute a work of art. In this case I am not really hearing the poem; I will have missed its meaning, its form. David Best makes exactly the same point concerning a dance performance by the classical Indian dancer Ram Gopal. The work in question (Gopal's dance) was, of course, art, but, as Best acknowledges, he was unable to see it in this way because he was not aware of the significance of the formal features of the work. He did not see its 'meanings' at all. Yet, as he said, 'I was enthralled by the exhilerating quality of his [Gopal's] movements. . . . So it seems clear that my appreciation was of the aesthetic, not the artistic' (Best, 1978a: p. 115). Here again we have aesthetic appreciation only, not the appreciation of art.

It will be worth saying a couple of points which elaborate this distinction between artistic judgement and aesthetic judgement, for the examples given above may demonstrate that there is some such distinction without telling us very much about it. To do so, we should remind ourselves of three points already implicit. First, the *details* of a work of art seen as art have a significance they lack when the work is seen as merely aesthetic. The logic of appreciation differs in cases where we are and where we are not confronting an object as art; for when we *are* confronting it as art, formal notions have an important role to play. So that, in the earlier example, listening to a French poem *as a poem* requires not merely understanding of poetical form: the significance given by sonnet form, and the structural devices that employs for example. Again, in the example of Ram Gopal's dance from David Best, we might imagine that slightly different movements might still have had an 'exhilarating quality' for Best, but the dance would only have amounted to what it did – would only have had that precise 'meaning' – with the gestures Gopal performed. Thus, as Best recognizes, to treat a work as merely aesthetic is, in one important sense, to denigrate it. For one is ignoring or failing to notice just those details that are crucial for its meaning.

Moreover (a point elaborated in Chapter 3), art has a conventional character. It has become a commonplace to say of art that it is an intentional activity. What this means, of course, is that one makes art deliberately, and not (except perhaps in rare cases where this is a compositional tool) accidentally. What is less commonly recognized is that it follows that the judgement of works of art, too, has a 'learned' character, that my appreciation of a work of art *as art* requires that I see it *as art*. This requirement means that I must distinguish (to take the case in point) between my appreciation or admiration of an interesting movement and my appreciation of a dance. And to see it as a dance is, among other things, to recognize a formal significance in some of its features. Such significance (for those features) is acquired from other works where similar features occur; for instance, the formal significance of the sonnet form – as it makes itself manifest in my seeing a certain set of words *as a sonnet* – is built up from other sonnets, and hence learned.

There is a great deal here to be said about aesthetic concepts and, for our purposes, even more about the character or nature of artistic concepts. In particular, we need to better understand their conventional character, and this is the topic of Chapter 3. For now it is sufficient to record that it seems plausible to draw a distinction between objects where we can meaningfully talk about a creator (leaving aside religious questions) and where we can meaningfully talk about the details of the work as intended and as crucial – and where we can take these features in a non-purposive way.

Conclusion

In this chapter I have identified three sets of ideas which I will be using throughout this work. There is a great deal of background philosophy not thoroughly discussed here, but two crucial notions would, in an ideal world, have been introduced. The first such notion is *explanation*, which I leave to the references given, and to what can be said about that notion as it occurs. Second is *understanding*. This is too complex a topic for much to be said about it usefully in this context (Baker and Hacker, 1980: pp. 69–85; pp. 595–620).

Recommended reading

Key texts here will be Best, 1974: pp. 15–55 (on definition); Best, 1978a: pp. 65–98 and Best, 1985: pp. 12–34 (on subjectivity and objectivity); Best, 1978a: pp. 99–122, and Best, 1985: pp. 153–68 (on artistic judgement). For some implications of these assumptions for dance studies, see McFee, 1989a.

PART II

The Nature of Dance

2

Dance as Action

(Is it dance . . . as opposed to gymnastics?)

The question approached in this chapter, and the next two, concerns the nature of dance. Having accepted that it is impossible, and unnecessary, to offer a definition of the term 'dance', we still need to clarify what dances are. But, asked the question 'What is dance?', we have no context in which to recognize an accurate answer. So the topic of this chapter can be put more clearly by asking what makes a particular movement sequence dance rather than, say, gymnastics. That is to say, *what* makes a particular movement sequence dance rather than something else?

A first thought might be that the movements performed were somehow characteristic of dance. A moment's reflection shows that what makes a sequence dance rather than, say, gymnastics, cannot be features of the movement; there cannot be any exclusively dance-type movements – that is to say, movements that could only appear in dances and never appear anywhere else. For we could imagine just those movements of the body being part of some activity other than dance: for example a ritual, a rite, a piece of gymnastics, or a child's game. The description of the movement by itself can give us no guarantee that we were watching dance and not some other thing. For example, it may be true that pointe-work, as a general rule, appears only in classical ballet. If one saw pointe-work, there would be some justice in one's claim that the activity was classical ballet. But this would not be an absolute guarantee. Something different could be occurring, for example, some peculiar ritual or rite, with which one was unfamiliar. Additionally, as we shall see in Chapter 4, features of the dance which one might think of as incidentals (costume, lighting and so on) play a key role here (Sirridge and Armelagos, 1977; Armelagos and Sirridge, 1984). But, again, specification of these would not guarantee that one was watching dance and not something else.

The importance of the issue

An objector might ask, 'Who cares?'. The answer is revealing, since a discussion of the importance of the issue makes clearer just what the issue is. Why should one care if a particular action is dance or gymnastics? Isn't this simply a matter of classification, or what the action is called? Of course, there is more to it than this.

In a sense, the importance of the issue of whether the performance I saw on Tuesday was dance or gymnastics follows directly from two of the theses developed in Chapter 1. There I urged (a) that what we experience depends on the concepts we bring to bear, and (b) that a battery of concepts appropriate to art works are appropriate *only* to them (and not to other kinds of objects). So that if dance is an art form (as it obviously is) we have a reason to insist on distinguishing dance from any other physical activities – even dance-like ones – which are not art. For only under those concepts can art, in this case dance, genuinely be experienced. Yet we must be sure that those concepts are appropriately applied to the activity in question. That means deciding just *what* activity it is.

Putting the matter thus bluntly raises two important questions. First, are, say, gymnastic performances art works (and if not, why not)? Second, what is it that distinguishes dance from any other physical activity? Now, partial answers to this first question, regarding art status, are suggested in Chapter 1, and expanded in Chapter 3 and Chapter 8; and so may be put aside for the moment. But such a strategy simply intensifies the other question: what distinguishes one activity from another?

Notice, though, that we have already ruled out two ways of responding to this question. First, it will not do to say that whether an activity is dance or not is just a matter of opinion. We rejected such subjectivism in Chapter 1. Whether or not a particular activity is dance may well be contentious, problematic, arguable; we may even have a border-line case here (when is a big shrub really a small tree?). But it cannot be a matter where any opinion is as good as any other. Second, it will not do to reply, 'It is just a matter of what we *call* it, of whether we use the word "dance" or not', for two related reasons: (a) we could make the point without using the word 'dance', by talking in a roundabout way or, perhaps, by using a word in another language; and (b) that treating the activity as dance (rather than something else) will have implications. In particular, it will bring to bear different ways of understanding the activity; in our case, whether or not we understand it as *art*.

To progress here, we must proceed slowly, presenting our reasoning as clearly as possible. Doing so will not only take us forward in respect of *this* issue, but will also allow us to focus on the nature of argument, so as to practise the kinds of argument, counter-argument and rebuttal characteristic of philosophical enquiry.

Dance as a 'special kind of movement'

As already suggested, it is at least possible (although not likely) that any movement that actually occurred in a dance nevertheless could have occurred in some other context; no movement pattern will, of itself, be uniquely distinctive of dance. In response to this point, it has been suggested (Hirst, 1989) that dance is indeed 'a special kind of movement', but that its distinctiveness lies in the way we look at it, that dance is 'aestheticized movement'. Such a claim is ambiguous however; we can take the expression 'aestheticized movement' in two quite different ways. Further, neither of them really answers our question. On the second reading, it is true that dance is aestheticized movement, but not informative. On the first reading, it would be informative if true, but it is in fact false. We can bring out the ambiguity with a simple example.

Suppose we consider a sweeping action (see McFee, 1989a). Two kinds of cases would be these: first, I see a person, broom in hand, sweeping the floor in a graceful, elegant, fluid way, and so I concentrate on the grace, line and so on of the sweeping movement. Now, I have lost interest in its purposive dimension, namely, the aim to clean the floor. I have aestheticized it. But it is still sweeping, and if the room is not cleaned, it is bad sweeping, however gracefully done. If this is what is meant by the expression 'aestheticized movement', then dance is *not* aestheticized movement. Second, having seen the sweeping above, I decide to use sweeping as a motif in a dance I am making. And because I am literal-minded, I actually use a broom. I have aestheticized the sweeping. Yet now it is not sweeping at all. It is dance. And this is so even if the performance area ends up remarkably clean. Now, this second use of the term 'aestheticized' could imply that dance involves the aestheticization of movement. But clearly that is a very inexact way of putting the point. What goes on there is the transformation of the movement in question (the sweeping) into something else, namely dance. So no doubt dance is aestheticized movement, but aestheticization involves a transformation. The activity *is* dance. And that means it *is not* sweeping.

Perhaps the most important difference between these two accounts is that the second, which transforms the movement, can explain the interest, importance or value of such a movement: namely, whatever interest, importance or value attaches to art. On the first version, where the action actually is sweeping, the only real value would be the hygienic one. No doubt we spectators can take an aesthetic interest in any activity (say, sport) and hence aestheticize it (McFee, 1986). That does not make it dance. Certainly (on such a conception) there would be no need and no place for the specialized movements of a dance technique. Taking an aesthetic interest in sport – enjoying, for example, the grace of a particular rugby player's running game – we do not translate the movement into something else. We simply enjoy it in its context. And the criterion for success here is *not* an aesthetic one (or, in the case of aesthetic sports, is not a wholly aesthetic one; see David Best, 1978a: Ch. 7). The bottom line, then, is that it makes no sense to think of dance as aestheticized movement, for that runs counter to our thinking of it as dance.

Understanding action

The discussion above highlights, of course, that making sense of the actions of persons differs in two important ways from understanding, say, the motion of clouds or the flight of birds. The first difference (the topic of this section) is that the meaning of human actions can change as the context changes. This is just another way of saying that actions of persons have this kind of meaning,[1] for an understanding of action draws on a web of rules that we know independently and that we bring to bear on the case in question. Second (a topic for the next section), we must recognize that, therefore, human action is not equivalent to the movement of an automaton, even when the 'automaton' in question is a human being, but viewed as just a collection of biochemical processes. Both these topics are wholly general, applying to the understanding of human behaviour generally, and therefore to dance as one form of human behaviour. We will consider first the abstract point and then its application.

The key point is that description of the actions of human beings is only possible if one takes account of the context of the action. For human actions are rule-governed or rule-related (in general terms). This point can be clarified by citing two kinds of examples. First, there are formal activities where the rules are fairly explicit. The action of marrying, for example, is an activity precisely bound by explicit rules. If certain formulas are gone through, then those people are married; if

52

not, then they are not. Notice that the context in this example is not solely constructed from the words or even from the location. An intelligent Martian who spoke English and arrived at a church on a Saturday afternoon might be puzzled by a marriage ceremony. He would not recognize that this exchange of words between bride and groom, together with words by the priest, had important consequences for the future – say, in terms of property rights and inheritance, and perhaps simply in terms of lifestyle. For he would not see those activities under the appropriate rules. He would not know what *action* it really was, because he would not see the meaning or significance of marriage, nor that this behaviour constituted marrying. But he would be even more mystified if he arrived at the same church on the preceding Thursday evening. Then he would see the same people saying the same words, when absolutely nothing would follow from it. For this would be the rehearsal. The point here is that formal activities such as marrying are only intelligible once the context of rules is understood.

Indeed, there is a quite general point here: that *understanding* such-and-such depends on locating it within a complex relation of things that one already understands. So that, if I understand all the other moves of chess pieces, it makes sense to explain the queen's move as compounded of the bishop's move and the rook's move (Baker and Hacker, 1985b: pp. 26–7). Also, we have a grasp of what is (and what is not) permitted by a rule. Indeed, as we will see in Chapter 3, the understanding of art works such as dances makes a similar demand on the tradition within which those works are conceived. One understands the work in question in terms of that tradition, and that means in terms of what one already knows. But this does not require knowing everything; knowledge (and learning) are not all-or-nothing. One can *learn* to understand, yet one's understanding still depends on what is learned. This is most obviously true for formal activities, but not only there.

Second, consider informal activities such as signing a cheque or voting. The description of the action makes reference not just to what one's body did (the making of marks on pieces of paper with a pen) but to a nexus of rules, in the case of cheque-signing, to do with banks, perhaps with international banking, with the transfer of funds and so on. All of this is captured in characterizing the action as the signing of a cheque. As Wilkerson (1974: p. 133) comments, describing a man as picking up pieces of paper from a wooden desk is not offering a poor description of his visit to the bank; rather, one is simply not describing his withdrawing money at all, any more than talking of the redistribution of elaborately carved pieces of wood on a checkered surface is really talking about chess.

In all the cases described above, one can make a mistake, do something wrong. For example, one can make bad moves in chess. Like all rule-governed or rule-related activities, even informal ones, actions are typically normative activities. Often we must decide that a certain way of proceeding is wrong. So that there are good moves in chess, bad moves and also 'moves' that are not moves in chess at all, for example, moving one's knight straight forward. Here is one feature of normativity: the contrast between doing a thing (well or badly) and failing to do it at all. Further, a person might by coincidence move the chess pieces in a way that an observer concluded to be playing chess. But there is more to it than that, which is a second feature of normativity. With any rule, there is not mere acting in accordance with the rule but, as one might put it, acting in that way *on account of* the rule in question. Only then do we see the rule itself functioning actively within our behaviour. The behaviour of a trained seal might accord with a rule, but a person who acts on the rule acts on his own initiative. Hence it is possible (in principle) to identify what it is right (or wrong) to do, as opposed to what is simply done. To explain such a difference (a crucial one) we must appeal to context. If we did not, we would simply be assimilating the normative notion of following a rule correctly with the statistical notion of acting in, say, the same way that most people are disposed to act in such-and-such circumstances. It is a statistical notion which could be applied to the trained seals (Baker and Hacker, 1984b: p. 71). So action is a normative notion in this sense.

These cases emphasize the need for characterization of actions to take account of the context of rules into which the action fits. What is thereby emphasized is the description under which the action is intended or motivated. The action is not intentional or deliberate under just any description. Someone digging in the garden is flexing certain muscles and also, for example, chopping up certain earthworms. But neither of these descriptions of the activity identifies the action. The first (flexing certain muscles) is just a causal description, while the second (chopping up earthworms) picks out an event which occurs coincidentally. To identify an action is to identify it under some description under which it is intentional or deliberate (Anscombe, 1981: pp. 208–19).

Let us briefly apply what we have learned so far to the case of dance. The centre of our account of human action emphasizes that explaining actions as actions involves contextualizing them, that the context allows the behaviour to be intelligible and hence to be the action that it is. The point then is that what makes a particular sequence of movement dance (rather than gymnastics) involves the context of performance and, relatedly, the description under which the action is intended. Only in certain contexts does the intention to perform a dance make sense. And only when dances *could* be performed (or made) does it make sense to ask if a particular sequence of movement is, or is not, a dance (see Carr, 1987).

People, not machines

One way to sharpen our attention to the action of persons is to contrast it with another concern which we might reasonably take on some occasions: namely, the concern with the person as a biochemical system, or, as I shall call it, with the movements of the body. To do so is, briefly, to move away from specifically dance examples, but only temporarily. For an action/movement contrast of the kind drawn above is at the root of much philosophical discussion of the freedom of the will (Nagel, 1987: pp. 48–58; O'Connor, 1971; Thornton, 1989; Van Inwagen, 1983) in the following way. If scientific laws govern the particles which compose the human body, then the motion of these particles is just as much a working-out of the laws of science as the motion of any other particles – say, those which compose the planets, or Halley's comet. But we expect to be able to predict the motion of Halley's comet, at least in principle. That is, we believe it could be done, if only more knowledge, more technology and so on were available, even when we accept that such things are not available at present, and perhaps never will be. So why are the motions of a human body not similarly predictable, assuming the same huge advances in technology?

Of course, to explore this topic would take us too far afield (see McFee, 1983). But three features are relevant, and move our argument forward. First, to accept that human behaviour is predictable in this sense would be to accept an absolute inevitability for it. To provide a rough analogy, if a gunman tells me to jump out of the window, it may seem inevitable that I will jump, but in fact it isn't. I could decide to stay and take my chances. Indeed, if his request instead were, say, that I blow up the world or betray a friend, it may even be that I prefer dying to obeying. But this is emphatically *not* the kind of inevitability under debate. For thinking of my behaviour as the result of inexorable scientific law leaves me no room at all for the exercise of my powers of choice. On the analogy, it would be as if six strong men siezed me and hurled me out of the window. I did not and could not choose, and that is true even if, as they rushed towards me, I shouted 'Please throw me out the window!'. That is to say, any feeling of choosing is simply an irrelevance, an illusion of the sort that might affect the passengers on an airplane flying over a railway yard. Looking down, with the train lines invisible from so high, it might appear that the trains were choosing to turn in this or that way. In fact, the motion of the trains is strictly governed by the track.

So, while it is certainly true that there is a physiological basis to dance (as to all human activity), to concentrate on that way of looking at dance is to view dance as (using one artificial contrast) movements of the body rather than as actions of the person, and to do so is to make the movement inevitable. This is not a perspective which can be taken of dance if one wants to keep viewing it *as dance*. For notions of creativity and of responsibility for one's work could no longer apply.

The second point is that the movement-of-the-body perspective takes us back to the particular movements performed by that physiology on a particular occasion. Yet we have already noted that movement as such is not what is distinctive of dance; that very sequence of movements could (in principle) have occurred as part of some other activity. So this perspective cannot be the one students of dance require. What it lacks, of course, is any way of referring to the context of an action.

The third point draws on the first two. It is sometimes suggested that dance is 'just' a sequence of movement, that such movements could equally well be performed by automata or by apes as by humans. David Carr (1984: p. 74), for example, critically discusses just such an attitude to the teaching of folk dance: if a group of students can 'go through the motions', get the steps (roughly) right, then the group has mastered that dance. As Carr notes, this way of treating the dance reduces it to 'a sequence of colourless movements'. Instead, one must recognize how human activities have specific purposes embedded in them; in this case, artistic purposes. Indeed, that is what it means to think of them as human activities. Thus, to claim that apes or automata were dancing would be to ascribe those (artistic) purposes to them. This is problematic. Apes are clearly not really candidates here (see Sparshott, 1988: pp. 217–20), and many theorists would accept that machines are not, either (Searle, 1984: pp. 57–70). At the least, such a contention is highly debatable, whereas it would not be were it obvious that simply making movements is equivalent to performing a dance. But if, in this way, we recognize that a dance is something other than just a sequence of movements, we must recognize that some ways of describing and explaining sequences of movement will therefore not be ways of describing and explaining dances.

Two ways of talking

As a means of sharpening our discussion, it is useful to introduce two ways of talking about our distinction between actions of persons and movements of the body. I have already implied that the action/movement contrast is not designed to correspond exactly to how we do use the words in English. Instead, to mark an important distinction, I have introduced technical senses of both these expressions. (In fact, this particular distinction is one commonly used in philosophy [Best, 1978a: p. 78; O'Connor, 1971: p. 100]). But we can augment it in two ways. First, we recognize that even my moving a pen to write a letter might be seen (by a doctor interested in manual dexterity) in terms of movements of the body, even though it is more properly seen as an action of the person. But there is only one 'thing' going on: there is just me writing away furiously (Anscombe, 1981: pp. 208–9). So the position is clarified if one speaks of the doctor as offering a *movement-description* and a *movement-explanation* of the event, while someone else might offer an *action-description* and an *action-explanation* of what happens. Thus the first way of talking focuses our attention on the different ways events are described or explained.

The second way of talking expands on the first, by introducing another technical contrast. For the movement description will focus on the sorts of explanations characteristic of the natural sciences. It cannot be far wide of the mark to think that such explanations focus on *causes*, and hence to call them *causal explanations*. But how are we to characterize explanations of action? A wide variety of terms crop up: 'reason', 'motive', 'choice', 'decision' and others. For ease of exposition, I shall call them *reason-type explanations*. So the second way of talking is a contrast between reason-type explanation and causal explanation.

It is accepted that the difference between explaining via causes and explaining via reasons is a technical one, not exactly corresponding to the uses of those words in ordinary language. For example, if I ask the reason that my car has broken down, I am actually asking for a causal explanation, since cars don't have reasons. Similarly, if I ask the cause of the breakdown of some political negotiations, I am probably asking for an explanation in terms of reasons or motives. Taken together, these ways of talking allow us to formulate a view of human behaviour, the two-language view, which urges that both of these kinds of explanation are essential to the description of human life, and that neither can be reduced to the other.

The two-language view argues for the distinctiveness of these two kinds of explanation – their logical independence – by arguing that one cannot 'translate' one kind of explanation into the other 'without remainder'. That is to say, if I had a complete causal story for a particular piece of behaviour, I could not with any certainty infer what the corresponding action story would be. Similarly, having a complete action story of the event, I could not guarantee what the causal story would be. In the relevant case, no causal description is ever exactly equivalent to the description employing notions like reason, motive, choice. The very same causal description in terms of one's arm going up could be any number of different actions: for example, buying a table at an auction, warding off a blow, asking to leave the room and so on. Also, the action of offending you could be performed in a number of ways, each with its own causal story: for example, I could offend you by talking to you, by not talking to you, by kicking your dog and so on. In each case, having one description, however complete, would not guarantee the appropriateness of some description of the other kind. Here we have argued for the independence of the two kinds of description or explanation urging that they are different in kind.

The importance of context

It is useful to review the argument of this chapter thus far, and to draw together its conclusions. What has been emphasized is that action-description is context-dependent and that it is essential to provide action-descriptions if one is considering what humans do. Further, that what distinguishes, say, dance from gymnastics is also provided by the context, built of a nexus of rules (not simply a location or a verbal formula). This way of understanding human activity picks out what is distinctive of human concerns. That point was made technically, using the action/movement contrast, by saying that the explanation of human action must be reason-type explanation. This is, in effect, a two-language view of human activity.

Here, then, we have a picture of the nature of action which draws out how *some* human activity – the action-type – can be meaningful, and how it can in principle be understood. As we have seen, that sort of understanding is appropriate to identify a movement sequence as dance, and hence to distinguish dance from other kinds of activity.

The following two sections, first, draw some general implications of this view of human activity – to offer an insight into ways of understanding dance – and then introduce a technical notion which offers a way of presenting complex points about the relationship between certain kinds of notions and the evidence or justification of them. For we are increasingly drawn to ask how one can be certain that a particular relationship holds – say, that a certain sequence of movements in a certain context really is, for example, *Black Angels* (1976). Here the (legal) notion of *defeasibility* will be brought to bear (Baker, 1977: pp. 26–57; Hacker, 1990: pp. 553–4, 565–6).

Insights from the two-language view

The first of two central insights from the two-language view is that one must always be clear whether one is offering reason-type description and explanation for a piece of human behaviour on the one hand or, on the other, causal (movement-type) description and explanation. That means being clear what kind of question one is answering. The dancer, for example, will need to be clear about the correct description of activities, distinguishing, say, stretching certain muscles from practising a certain kind of extension. The first will clearly be a causal description, while the second may be a reason-type description.

The second insight concerns the place of context and of the description under which the action was intended. For it is the context that determines what action is constituted by a particular sequence of movements. In different contexts, the very same sequence of movements could be different actions. To apply, in characterizing a certain activity as dance, I am not talking solely about what the sequence of movements is; that very same sequence of movements might occur in gymnastics or in some ritual or rite. Rather, I am characterizing the action, taking into account the description under which the action is intentional or deliberate; I am bearing in mind the context. Of particular relevance here might be the context of presentation, say, in a theatre or in a town square where the audience is expecting a dance presentation, and so on. These are not the only areas where dance could be presented, but certainly these will be characteristic or typical areas. Notice, too, that this context brings with it a vocabulary of discussion, analysis, appreciation, criticism and appraisal. Indeed, to speak of the audience as expecting a dance performance is to imply that they will take these critical, analytical concepts to be the appropriate ones in this case. Even if they do not, or cannot, use them personally, still they recognize their relevance or appropriateness in the writings and sayings of, for example, dance critics and dance theorists. Having characterized an event as dance, we would expect it to be appropriate to talk about the line and grace of the movement (or action), about some of its structural properties and, perhaps, about its expression or communication. And if we characterized it instead as gymnastics, we would expect that some similar concepts would apply (line and grace, for example), and others (such as communication) would not apply. This takes us back to the discussion, in Chapter 1, of the distinction between artistic appreciation and appreciation of the merely aesthetic.

To repeat something said earlier, characterizing an event as dance is of fundamental importance, for such a characterization operates as reason-type description rather than description of events solely as physical movements. This seems to me to be a very powerful insight of the two-language view. Notice too how the two-language view works against the worship of measurement and other crude versions of science. For it affirms that reason-type descriptions are genuine or real descriptions: they do describe features of the world, and features not amenable to the sorts of causal description commonly favoured by science. To repeat a familiar example (Best, 1974: p. 64), if asked by his wife why he is drunk, the husband giving the *causal* answer, 'Because I drank ten pints of beer' is simply not answering the question. Of course, what he says is true (it is even quantifiable), but it doesn't explain what the wife wants to know. She wants a reason-type description: 'I've been celebrating my promotion'; or 'I was drowning my sorrows at being fired', for example. Just because everything in the world can be examined scientifically, without anything being left out (to see this clearly, think about physics explaining all the fundamental particles and forces in the universe), it does not follow that this is the only sort of acceptable examination or investigation (see Best, 1978a: pp. 90–3). The two-language view undermines such a conclusion. If reason-type description is legitimate, it follows that there are other acceptable ways of explaining facts about the world, that is, ways other than the causal.

This conclusion is of particular importance for those, like dancers and choreographers, with a commitment to the arts. For (to repeat some remarks made in our discussion of objectivity) the fact that investigation by the hard sciences fails to reveal the grounds for aesthetic judgement does not imply that those grounds are somehow not there in the world, or are subjective in some way. Rather, it implies simply that there are other legitimate forms of investigation. Moreover, it suggests that the standards in those other forms of inquiry will operate differently from those characteristic of the hard sciences, for there is a diversity of questions or issues to be addressed, each with appropriate standards of correctness, just as questions (and hence answers) of physics differ from those of chemistry. Of course, truth, objectivity and validity are still sought, but they are no longer identified with one way of finding truth.

Again, it follows from the usefulness of the two-language view that there is no uniquely correct classification of behaviour. The search for a set of *basic* actions is just an argument for one taxonomy of action over another. And this would be argued for on grounds of usefulness, as driving instructors might take 'when changing direction and/or speed' as an occasion for looking in the driving mirror, while the rest of us might say things like 'before changing lanes', 'before pulling out', 'before slowing down'. The instructor's taxonomy may be more concise, but it is not more accurate or basic. The view developed here takes us further, for it makes it plain that the situation is exactly the same for causal descriptions: causal taxonomies are as arbitrary as any other. Thus one taxonomy could only be preferred to another for some ulterior reason or purpose.

Also, consider the nature of systems of notation, as viewed from a two-language perspective. It is often urged by their defenders, with much justice, that one advantage of a particular notation system – say, Labanotation, Benesh, or Eshkol-Wachmann – is that it can characterize all human movements, and hence can be used (for example, by anthropologists) to compare very different kinds of actions. For example, a study might compare the Roman Catholic mass with the Tai Chi Chuan solo exercise and the ballet *Checkmate*,[2] using the notated scores of each. (Notice that I am neither asserting nor denying that these notation systems can do this, I am merely recognizing the advantage there might be if they could.) But that tells us something about the character of such notation systems: they offer descriptions of what we have called movements rather than descriptions of actions. They are not context-sensitive descriptions. Indeed, if a notation description could only be used for, say, dance (that is, it characterized the activity as the action 'dance') it would for that reason be unfit for the description of other activities, and hence of no use for the anthropological purposes described earlier. Of course, this is no criticism of notation systems. We use, and need, both causal and reason-type description. Still, it should give us pause when faced with the worst excesses of enthusiasm for notation systems; it should make us recognize both what they can do and they cannot do.

A technical point: defeasibility

The difficulty with the whole view developed thus far is that we cannot readily describe the relationship between our remarks about human action and those about bodily movement; at least, we cannot do so if we assume that there must be a fixed, always-or-never kind of relationship here. On such a view, if a movement sequence were sometimes a particular action, then it must always be. Or, if not, then it really never is. Philosophy has often been concerned with such relationships, explained as *logical entailments* (Toulmin, 1976: pp. 53–81). But we know that here, as elsewhere, such a model does not reflect the real situation. To repeat an example: the intelligent, English-speaking Martian could not distinguish the real marriage from the rehearsal. We can, but not because the movements or the words or the location is different. This is a different context. But how can we describe the possibility of such a change of context, while still insisting that contexts are composed of movements, words, and locations, as well as rules? Luckily, a model which can stimulate our thinking on this topic is available. And adopting it allows us to explain some of the conclusions drawn in the previous section.

The technical way of elaborating this model employs the idea of defeasibility, for the application of certain concepts is defeasible. Here the picture comes from the law. If certain conditions, C, are fulfilled, then there is a contract between us. But 'contract' is a defeasible notion, which means that built into the idea of a contract are certain 'heads of exception' under which the contract would be undermined. These are usually expressed in a positive form – contracts must be 'true, full and free' – but in fact represent negative heads of exception (Baker, 1977: p. 33): if any is fulfilled, the contract is null and void. In a particular case, the onus of proving the satisfaction of such heads of exception is on the person who objects to the contract, given that conditions C are fulfilled, or who denies that there is a contract. But he must raise it as more than a mere possibility, as something which might occur. Rather, he must give reasons to think that, in this case, it will be realized. The situation resembles that of, say, a mathematical proof. Objecting to a supposed proof of mine, you must show exactly where I went wrong. You cannot simply voice the possibility that I did so, nor dispute the conclusion by disagreeing with it.

In the relevant case, suppose that I asked if a person did such-and-such, say, performed Martha Graham's *Lamentation* (1930). Or if a movement sequence is a particular action, say, a dance. Suppose, further, that it is accepted that a certain sequence of movements occurred, a sequence of movements which typically instantiated *Lamentation*. So, yes, the person did perform *Lamentation*. And, since *Lamentation* is a dance, yes, the sequence is a dance. Here we have a very simplified example of the application of the relevant concepts in the context. Since such action-concepts are defeasible, it follows that if the activity seems in this way to be *Lamentation* – the context is appropriate and the movement is apposite – there is no further question to answer. The conditions, C, are satisfied.

The importance of the defeasibility of concepts is this: if someone now chooses to dispute my claim, he cannot do so simply by raising the possibility that this sequence is not in fact *Lamentation* (or, even, that it is not dance). It is not my task to rule out mere possibilities that might undermine my claim. These counter-possibilities, especially the fanciful ones beloved of philosophers, must be shown to be relevant, which makes them more than mere possibilities. The objector must show reasons why, in this case, this movement sequence is not actually *Lamentation*, despite its similarities. If he can do so, he will have raised a head of exception to my claim that the activity is *Lamentation*. And one way to do so would be to show that the context was not, after all, an appropriate one.

Further, any reason I offer (say, for a critical judgement of a dance) is defeasible in a similar way: it assumes a context of puzzlement. So that a satisfactory account for one audience might not be adequate for another audience. Yet this could depend not on the completeness of the answer, but on the point of view of the person to whom the reasoning was offered. So my remarks on Rambert to a balletomane would differ from those I offer to a beginner in contemporary dance, and again from those I would offer to a person with no experience of dance.

Thus, even when the point of view of a question or investigation is clear, one does not attempt to rule out all counter-possibilities, but only those which that point of view places in the foreground. And one behaves in that way in the certain knowledge that, if the defeating conditions were satisfied, one's claims would not be justified.

Another point identified in the previous section develops from this one. For one might think that the point of view given by natural science is paramount. This thought is undermined once one recognizes that causal explanation is also point-of-view dependent, and in ways that render its explanations as defeasible as those employing reasons, as we will see in what follows.

In science, as in art, it is not necessary to check all counter-possibilities, all those events whose occurrences would alter the initial conditions in so drastic a fashion as to render different causal laws appropriate. Rather, I need check only on those possibilities given substance by the point of view implicit in this particular investigation. And this is as true for causal inquiries as for those to do with action: scientists control only for those variables which theory leads them to believe are the relevant ones. So that, for example, typical experiments in biomechanics take no notice of the position of the moon, and might well dismiss the suggestion that they should as mere astrology! But when we think about tides, we see that the moon is not (always) an irrelevance. Rather, theory tells the biomechanics experimenters that the moon is not relevant in this case. There is a temptation to think that all variables must be controlled for, but then one realizes that what are and what are not variables in a given context cannot be sorted out independently of the theoretical constructions one takes to be relevant: these imply a point of view. Similarly, one may think that there is always a right answer to questions about, say, the size of an object, independent of any point of view. Asked how long a table is, one may have the impression that a reply taken to six decimal places is somehow always more precise than the answer, 'about three feet long'. But if our interest lies simply in getting the table through a particular doorway, this second answer may be just what I need to hear; it may be sufficient. Then the answer to six decimal places won't be more precise, it will be plain silly! In terms of the point of view of the question, the purpose of the question, the answer 'about three feet' is perfectly precise. What I am urging then is that an answer which may be perfectly precise for one purpose, in answer to one question, may not be precise for some other purpose, even though the same words are used in both cases. What is fine as a reply for getting the table through the door, may be useless for, say, checking the accuracy or calibration of one's new microscope.

One way of making this point would be to consider a question like, 'What is *really* there?', pointing to a table or a human being, where, a scientific answer such as 'collections of elementary particles, in such-and-such configurations' might be offered (Wilkerson, 1974: pp. 165–6). The associated presumption might be that there is really just one answer to such a question. But the word 'really' in the question does not imply (as it might seem to) that the answer gives a deeper or more profound account of 'reality'; rather, it serves principally as a warning against being led (for example, by our senses) into some other view – and it does so in the context of a prior interest in finding an answer from, say, physics. That is to say, when we ask 'What is really there?', the context supplies the kind of answer needed. If we had asked the same question at a magic show the answer might well have been, for example, 'A woman with a black bag over her head' (as a description of the 'headless woman' illusion). And this would be the 'right' answer, even though she too is a collection of elementary particles!

In fact, there is no primary or basic description of 'how things are' or 'what is really there'; in particular, the causal description is not the primary one. Rather, the character of the appropriate description depends on the question being asked. And that in turn depends on the context of the utterance in question. So such descriptions and explanations are typically point-of-view dependent, because, as noted previously, the context brings with it a particular point of view. This point is made neatly by Wittgenstein (see Baker and Hacker, 1980: p. 352n) using the notion of the sharpness of knives. He imagines someone who asks for a breadknife but is given a razor 'because it is sharper'. It is not, of course, that one wants to deny that sharpness is important in knives nor that razors are sharp; rather, what one requires from a knife here is not given by some absolute conception of sharpness and hence is not better served by the razor than the breadknife. As this case illustrates, this context-dependence is equally the case with causal explanations and descriptions as it is with reason-type ones.

Of course, such kinds of descriptions do not depend on points of view in precisely the same way. Some, characteristically the aesthetic ones, involve the view of a particular person or group. This is typically not the case with descriptions from science, which have a more detached 'feel': they appear more 'objective', in just this sense of being more distanced (Nagel, 1986: pp. 25–7). However, the distancing does not lead to no point of view, but rather (at best) to no specific person's point of view: that it is, for example, the view of science rather than (merely) the view of certain scientists. Of course, I have not said enough to show conclusively that causal descriptions are point-of-view dependent (I would need to say a lot more about the notion of causation to establish that) but I have offered examples that give one reason to think that this is the right way to treat causes.

Conclusion

Despite the abstract character of this chapter, it will be helpful to pull together some of the strands of the argument to apply to the case in point, dance, and see just how we are answering the questions with which the chapter began. We have learned that what distinguished dance from gymnastics involved the *context* within which the activities are performed and perceived, and, as an extension, the concepts used in criticism and appreciation of those activities. For making sense of a piece of human behaviour is seeing what *action* it is: only then can we begin to understand it. And this is true of dance as of other actions. This means that what we *understand* as dance *is* dance, and so on. This may seem a weak conclusion, but we have ruled out some tempting ways of analysing dance, if one wants to concentrate on dance and not just, say, on the movements of the body that comprise a particular dance. We have seen that any analysis of dance must be a reason-type analysis; that causal analysis will be beside the point, or anyway not central. We have concluded that there is nothing that makes a particular sequence of movement really dance rather than something else; that is, nothing over and above people's activity (such as criticism and appreciation), the context, the interests and the analytical notions employed. We have seen that these sorts of concerns, manifested in reason-type description, are fundamental in human life. They cannot be dismissed as not real, not objective, not 'facts of the matter'.

Notice finally how the argument here reinforces the starting point of this chapter. We initially concluded that a question like 'What is dance?' lacked a context, and so we could not recognize an accurate answer. It may have seemed strange at that time to place such an importance on context. But the ensuing discussion has clarified the importance of understanding the context of questions if one is to know how to answer them. This general point about understanding should be borne in mind throughout our consideration of the understanding of dance.

Recommended reading

The best brief discussion is Carr, 1987. Carr, 1984 also provides a perspective. A discussion of much of the complexity is Sparshott, 1988: pp. 167–268, 380–96. Some key distinctions are found in Best, 1978a: pp. 74–98.

3
Dance as Art

In Chapter 2 we asked 'What makes a particular movement sequence a piece of dance rather than, say, a piece of gymnastics?'. And we concluded that the context was strongly important. Further, our concern was with dance as art. It may seem, therefore, that there is another issue here. Given that a certain sequence is offered as dance, what makes it really or genuinely dance? That is to say, what makes it art? Such a question might be prompted by cases of avant-garde or modern dance: for example, works by Twyla Tharpe (*Push Comes to Shove*, 1976), Yvonne Rainer (*Trio A*, 1967), Laura Dean (*Changing Pattern, Steady Pulse*, 1974) or perhaps – since audiences typically seem a little behind in the times, having trouble with things other artists find unproblematic – some work by Merce Cunningham. Certainly, in the visual arts, examples would include the Carl Andre firebricks (see Ground, 1989), and in music, the John Cage piece *4 Minutes 33 Seconds*. But similar pieces of (arguable) 'minimalism' do occur in dance. For example, David Best (1985: p. 14) describes a case in which a group sat in the middle of the dance studio eating crisps (American 'chips') as their dance presentation. Why wasn't this dance, if it wasn't; or why was it dance, if it was? Clearly one part of the answer here involves a general consideration of why things are dance, and hence why they are art. In part, the relevant answer will appear as we go along. But one segment of our answer is worth noting: the contrast (from Chapter 1) between artistic appreciation and the appreciation of the merely aesthetic; also the discussion of context and the importance of appropriate concepts in the consideration of a movement sequence (from Chapter 2) – particularly when combined with the thought that neither the term 'dance' nor the term 'art' is susceptible to definition (again, from Chapter 1).

Tradition and conventions of art

First, let us be clear as to the importance for understanding art of a grasp of the traditions and conventions of an art form. This topic was introduced briefly in Chapter 1, and is implicit (also explicit) at other points in the discussion. For the difference between knowing what to make of a dance, picture or play, and failing to see anything in it depends on just such a grasp of the traditions and conventions of the art form. We can see this clearly in a case where it breaks down, one so brilliantly discussed by Richard Beardsmore (1971) that I shall merely recapitulate his discussion. For it was lack of such a grasp of traditions and conventions that led Tolstoy (in *What is Art?* [1895] 1930) to completely misconstrue the opera he describes. It was, Tolstoy tells us:

> one of the most ordinary of operas for people who are accustomed to them, but also one of the most gigantic absurdities that could possibly be devised. An Indian king wants to marry; they bring him a bride; he disguises himself as a minstrel; the bride falls in love with the minstrel and is in despair, but afterwards discovers that the minstrel is the king, and everyone is highly delighted.
>
> That there never were or could be such Indians, and that they were not only unlike Indians, but that what they were doing was unlike anything on earth except other operas was beyond all manner of doubt; that people do not converse in such a manner as recitative, and do not place themselves at fixed distances in a quartet, waving their arms to express their emotions; that nowhere except in theatres do people walk about in such a manner, in pairs, with tin halberds and in slippers; that no one ever gets angry in such a way . . . and that no one on earth can be moved by such performances – all this is beyond the possibility of doubt. (Tolstoy, 1930: p. 78; also quoted in Beardsmore, 1971: pp. 41–2)

Tolstoy's description reduces what he saw to a 'gigantic absurdity', at least in part, by emphasizing how what he saw and heard was not commonplace, everyday, 'natural'. Yet, Tolstoy's complaint is groundless, given the importance of, in this case, theatrical and operatic traditions and conventions. Indeed, it highlights just what one should expect: that the formal features crucial to artistic appreciation acquire their force from traditions and conventions. For, within opera (or any art form), formal features have an importance which cannot be understood apart from such conventions. And seeing this is integral to seeing the activity as opera. But Tolstoy really fails to do this. Naturally what takes place in a theatre does not have the importance (if any) that otherwise similar activities have elsewhere. They could not; any more than, say, the significance which attaches to the movements of the pieces within a game of chess could be considered divorced from the game. As we saw in

Chapter 2, only in the context do those movements amount to that particular action. As Beardsmore (1971: p. 42) puts it:

> To complain that it is only in a theatre that "people converse in such a way as recitative" is as absurd as complaining that only in a chess game do people try to check-mate one another. For just as it is only given the traditions of chess that check-mating is even conceivable, so it is only given certain operatic and theatrical traditions that recitative can have the significance which it does.

As Beardsmore diagnoses, positions such as Tolstoy's result from a failure to draw crucial distinctions between what is relevant to appreciation of, in this case, opera (that they converse in recitative) and what is irrelevant. For example, it is simply irrelevant that the halberds are tin foil and not steel, or that the footwear is slippers – just as the colour of the actor's eyes (Beardsmore's example) is irrelevant. There are operatic conventions that give sense to conversing in recitative, although none which relate to halberd construction. By ignoring such conventions, Tolstoy makes the proceedings on the stage seem arbitrary: the 'pointlessness' of the halberd construction then attached to the conversing in recitative, which, given the conventions, is not pointless. To put it roughly, Tolstoy does not recognize that the conventions give one thing (but not the other) the status of a reason for some artistic judgement.

We can apply this point to our case by asking, 'What is required in order that I take a particular movement sequence to be dance?'. We have already implicitly answered this question in Chapter 1. I must take the movement to be the sort of thing that can be understood or made sense of, of which the precise details mattered, that has a background of conventions and traditions. In short, I value it as I value art.[1]

This discussion illustrates ways in which the understanding of art, because of its conventional character, stands in need of elucidation. Having identified the role of conventions in our understanding, however indirectly, we need to say more about how those conventions and traditions operate.

Conventions and understanding

One point already seen (Chapter 1) concerns the role of the history of an art form for our understanding of works in that form. So that we draw on our knowledge of previous works when we come to confront

69

a particular work. In part, this results from the importance, in works of art, of formal or structural relations, as we have said. And one cannot learn to recognize such relations, much less learn their importance (in particular their expressive importance), from just the work under consideration. Rather, we necessarily draw on our knowledge of other works (and perhaps other forms), although we may be doing so implicitly. In this way, we can find elements in a new dance intelligible to us if they are related to familiar elements from previous dances. And this point applies whether the elements in question are formal, or whether they employ content. Indeed, such a point is regularly made about the understanding of art works, even of dances: for example, Susan Leigh Foster (1986: p. 2) remarks that Martha Graham's *Acts of Light* (1981) 'represents an inventory of the now well-established Graham lexicon – from simple articulations of the spine to dazzling jumps and leaps from the floor'. The implication here is that we can make sense of *Acts of Light* because we can make sense of these movements and sequences (and their place within the whole); and that we can make sense of the movements and sequences because they are part of a 'well-established lexicon'. This is just the point I am urging.

This point is most easily seen if we consider a case where ideas from one work are employed in another: a valuable source is jokes (that is, 'humorous quotation'). For example, in the film *White Christmas* (1954), the Danny Kaye character performs a dance number (with a cast of female dancers) entitled *Choreography* which makes fun of the Martha Graham style. The 'quotation' is obvious, the costumes and hairstyles a giveaway, and the point is that tap-dance in hit shows has been replaced by what they call 'choreography', typified by this reference to (or quotation from) Graham. The period suggested is the late 1940s, *Errand into the Maze* (1947) and *Cave of the Heart* (1946) most of all. But the point is a more general one, for, to understand the joke, we must recognize the Graham style and hence see that it is not really being used here. Thus the quotation serves to locate (some of) the context of our understanding.

We see a similar point when there is a comparably clear relation between elements in two works, and especially between two works within the *ouevre* of one choreographer. So that we might ask how much the woman in a kind of stretchy sack in Martha Graham's *Acts of Light* owes to her *Lamentation* (1930)? Here I am not considering its composition, but our experience of it. Even if we – as critic or audience or members of what I shall call the Republic of Dance (see pp. 72–3) – decide that this is not genuine quotation, our understanding of it is certainly coloured by *Lamentation*. We might also think of the wrapped

70

figure of Medea in *Cave of the Heart*. So that even if *Acts of Light* is (as Robert Cohan called it[2]) 'one of her abstract, pure dance works' (as, I take it, *Lamentation* was not), the expressive potential of the movements of the woman in the sack in *Acts of Light* is dependent on the ways those sorts of movements were used fifty years earlier.

If these movements in *Acts of Light* are to be understood in terms of some specific earlier work of Graham's such as *Lamentation*, then obviously we must have some sense of *Lamentation* if we are to understand the later work. And this would be even more true if we think of the reference as not to some specific work, but rather to (say) Graham's work as a whole. I put the matter in this guarded way because, except in cases of actual quotation, one clearly does not need to have seen *Lamentation* oneself. It is sufficient to be part of a tradition that knows that work. Seeing the traditions and conventions of art as operating in broadly this way, we now ask ourselves how the concepts of art implicit in such traditions and conventions operate: how they are employed in our making sense of the particular art works before us.

It must be acknowledged that there is a variety within what counts as art, but this variety is not as great as is often supposed. A man who appreciates classical music must admire someone from a list of established composers – Bach, Mozart, Beethoven, Wagner – or, if he does not, he must have some explanation, if we are to accept his claim to appreciate classical music (Cavell, 1979: p. 13). So there is a broad consensus here. But how is it maintained? What is it that makes the objects in question art?

An institutional account of art

Having accepted (Chapter 1) that the term 'art' cannot be defined, we cannot go on to describe in detail what it is to be art. So what can we do to fill in our account here? We cannot hope to completely articulate any answer to questions about what makes art really art. However, we can introduce the style of answer to be offered to such questions: that style is an institutional one.[3] This idea will be outlined, and then some objections will be confronted.

The central thought here is, roughly, that something is art if the right people say it is art. That basic thought has to be complicated further for art in general, and still further for dance in particular. Such complications will emerge later in this chapter, and in this work as a whole, but the first point to recognize is that the process we are describing – or, rather, offering an abstract model of – should best be thought of in two

71

stages. In the first stage a work is offered as art. We can call that stage 'self-election': someone puts an object forward as art. The second stage might be called 'other-acclamation', and amounts, roughly, to that work being accepted by others. In the case of art in general, that group of others will be fairly wide, including other artists, critics, performers (where relevant), gallery owners or theatre managers, as well as historians and philosophers of the arts. Terry Diffey (1969) has extended the eighteenth-century idea of a 'Republic of Letters' to catch just this sense of variety. He speaks of a Republic of Art, a vivid phrase which I propose to adopt, along with much of his argument. In the specific case of dance, the 'Republic' will be composed of choreographers, producers, dance-theatre owners and so on, and, in particular (other) dance critics and dance theorists. Any movement sequence put forward as dance (self-election) and accepted by others (other-acclamation by the Republic) is indeed a dance.

If a work that is put forward as dance does not receive this other-acclamation, two courses of action are open to those putting the work forward (apart from simply accepting that the movement isn't dance after all and letting it sink into obscurity). The first is to wait for the judgement of posterity: to assume that one is right and wait to be proved right, when later dance theorists and dance critics regard the work as art. That is to say, when the judgement of the Republic changes. But this is a doubtful path to success, particularly if one reflects on the history of the art form.

A more enlightened course of action could be to attempt to shape taste, so that one's work is accepted as art; that is, so that it will receive the necessary other-acclamation. This can either be done oneself – as in the case of T. S. Eliot, whose criticism created the taste by which his own poetry was admired – or by others. So Clive Bell created a climate of criticism appropriate for the appreciation of Cezanne, and Ruskin did the same for Turner. In the dance case, we might be thinking of the changes in aesthetic values, and hence in what is thought about dance, brought about by the critic XXX through his writing in the *Journal des Debats* from 1828 to 1832 (Chapman, 1984). In contrast to other critics of the time, who emphasized the narrative, literal and dramatic elements of the ballet, XXX enjoyed the dance for its non-literal appeal. So his writing emphasized the expressive quality of the dancing itself; and it is not too fanciful to see the subsequent shift in critical interest from pantomime effects in ballet to a (pure) dance as resulting from XXX's writing, for the reviews and articles amount to a sustained polemic for that view. The outcome of such a shift in taste would be the other-acclamation of works previously not seen as art.

72

Notice that what is actually done here is a kind of public relations job. But it involves the validation of certain critical concepts: the vocabulary of criticism is changed in these events and, with it, the sorts of things which count as a reason for an artistic judgement. So the other complications needed, in general and specifically for dance, can be introduced when we see the nature and role of such critical concepts (in Chapters 6 and 7). For now, we must record some features of our institutional theory before returning to the central task, expanding our account of the institutional character of art by confronting a major objection.

There are four aspects of our institutional account of art that are worth noting briefly here, since they conflict with George Dickie's (1974) position, which is typically used (for example by Wollheim [1980b: p. 157]) as representative of institutional theories of art. First, Dickie offers a definition of art. We do not. Although we accept that something can and must be said about the nature of art such as dance, we also accept that this cannot amount to a definition of art. (It may be that Dickie actually agrees here, but he still uses that way of speaking, with all its implications [Dickie, 1984: p. 77].) Second, Dickie's theory concerns the term 'art' in, as Dickie puts it (1974: p. 34), 'the classificatory sense'. That is to say, his theory employs a firm distinction between classification or description on the one hand, and evaluation on the other. As will become clear, our account does not employ this distinction in a rigid way. Defeasibly, the assignment of art status to an object brings with it both the possibility of evaluation, and the implication of a minimal evaluative content. Put roughly, when we say something is art, we are suggesting that it is, to that extent, a good thing.[4] Third, Dickie's theory is a one-stage theory (see Dickie, 1984: p. 9); our has two stages, namely, self-election and other-acclamation. Finally, Dickie explicitly contrasts his institutional ideas with what he calls an aesthetic attitude type of theory. Indeed, he cites his dissatisfaction with that sort of theory as a key reason for elaborating his institutional one (Dickie, 1974: p. 10). The aesthetic attitude theory urges that an object is art if it is seen or approached in some characteristic way, for example, with disinterested, contemplative awareness.[5] But, if we articulate this kind of theory in certain ways, there is nothing in our institutional theory that requires us to reject this idea wholly. Certainly we cannot (as we shall see) allow that objects become art because of some aesthetic attitude, but that does not mean that we cannot, for example, speak of art as 'proving itself on our aesthetic pulses' (as I did elsewhere [McFee, 1980b]). To make such a claim is just to recognize that bringing aesthetic concepts to bear on seeing an object and taking that object to be art are not really distinguishable. To find the argument for this claim, however,

73

we must turn to a powerful objection to all institutional theories. Our reply to it will allow us to substantiate this claim.

A fundamental objection to institutional theories of art

There are many difficulties for institutional theories of art, even when those theories are presented in as sketchy a way as was done in the previous section. Here, however, I propose to consider an elegant argument which promises to show, once and for all, that an institutional account of art is impossible. Richard Wollheim (1980b) argues this by dilemma in the course of his discussion of institutional definitions of art. As we have seen, on institutional accounts one learns about the nature or character of art by considering how objects become (acquire the status of) works of art. The institutional answer has traditionally involved this status being conferred on the object by some group of people 'whose roles are social facts' (Wollheim, 1980b: p. 157). Some thought of this kind is a central part of any institutional account of art deserving of the title, for such conferring is (or, at least, models) the institutional actions whose importance is emphasized in such accounts of art. So Wollheim's dilemma, which (if successful) squarely undercuts such a model, strikes at the heart of institutional accounts. The argument is relatively simple. Wollheim (1980b: p. 160) asks:

> Is it to be presumed that those who confer status on some artifact do so for good reasons, or is there no such presumption? Might they have no reason, or bad reasons, and yet their action be efficacious given that they themselves have the right status – that is, they represent the art world?

Wollheim attempts to use this question to generate an insoluble dilemma for any institutional account. Here is the first horn. If the 'conferrers' have good reasons for taking the work to be art – reasons, that is, that antedate the conferring of art status – all they do is to confirm by their action that the object enjoyed art status prior to that action. Hence something other than their action makes the object art. Thus to take this option is, Wollheim thinks, to acknowledge that art works are not, after all, institutional objects, for their art status antedates their 'conferring'.

The other horn of the dilemma comes from denying that any reason is required. All that is required is that the conferrers have the appropriate status. For this reply violates what Wollheim (1980b: p. 163) speaks of as 'two powerful intuitions that we have'. These are, first, that there is an interesting connection between being a work of art and being a good work of art, and second, that there is something important to the status of being a work of art. Any aesthetician will surely want to acknowledge both of these. Yet really they come to the same thing in this context: that art status (taking something to be a work of art) minimally implies a commendation of that thing, and also places it in a category which allows for commendation. But, Wollheim urges (1980b: p. 164), if art status can be conferred for 'no good reasons', the importance of that status is placed in serious doubt. For surely what can be conferred for no good reason cannot be of any great importance; yet we do not doubt the importance of art status. So this is the dilemma. Choosing the first horn endangers the claim of the account to be institutional. Choosing the second endangers its relation to art, at least as traditionally understood, by making the value of art status arbitrary.

Nor can this objection be avoided by reformulating the institutional theory. If one dropped the idea of 'conferring' art status, as some recent writers have (Dickie, 1984: pp. 11–12), a similar objection can still be raised, for nothing particularly turns on the notion of conferring as such. The dilemma can be restated as follows: 'Is work X presented by the artist to the art world public for some good reason, or might there be no reason?'. One cannot avoid this dilemma simply by reformulating one's theory, as this example illustrates.

A reply to this objection

If this dilemma can be foisted on any institutional account of art it will succeed in making that account at least very implausible. And while it may be necessary for the institutional theorist to grasp a few of the nettles of implausibility, too many destroy the account. What I will try to show here is that a member of the Republic of Art can confer status – or, better, take an object to be a work of art – in a way which both allows that nothing other than his so taking it makes it a work of art (apart from others in the Republic so taking it, thus accepting his claim) and then he can still offer reasons, give explanations and so on in justification of that work's art status. In short, we need to relate the discussions and explanations he would give to the conferring. If one can speak at length, giving reasons and so on, as critics do, about works that are art for no prior reason than one's institutional action, one does not violate the two intuitions Wollheim mentions in developing the second horn of his dilemma.

75

At first sight, it may seem impossible to develop this option, for surely, if there are reasons or explanations to be offered, they could be used in support of the art status of the work prior to the institutional action. To follow this line would be to accept Wollheim's conclusion. But a first thought here would be that the categorial difference, whether or not the object in question is a work of art, may itself play a role. That is to say, whether or not the concepts one uses are artistic concepts may itself be important. Perhaps acceptance (or acknowledgement [Cavell, 1979: p. 157]) as art brings with it sets of reasons or explanations otherwise unavailable. For example, one might argue (as Danto has done) that there is a crucial difference of category between a necktie decorated with paint by a child, and an indistinguishable tie painted by Picasso:

I would hesitate to predict a glorious artistic future for the child merely on the ground that he had produced an entity indiscernible from one turned out by the greatest master of modern times . . . I am prepared to go further and insist that . . . what the child has effected is not an art work; something prevents it from entering the confederation of enfranchised art works into which Picasso's tie is accepted easily, if without immense enthusiasm. (Danto, 1981: p. 40)

The outcome of the difference of category – which means the appropriateness of certain concepts being applied – is that what could be said of Picasso's blue tie, the set of reasons employed in interpreting it (say, its absence of visible brush strokes) is simply not available on the child's effort.

This means that institutional action with respect to some particular works might be said not merely to confer art status on those works, but also to create categories of art (see Chapter 1) which bring with them a universe of critical discourse. But only the actual 'conferment' takes place. To make this discussion more concrete, let us employ an actual case.[6] As an example of the sort of reasons operative here, consider a brief critical discussion by Marcia Siegel of work by William Dunas, whom Siegel (1977: p. 313) calls 'the most important dancer we could support today . . . the most consistently creative person in all of dance'. She discusses an hour-long piece, *I Went With Her and She Came With Me* (1973):

in which Dunas merely walked around a space. Following straight, diagonal, or slightly curving paths, he slowly lifted one foot, then the other, going continuously except for brief rest stops. (Siegel, 1977: p. 314)

76

It is not difficult to imagine a cynic dismissing this as 'just a guy walking about for an hour'. But Siegel remarks:

> I never lost interest in the piece...I enjoyed examining Dunas' movement, which is very complex as to the way he distributes his weight, rearranges his tensions, contains himself in space. Since the step itself changed so little, I could pay full attention to its ingredients and discover new aspects of it...(1977, p. 315)

Siegel explains the interest of this dance: 'Maybe he's trying to lower my threshold to differences' (Siegel, 1977: p. 313). Later she comments: 'The piece has a meaning as metaphor. The narration suggested exile and war to me' (Siegel, 1977: p. 315). And, in summary of Dunas' work (although specifically about another piece), Siegel concludes:

> His dancing always conveys to me a fanatic determination to do more, to last longer than anyone humanly can, together with a holding back from complete commitment, an implied fear of unleashing his full strength. (1977, p. 318)

A serious spectator to *I Went With Her and She Came With Me*, duly puzzled by it, might find in Siegel's remarks a way of making sense of it, a way of finding it intelligible. That is to say, such a person might come to regard the Dunas dance as art as a result of reading this criticism (see also Mothersill, 1975). And this is true even when the person in question is one whose other-acclamation would, on an institutional account, make this a work of art. Indeed, if self-proclaimed artists are to conduct a public relations exercise on behalf of their work – as we have seen, an idea surely central to the institutional model – such conversion is exactly what is predicted. And the person's coming to regard the Dunas dance in this way will allow him to say at least something in its defence if asked whether or not it is any good. For here we see that aesthetic status and aesthetic value, subjects of Wollheim's 'two powerful intuitions', are connected.

Yet notice two things. First, the familiar point that there is nothing general about Siegel's comment on Dunas. She clearly admires this work, thinks it of high artistic merit. But another work which might be crudely characterized in exactly the same way might not also be meritorious; it would not necessarily even be art. It might seem that this fact derives from the crudeness of the characterization, but actually it explains why any characterization will always be open to the charge of

77

crudeness. For the comment is only fully specific when it is seen in conjunction with the work in question, and this seems a general fact about art criticism. Yet the second point is more central. For Siegel characterizes the power of the Dunas dance in two ways: first, by reference to the complexity and interest of the movement itself – by reference to the manipulation of the medium, as it were (see Chapter 9) – and second, in terms of the metaphorical dimension, of what the dance 'suggested'. In both cases, reasons are offered which, if accepted, explain the power of this Dunas dance, a power Siegel acknowledges. In both cases, the reasons draw on explicit or implicit comparisons with what might be said of other dances – as it were, of more traditional dances. So that the concern with movement-detail links these remarks to a tradition of such concerns in dance criticism, going back at least to XXX around 1830 (Chapman, 1984), and exemplified by Siegel on, say, Graham's *Dark Meadow* (1946):

> The chorus invokes the life force springing from these natural phenomena – the urge to dance and to mate. Graham created for these four couples a wonderful series of duets, which they perform mostly in unison, that combine rhythmic drive with beautiful intertwinings of bodies... But... this sensuality was very carefully controlled; the couples don't act out love scenes, they portray the modes of love. (Siegel, 1979: pp. 192–3)

Here we see a concern with movement as such, with its expressive potentials. Yet a concern with movement as such is just what Siegel finds in Dunas.

But the claim that the Dunas dance is 'about' war also connects it with a traditional concern of dance; indeed, of art more generally. So that, for example, a critical tradition including Alvin Ailey's *Adagio for a Dead Soldier* (1970)[7] is thus brought to bear.

What might we learn by accepting the accuracy of Siegel's remarks about Dunas, by having our taste shaped by them? The answer is that these remarks simultaneously treat the work as art and give us a critical vocabulary for discussion of it, namely, a vocabulary drawn from other works in the critical tradition thus established. That vocabulary will locate the discussion in a particular period, for the exact force of the implicit comparisons will change as critical opinion on Graham, Ailey, and so on, changes. At some other time, informed criticism of the Dunas piece might even find the reference to war, with its implied comparisons, a ludicrous one. On the option I am sketching, should this happen, one reason for the art status of the Dunas, and one set of critical tools for its discussion would have been removed. And both removed at a stroke, as it were. For what allows purchase to the critical tools is the art status of the object – and, we might say, what makes the object art is the purchase of these critical tools.

Notice, then, that taking this option does not require that, given that we think art valuable for certain reasons, there is still no reason why certain things are considered art. Rather, there is no such reason antecedently for their being so considered. Once we take the objects to be art, a wealth of analytical tools becomes available, and our taking the objects to be art may be no more than our taking those tools to be appropriate for the analysis and discussion of those objects.

A diagnosis of the origin of the objection

To recognize the possibility of taking this option in response to Wollheim's objection is not to have compelling arguments. Given that one can ascribe this significance to the difference in categories, why should one prefer the resultant position to Wollheim's view of the matter? What, apart from an attachment to the institutional, should drive one in that direction? Such questions point to a fundamental issue here: the presuppositions which generate Wollheim's powerful yet simple argument.

Wollheim has made it clear that, in the relevant case, questions of whether or not object X is a work of art can always be correctly answered either 'yes, it is' or 'no, it isn't', even though we don't know which. As I shall put it, Wollheim thinks there are determinate answers to such questions. And those answers do not change at different times in history; they are ahistorical. Further, Wollheim claims that questions of whether or not there is a reason for object X being a work of art have determinate answers, independently of anyone asking, or answering those questions – hence ahistorically. When (and whether) the question is asked or answered would be beside the point on such a view. Rather, if there is a reason found at some particular time, then there *is* a reason, and that is all there is to be said. A moment's reflection shows the importance of this assumption in Wollheim's picture of reasons and explanations, for such things are reasons, he thinks, antecendently of other people – indeed, anyone ever – finding them reasons. In taking such a view we would be implicitly assuming that an object could be art without our say-so. By this I mean that, on this view, whether or not there is a reason for such-and-such does not depend on our knowing that reason, or even our knowing that there is such a reason. If reasons work as Wollheim suggests they do – or, more exactly, as he assumes they do – one might expect his dilemma to be a real one for any institutional theory. For that picture of reasons is quite explicit in the first horn of the dilemma, as it was articulated above.

I shall not argue here that this conception of reasons is wrong, although I wish to assert that it is. But notice three features. First, it is ahistorical: it takes no account of the position of the audience for art in history. As we will see, this is a commitment which we may prefer to give up. Second, it would oblige us to treat the cases where a difference of category seems to make a difference, as given above, in some other way. Such an outcome may seem a little surprising, not least because works of art are man-made objects. What category a particular object belongs to, when that object is man-made, does seem to be the sort of thing that human 'decision' might resolve.

It seems right that artistic objects are objects as experienced by us, objects construed by us – or anyway by people. Surely it seems very plausible in the case of something so transparently man-made as art to limit meaningful claims about art to those within the scope of human knowledge or human participation. And this means, in contrast to Wollheim's picture, that what are reasons will be reasons for particular groups of people, at particular times and places, with particular interests and so forth. And of course, this is one reason why we might conceive of such reasons rather differently than in the ahistorical manner Wollheim suggests.

The third point – which, of course, will carry little weight with opponents of institutional accounts – is that this view of reasons will conflict with the standard characterization of institutional concepts: for example, that given by Quinton (1963: pp. 190–1):

> Institutional concepts . . . are those that apply to the fruits of human contrivance. First and foremost artefacts (tools, machines, houses, furnishings); then institutions proper (marriage, property, the state): the social roles associated with them (king, priest, creditor); customs and practices (manners, games, meals).

What is and what is not a work of art is surely determined by humans and for humans. If art status is the product of some kind of human consensus, one might expect that what is and what is not a relation to the 'fruits of human contrivance' is itself a matter of human contrivance, of what one wished to do with an object, of how one sees it.

However, one important idea implicit (or mentioned) here but not sufficiently stressed is the difference between institutional matters and (other) rule-governed ones, for example, language (Baker and Hacker, 1984a: pp. 272–3). For institutional concepts, an authoritative body, although perhaps of an unstructured kind, is required to pronounce on its rules. So that, for example, language is rule-governed and the normativity of language is directly established in language-using behaviour, so that all such behaviour is potentially relevant. By contrast, the normativity of an institutional concept (like art) requires that some, but not others, can pronounce on its normativity. It is the activity of this 'institution' that marks the concept as institutional. Again, the parallel with the concept 'machine' is close. For it is generally accepted that not every Tom, Dick or Harry is competent to judge on matters mechanical. And this point is crucial, for it is this feature that marks out our understanding as institutional.

The final thing to note here is that Wollheim's picture too is not self-evident. He thinks of reasons in certain ways, because he thinks of knowledge and of understanding and, in particular, of meaning in a certain way. An important point to recognize here, then, is that Wollheim's view is plausible only if one wishes to go along with other philosophical views to which he subscribes. But for now it is sufficient to recognize that adopting a different picture of meaning and understanding allows us to combat Wollheim's otherwise appealing argument. What I am saying is that Wollheim's argument can be defused by a rejection of the views it presupposes, but that this cannot be given up independently of other views, particularly those in the philosophy of language.[8]

What must be recognized at this juncture is that I am not offering some general thesis about all concepts. To put it at its simplest: even if there were no people, still there would be mountains and red things and bushes. So that if we think about such concepts – 'mountains', 'red', 'bush' – there is a clear sense in which we can call them 'world-dependent' (whatever other theses we produce for them). But some concepts are not world-dependent in this way. Rather, they are person-dependent. For some concepts – for example, the concept 'machine' or equally, of course, 'art' – if there were no people there would be no machines and no art. These are, as one writer quoted above rightly termed them, 'fruits of human contrivance'. And I am suggesting that, for such concepts, institutional concepts as we are calling them, an institutional analysis of the sort outlined above is right and appropriate. One could summarize the conclusion by saying that institutional facts (that is, facts whose descriptions employ institutional concepts) depend on what people do and say. But that does not make them any the less true, or any the less facts.

Digression: the 'community' view of concepts

At this stage it is advisable to say something, briefly and dogmatically, about other concepts, since there is in the philosophical literature a growing view (perhaps one I held earlier[9]) that all our concepts should be given some kind of 'community' analysis. This is clearly wrong.

As Baker and Hacker (1984b) show, it is to combat such a view, among others, that Wittgenstein undertakes his discussion of rule-following in *Philosophical Investigations*. And what I say here follows Baker and Hacker's discussion. For if we think of meaning as depending on certain rules (say, for the use of expressions) then the crucial question will be what it is to follow such a rule: and the community analysis will reply that following a rule amounts to doing what the linguistic community does. Thus, in the case of a completely isolated Robinson Crusoe figure, his words will have meaning, his sounds will indeed be words, if we can 'take him into our community': roughly, if his use of the rules coincides with ours. On such an account, the normative notion of following a rule is assimilated to the statistical notion of acting in the way most people would in such-and-such conditions. Against such a community view, we should urge instead that, in order that Crusoe's words have meaning, he must follow the rules correctly. This means disentangling the idea of normativity – of right and wrong – from that of mere statistical regularity (see Chapter 2). Applying a rule-governed expression correctly just is applying it in accordance with the rules of its use. And this means that we need to concentrate, not on what we understand by a rule, but on the correct understanding, or perhaps on cases where we evidently understand correctly.

Such understanding can be manifested in two ways, both emphasizing the connection between understanding the rule and recognizing correct application of it (see Baker and Hacker, 1984b: p. 75). The first is through the giving and explaining of formulations of that rule. Thus, if asked about the rules or conventions ramblers adhere to when crossing cultivated land – say, you ask why one shouldn't walk in a certain ploughed area – I can tell you that it is wrong to do so, and why. I can formulate the rule for you, and also explain the rule.

But a second way in which understanding is manifested is through applying that rule in practice. That is, I display my understanding of the 'rules of the ramble' if I cross the ploughed area in the prescribed way, or at least, if I do so for that reason. So these are two ways in which the understanding of rules can be manifested. Neither of these is a statistical matter. Rather, each is to be interpreted bearing in mind that 'the concept of a rule and the concept of what accords with it (what is a correct application) are internally related' (Baker and Hacker, 1984b: p. 72). When I understand a rule I typically know what would count as satisfying it, just as when I intend something I typically know what would count as fulfilling my intention. And the qualifying word 'typically' in the first case, as in the second, is only there to mark two difficulties: first, I may not be able to say what would do this satisfying or fulfilling, although I must surely recognize it; and, second, there may be certain hard cases where it is beyond my powers to determine whether or not the rule has been correctly applied. But the possibility of such hard cases need not concern us unduly, for we have an ample supply of straightforward examples, where I do know what to do and say. Yet if understanding of a rule is demonstrated both through giving and explaining formulations of that rule, and through applying the rule in practice – which even the community view surely accepts – our account of the features of rule-following serves to emphasize that these are not mere indicators of rule-understanding but are, rather, criterial of it. It is this emphasis on an internal (or necessary) connection which distinguishes our account of normativity from the empirical one which identifies it with statistical regularity. We can see this point clearly when we realize that, in some straightforward examples, the majority of judgements made may generally be wrong, for example (Baker and Hacker, 1984b: pp. 71–2), most long division is done by school children, largely incorrectly, and then corrected by their teachers. Statistically, therefore, the majority of attempts to 'follow the rule' for long division fail, but this does nothing to undermine the rule. It is what people do in acting in accordance with a rule, 'the *practice* of normative behaviour' (Baker and Hacker, 1984b: p. 53), that underlies our language, and hence underlies meaning and understanding as such. It is in this context that Wittgenstein often quoted Goethe: 'Im Anfang war die Tat' – 'In the beginning was the deed' (see McFee, 1991).

Ideally, what is required is a competent follower of a certain rule, for his or her acts would provide a guide to correctly following the rule. Such a manoeuvre is of no use in general, for we must characterize such competence in terms of a previously understood notion of correctness. For aesthetics, however, it has some place. Indeed, the idea of an institutional account of art amounts roughly to specifying some competent rule-followers prior to (or constitutive of) some such notion of correctness.

Discussion of the flaws of the community analysis of concepts is of relevance here, because, while not generally applicable to understanding, something quite like a 'community' analysis is given for institutional concepts. But two differences must be noted. The first is that the institutional account of the concept 'art' is part of a non-institutional account of other concepts, so there is no general theory offered here. Second, the institutional account only resembles a community analysis, not least because, at its centre, the institutional analysis has a certain 'authoritative body' of those whose decisions matter (the Republic of Dance, in our case). As noted earlier, nothing similar can be said for understanding more generally (Baker and Hacker, 1984a: pp. 272–3).

Outcomes of the institutional analysis

The upshot, then, is that institutional concepts work differently from other concepts,[10] even when the institutional concepts have a normative dimension, as in the case of art. Notice how the institutional analysis places considerable weight on the work of theoreticians of a particular art form, that is to say, art critics, theoretically inclined artists, art historians and the like. These are central to the Republic. For these are the people who, first, will be chiefly involved in the other-acclamation of putative works and, second, will be involved in the kind of public relations task that shapes taste.

Placing this importance on theoreticians has two important consequences. The first consequence to be noted is an *historicism*: art has an historical character. By this I mean to say that the meaning of a work of art at one particular time may be different from that which it has at some other time, solely in virtue of theoretical changes – and that means changes in the views of the theoreticians of the art form, as mentioned earlier (McFee, 1980b). To see that this is indeed a consequence of institutionalism, we must consider the second feature noted above; for, as was argued earlier in Chapter 1, one only genuinely confronts works of art as art when one applies artistic concepts to them. What does this mean? It means that to be experiencing a work of art at all, we must be bringing it under a certain battery of concepts. And those concepts are typically interpretive: they yield interpretations of the work. Thus one way of putting this point would be to say that works of art are essentially interpreted objects, for unless one is engaged in the kind of interpretation of the 'object' that I have called 'making an artistic judgement', one is not confronting a work of art at all. Instead, one's appreciation is (at best) 'merely aesthetic'. There is a lot more to be said about this notion of interpretation (see Chapters 4, 6, 7).

84

Now we ask what may bring about changes of interpretation. And one reply, which leads to the historicism mentioned above, is that changes in art theory might lead to changes in interpretation. To see this most clearly, we need to see that the reasons one gives for an interpretation are not mere adjuncts to that interpretation. These reasons are best thought of as part of one's interpretation, rather than merely as what leads one to offer that interpretation. Consider the following example. Two spectators to, say, Picasso's *Guernica* offer what might be thought exactly similar interpretations of that work, that is, they both describe it in exactly the same (judgemental) terms. For example, they both identify elements of man's inhumanity to man, of the crushing of the human spirit and the like. But are these in fact the same interpretations of that work?

I suggest that one case in which our intuitions would lead us to say that they were not the same interpretation would be when the two offered entirely different reasons for those interpretations – say, one in terms of symbolization of events in Spanish history, the other in terms of purely formal features of the work. Once convinced that these were, in fact, the bases on which their interpretations stood, surely we would want to say that these were different interpretations, different judgements. Thus we emphasize the importance of the reasons offered for an interpretation. For, if asked to say which of two interpretations is being offered, when the same words are used, we must look to the reasons offered for each. Hence the connection between reason and interpretation cannot be merely a symptomatic one. What this example shows is how the reasons are relevant to when we do and when we do not have a different interpretation. And this in turn bears on the temporal character of interpretation, for when a new reason becomes available to us, we may be able to offer a new interpretation. For example, the development of psycho-analytic theory may make possible Freudian interpretation of art. Surely it is clear, then, that later events can make new reasons available to us, in a variety of ways, or subtly affect the reasons we give for a particular interpretation (if this is different).

Thus we have a unified package here. Works of art are essentially interpreted objects, because to confront the work of art itself I must make an interpretive judgement. The reasons one gives for one's interpretation should not be thought of as distinct from one's interpretation, and hence these reasons are not conceptually distinct from the work of art ('itself'). And this means, as we have seen, that two interpretations can be superficially the same – can use the same words, for example – but if they have a different 'source' (different reasons) they can be two different interpretations.

85

In this context, it seems to be natural to speak of the *meaning* of works of art, not least because works of art can be understood – and meaning and understanding are correlative notions. Certainly critics regularly speak of the meaning of works of art. Now, this is a topic on which we must spend more time (see Chapters 5, 6, 7). But two points we would make in respect of it are directly relevant now, and bear repetition. First, that speaking of 'the meaning' of the work of art is misleading; it may make us think that there is only one. As the discussion of objectivity (Chapter 1) makes clear, it is no part of my view of artistic judgements that there is necessarily one 'correct' judgement of any particular work. Indeed, I would want to stress the variety of possible judgements of a work, all of which are acceptable if they are answerable to the perceptible features of the work. So to speak of 'the meaning' should not be taken to imply only one. Second, we must distinguish meaning from association. Perhaps I recall a particular dance with affection because I met a beautiful woman at a performance of it. It would be good English to say that this dance meant beauty to me, but this would not be a comment on the dance at all. Here I associate certain things with the dance which are not (strictly) part of it. This is mere association, not meaning in the sense of that term I am using. (Another example of association: I think of a dance as rewarding because I put money into financing it, and it was very successful. Here I might admire the dance without having even seen it!)

Conclusion

In this chapter I have developed an account of art which distinguishes artistic judgement from aesthetic judgement, which acknowledges that 'art' is an institutional concept, with a constructed, conventional character. Further, works of art, such as dances, are essentially interpreted objects; indeed, this is part of what it means to speak of them as objects of artistic (rather than aesthetic) judgement. I began by asking what makes a movement sequence a piece of art, that is, dance? I have answered that this is accomplished by an institution, the Republic of Dance, in two stages: self-election and other-acclamation. And I have urged that art status brings with it a minimal *evaluative* element, at least typically.

Recommended reading

Any discussion of the Institutional Theory of Art must consider Dickie, 1974; Danto, 1981: pp. 1–31, 115–35; Dickie, 1984. For criticism, see Beardsley, 1976; Wollheim, 1980b. My preferred version of the institutional theory is Diffey, 1969.

On the 'community' account of language, see Baker, 1981: pp. 57–8; Baker and Hacker, 1984b: pp. 71–85.

4

Dance as a Performing Art

(Is it the same dance I saw last night?)

We have learned (from Chapter 2) that identifying a sequence of movement as dance rather than, say, gymnastics is a matter of employing action concepts and taking into account the context of that sequence. Further, from Chapter 3, we have seen the institutional force, given by the Republic of Dance, implicit in regarding dance as an art form. But dance is not just an art, but a performing art: and that is our topic here.

This chapter is in two parts. In the first half (pp. 88–103) we investigate some of the assumptions implicit in recognizing dance as a performing art. Then some of the consequences of these assumptions are considered. Such consequences are not (as is sometimes assumed [see Redfern, 1983: p. 19]) trivial or unproblematic but, rather, important and neglected. The background is provided by the question: 'Is the dance I saw on Tuesday night the very same dance as the one I saw on Monday?' (that is, are they both *Swan Lake*?). If we understand how to answer such a question, we know rather a lot about performing art – or so I shall urge. And, as we will see, philosophers call such questions *identity questions*.[1]

Performing arts, multiples and identity

Speaking of dance as a performing art is, implicitly, appealing to a contrast between visual and performing arts (Urmson, 1976: p. 239). Such a contrast leads us naturally to two important points concerning the nature of the performing arts. First, in general, the idea of a performing art implies the possibility of a number of performances. Second, the work of art is encountered only when one attends a performance, for only then is the work instantiated. In particular, one is not confronted with a work of art when one confronts only a notated score or a film or video. The point here is that this contrast tells us something important about performing. In contrast to visual arts like painting and sculpture, which are atemporal, performing acts like dance take time, not just in the trivial sense that it takes time to see or experience them, but in the more profound sense that they centrally involve events, which are in the flow of time, occurring at a particular moment and so on. Moreover, visual arts are fixed, as it were, after their creation, whereas performing arts are inherently underdetermined by their creation: they must be brought into completeness – as the name suggests – by being performed. And, as we shall see, this implies a different sense of the term 'interpretation' (what I shall call 'performers's interpretation'), the aesthetic significance of which we must gauge.

One feature of recognizing dance as a performing art is recognizing its evanescence. As the dance critic Marcia Siegel (1972: p. 1) suggests: 'Dance exists at a perpetual vanishing point', for, she continues, 'At the moment of its creation it is gone'. My point is that, once we accept the transience of dance in this sense, we must still acknowledge its permanence: that the very same dance can be re-performed at some later date. But that fact itself must be explained. And if we want to understand the performing arts a little better here, it is first necessary to say something about the arts more generally.

For the purpose of our discussion (see Wollheim, 1973: p. 256), works of art can typically be divided into two classes. Lacking clearer names, I will call the first kind 'particular objects' and the second kind 'multiples'. Typical of the first sort would be paintings, for example, the *Mona Lisa*. Typical of the second would be novels, for example, James Joyce's *Ulysses*. And we will stick with these as examples for the moment, as cases simpler than dances.

If we ask 'Is work A seen on Tuesday the very same work of art as B seen on Thursday?', in respect of the particular object kind of art, for example the *Mona Lisa*, this question – an identity question, as philosophers call them – will be answered in a way very similar to (perhaps exactly the same as) the same kind of question about a chair, a pen or a car. Roughly, the idea is that if no one *moves* an object, then it is now where it was yesterday. So the one here today is the very same one as was here yesterday. And if it is moved, we can follow its path to its new location. We can focus on this very same object and follow its space–time path, as we might say (see Wiggins, 1980: p. 76).

Just to be clear: when philosophers write of identity questions they do *not* mean questions like 'Is A very similar to B?', 'Is A of the same sort or the same kind as B?'. Rather, identity questions ask 'Is A the very same *one* as B?'. For example, 'Is the old man getting the Nobel Peace Prize today the very same person as the young boy who bullied me at school years ago?'. So identity questions ask 'Is it the same one?'.

Two features are especially important. First, identity questions are characteristically questions across time: questions relating what we see now to what we saw then. Second, they are not questions about similarity. In the example above, the man is short, bald, old; and the boy was tall (for his age), hairy, young and so on. We know the boy did not look as the man does, but, still, are they they the same person? This is an identity question: a *numerical* identity question. (As with many categories drawn by philosophers, this seems an inappropriate name, but the point is clear enough.)

To see the importance for us of this sort of question, we must consider its use for works of art: for example, novels. When we ask about the identity of the novel ('Is the novel I was reading this week the very same novel that I was reading last week?'), and if our interest is solely in its being the same work of art, it will not matter that this week I am reading the Bodley Head hardback edition, whereas last week I was reading the Penguin paperback edition. That is to say, we will have the very same work of art in circumstances where we do not have the very same physical object. So, for now, we can identify multiple works of art as those where the work of art itself can be in numerous places at once. Notice that here we are making a numerical identity judgement: we are not saying that, in the case of multiples, there are works of art of the same sort in different places. Rather, these are the very same work of art. The Bodley Head *Ulysses* and the Penguin *Ulysses* are both James Joyce's *Ulysses*: the very same novel, the same work of art.

Typically, novels, pieces of music and dances are art of the multiple type. But, to repeat, I shall begin by concentrating on novels, since this seems the easiest way to clarify the category. As we shall see, the extention to performing arts introduces further complexities. Notice too that works in this category need not be performing arts even if/when one puts aside the case of literature (see Shusterman, 1978). For cast sculpture would equally be a multiple art.

Type/token

At this stage I introduce a way of talking about the multiple arts, although, as we shall see, this way of talking has implications for our study of the works of art themselves, implications not always recognized (see Redfern, 1983: p. 19). The technical device I shall use is a distinction between *types* and *tokens*. This distinction can be clarified using the example of flags (Wollheim, 1980a: sections 35–6, pp. 74–84). Suppose I distribute a flag to each of ten people. Now I ask how many flags there are. Clearly there is a sense in which there are ten flags: each person has a stick with a piece of cloth attached to it. This we call the token sense. Equally clear is the sense in which there is just one flag, for each person has the Union Jack; or two flags, because five have the Union Jack and five have the Stars and Stripes, and so on. This we call the type sense. We describe the particular flags the ten people have as tokens of a certain type. Now I can reformulate my initial question. If I have given five people the Union Jack and five people the Stars and Stripes, I can ask how many type-flags there are, to which the answer is two. Or again, I can ask how many token flags there are, to which the answer is ten (unless I ask a more precise question, such as 'how many tokens of a particular type, say, the Union Jack, are there?', for then the answer would be five).

This type/token language provides us with a clear way of talking about works that are multiples. We can have a discussion of one sort about James Joyce's *Ulysses* – the novel in the abstract, as it were – and another discussion about the particular Bodley Head hardback that is on my shelf.[2] At least two important features from the type/token distinction will be carried over to my discussion of multiples, if that way of talking is used. The first of these two points is that the type is an abstract object. One never meets or confronts the type directly. To clarify, think again about flags. The flag on top of Eastbourne Town Hall, the flag on top of Buckingham Palace, and so on, are all tokens of the type Union Jack. But where is the Union Jack, the type? Here the answer is that this is a foolish question. The Union Jack is an abstract object. The second point is that all the tokens are of equal importance; all are equally the type. Again, consider flags: there is no flag that is more the Union Jack than any other.

Why should these points be of any significance to us? The answer comes when we apply them to our art case, and again, let us begin with the novel. What this means is that James Joyce's novel *Ulysses* – the type *Ulysses* – is not uniquely instantiated in any of the texts of it: each is as much (or as little) the work of art as any other. In particular, it is not uniquely instantiated in the version that Joyce himself wrote by hand (always supposing that he did this). Each token is equally a token, and the handwritten token is no more so than the printed ones. If we are not prepared to regard the work in this way, we cannot use the type/token contrast to characterize it.

Once we apply this point to dance, we begin to see the complexities closing in. At the very least, it means that, if we genuinely encounter *Troy Game* (1974), that is as much (or as little) *Troy Game* as the original production staged by Robert North (from his own choreography) for

91

London Contemporary Dance Theatre. (It is interesting in this case to recollect that North himself prefers the version of *Troy Game* staged by the Royal Ballet Company.) Yet if they are all *Troy Game* and if we are right to talk of multiple art in a type/token way, then each is equally the work of art. But these performances will differ in detail; it follows that work identity cannot require indistinguishability (a point to which we will return). If we talk instead about *Black Angels* (1976) or *Swan Lake* (1895) and not about a particular performance, we are required to recognize that certain features of the work will be underdetermined. Not all the features of the performance will be required by the dance itself. We realize this when we recognize that the performances could differ in these respects without work identity lapsing. If it is possible to perform *Swan Lake* with differences, creating some changes between different performances, or with a different sized *corps de ballet*, it follows that the work itself cannot be determinate on these features.

We have said that, for works of art that are multiples, we will make use of a type/token schema. So if we were to ask an identity question it would become, 'Is A a token of the same type-F as B?'; 'Is the ballet I see on Tuesday night the very same type, *Swan Lake*, as the ballet I see on Wednesday night?'. And this is not a matter of mere academic interest. The answers to such questions must be determinate, at least in principle. For if it were in principle impossible to answer these questions, whether or not two performances were of the same dance would simply be a 'matter of opinion'. And that leads to a quite unacceptable subjectivism.

It might seem that this question is relatively straightforward to answer. And, as we shall see, the answer that one gives unreflectively is not so much wrong as inadequately formulated. The snap answer would be that A and B are tokens of the same type if A involves the same sequence of movements as B. But a moment's reflection shows us that this cannot be right as it stands, primarily for reasons to do with the nature of action (discussed in Chapter 2). Unless we characterize both sequences of movements as dance and, moreover, import some other considerations – for example, music, costume, lighting, staging – we will not characterize them as proper objects for artistic appreciation. And this will involve more than just sameness of movement (as we have seen).

There are two points here. First, sameness of movement is compatible with one event being a dance and the other not. And, second, when we do not have the same movements within dance A as in dance B, that does not guarantee that they are not the same dance. We cannot expect the 'same work' judgement to be confined to cases where there is the same sequence of movements, if we mean by this that any difference between two performances implies that these are not performances of the same work. It may, but equally it may not.

It might be objected that our everyday practice here is too lax, that one *should* insist on indistinguishability of performance in order to guarantee same work continuity. And, although this might be done, a serious look at its consequences suggests that it is neither possible nor fully intelligible. Here three considerations are operative. First, such indistinguishability will never come about as a point of actual fact, especially if we consider the empirical differences with which performers inevitably find themselves, for example, the different faces and physiques of dancers, the different emphases in training, the differences between performance areas throughout the world. So to insist on this 'tough' line would probably be to render each performance a separate work, since each is distinguishable from the other, and hence to make dance a particular object art form after all.

But, second, requiring indistinguishability for identity would render practise and rehearsal impossible. For the rehearsal would never be indistinguishable from any performance. Suppose one rehearsed all day Monday and performed Tuesday and Wednesday. For which of these two performances is the Monday activity the rehearsal? We might expect the Monday rehearsal to differ markedly from both performances, even if it is a full dress rehearsal. And some of the mistakes from the rehearsal might crop up in Tuesday's performance, others in Wednesday's. If one required indistinguishability here, one must conclude that the rehearsal is not *of* either performance, and hence can never be counted as a step towards a token of that particular type. This seems too huge an anomaly to accept.

Third, we should ask ourselves the question, 'Indistinguishable from what?'. All we seem to be able to say is that Tuesday night's performance differs from Wednesday night's. But which is 'the work' and which the deviant? Such a question cannot always and in general be answered, for the work itself, the type, is indeterminate in certain dimensions. To see this, let us consider some putative answers. First performances might be appealed to, but they are notoriously unreliable, with choreographers often furious at what has happened to the steps that they have set. And it will not always do to appeal to the choreographer, since he may not be around to ask, or since he may see something in one of the performances that strikes him as an alternative or a development or an irrelevant change, and so on. That is, he may decide at any time that the 'evolution' of that dance is complete: and hence not be sure before that time (he may be sure, but equally he may not). No, there is no infallible source of *the* performance to which others must conform if they are to count as that same work of art; or at least, there is no such performance for most dances.

At this stage, an objector[3] might point to what could be called, with justice, quintessential performances: Pavlova's *Dying Swan*, or Nijinski's *Firebird*. 'Surely', he might say, 'these can be used as standards'. Now, the importance of these performances cannot be underestimated, for they can indeed be taken as standards to which other performances will be compared. But notice, first, that this is an historically specific use: the quintessential performances of one age will not necessarily be those of another; and, second, that this use of standards locates itself within art criticism, that is, across acknowledged tokens of the type. Even if criticism of a particular time does not take, say, Baryshnikov's *Firebird* as quintessential – and hence compares it unfavourably with Nijinski's – that judgement does not undermine in the slightest that it is a bona fide performance of *Firebird*.

The source of this objection is the different roles that the different works of art can play in criticism, sometimes as (temporary) paradigms of art, sometimes as critical standards. And, even when we can be sure which of these roles is embraced, we cannot typically describe which of the features of a particular work are functioning in this 'standards' way. To make this point clear, consider a case of two performances of a particular piece of piano music, one which we think of as evocative, emotional and so on, the other we consider 'merely' technical. It is a fine difference, one of touch, yet it is a difference in the performance, not simply in the thoughts or feelings of the performer. Since we cannot say precisely what it is about performance B that makes it 'merely technical', we cannot describe the standard performance A sets for us. These differences are the sorts of things one learns to discern when one learns to understand music – or equally, dance.

The creation of the type-work

Where have we arrived? We have seen that the type/token language can offer us a way of talking about works of art of the multiple sort – a way of talking with certain implications. And we have recognized some of the difficulties implicit in seeking to decide whether or not a particular performance is indeed a token of a certain type. In particular, the abstract character of the type made it difficult for us to derive from it constraints which would help us with identity questions. As one might say, it was difficult to arrive at *determinacy* for such constraints.

94

To take us forward *vis-à-vis* the question of determinacy, we need to recognize that multiple arts are of at least two kinds or, more precisely, that they can be made in at least two ways (Wollheim, 1973: pp. 357–8). Notice that what we are describing is how one sets about creating the type but, since it is an abstract object, one cannot make the type directly, as it were. First, one can make the type by making a token, as in the case of novels. What one does is simply to produce one token of the work – say, the handwritten token – which allows the creation of other tokens of the same type. And it provides a test for whether or not putative tokens are really tokens of that type, for they must conform to that original token, in some way yet to be explicated. Similarly in dance, one might 'push around' the bodies of particular dancers in order to create one's token. This will allow creation of other tokens of the same type: the first construction of the dance (through performance) allows successive performances of it, and so on. The second way one can make the type is by making a recipe or mechanism for producing tokens. For example, in the case of music or dance one might write a score. The score then serves as a recipe: if one follows it correctly, one gets the music or dance in question. That is, following the recipe allows one to create tokens of the type. But not all recipes or mechanisms would be of the same form. For example, it seems right to regard the copper plate from which prints are taken as a recipe for etched prints, in just this sense.

Notice that some art forms that are multiples can only have types brought about in one way. For example, a novel can only be brought about by writing strings of words: that is, by creating a token. Of course, one could produce those strings of words onto a tape rather than onto a page, but in any case one is making a token. So here is a kind of art form which only admits to the creation of the type through creating a token. By contrast, an etching must be made by making a recipe – the plate – which is then allowed to generate tokens. Yet here too there is only one way to make the type (although it is a different way). But for some of the works of art that are multiples – here dance and music are examples – one can create the type in either of the ways described above: I can direct the dancers or I can write the score. So that, for example, Christoper Bruce did make *Black Angels* by 'manipulating' Zoltan Imre, Lucy Burge and the rest (see Austin, 1976), but it is not entirely fanciful to imagine a choreographer bringing that dance into being by writing a score. And this feature is characteristic of performing arts: they can be made in either way.

Now we should go on to ask what is achieved when a work is made (the type is made) by making a token, that is, by actual performing.

95

And the answer is that from this performance other performances can now be generated. And these either will or will not be performances of that work of art. The performance the choreographer extracts from his dancers serves as a kind of example. And from that example we must know (or learn) which of its features are the crucial ones in deciding whether or not a particular performance is of that work of art: that is to say, which features are the crucial ones determining work identity.

Of course, if we make the dance (the type) by writing a score, then again the score serves to allow us to make other tokens of that type, other performances of that dance. But here the work of art, the dance, is underdetermined by the score to a greater degree than in music (Carr, 1987: pp. 346–7); perhaps this is why dances are typically created by working on the bodies of the dancers. For a score will not, typically, be immediately accessible to the dancers. Rather, the choreographer will have to teach them the dance from the score. The crucial point is just that the dance could be made by making the score, and this means that the score could be used to answer questions about work identity.

This suggests, then, that although we can make the type for a dance in either of the ways described above, the second of these ways is, to some extent, preferable. And for two reasons. First, and especially, creating a dance by creating a token leaves the future of the dance uncertain. Of course, it can be repeated, performed again, but such repetitions will depend on the memories of those people involved, the choreographer, the dancers and so on. A practical example: Marcia Siegel (1979: p. 81), discussing an effort by Charles Weidman in 1972 to revive Doris Humphrey's *New Dance* (1935), to 'piece it together from memory' with the help of dancers from Humphrey's group, notes: 'What they could remember, they remembered'. Only some sections of this 'masterpiece' could be retrieved in this way. 'The rest of the dance . . . disappeared when Humphrey was no longer alive to do productions of it'. Clearly, it is unsatisfactory, for the continued existence of works, to depend in this way on recollection. If we are to have permanent works of art of any high level of complexity, we should prefer to have scores for those works.

Second, notice that if I had written scores for a dance, then any dance which conforms to that score – and which is seen as dance in the appropriate ways mentioned above – will be a token of that type. That is to say, if I create the dance, the type, by creating a token, this procedure may leave open *which* features of this particular token are crucial for other dances if they are to be tokens of the same type. But, in creating a recipe, I specify which features are the crucial ones. So it seems advantageous, for sorting out identity matters for performing arts, if types within those arts are (or anyway, can be) created by making recipes or mechanisms: that is, scores. It is this that is meant when, adapting a comment from Pater,[4] we claim: 'All performing arts aspire to notationality'. By this, I intend that even when the production of a work of art in a performing art is actually brought about by the creation of a token of that type (that is, by a performance) it would not be far wrong to take it as a precondition of the production of a 'performable', as we might say, that there was available a notation for that art form.

Notice that what makes it a notation for that art form depends, in ways identified in Chapter 3, on the traditions and conventions (that is, the history) of that art form. We have an 'object of artistic interest' only when the traditions and conventions of that art form allow us to see the movement as within that art form, to take an artistic interest in it. Of course, in respect of the creation of that work, just this object of artistic interest could have been created directly, by creating a token of that type. Yet this fact cannot be crucial. Even though the notation for that art form need not have been employed in the creation of a particular work, the possibility of its employment is central to the ability to create works of performing art. For though we did make the work by making the token, we could have made just that work by creating a score or mechanism. And this fact reinforces our sense of the work itself as an abstract object.

To be clear: I accept that dances are very often, perhaps even always, made by making a particular token. The upshot of my discussion, though, is to show how uninformative that fact is concerning the nature of dances. By contrast, the possibility of making the type by making the score offers us a useful insight into the character of performing arts; in particular, it suggests a relationship between the type and the notated score.

The thesis of notationality

Our identity problem, it will be remembered, lies in answering the question, 'Is A a token of the same type-F as B?'; and that means in finding constraints under which A will be a token of the same type-F as B. The thought I am offering is that these constraints might be provided by the score. So one might begin by expressing a 'thesis of notationality' in roughly the following way: *performance A and performance B were performances of the same work of art (in any performing art) just in that case where both satisfied or instantiated some particular 'text' in a notation agreed by the knowledgeable in the art form to be an adequate notation for that*

97

form. Such a thesis makes the notation important, just because it allows us to decide in principle whether or not the object in question is a token of a particular art-type. And this idea has its origins in the work of Richard Wollheim (1973, p. 257), who says: 'Where such a notation is available, then there is a clear and determinate way of individuating tokens of as a given type, and hence of identifying the work of art with the type'.

In respect of this thesis of notationality, two points are of central importance. The first of these is that notationality does not, as it stands, guarantee that the object – the work, which in this case would be a performance – is indeed a dance. We will need to specify that it is a dance, and also perhaps to specify the story, the music, perhaps even the costume, and so on, a number of features sometimes thought of as incidental to works of art, but which certainly are *not* incidental. While it is doubtless true that most dances are best explained as sequences of movements, the relative importance of other features, such as music and costume, varies from one work to another. As has been said, it is no longer true that music is always a primary determinant of a dance work (see Armelagos and Sirridge, 1984). For example, Twyla Tharpe's *The Bix Pieces* (1971) has a variable music element. Similarly, many works of Alwin Nikolais require a particular costume (McDonagh, 1970: p. 189; Siegel, 1979: p. 320). Here we have examples of, first, a feature generally thought to be constant functioning as a variable and, second, a feature generally thought variable acting as a constant. These and similar examples should make us hesitant about ever claiming a general necessary condition status for any of these features of dances: that is to say, there are no such features which apply equally in all cases of dance. And these facts mean that specifying, for any sequence of movements, that it is a dance may prove a complex procedure. One cannot appeal to any general properties of the movement or the context which guarantee that this sequence of movement is indeed a dance. But, in respect of a particular dance, the thesis of notationality is operative. So, while the thesis of notationality does not give us a way of determining absolutely whether or not a particular performance is a token of the same type as another performance, it does seem to give us a necessary condition for dance identity.

The second point concerns the need for something standing in the same place as the thesis of notationality. That is, suppose that we rejected the thesis of notationality. We would still, I am urging, need some other mechanism for providing constraints on possible performances which are to preserve same work continuity, and on possible interpretations of such works. Clearly, one does not wish to arrive at the situation where it is in general an open question as to whether or not performance A is the very same dance as performance B. We do not wish this to be merely a matter of opinion, or a matter for individual decision, or a subjective matter. No doubt there are borderline and problem cases here. Still, this should be a matter for which the relevant considerations can be articulated, even if we cannot always arrive at a satisfactory conclusion. But if the thesis of notationality is accepted, one has a way of accommodating the second of the consequences outlined above. For we might expect the notation to underdetermine the performance; and yet still to constrain it. This is exactly what is required if subjectivism is to be avoided.

It is, of course, an oddity of dance, especially given the way dances of the past have been lost, that such an importance can be placed on the possibility of notation. Marcia Siegel (1972: p. 178) picks it out as follows: 'It seems absurd to be talking of trailing after the artist, gathering up dances as if they were crumpled memos he'd made to himself and discarded... Only dance requires such elaborate procedures to effect the simplest type of retrieval.' But she is right, and the thesis of notationality shows why. For the possibility of re-performing art works in any performing art does depend on an adequate notation. And this has not been widely available for dance until recently. (Even now notators are not in fact universally employed, which is why it is the possibility of notation that is stressed here.)

Interpretation and performance

Thus far I have articulated a conception of the performing arts, and of dance as a performing art, which emphasizes that dances are multiples and should be treated as abstract objects, using a type/token distinction. This conception has a number of consequences for aesthetics, each generating a potential problem. I will mention four: two deriving from the 'multiple' status of dance, two from its 'abstract object' status:

- It is necessary to find a way to talk about the relationship between the various instantiations of a dance, otherwise we will lapse into treating them as separate objects.
- It is necessary to show how to relate performances together, and to accommodate differences in performance. If not, we will be in the 'anything goes' position characteristic of subjectivism.
- There is a need to explain how the abstract object is related to the particular instantiation, that is, to the particular performance.

● There is a need to show how we have access to the abstract object *through* the performances, otherwise discussion can only be of the performances, not of the work itself.

The first of these is easily dealt with, for seeing dance as a multiple-type art form raises whatever questions follow from multiple-status; and these depend on how we treat such art forms. For me, the type/token language provides a clear way of talking about multiples. We have already discussed some of its consequences, and we are going to discuss others.

The second point repeats, in some senses, a nettle to be grasped. We cannot offer a general account of how the type/token relationship serves to constrain the tokens, so as to subsume them under the type. But our practical concerns here are at least clarified by what I have called the thesis of notationality. We have seen that the notation can, as it were, offer us an insight into the constraints from the type. In this way, if we have a notated score (or equivalent) we can at least begin to make identity judgements in actual cases, at least in principle. Again, this will work primarily negatively, allowing us to rule out candidates as tokens of a particular type if they fail to satisfy the score.

The other two consequences relate directly to our conception of dances as abstract objects: we need a way to relate that abstract object to particular performances, and to criticize the abstract through the performances. A clearer way of asking both these questions about the relationship of abstract object to performance focuses on the idea of interpretation. It is natural to speak of interpretations of art works; and then the question naturally arises, 'Of *what* are these interpretations the interpretations?'. Here we are asking how the work itself provides constraints on understanding (for example on criticism); how inappropriate interpretations are to be ruled out.

The term 'interpretation' is used in two distinct senses here. The first, typified by a critic's interpretation of a particular poem – or equally, a particular dance – would typically consist of a string of sentences discussing the structure and value of the work in question: that is, it would usually be composed of words. But also we speak of a kind of interpretation typified by a pianist's interpretation of a piano piece – say, Pollini's interpretation of Schoenberg's *Six Little Piano Pieces Opus 19*. Here the interpretation typically consists in some set of actions performed, or, as we might say, in producing that object in which the witnessable works consists. In the case of a piece of music, it consists in producing sounds; for dance, in performing (at least) movements of the body. So here we have two kinds of interpretation. Notice that the second kind – performer's interpretation – is unique to the performing arts, while there are critic's-type interpretation of all works of art. Indeed, when we speak of works of art as 'essentially interpreted objects' (see Chapter 3), we are referring to the kind of interpretion implicit in critical judgement or appreciation, here called 'critic's interpretation'. Hence any difficulty or problem we have in giving exposition of, or in understanding, the idea of critic's interpretation – or in seeing the basis for such interpretation, or its relevance – are equally problems for all the arts. So it is as much a difficulty in painting or sculpture as in dance or music. Then the problems mentioned earlier – how to make the interpretation an interpretation of that particular work of art and no other, and how to rule out inappropriate interpretations – can be seen, in the case of performing arts, to have two dimensions. We now realize that the difficulty will apply not only to critic's interpretation – a difficulty shared with other art forms – but also to performer's interpretation.

One tempting route here would be to assume that there were some 'facts of the matter' to which any critic's interpretation had to conform, and which had to be instantiated in any performer's interpretation. This line of thought can be rejected for two related reasons. First, we have urged that works of art are essentially interpreted objects. Hence it would be impossible, even in principle, to confront the works uninterpreted: there can be no 'facts of the matter' different from interpretations while we are considering the objects in question as objects of artistic interest (Danto, 1986: pp. 50–1). To recognize this point, consider any of Marcia Siegel's 'descriptions' of dances in her book *The Shapes of Change*, her account of Martha Graham's *Errand into the Maze* (1947) for example (Siegel, 1979: pp. 198–202):

> Seeing the rope on the floor, she picks her way along it, her legs so narrowly close together that they often cross as she follows the twists and turns of the path. When she comes to the branching structure that is the heart of the maze, she steps inside and can expand for the first time, opening her pelvis and swinging her leg in figure eights, as if she could be safe there in the depths – of what? Herself, perhaps. But while she is there, the Creature enters for the first time. The fact that he appears when the woman has withdrawn into her most private refuge indicates to me that he is a product of her own pysche, not something that threatens her from the outside.

Although this is certainly intended as a descriptive passage, it also leads us into an understanding of the work. In particular, it guides us as to how to see the Creature. So the first point is that any (critical) description of the work is essentially interpretive to some degree. The second is this: when one witnesses a work in the performing arts, it is already a performer's interpretation; it is already a particular token of the type-work of art, and hence cannot answer for us questions about the grounds from which such interpretations begin. However, this line of reasoning does take us forward: once the performer's interpretation is completed, a work of art in one of the performing arts is then in the same position as a work of the particular object sort, or a non-performing work of the multiple sort, such as a work of literature. Each has a physical instantiation which is then the subject of critics' interpretation.

What, then, are the constraints on a performer's interpretation? Since we employ the type/token contrast, we might reply that the constraints governing whether or not one particular performance is a token of the same type as another particular performance were provided by the type, by its features. But such metaphysics takes us nowhere. We have already accepted that the type underdetermines performances, so that a variety of perceptible differences are quite acceptable within same work of art continuity. Moreover, while the idea of a type provides us with a useful way of talking about multiple arts, it is unclear precisely what the consequences are of employing this idea in our discussion: we have no idea what features the type will offer for us. So it is best to recognize that the constraint on performance is actually provided either by the notation or some notation-equivalent. It is in this sense that notationality is so crucial a feature.

The thesis of notationality provides the potential constraint on performer's interpretation: the performer's interpretation must be amenable to the notation, it must satisfy that notation. And any performer's interpretation which fails to do so is therefore an inappropriate or incorrect interpretation. For works in the performing arts come as a recipe, as it were, with a note attached saying 'And now perform it!'. And that amounts to an instruction to produce a performer's interpretation.

Certainly, scores underdetermine the features of the work. But they regulate possible lines of fulfilment, so that there are varieties of unacceptable response to that score. In this sense, any such 'performance' does not fulfil/satisfy the score at all. For such performances do not generate tokens of the particular type. This in turn indicates the degree to which the performer's interpretation is circumscribed by what may rightly be called the features of the dance itself. Thus it is surely better to think of the relationship between type (abstract object) and token (performance) as mediated through the routes to that performance; that is, through the various ways of realizing that score, which is, to put it another way, through the performer's interpretations.[5]

Suppose this point were accepted. What does this give us? The answer is 'very little'. It does offer a response of sorts to the question, 'Of what is the performers' interpretation an interpretation?': namely, that it is an interpretation of the type, where the constraints of the type are supplied by the notation. Of course, the role of this feature of notationality for the performing arts is thus limited; it only provides a necessary condition of work identity. Yet this role is important, for it allows some positive constraints to be applied to performer's interpretations. No massive task is undertaken in formulating the thesis of notationality, but a genuine problem is avoided.

Performers' interpretations

Has this discussion really dealt with the relevant two consequences identified in the last section of this chapter? Can we now see how to relate the abstract object to the performances? Yes, for the thesis of notationality provides constraints (from the type) on performances. These constraints are, at least, capable of ruling out putative performances of that dance. Can we now explain how it is possible to discuss the abstract, though we only confront the performances? Again, it seems that we can, and for two reasons. First, the thesis of notationality assures us that some of the key characteristics of the work of art (the dance) will be locatable from the notated score, and hence can be used to give insight into (and provide a basis for criticism of) particular performances.

Second, the dance itself is underdetermined, and the performer's interpretation makes it determinate. But we can see which features of the performance will typically be those provided by the performer's interpretation and – though we may well be wrong here – viewing other performances may be expected to help. Thus, there may be some advantage to be gained by thinking of some performances of, say, Pollini's interpretation of Schoenberg's *Six Little Piano Pieces Opus 19*, or Nureyev's interpretation of *Sleeping Beauty*. And notice that any advantage here would need to relate to an understanding of those works or those performances: it somehow made what is 'going on' in *Six Little Piano Pieces Opus 19* clearer if one thought of a particular performance as Pollini's interpretation – for example, because it grouped this performance with others, or perhaps because it was then

103

seen to exhibit characteristic Pollini features which could then be discounted or minimized, if one's interest is in the type. In any case, the difference here would be an art-critical difference, a difference of how one should/could discuss or describe the work (see Chapman, 1984). I am suggesting that we do not need a central explanation of how the performer's interpretation functions, for no such explanation is, in principle, possible. The performer's interpretation comes about when what I earlier described as the 'And now perform it' label on a particular score is acted upon, the way in which a particular performance is realized or created.

This position highlights, and diagnoses the flaw in, a view typically found in discussion of dance: that the realization of the work of art – the performer's interpretation – is itself creative. One can mean a volume of things by the term 'creative' here. But the interesting claim would be the one often implicitly made (for example, by Davies, 1987: pp. 47–8) for the music case: that the elaborations of performer's interpretations are creative activities in the sense in which choreography (for dance) or composition (for music) are creative. These are the relevant senses of the word 'creative'. And, taken that way, surely such a claim is plain crazy. For if one's efforts result in the performance of *Swan Lake* or *Black Angels* (in tokens of a type which has a creator), or equally, Beethoven's *Ninth Symphony* or Schoenberg's *Six Little Piano Pieces Opus 19*, it is hard to see how one's work could be creative in the sense in which the construction of works of art is creative – for those works of art are the creations of Christopher Bruce or Schoenberg or whoever. As was noted, the scores may underdetermine the features of the work. But they also regulate possible lines of fulfilment, thus only certain actions by the dancer could count as performing just *that* dance. The real creative activity is that which 'sets' those constraints; and the constraints are provided by the type.

Further considerations

Two importance objections arise at this point. First, it might be suggested that an unacceptable consequence of the position advocated here is that the performer's interpretation is not after all an interpretation of the work of art, but rather an interpretation of something *not* the work of art, namely, the notation. Second, it might be urged that, if accepted, this position plays havoc with the notion of a type by allowing its constraints to change as different notation systems are employed.

The first of these objections prompts two related replies, for it has already been accepted that the notation is not the work of art, that one only confronts the work of art when one confronts a performance. In the first place, is the consequence pointed to really unacceptable? We have accepted that the work of art is instantiated by the performance, and hence by the performer. His performance really is the work of art. The apparent difficulty arises because we also want to call this performance an interpretation. If we did not think of this as an interpretation of something, there would be no difficulty. And the temptation to regard it as an interpretation comes just because we recognize the possibility of perceptible differences between tokens of the same type, differences for which reasons might be given.[6] So it seems perfectly in order to say that, for performers' interpretations, this question, 'Of what is it an interpretation?', is a nonsense question, at least if the answer, 'Of the work of art', is ruled to be unacceptable. That is all the answer one could give, even in principle.

In the second place, the position did not locate the object for interpretation within the notation. It said merely that the notation made explicit for us the constraints of the type. If one continues to use the type/token way of speaking, and if the type is to count as the work of art – and surely it must, otherwise *Swan Lake* would cease to exist the very instant the curtain came down on performances of it – the performer's interpretation is indeed an interpretation of the work of art, because it is an interpretation of the type. As the first part of the reply recognizes, it is an odd sort of interpretation when compared with the critic's, but if we were to insist on calling it an interpretation, there would be no inherent contradiction in so doing. Notice, as a first approximation to seeing our way through this oddity, that the critic's interpretation is essentially based on some extant, instantiated object or objects – some particular token (or set of tokens) of a particular type – while the performer's interpretation brings those tokens into being. When I, as a dance critic, discuss *Black Angels*, I am characteristically producing a critic's interpretation. But, or so one might think, *Black Angels* exists independently of my (critic's) interpretation. On the other hand, the dance's existence depends on certain performers' interpretations, namely, the interpretations of those who perform it, together perhaps with the interpretations of stagers and the like. Thus the first objection could be defused. The motives behind calling the performance 'an interpretation' do not conflict with its relation to notation (and to the type).

The second objection is important and powerful. Recall it raised the difficulty that the thesis of notationality made work identity dependent on a particular notation system; hence a performance which satisfied a notation of *Black Angels* in one system (say, Labanotation) might not satisfy the notation of *Black Angels* in another (say, Benesh). But did this fact undermine the idea of notation providing 'constraints from the type'? Notice here that nothing is gained by a recognition that a general constraint on notations might be used to rank notations, or even to reject some – such that only some notation systems could provide constraints from the type (see Goodman, 1968: pp. 127–54, 211–18). In the first place, we have already allowed some 'ranking' of notation systems – or at least some ruling out – through our commitment to the idea that any notation system must be acknowledged by the knowledgeable in that art form to be an adequate notation for that form (in the thesis of notationality). Second, we must see that a number of notation systems might do equally well in these 'tests', and hence nothing be shown. Finally, and most importantly, we must see that the particular notation systems are chosen at particular times for particular purposes of a quasi-interpretive kind: one uses Benesh notation for classical ballet when one wishes to emphasize a 'flat', lateral quality in such ballet (at least, if one had a choice one might do this). So it must be conceded that what counts as a performance of a particular dance – a token of a particular type – does indeed change as notation systems change or as different ones are employed. This is simply a place where one must be historicist about the matter, and grasp the nettle of implausibility which this acceptance may bring with it.[7]

Re-evaluation

Thus far I have suggested treating works of art in the performing arts using a type/token contrast, with the type being the abstract work of art and the performance the witnessable token. However, I have emphasized that a role is to be ascribed to the performer's interpretation. For the performer's interpretation characteristically amounts to producing that in which the witnessable work consists. This leaves me in need of an account of the role of the performer's interpretation. It can be given by returning to the beginning. For it is important to recall an oddity about this interpretation, noted earlier: that it consists in doing or producing that in which the witnessable work consists (in the relevant case, the bodily movements). As such, it is better thought of as a route to realizing a token of a particular type, and hence different performers' interpretations should be thought of as different routes, each of which produces a token of that type. Just as one might travel from London to Edinburgh by a number of routes, so one might produce tokens of a particular type in a number of ways. There may be some virtue in grouping those ways, just as, in the road case, there may be some virtue in classifying routes as, say, motorway routes or A-routes or minor road routes.

There are two minor points which must be mentioned here. First, the analogy with roads is far from perfect. It breaks down when one asks for an equivalent for the destination of the various roads. For each of the tokens may well be different; hence we cannot think of them as 'the same place' for an arrival. Still, the analogy with roads does provide an informative picture because it illustrates how an important role may be given to a means of realization of a goal, and how such means of realization may be grouped. The second point may be more substantial. It is characteristic of the differences between tokens of the same type for any non-performing art that such differences are of no aesthetic relevance. Typically, for a novel, these irrelevancies would be colour of page, pagination, typographical errors, small omissions of, say, commas. No aesthetic explanation of these can be offered, nor is any needed. Now, some differences between tokens of the same type in the performing arts may be of this kind. For instance, differences caused by using a different cast might be of this sort. But those differences we think of as characteristic of a performer's interpretation will not be like this. They will have features which *can* be explained, for which artistically relevant reasons can be given. I will return to this point in the next section.

Here performers' interpretations, characteristically actions, are tied into critic's interpretations, characteristically words. Now recall a fact used earlier in this chapter: that, while the critic's interpretation of literature is typically of the type, in the case of the performing arts it is characteristically of the token, that is, of the performance. The explanation here is that the object the critic uses in formulating his interpretations is, one might say, the physical realization of the work of art. But in the performing arts this is necessarily the token in a strong sense. It derives from the type by performer's interpretation, and hence might be radically different from other tokens of the same type. This cannot be said of the interpretation of literature, where the constraints of the type are fairly visible in the token, and there are none of the aesthetically explicable sorts of difference. The upshot of this contrast is that there can indeed be aesthetically (artistically) relevant differences between tokens of the same type work of art in the performing arts, but not in literature. But this is something we can explain, for the differences will be reflected in differences of critical and theoretical discussion (of just the kind considered in Chapter 3). So that this may seem odd, but it is in fact perfectly consistent, given the whole context of our discussion of the character of dance.

Before concluding, I want to put aside two or three small objections which might arise. The first concerns the possibility that a particular performer's interpretation might take us beyond the type. Let me explain with an example. One might feel that Nureyev's (1966) re-choreography of *Sleeping Beauty* (greatly increasing the role of the Prince) results in a work with unacceptably huge differences from the original (1890) choreography by Petipa (Brinson and Crisp, 1980: p. 51). Of course, it may still be possible to treat this case as just another performer's interpretation, and hence as generating tokens of the type *Sleeping Beauty*, in the ordinary way. But one may feel that this is quite inadequate to deal with such a degree of difference. Here it may be preferable to treat this as a case where a new work of art is brought into being: a new type created through the production of a token of that new type. (Of course, this new work would have a great deal in common with the other work – story line, music, and so on – but such overlap is not unknown, for example, between ballets which use extant music and the music itself; or between concerts and performance versions of operas.) The point here is that whichever of these options is adopted, either performer's interpretation or new work, it can be accommodated within the analysis offered here. It is a matter for art criticism and art theory. Given the historical character of art (McFee, 1980b), critics and theorists might, at one time, offer one solution, at another time the other solution in respect of a particular case. So there is no difficulty here for our thesis of notationality.

Variety among performances

Although the position described here allows that all tokens of that type work of art are equally tokens, still our ordinary discussion of different performances of a particular work seems to involve comparison of those performances – saying either that (for some reason one goes on to give) Tuesday's performance is better than Wednesday's, or that one company's performance is preferable to that of another, and so on. How can this fact be accommodated within our view of the nature of dance?

In fact, the points needed are fairly familiar.[8] With respect to many general terms – for example, terms for naturally occurring kinds, such as 'dog', 'lion', 'elephant' – objects can be good examples of that kind in at least two ways. They can be good by exemplifying all the characteristics of that type, or by exemplifying these characteristics in a vivid way. This is not true of all types: for example, it makes no sense to

108

speak of something as a red object and yet not a particularly good red object. One feels like saying 'It's either red or it's not!'. But for lions and for art works, this distinction does make sense. Thus, for something to be a good example of a lion, say, it must have four legs, two eyes, a tail, a mane and so on. That is to say, one might with justice remark that a one-eyed lion was, for these purposes, not much of a lion, or not a very good lion: it would not do as a model in the zoology class. It would be undoubtedly leonine, nonetheless. In this case, to be a good lion is to well or clearly or completely have the form and features of a lion. Of course, there is another way in which we might speak of 'a good lion': for a perfectly formed lion might perhaps be weak or sickly. Here our one-eyed lion, if it were otherwise healthy, might be preferable – for example, for purposes of breeding or defence. That is to say, some of its leonine qualities are the ones we most value, in this particular context; hence our one-eyed lion is a good lion because it possesses just those qualities very strongly.

This discussion is fairly easily applied to the case of dance (or of music). Anything which satisfied the thesis of notationality is a token of that type; for some 'critical' purposes and with some works, we may prefer or even require that the performance be in some particular fashion, say, in the original costumes. We might have this purpose or interest if we wanted to use the performance in a class on the history of dance. We might be looking for, as it were, the lion with the 'right' number of legs, eyes and so on. Equally, we may feel that, for other critical purposes and for other works, perhaps, we may prefer the 'one-eyed lion' case: the performance that is particularly vivid or powerful for us, even though it does not fulfil to such a high degree the typical features of that particular work of art. For example, one might urge that, in comparison with the version of Glen Tetley's *Pierrot Lunaire* (1962) originally performed by Tetley's own company, the Rambert version (1967, with Christopher Bruce as Pierrot) was less accurate or precise, that it less closely approximated the steps and moves as Tetley had set them down. (I have heard this said.) Yet one might feel that it was more desirable in spite of (or perhaps, because of) its deviations from a 'pure' version. It is a 'one-eyed lion', perhaps, but a very attractive one – and certainly a lion.

The thesis of notationality gives us a guarantee, for it guarantees (in this analogy) that we have a lion. What it leaves open, of course, are matters of critical interpretation of the particular performances, even granted that they are all dances, and all tokens of a particular type work of art.

Conclusion

To conclude, I have urged that the thesis of notationality allows us to give a minimal answer to the identity question for dances. If a perform- ance satisfies an acceptable notation for particular work, a particular dance – and given that it is seen as a dance, and so forth – then it *is* that same dance. Perhaps one might not insist on this positive point, for the use of the thesis of notationality is minimal in just this way. But cer- tainly, if a performance fails to instantiate the notation, it clearly is not the particular dance. We have a necessary condition for 'same dance' identity, since unless two performances both satisfy the particular notated score, they cannot be the same dance. (Notice how this refor- mulates, in a more sophisticated and also more adequate way, the initial thought: that performance A and performance B were perform- ances of the same work if they contained the same series of movements. We no longer require that, but we do rule out identity if they do not satisfy the same notation.)

What has arriving at this conclusion taught us about the nature of dance? Two things are particularly worthy of mention: first, the role given to various notation systems, each with a different conceptual structure, emphasizes the variety of taxonomies of movement, and hence the underdetermination of dance performances in general, by the work of art itself; that is, by the type. As we've seen, the constraints from the type can usefully be found in the notation. Second, we have seen how identity issues force us to recognize the importance of inter- pretation. Does this enable us to break the hold of the mythology about the importance of the artist's intentions? We shall see in a later chapter how the intentions of the artist may be seen as important. But the thesis of notationality insists on the possibility of perfectly public constraints which allow for accurate interpretation of the work (and the ruling-out of inaccurate interpretations). Hence whether or not performance A is a performance of the very same type as performance B becomes a matter which depends on critical judgements in important ways, but which is nevertheless perfectly public.

An important point to recognize is that, from discussion of these rather abstract identity questions, we are beginning to characterize dance, to say what dance is, or what dances are. For not merely have we characterized dance as a multiple art, a performing art, an art form to which the type/token contrast can usefully be employed, but we have also elaborated the role of performer's interpretation and, to a lesser extent, critic's interpretation in the construction of that particular dance as an object for understanding and appreciation. Additionally, the nature of the uniqueness of dances is clarified through our elaboration of the identity conditions.

Recommended reading

For further discussion, see Sirridge and Armelagos, 1977; Armelagos and Sirridge, 1984; Margolis, 1984. A key text is Goodman, 1968: pp. 127–224. See also Levinson, 1980.

5

Dance as an Object of Understanding

(*The Dance/Language Analogy*)

The aim of this chapter is to round off our examination of the nature of dance by exploring the character of dance as an object of understanding. This will involve some consideration of the centrepiece of our account of dance, namely, a picture of understanding that draws on a model of the understanding of language. We will give some attention to the analogy between understanding dance and understanding language. Our exploration will begin by distinguishing three (related) motivations for looking at this issue.

The first is that, if dances are indeed the sort of thing we understand, and if understanding and meaning are correlative notions,[1] it follows that dances are the sorts of things with meaning. But that raises the question: how is understanding to be understood? And if we look for models for the understanding of *meaning*, we may well look towards the understanding of *linguistic meaning*.

The second motivation is that dance, like the other arts, is meaningful or meaning-bearing. Here one should notice books entitled *The Meanings of the Modern Art* (Russell, 1981) and so on. It is far from clear how one could really *argue* for this claim. Certainly it seems an extremely plausible idea, given the artistic/aesthetic contrast which, it will be recalled, is partly made in terms of possibilities of meaning. Moreover, this connection between meaningfulness and understanding (and a further association with value) is widely argued in the recent literature of aesthetics (Scruton, 1983: p. 77; Budd, 1985: p. 151). So the second motivation lies in our tendency to take dance to be meaningful or meaning-bearing, for when we investigate this notion of meaningfulness we will inevitably look towards the meaning of language. The third motivation lies in expressions like 'dance vocabulary' which suggest a parallel or analogy between dance and language, since language is the natural home of the term 'vocabulary'.

112

Motivation one is the topic of Part Three of this text. Hence, in what follows, I shall concentrate on motivation two, to give us a sense of the positive values in considering the dance/language analogy; and then turn to motivation three when I consider difficulties in the articulation and elucidation of that analogy.

The second motivation is, as remarked earlier, of a piece with Best's (1978a) artistic/aesthetic contrast, for it distinguishes our understanding of the art form *dance* from our understanding of other kinds of movement. (This is a point that we will further elaborate in Chapter 8.) But it can easily lead one into other, confused positions. For example, the differences between dance and other movement activities is sometimes explained by using a threefold distinction between *functional* movement (such as work actions), *expressive* movement (such as gestures) and *symbolic* movement (dance – and some supporters might include gymnastics). I shall not discuss this proposal here, beyond the remarks I make later about the idea of the *symbolic* later on. For our purposes we can say that this plan is right if it marks Best's artistic/aesthetic contrast, but wrong if it is thought of as saying more. For no real sense can be given to this threefold distinction.

Meaning, understanding and explanation

If we are pursuing the second motivation for an interest in the dance/language analogy, the question then arises, 'How is meaning understood?'. And really the only place we can look for a model for the understanding of meaning is language, for language is the prime source of questions, and answers, about the notion of meaning. Thus our question becomes transformed: 'How is meaning *in language* understood?'. (Here we introduce the idea about the nature of understanding central to the whole text.)

Throughout in this book I propose simply to assert an answer to that question, in terms of a slogan from Wittgenstein: 'Meaning is what explanation of meaning explains'.[2] The thought is a simple one. When we say 'He knows what the word X means' we should think not that there is some thing that he knows, that is what X means, but rather than he knows how to *do* something: namely, answer the question 'What does X mean?' (or, at least, to recognize the correctness or otherwise of an answer to this question, if presented with one). And answering such a question is *explaining* the meaning of X.

The (related) advantages of my Wittgensteinian slogan (that meaning is what explanation of meaning explains) are as follows:

- It makes meaning something public, 'out there'. That is to say, we are directed to written or spoken words on paper when we look at meaning in the arts, or indeed, meaning in language.
- It demystifies the notion of meaning. We are no longer obliged to think of meanings as somehow abstract entities; and this may help us avoid the mistake of viewing meaning as something inherently private.
- It makes meaning something humans do know in typical cases and, moreover, must know. This connects up with points made earlier about definition: that even if something common could be discovered by analysis, this wouldn't be what I meant by a particular term since I couldn't/didn't know it.
- It rules out 'association': the sorts of things that might be triggered in my mind by a certain word. For these are not its meaning, and we recognize this by seeing that they are not part of any explanation of that meaning. That is to say, they are not appropriate. (This may lead some to ask 'Who decides what is appropriate?'.)

What the slogan 'Meaning is what explanation of meaning explains' amounts to is a discussion of the meaning of a particular word through discussion of what people would describe or discuss as its meaning. So if we understand meaning at large in terms of that slogan, what about meaning in dance? This amounts to asking where explanations of the meaning of dances are typically given. The answer to that question is 'In dance criticism and the like'. And this explains why Chapter 7 will spend considerable time discussing dance criticism: it will fill in this point. For now, it will do to say that the meaning of dances is identified with, roughly, the sum of criticism of these dances. Of course that rough idea will need to be augmented in at least two important ways. First, a great deal more will need to be said about the idea of 'criticism' at work here, so that, for example, it is criticism by those who have seen the dance itself (see Chapter 4). Second, we must dispel from our minds any thought of *the* meaning, in the sense of there being one unitary meaning (see Chapter 3). Again, a comparison with language reveals our point exactly, for when I ask for an explanation of a particular word in language, then you are entitled to respond in terms which explain that word for me, with the particular interests and purposes that I have. It will be a complete explanation if it answers all my perplexities: that is what completeness amounts to here. With a different set of interests and purposes on my part you might reasonably explain it to me in a different way. And then something quite different would be a complete explanation. Nor should we think that these explanations can

114

necessarily be added together in any sensible fashion. And this may seem odd, if both are complete, since we would expect such explanations to differ fairly radically.

A similar point might be made for dances. With different interests I would expect to be saying different things about those dances, and that means identifying different things, all of which are part of *the* meaning of the dance (with similar remarks about completeness). We have some guarantee for the objectivity of these judgements already (from Chapter 1). But this is clearly a point to be taken up in great detail in the next two chapters.

As we will see, much discussion of the dance/language analogy has focused on whether or not there are equivalents, within dance, of specific words; whether or not, roughly, a certain movement functions in dance as a word does in language. And, as we will come to, a detailed response can be offered on this issue. But another level of response is more appropriate. If the central issue *vis-à-vis* meaning (and understanding) is the one relating to explanation – the one Wittgenstein refers to – then those features of linguistic meaning will be less crucial, perhaps not crucial at all. Certainly, applying Wittgenstein's slogan to the case of dance seems to focus our attention on features of dances which have little or nothing to do with a movement/word equivalence.

Applied to aesthetics in general, the point that meaning is the correlate of understanding and understanding the correlate of explanation[3] is no less helpful. It makes us see that to study the understanding of a particular work of art – or, more concretely, explanations of that work – is to study the meaning of the work, and hence the work 'itself'. We would not simply be considering 'states of the observer', or any such, contrary to the views of some theorists of aesthetics.[4] Moreover, one receives guidance on how to deal with a variety of hoary aesthetic difficulties; for example, the difficulty concerning what is, and what is not, reading something into a particular work of art, rather than just interpreting or criticizing it (see Chapter 6).

It is important, however, before accepting this view of understanding and meaning, to ask if it is correct. This amounts to asking what alternative pictures of meaning we could have. The philosophy of language offers a great many, but the one that has been most widely adopted for application to meaning in dance has been in terms of *symbolism*: that is, of some symbolizing type of relationship (Best, 1974: pp. 179–89; Best, 1978a: pp. 123–37). Such a widespread currency warrants our discussion here. But such an account is demonstrably wrong applied to meaning in language, for the sense that we have of the term 'symbol' here cannot be generalized. If the term 'symbol' is to mean anything in uncontentious cases of one thing symbolizing another (for example, fish or lambs symbolizing Christianity in pictures) then no similar relation holds between, say, word and meaning. The word does not stand for the meaning. Rather, it *is* the meaning. The popularity of a symbolic account of meaning has greatly waned. It is still applied in the case of the arts but, as we can see, must surely be mistaken. And since it is a mistaken account of meaning in language, it would be misguided for us to employ it for meaning in dance (Best, 1974: pp. 179–89).

Meaning and institutional concepts

There is a major complexity here. Recognizing it answers a question raised earlier over words in English. A 'native speaker' of English will be able to offer explanations of the meanings of those words, or at least recognize explanations as correct if offered by some other person; that is to say, when we ask about meaning for words, recognizing its shared character amounts to saying that, roughly, all native speakers have some 'hand' in it. Indeed, that is what makes them native speakers: they have a grasp of the words, usages and so on in the language. And, technical expressions aside, they can talk about the words – explain them – as well as talk with them. If the words we use are words we have grown up with, words which 'come to us from a distance' (Cavell, 1981a: p. 64), then we might reasonably expect all native speakers to have something to say in explanation of the meaning of ordinary concepts.

Consonant with points made in Chapter 3, this will not be true in respect of the arts. Art is, we have argued, an *institutional* concept. (Recall our remarks about institutional concepts from Chapter 3.) Roughly, object X is art if the 'right people' say it is. We employed the idea of an 'authoritative body' (Baker and Hacker, 1984a: pp. 272–3), the 'Republic of Art' drawn from the writing of Terry Diffey (1969) and based on the eighteenth-century Republic of Letters. We acknowledged that there was not one Republic but, rather, a set of overlapping republics, so that those crucial to dance might have no place in some other art form. We raised questions concerning the membership of this Republic, and said that, at the least, it contained practitioners in the arts, theorists of the arts, together with those involved in the display or audience of those arts. Moreover, we added historians and philosophers. We saw how institutional concepts operate through two stages: first, self-election, and then other-acclamation. Further, this implied that artist's work would become art (be accepted by the

116

Republic) on the basis of a public relations exercise on the artist's behalf, either by himself or by some critic. Of course, an artist might wait patiently for the judgement of posterity if he did not receive other-acclamation from the Republic of his day, but reflection on the history of art would convince us that this would not be a promising procedure. And we recorded as examples the excellent public relations job undertaken on his own behalf by T. S. Eliot, by Ruskin on behalf of Turner, and by Clive Bell on behalf of Cezanne.

This means, for dance, that it is the explanations of the Republic that count as contributions to the meaning of dances. Thus there is a disanalogy here with the language case, but one explained by the conventional, constructed character of art. (However, ordinary language is by no means homogeneous. Some terms are only understood by particular groups. And ordinary language contains institutional concepts, for example, 'machine'. So perhaps this dichotomy is less important than it seems.) So far, what we have said is that art has a conventional, constructed character that distinguishes it from language: that the concept 'art' is an institutional concept, whereas typical concepts in meaning are not in this sense institutional. We have not said a great deal about explanation – this is a very complicated topic (Baker and Hacker, 1980: pp. 69–85) – but we have located such explanations as typically the business of members of the Republic of Art and, particularly, of critics. We have seen, further, that employing Wittgenstein's account of meaning, in terms of explanation, allows us to make 'meaning' a perfectly public phenomenon for dance. In summary, then, exploring the second motivation, the meaningfulness of dance, allows us to emphasize the importance of dance criticism and of the kinds of discussion and explanation of dance that we find most characteristically there, but equally in other discussions.

A parallel between understanding dance and understanding language, then, seems both inevitable and appealing. But let us catalogue the difficulties. There are two sets of major difficulties: the first having to do with any picture of language; the second deriving from a particular view of language – that found in structural linguistics.

Two difficulties for the dance/language analogy

The first difficulty concerns the fact that, it seems, the unit of meaning in language is the word, but in dance there is no equivalent unit. There is no independently meaningful element of a dance. We find the meaningfulness of particular segments of the dance in terms of the meaning of the whole dance. The second difficulty concerns translation, for we can typically translate a passage of language into another language, or (and this is paraphrase) into another set of words in the same language. But, as is widely agreed,[5] it makes no sense to speak of constructing an exact equivalent for some work of art. Unlike the reports of, say, car accidents, exact equivalents of works of art are not possible, neither in ordinary language, nor in the forms of other works of art in the same media or in different media. To think otherwise amounts to urging that works of art might be interchangeable (see Beardsmore, 1971: pp. 15–18). Suppose, for example, that when you fail to get to see Martha Graham's *Night Journey* (1947), I say to you 'Well, see Sophocles' *Oedipus Tyrannus* instead. It says the same thing'. This view is transparently absurd (Redfern, 1979: p. 18). So, if we wish to speak of a dance/language analogy, or of a 'language of dance', this 'language' appears to be neither translatable nor paraphraseable. How can that be?

Let us look at these difficulties in turn. What must be seen in the first difficulty is that the apparent meaningfulness of words in isolation is illusory: rather, a word has meaning only in the context of a sentence, and a sentence has meaning only in the context of a whole language and a whole set of human practices. I do not propose here to discuss this normative account of language (see Baker and Hacker, 1984a). The point is simply that the objection has no grounds, for it assumes that word-meaning is understood in ways which, on the conception of meaning adopted here, it will *not* be. Moreover, as was said earlier, our aim in drawing the dance/language analogy may not be, if we follow Wittgenstein's account of meaning, to make points like this: although the third motivation is about them!

The second objection is more fundamental, and gets to the heart of talk of a 'language of dance' or of the dance/language analogy. It highlights how, in speaking of 'the language of', some writers concentrate too exclusively on natural languages, such as English and French. The parallel, it seems to me, is more exact when one speaks of, say, the 'language of mathematics' or the 'language of science'. There are important differences between these two uses. (This idea is so clearly discussed by Peter Winch [1987] that this paragraph and the next draw heavily on his work. The quotations are from pp. 197–8). Those differences turn on the role of new concepts: 'An Englishman who wants to learn French will have to master a new vocabulary, having varying degrees of equivalence with the vocabulary of English, new grammatical rules for sentence construction . . . and the like'. These will be varyingly proximate to the rules of English, and so on. So there may be difficulties concerning the translation of sentences from one language to another, and these will turn on 'the kind of material to be translated and the purposes of the translation . . . But by and large, such differences are marginal; there is so much common ground', which one might describe as a shared culture. So Winch suggests, 'learning French does not consist, for the most part, in learning to express radically new ideas, but in learning to express in a different medium . . . the kind of thing which an Englishman is perfectly well able to express' – and of course inclined to express. So that, in Winch's clear example, learning imperative forms is learning how to express commands in French, but not learning how to command, or what it is to command.

In contrast, learning the language of mathematics amounts to learning mathematics. Learning 'how to formulate a mathematical proof (as distinct from how to operate with particular notation)' is not acquiring a new way of expressing something already grasped (mathematical proof). It is learning *how* to prove something, or 'even *what it is* to "prove" something mathematically'. Recall that the problem that introduced this discussion was the difficulty of translating or paraphrasing the 'language of dance', which was contrasted with translating from English into French. When one turns now to the 'language' of mathematics, it seems impossible 'to speak of a translation from mathematics into . . . well, what? There is no such thing as translation into non-mathematical terms of the phrase "solution of a differential equation". The concept of a differential equation belongs to mathematics and has to be expressed in the language of mathematics'.

Like mathematics, understanding the 'language of dance' is not fully separable from understanding dance. It is not that one is learning to express in a different way ideas already perfectly understood; rather, one is learning (or acquiring) new ideas.[6] Moreover, this sort of outcome is to be expected. For concepts of mathematics and of science are often (perhaps always) institutional concepts in the sense of that expression as we have been discussing it (see also Chapter 3). So it is hardly surprising that they share these features with the 'language of dance'. The role of the movements which comprise the dance is also centrally important here. For dance-critical purposes, the explanation functions not *instead* of the movements, as it would if we thought of the dance as translatable into words, but rather (at the least) as an adjunct to the movement. One may even think of that explanation as *part of* the movement. For seeing it as dance is seeing it as the sort of thing which can be explained in these sorts of ways (see Chapter 4).

At this point two further brief (and related) objections must be met. The first urges that there *is* a translation equivalent in some cases. First, in sign language for the deaf and, second, in some dances, particularly those of other cultures (say, the Kathak North Indian form). The second objection points out that the story of many ballets can be put in a variety of ways, contrary to the spirit of the remarks above. But both objections fail to do justice to a distinction, crucial to the character of the arts, between content and the use of content. So that a ballet does more than just tell its story (although the story is portrayed). And while we may have an interest in the story, our artistic interest is not exhausted there. Moreover, to return to the example above, one might contrast the story of Oedipus (generally) with the story of Sophocles' Oedipus. The subtle differences here will be crucial, for they will be a part of what Sophocles manages to make us see which other tellings of the story do not.

Objections from structural linguistics: an example

Now, let us turn to the specific difficulties raised by viewing language from the perspective of structural linguistics. And here I am implicitly meeting some objections raised by Paul Ziff (1981). His arguments will serve as examples of the sorts of criticisms to which this perspective typically gives rise.[7] Ziff argues that dance should not be conceived of as a language for two kinds of reasons, although each of these reasons has numerous aspects. The first sort, the ones for discussion here, are reasons of a syntactic kind. It is difficult to fully appreciate the force of this kind of objection unless one accepts how completely Chomsky has succeeded in articulating the structure of language on the basis of its syntactic structure (Lyons, 1970). However, since our interest in a comparison of understanding dance with understanding language (as seen through the second motivation mentioned initially) deals with dance only in so far as it is meaning-bearing, it has little or nothing to do with the possibility of syntactic structure for dance. Or so I shall argue. It is not clear how syntactic structures correspond with the semantic structures with which we are primarily concerned. As Searle (1984: p. 39) puts it, 'Syntax is not sufficient for semantics'. While structural linguistics gives a meaning-bearing role to syntax, it also imports semantic elements through a lexicon (or some such) (Lyons, 1970: pp. 78–9), and this might be a feature we exploit in drawing the dance/language analogy.

Having mentioned that general point, let us consider one of Ziff's specific remarks concerning syntax: it identifies, as a characteristic of language, *recursiveness*. By this Ziff means the way in which one sentence can be imbedded in another, and the whole further embedded in another sentence, and so on. This allows for infinite extension of sentences. It means, too, that we are able to encounter sentences that we have not encountered before. But because they are made up of elements with which we are familiar, we are able to understand them. It is this feature – the ability of language to generate new but intelligible combinations – that Chomsky calls 'creativity' (Lyons, 1970: p. 86). And indeed, the elements of syntactic structure highlighted by Ziff as belonging to language but not to dance, all relate to this idea of creativity. Ziff's argument is that language has these features and dance does not, therefore the analogy between dance and language should be given up. My counter-argument throughout has been that these features are not those on which the analogy is based. My reply is to ask whether or not recursiveness is indeed a feature of language.

In respect of syntax, recursiveness is a harmless, if irrelevant, feature. But the same cannot be said of semantic recursiveness. For semantic recursiveness requires that these transitions from sentence to subject-of-sentence, the embeddings, be done without change of meaning. The guarantees here are by no means obvious for sentences, let alone for language in general. To suggest that it does not hold, I shall mention one feature that is arguably integral to meaning: what Charles Travis[8] calls *speaking variability*. Travis urges that the meaning of a particular sentence depends to such an extent on its context, on the particular *speaking* of it, that a discussion of its semantic properties that ignores this is bound to be misleading. An example of the following sort explains, in respect of the word 'red'. I am involved in a marine biology experiment where the head scientist and I go scuba diving, catching a number of fish which, at the depth of 100 feet where they live, are brightly coloured: green, blue, red and so on. On the surface all look a dull grey colour. This expedition is, typically, short of funds. So, in an addition to my role as assistant to the scientist, I am also assistant to the cook. The cook has been fishing over the side of the boat, catching surface-swimming fish – in particular, a tasty red fish. Now I receive the instruction 'Bring a red fish'. As Travis (1984: pp. 78–81) urges, this order is unclear if I do not know which of my two masters has issued it. But, first, all *is* clear if I do know which and, second, the problem here is *not* about the word 'red'. The word 'red' means red, coloured red, and that is all there is to it. But it amounts to something different when said by the cook and by the scientist. Here we have an example of speaking variability: the satisfaction conditions for the word 'red' vary with these different speakings of it. Yet the word 'red' is not ambiguous (as, say, 'bank' is) and the variability does not depend upon names (or indexicals).[9] The point here is that we cannot adequately describe recursiveness for the semantics of a particular term, if that term amounts to something different on different speakings. This will count heavily against the application of the idea of recursiveness to questions of meaning.

The conclusion to be drawn is that this sort of objection, drawing on supposed features of language, is not to the point unless it can be shown (a) that it genuinely is a feature of *all* language (a point open to debate) and, more importantly (b) that it is a feature of language on which the analogy draws. But this second feature is absent.

An area of disanalogy?

However, my use of the Wittgensteinian slogan ('meaning is what explanation of meaning explains'), characterizing the notion of understanding via the notion of explanation, might itself seem to generate a problem. For such explanations of dance will be substantially linguistic in character. Does this not give too much weight to *accounts* of dances, too little to dances themselves?

The reply is in two parts. First, we must recognize the gains in clarity from adopting such a position. If these are not to be lost, if one is not to sink into a miasma of feelings, the primacy of the linguistic element in explanation must be acknowledged. But that is not all the story. For the slogan (that meaning is what explanation of meaning explains) also serves to reinstate the claims of the non-linguistic. For an explanation of dance might involve things other than words. Gestures might be used. After all, the only complete realization of the meaning of a dance is that dance itself. Still, those gestures *can* be described in language, even if that is not the most effective method of explanation. The linguistic is not thereby unseated from its conceptual supremacy (but the pedagogy may be quite another matter).

Indeed, if we are interested in producing creators of dances – speakers in the language, as it were – it seems obvious enough that successive concentration on verbal reports of dances, or even on notations of those dances, will be unwise. Here there are three points. First, even for the most basic understanding, it is *the dance* that is to be understood, and the dance is only confronted when one confronts (minimally) an assemblage of moving bodies. So that by itself the notation, for example, will not do. Of course, it may be that I can get a group of dancers to perform my choreography without myself being able to move at all. My choreography, after all, is predicated on the technique of some such dancers. That is, technique in dancers is a precondition

122

of style in choreographers, as argued in Chapter 9. This leads to the second point, for those dancers must be taught that technique. That is essentially a practice on their bodies, for a technique might roughly be characterized as a set of fairly specific bodily skills. But the dancers are not thereby taught to 'speak' the 'language' of dance. Rather, they are trained to be the medium of the 'speech' of the choreographer. Yet, as with language, one develops one's fluency of such speech by practise. Thus the third point is that trainee choreographers will need bodies on which to practise. One can see how being able to begin with one's own body would offer, first, an easy method of explaining what one wants to do – the 'do this' method – and, second, a very basic supply of a limited (to one) number of such bodies always at one's disposal.

But all of these conditions are *conceptually* irrelevant. What is learnt from the art of dance – as opposed to, say, what exercise one gets or what friends one meets – is essentially a function of observers of that dance. A training in the bodily skill might make one a better observer, perhaps by teaching one the sorts of thing to look for: yet surely that can be taught in other ways. Again, a performer may be in a rather worse position to actually see what is going on at a particular moment in a dance performance than a well-situated audience, since the dance is, after all, staged to provide the view to that audience.

Interpretation and performance (again)

Such reflections on the dancer take us to a central aspect of performing arts such as dance. And to a difficulty for the notion of a 'language of dance'. The difficulty can be introduced via the notion of an interpretation as discussed in Chapter 4. For, remember, there are (at least) two uses of the term 'interpretation' in this context. The critic writes an interpretation of a work of art – a poem, a painting or a dance. These interpretations are centrally, often exclusively, verbal in character, even when they are interpretations of dance or music. We call these 'critic's interpretations'. Second, there is the interpretation of the performer in a performing art: to continue the example from Chapter 4, we speak of Pollini's interpretation of a piece of Schoenberg. This is 'performer's interpretation', constituted by doing something, that is, by creating that object in which the witnessable work of art centrally consists – sounds in the case of music, movements in the case of dance (Urmson, 1976). Yet, to continue the music example, Pollini plays the Schoenberg in such-and-such a way to bring out a certain kind of expressiveness in this piece of Schoenberg, at the expense, one might say, of the kind of expressiveness other pianists might bring out in their interpretations. So it will not do to conclude simply that the performer is irrelevant to what the work of art (in a performing art) means, although my earlier remarks may have tended in that direction.

It is plain that in language there is no analogue for this feature. One might perhaps point towards the different nuances given by different inflections; these at least involve the 'doing' of language. But since these nuances make a clear contribution to the meaning of strings of words (in utterance), this does not seem the right way to proceed. There is not, as it were, a second tier of interpretation here.

But, recall, the view developed in Chapter 4 offers an alternative picture here. It is not as though something that could be interpreted by the critic is instead interpreted by the performer. Rather, whenever the critic confronts the work of art itself (rather than the score, say) he necessarily confronts something already interpreted by some per- former, if this is a work in a performing art. Works in the performing arts come, as we have seen, with a label reading 'And now perform it'. The content of such a label is always relevant to the meaning of such- and-such a work of art. For only in performance is a token of that type- work available for criticism. This means that the performer's interpretation does not really constitute a level of interpretation at all. For one cannot confront the work of art except in this 'interpreted' form. So speaking of the dance/language analogy, and of the linguistic character of our understanding, emphasizes that the place at which the meanings of dances are most readily located is in discussions of those dances, that is to say, in the linguistic element which is the critic's interpretation.

Literature is not, or not centrally, a performing art (Shusterman, 1978). Those who urge the anomalous nature of literature have their finger on an important pulse here. Any analogy for understanding dance with understanding literature is bound to break down at just this point. But that highlights another shortcoming in speaking of a 'language of dance'. For dance works are art; language is at best the medium of art (the art of literature). This is, of course, why dance has conventional character relevant to its understanding and language does not – why the understanding of dance, as manifested through expla- nations of dance, is conceptually derivative of linguistic explanation, as noted earlier. As with the language of mathematics, one does not entirely escape from the language of dance in presenting these expla- nations, but here, unlike the mathematics case, neither does one necessarily present them by dancing. And this explains why teaching a technique is not fully equivalent to teaching a language, for the technique is not central to the 'presentation' of explanations of the meanings of dances.

However, one must not become infatuated with these differences to the exclusion of both similarities and other differences. The words on a page are a token of the type-work of literature, in the case of a poem; the dance score (the notation) is more like a recipe for the work of art (Urmson, 1976). A second difference is no less important. It concerns differences in our ability to understand the two texts; they are not equally comprehensible to the layman, even the intelligent layman. With the poem, there is at least something (that is, the words) which in general we can understand – although perhaps (say, in the case of a T. S. Eliot poem) not those of inordinate length, or in a foreign tongue. By contrast, a dance score can mean literally nothing, even to an interested spectator. Of course, you haven't got the poem, even when all you have is the words (merely). But at least you have something. Just what that 'something' is can be made explicit by recalling the passage in Virginia Woolf's *Mrs Dalloway*, where Septimus Warren Smith sends love poems to his beloved, an English teacher, only to get them back neatly corrected in green ink. There is little doubt that the words, but not the sentiments, were understood. Here the words were not being treated as poems, but at least some sense is being made of them. We might say that they are not being viewed using artistic concepts.

Conclusion

That concludes our characterization of the nature of dance. In this chapter we have further explored the view of dances as essentially interpreted objects, and have done so using the *key* slogan that 'meaning is what explanation of meaning explains'. At the root of our analysis are two thoughts: (a) that this way of conceiving dance is central to the nature of dance; and (b) that this conception of understanding is revealing. This point is elaborated in Part Three of this text.

Recommended reading

The account of Wittgenstein and of understanding defended here is that in the (difficult) writings of Baker and Hacker, 1980: pp. 69–85; Baker, 1981: pp. 36–49. The criticism of traditional views of language is largely from Baker and Hacker, 1984a. Those traditional views are represented both by Lyons, 1970 and by Blackburn, 1984: pp. 3–109.

PART III

Understanding of Dance

6
Understanding and Dance Criticism

At the centre of the account of dance developed here is dance seen as an object of understanding, developed (in Chapter 5) via the explanation of dance. But where are such explanations characteristically found? The answer, of course, is that they occur in dance criticism. As a result, this chapter and the following one explore the nature of such criticism, arguing that dance criticism has a crucial and central role within the understanding of dance. So the reading of dance criticism is no longer something a dance student might do if he chose, or equally, might decide not to do. Instead, it is argued that only the kind of informed confrontation with the dance that critical concepts entail will really be a confrontation with the work of art.

The sharpest way to identify the topic of this discussion is by considering a kind of remark heard fairly widely about the arts. It is often said that criticism inhibits one's appreciation of art, or that criticism spoils one's experience or confrontation with works of art. In this chapter and the next, then, I urge that such an idea is nonsense: that, as Ezra Pound put it, one should give sixpence for any bona fide example of criticism preventing appreciation of the arts. As Pound continued, one might as well say of a train that the rails stopped the train running – no one ever said that they would make it go. As will be apparent in Chapter 7, we can say something even stronger and urge that, in the relevant sense, understanding dance and dance criticism are very much of a piece. And though, by the end of the next chapter, I shall introduce some reservations around Pound's challenge, it seems to me to be making the right point.

Three topics for the understanding of dance

This suggests three major topics for this chapter and the next, at least superficially. The first concerns the character of criticism: what precisely criticism is and how it works. This amounts to a question about what

129

we take as evidence for any interpretation we might make of a certain dance. For how are we to rule out invention on the part of the interpreter (or critic)? How can we be sure that the remarks we make about dances are really comments about them? These are questions about the nature of the critical enterprise. And that is our topic in this chapter. Second, the relevance of criticism to understanding. And third, the relevance of criticism to experience or appreciation. These are the topics of the next chapter.

But it is necessary, before we consider any of these three topics, to clear away some of the ground. For example, these questions and issues arise for criticism in the arts in general, although our interest here is in criticism of dance. Moreover, the term 'criticism' itself stands in need of some comment. As Wollheim has noted, the English language seems to have no single word, applicable over all the arts, which applies to 'the process of coming to understand a particular work of art' (Wollheim, 1980c: p. 185). Certainly, the term 'criticism' is used in literature to mean exactly that, although in the other arts – particularly visual art – the word 'criticism' has a narrower usage, more closely located around evaluative questions. So, when we speak of criticism we are describing the general process by which one comes to understand works of art. A final piece of ground-clearing here would be to put aside questions about the subjectivity or otherwise of criticism. This topic has been discussed in Chapter 1; but for now the important thing to realize is that the idea of understanding itself brings with it the possibility of, first, misunderstanding (that is to say, of understanding incorrectly or mistakenly) and second, the possibility of other people understanding. Both of these require a greater generality than some subjective account of criticism would allow.

With those remarks putting aside some possible objections, let us turn now to the first of what I previously identified as our three major topics. It concerned the character of criticism. In this chapter I shall argue that criticism should be thought of as a kind of 'noticing': the recognition of aesthetically relevant [and hence tertiary (Scruton, 1983: p. 28)] features of art works. It may be worth demonstrating the potential importance of such a conclusion by noting that such a view implicitly rejects two other views of criticism. First, this view will reject a picture of the critic as arriving at the work with a set of rules for successful aesthetic performance or criteria for aesthetic success – that is, it rejects any kind of 'check-list' view of criticism. If criticism is a kind of noticing, then it does not follow that there are general rules applicable across categories of works of art, nor that there are any otherwise specifiable foundations upon which critical judgement is based. Rather, one notices features of aesthetic value and one learns to do so because one has an appropriate background in the art. Secondly, to take criticism as a kind of noticing is to reject a view of criticism as somehow approaching works of art with no preconceptions, or with no peripheral knowledge. It says instead that any appreciation of works of art draws on the knowledge and experience of the critic. We will see later how this is an important point. Finally, this idea of criticism as a perceptual process, as a kind of noticing, coheres very well with the view of the aim or goal of criticism that I built into my account of what criticism is, as presented originally. As Wollheim (1983: p. 550) put it: 'For the purposes of this paper I should assume what in fact I take to be beyond question: that the aim of criticism in the arts is, in the broad sense of those terms, to *understand*, or to grasp *the meaning of*, the work of art'. That is to say, the aim of criticism is understanding.

The next chapter will deal with the other two topics identified initially, namely, the relevance of criticism to the understanding of dance, and the relevance of criticism to the experience of dance. These will be argued to be inter-connected because experience is concept-mediated, as we will see here: that is, mediated through the understanding. So, although I talk in terms of understanding, of thoughts, and so on, this must be seen as also talking about feelings, emotions and so on, in ways we shall come onto.

I wish to introduce my view of criticism as a kind of perceptual process, a kind of noticing, via the analysis of competing views. And as I have said, this chapter is exclusively concerned with the nature of criticism in the abstract; that is to say, it deals with criticism in general, rather than dance criticism in particular – though of course I expect the points that it makes to be directly relevant to dance criticism, and I will bring out that relevance in the next chapter. In doing so I will build on ideas from Chapter 5, in particular on the discussion of the following of rules.

Two unsatisfactory accounts of criticism: 'rules' and scrutiny

We begin with two superficially plausible views of criticism, and show why they are entirely unsatisfactory. The first view takes the critic to have a set of criteria, or a check-list of rules or principles for aesthetic success. Although this view has a wide currency, it has never been possible to articulate, to any satisfactory degree, what exactly these rules or principles are. So, although this view has an initial plausibility – deriving no doubt from the view that if one can judge A to be better than B, then one does so on the basis of some criterion – the view cannot be said to be particularly well articulated or well supported in the available literature. In fact, the difficulty is a far more fundamental one; its conception of what it is to prove or establish something is a confused or mistaken one. To see this, consider how these principles or criteria are acquired. Typically, they are learned when prospective critics are introduced to works and have features of those works pointed out as valuable. But when that is done, in what we might with justice call 'the criticism lesson', there is no suggestion that every work bearing exactly those features will itself be aesthetically valuable. So, contrary to this view, criticism is not taught in terms of some kind of check-list, and the relevance of questions of teaching here is, of course, that criticism is successful, even though no such rules, principles or criteria are inculcated. Nor can we reasonably expect critics to have formulated such rules – not rules which might be expected to run over all works and all generations anyway. Once we accept the possibility of artists surprising us, we accept that if we did have rules, they would be somehow inadequate.

The most fundamental objection, however, concerns the need for such rules if one is to judge. The argument seems to be 'In order to make a judgement, I need a rule'. But of course, this position cannot be sustained. For if I need a rule to make a judgement, then presumably I need a rule about how that rule is applied, and a rule about how *that* rule is applied, and so on indefinitely. No, we must begin from a position where humans make judgements. Though as we shall see, this position becomes increasingly complicated as we attempt to articulate it more fully.

I want now to look at two more views of criticism. The first I shall call, with justice (and following Wollheim), 'the scrutiny view', for reasons which will be obvious. The second is Wollheim's own view, which mine closely resembles. And it is from there that I begin.

Wollheim (1980c; 1983) remarks that his arguments tend both to support and to elucidate the idea that criticism is, in an interesting sense, a *perceptual process*. By this is meant that criticism should not, for example, be modelled as an approach to works of art armed with sets of criteria or rules for aesthetic excellence which are then applied – as we have seen. Rather, criticism should be modelled as a kind of noticing: a survey of both large- and small-scale features of the object in question. (Later discussion will provide elucidation of this point.)

To fully understand both the importance and the accuracy of Wollheim's remark that criticism is a perceptual process – and to allow it to lead to my own view – I begin by rehearsing a set of familiar considerations. For there is a view which, in this simplistic formulation, might be mistaken for Wollheim's view: the idea that, as Wollheim puts it, criticism is a matter of scrutiny (Wollheim, 1980c: p. 188). This thought amounts to the idea that criticism consists in: 'scrutiny of the literary text, of the musical score, of the painted surface' (Wollheim, 1980c: p. 188). And the view conceives of scrutiny as an essentially perceptual process (Wollheim, 1980c: p. 193). Perhaps the ideal case for this scrutiny view of criticism would be as follows: I arrive in a house of indeterminate age and on a desk find, written in script of indeterminate age, a poem. I simply look at the poem, scrutinize the literary text, as it were, and this allows me to arrive at an articulation of critical judgement. In such an example, my critical comment is based only on the work itself, on features internal to that work and not on extraneous or extrinsic features. And my route to understanding here is a perceptual one.

The error familiarly (and correctly) attributed to such a view amounts to a criticism of its account of perception: that it takes perception to be a *direct* process, or to put it another way, it believes in the myth of the innocent eye. Our rehearsal of the argument here will be facilitated by putting it in that form. Let us therefore briefly rehearse the familiar considerations surrounding the myth of the innocent eye. This idea too can be formulated in a number of ways. For example, used in the context of aesthetic education, say, it might appear as the view that the 'vision' of children is purer or clearer than that of adults, because it is unsullied with preconceptions; or, in the context of criticism, as the view that one needs bring 'nothing but oneself and an open mind' to a work of art in order to understand it; or, again, as the view that great art must be available to everyone, hence cannot depend on knowledge or experience open only to an elite. As this last formulation makes clear, there is an attractive egalitarianism about this view.

Yet this *is* a myth, in all its formulations. As Wollheim remarks, referring to what he describes as the 'heroic proposal' that one can have understanding in the absence of any conceptual background: 'the aim of which is to ensure the democracy of art . . . This proposal . . . has little to recommend it except its aim' (Wollheim, 1980c: p. 194). For such a proposal in fact rules out the possibility of understanding. To see why, we need to recognize the connection between what one can see (or understand) and the battery of concepts one possesses – what is sometimes called one's 'cognitive stock'. To take the argument a little further, we can explore some implications of the formulations given above, they amount to saying that one can understand art without anything (or at least not much) in the way of a cognitive stock.

When one confronts this suggestion, one gets to the heart of the mythology here. For any understanding, indeed, even seeing and hearing, takes place under concepts. The desire to do without a cognitive stock is, on investigation, an incoherent one. To repeat an example from Chapter 1, when I see what is before me as a dog, I am implicitly contrasting it with a cat, a horse and so on. Anyone who fails to draw such contrasts is not seeing dogs as such at all; what he is seeing are, undifferentiatedly, dogs, cats and horses. What I see depends on the concepts I have, and that means that in the absence of any such concepts, there is no interesting sense in which I am seeing at all. For what am I seeing? If I can answer that question, I can subsume my perception under some concept. To say this is to repeat some points made in an earlier chapter.

Yet this point is of special relevance if one considers one's perception of a work of art, for now one must see it *as* a work of art. Thus, as noted earlier (Chapter 1), if my ignorance of the French language means that my delight in hearing a certain French poem recited is merely delight at a pleasing succession of sounds, then there is a clear sense in which I am not confronting the poem at all. And merely understanding the language is not sufficient here. I must see the formal significance of certain of the work's features, for if I do not, I will be merely frustrated by the fact that certain words at the ends of lines have sounds similar to those at the ends of other lines, or annoyed that the writer has only used up half the page in writing these lines. And, more generally, I must see this poem (this work of art) as manipulating formal elements – for example the sonnet form – which contribute to my understanding of what the work of art is about. To repeat points made earlier, this will involve my cognitive stock allowing for the use and understanding of 'categories of art' (Walton, 1978).

Of course, the conclusion that some cognitive stock is needed does not, of itself, tell us how much or of what kind. This is a complex and difficult question for aesthetics. Thus far we have learned from the scrutiny view that one cannot give an account of the understanding of works of art unless one allows that the critic bring with him some cognitive stock. In what follows, I will speak of what the critic may or must bring – but I mean by this what he will need if he is to understand. And surely, as remarked earlier, such an understanding is a prerequisite of criticism.

134

A modest proposal for the extension of the critic's cognitive stock

If, as Wollheim plausibly urges, we think of the major aim of criticism as aiding in the understanding of a work of art, the grasp of the work's meaning, it seems we may now have a way of deciding how plausibly to extend cognitive stock. For any addition will need to be consistent with, and where possible to forward, this aim. And since meaning and understanding are correlative notions (see Chapter 5), I shall speak indifferently of 'understanding the work' and of 'grasping the work's meaning'.

Worth noting also, since it colours the exposition here, is the tendency within philosophy to discuss powers of persons in terms of knowledge (supposedly held by such persons). So that, here, we are asked to think about the critic's use of particular concepts in terms of his having (or not having) certain facts or truths that are internal or external to the work of art. In this way, the critic's judgement of the work may appear correspondingly reduced to his or her capacity to employ – or, worse again, to state – certain truths. Although I continue to present the issue in this way, it is important to see, first, that it does not reflect my view of the matter and, second, how distorting it can be. To see these points, consider the learning of a foreign language. This is certainly not reducible to the acquisition of truths about the language,[1] whatever else it may be. Nevertheless, ease of exposition suggests that we proceed (carefully) using the traditional method of characterizing such powers.

Let us consider another relatively modest proposal. First (as Wollheim urges) we can scarcely avoid acknowledging that any person will know general truths about the world, such as the workings of causation, some natural history, some cosmology and so on. And in this grouping we must accept that the viewer of art knows something about some aspects of human social behaviour. For example, if he knew nothing of war (or at least violence on a largish scale) he would make nothing of Picasso's *Guernica*. We recognize that any viewer will bring this knowledge with him, not least because it is difficult to imagine what it would be like for someone *not* to know these things. But this is still not enough information to allow the understanding of art. Some of the prevailing conventions of art must also be grasped, if one is not to misperceive the works in question. (This is what is involved in having an understanding of the *categories* of art.)

So now we have a modest proposal formulated: the viewer brings general truths about the work and knowledge of some of the prevailing conventions of art. Yet, as Wollheim noted, once formulated it seems difficult to keep this proposal genuinely modest. For what knowledge can actually be ruled out? What is it that, on this proposal, one might not usefully know? (By 'usefully' here, I mean simply that the knowledge is used in one's understanding of the work.) Of course, one might attempt to be parsimonious by returning to the aim of criticism, as given above. Yet this is not effective, for all cases still seem plausible. This is surely what Wollheim (1980c: p. 194) means when he says that we cannot solve the problem by returning to the idea of the 'ideal critic'. But perhaps there is one line of defence that can be maintained. No doubt the critic may, and must, bring with him a great deal of information external to the particular work under discussion – general truths about the world, prevailing conventions of art, and the like – but surely he doesn't bring with him information about this particular work of art: any information 'internal' to this work of art. Surely any internal truths must be gained from looking at the work. While it may be no indictment of the artist that he does not provide the critic with external truths, surely the work is flawed if it cannot be understood simply by looking at it, given that the viewer has a grasp of these external truths. Or so one might argue.

It is to be noted, of course, that just such a contrast between the internal and the external is central to the scrutiny view. Indeed, it is thought by many to be the contribution of this view to understanding of criticism that it makes us aware of the need to distinguish between truths internal and those external to the work itself.

Wollheim (1983) has offered an interesting discussion of this proposed bulwark against the expansion of the critic's cognitive stock. For the restriction here does not rule out internal truths (or internal information) passing into the critic's cognitive stock. Rather, it says simply that this passage must be through perception. That is to say, the critic may understand things – may (perhaps even must) understand truths internal to the work – but he must acquire that understanding by looking at the work and in no other way. Here Wollheim made two comments to accurately illustrate that this point was *not* unproblematic. The first comment accepted (temporarily) as a reasonable restriction the idea that internal truths about the work must be perceptible, but then pointed out, first, that it is very unusual for the causal history of knowledge to be a relevant consideration, and second, that what are and what are not the perceptible features of works depends upon our having a certain cognitive stock: that without an appropriate cognitive stock, certain features would not be perceptible for us. This is one of the two related aspects Wollheim brings before us by drawing attention to the similarity between attribution of paintings by connoiseurs and those

136

children's pictures that have line drawings of animals hidden in the trees. Adults can generally see the animals easily, although it may take the children some time. Similarly, experts can see easily those features on which attributions are based, while we do not. The question of perceptibility is thus both important and open (Wollheim, 1973: pp. 188–92; Wollheim, 1983: p. 555).

Wollheim's second comment builds on the first. If the claim is that the entry of truths internal to the work can only be through perception, it is implicitly conceded that there can be such internal truths in the critic's cognitive stock, just so long as they are perceptible. But now the question arises: 'Perceptible on the basis of what cognitive stock?', and this question shows us that there is really no restriction here at all. The point of the restriction was just to limit what could appropriately be and what could not appropriately be in a critic's cognitive stock. As Wollheim (1985: p. 104) puts it: 'The spectator's role is perceptual, but the preparations he makes to prepare himself for it need not be perceptual'.

What we find, then, in investigating the modest proposal, is that it generates no unproblematic account of what the critic may/must know in order to understand a particular work of art. Indeed, it gives no way of maintaining its modestness. However, one line is suggested – though not much more than that – for the motivation behind the idea of understanding a work of art on the basis of zero cognitive stock, which we now see to be an incoherent idea, was that understanding works of art was centrally a perceptual process rather than an *inferential* one. But this thought is not actually undermined by the rejection of the 'no cognitive stock' view, and the failure of the modest proposal. Indeed, it may even be supported. For now we need no longer think of the procedure by which our understanding of a work of art (or our interpretation of the work) derived from our perception of it as an inferential process. Rather, we recognize that there is no significant step between how we perceive the work and how we understand it. Or, at least, there need not be. The worry here of course is that to place too great an emphasis on the perceptual character of understanding is to import *arbitrariness*. But we thought of understanding as rooted in scrutiny of the 'aesthetic surface' of the work, uncontaminated by our concepts, so the clear response to the charge of arbitrariness was possible. Any interpretation could be 'checked' against the features of that aesthetic surface. What can we say now? The answer lies, of course, in recognizing that perceptual processes are not necessarily arbitrary, and indeed that their dependence on shared concepts opens up the possibility that they are necessarily non-arbitrary.[2] While this does not deal

137

with the whole worry of arbitrariness, at least it gives us one less dimension in which that worry is operative. It is only when we fail to recognize the non-arbitrariness of the perceptual that we begin looking elsewhere for the will-o'-the-wisp of some other guarantee of non-arbitrariness.

This gives us a useful characterization of the disagreement between Wollheim and the scrutiny view. For Wollheim urges that perception is what gives us understanding of a work of art. That is to say, this picture is not an inferential view of criticism. He sees a direct transition from perceiving a work of art on the basis of a certain critically relevant cognitive stock to grasping the meaning of that work. By contrast, on the scrutiny view, perception supplies premises for an inference of the meaning of the work of art. On such a view, a certain cognitive stock allows the construction of critically relevant evaluations, from which the judgement of meaning can then be deduced. For this view Wollheim (1983: pp. 557–8) has no time. As he puts it, 'I cannot accept the view that perception of the work of art is primarily an evidence-gathering activity, the evidence thus gathered then being utilised in the determination of the meaning of the work of art . . . On the contrary, I think that the perception of the work of art *is* . . . the process of understanding the work of art . . . '. This summarizes the basis of our criticism to this point of the scrutiny view (see also Wollheim, 1985: p. 104).

Two provisos for an account of criticism as noticing

It is one thing to claim, however, that perceptual judgements are necessarily non-arbitrary (in the sense under discussion), quite another to prove the point. Our proof begins by continuing Wollheim's lead. At this stage, Wollheim provides what he calls two provisos for his account of criticism. First, the question of critical *relevance*. Clearly critical judgements may work in at least two ways: they may involve or suggest perceiving certain things in a particular work. For example, discussing Martha Graham's *Deaths and Entrances* (1943), Marcia Siegel (1977: p. 200) remarks on the way we see 'three women trapped by their own indecisiveness and gentility. The women fondle objects that seem to suggest action, but they're unable to act. Characters not definitely real or fictional run in and out, little encounters take place and are broken off, rivalries are intimated but quickly contained'. In all these comments, the focus is on finding certain things – formal or in terms of content – in the dance, certain insights of detail. Or again, critical judgements may involve or suggest perceiving the work in certain

138

ways: for example, in Martha Graham's version of the Joan of Arc story, *Seraphic Dialogue* (1955), we should see that the Joan character 'knows the whole venture will be dangerous: every step is a risk and every success will bring her nearer to death. In Graham's universe, Joan wins her own beatification' (Siegel, 1977: p. 206). And this is to be seen in the context of a 'personalized' vision of Joan, one on which she 'sees her former selves . . . enact her interior struggles, doubts and spiritual joy' (Siegel, 1977: p. 205). Thus we are offered a way of interpreting the whole work. Here we find the 'cosmic' aspect of the work discussed: major themes like man's relation to man, to nature, God and the like.

On Wollheim's account (and he is surely correct) either kind of judgement would be critically relevant. Indeed, the distinction is not easy to maintain. Consider, for example, Marcia Siegel's remark about Martha Graham's *Errand into the Maze* (1947): 'Gone is the standard tale of the hero who saves his people by seeking out an oppressor in its lair. Now it is an investigation of the hero's – heroine's – mind; her inner state of fear and tension, her positive action to confront the thing she fears' (Siegel, 1977: pp. 203–4). Here there is a blending, for we talk about both how the dance as a whole might be seen – what it is about – and how to construe its details (for example, how the role of the heroine is to be interpreted). As Wollheim (1980c: p. 199) might express this proviso, anything that does not contribute to our understanding in one or other of these ways is not critically relevant. Hence, by implication, information that failed to allow one of these sorts of changes in our understanding would not be critically relevant. So that, for example, if Ezra Pound's connection with Italian Fascism – given that it became well-established – did not lead me to see anything more (or less) in his works, nor to see his work in a different way, it would be right to regard that information as critically irrelevant. (This of course, is what one needs to do, in general, with information about artists' shoe sizes, lunch menus and the like.) So while it is necessary to make some restriction here – not everything a critic says or does falls in the ambit of this discussion – the proviso is, to use Wollheim's word,[3] 'amplitive'.

Second, a general difficulty must be noted; not just any view of a work of art is automatically acceptable. This is what it meant, earlier, to speak of 'misperception' of a work; for example, taking a work of Schoenberg to be unstructured because one is not hearing it as serial music (that is, in the category 'serial music'). Of course, there is no easy answer as to what are and are not misunderstandings or misperceptions. In effect, one has to listen to the story or explanation offered, and evaluate that. But once the possibility of misperception or misunderstanding is accepted, it becomes important to think about what Wollheim calls a 'restrictive proviso', to the effect that nothing is critically relevant *merely* because it allows some change in understanding; rather, it must lead to a correct or acceptable (Wollheim says 'true') interpretation. Thus, Wollheim (1980c) considers the case of so-called perfect forgery of a Rembrandt. He concludes that, if interpretations really did not distinguish the accurate from the inaccurate (or indeed, if Wollheim-style retrieval of their intentions did not really distinguish Rembrandt from the forger), in such a case 'we will be forced to downgrade our views, first, of Rembrandt, then of art, very considerably' (Wollheim, 1980c: p. 197). Instead, we must recognize that to fail to see the Rembrandt and the forgery differently, and hence to fail to interpret them differently, would be to *mis*-see them. So there is some canon of 'correctness' at work here. Thus the restrictive proviso sets limits on the acceptability of an interpretation, and if we can indeed make out this restrictive proviso it seems we are well on our way to showing that perceptual judgements are necessarily non-arbitrary.

Up to this point, this chapter has done little more than give exposition of Wollheim's ideas, drawing extensively on his examples and arguments. But here we must part company with Wollheim, for his way of making out this restrictive proviso employs ideas of retrieval which are the subject of much criticism. Wollheim says that a correct interpretation is one that takes us 'back to the creative act', that correctly or truly reconstructs 'the creative process, where the creative process must . . . be thought of as something not stopping short of, but terminating on, the work of art itself' (Wollheim, 1980c: p. 185). Of course, on Wollheim's view, it may be problematic whether or not any particular interpretation does indeed retrieve the creative process, that is to say, it may be difficult for us to know whether or not any interpretation is a 'correct' or 'acceptable' one. But, for Wollheim, there will be a true answer to the question, whether or not we humans know it. This view of Wollheim's is very difficult to sustain. I shall have something more to say about it when I consider the question of *intention* in Chapter 11. But for the moment, I shall assume that we find it, at the very least, unpalatable and, therefore, not an acceptable way of making out the necessary restrictive proviso.

The restrictive proviso reconsidered

It follows that we must look for another way of making out the restrictive proviso, for clearly we do need some method of arbitrating among the interpretations. I suggest that we can do so, and, moreover, that our arguments will be very much of a piece with the general tenor of the view of criticism as a perceptual process. The first step is again to remind ourselves of some familiar remarks. In discussion of the duck/rabbit figure, the point made is that one can see this figure in a number of ways, but not just in *any* way one chooses. And earlier (Chapter 1), I told the story of David Best in a lecture, remarking that one could not, for example, see the figure as a clock, whereupon a wiseacre in the audience quickly responded that one *could*, and it was a quarter to nine! But, although dealing with Best's particular example, a comment like this supports his overall case. Just as one can see the figure as a picture of a duck with certain lines depicting the beak, so those same lines could be seen as the hands of a clock. Implicitly, the wiseacre was agreeing with Best that, in order to be an acceptable interpretation of the figure, one's account of it must depend on taking those lines in some way: it must be, to use Best's phrase about art, '*objectively* supported by features of the work' (Best, 1983: p. 154).

Now, clearly, this answer is inadequate as it stands, for we need to know on the basis of what cognitive stock the figure can be seen in this way or that way. Hence we are immediately back among other problems raised earlier. Yet there is clearly something very right in this view of interpretation as answerable to the features of the object, in this case of the design. In particular, if it could be made out more fully, it allows an obvious reply to the charge that one's interpretation *reads into* a particular work of art something which is not there. But we can only return to the notion of *reading in* when we have said a little more about the perceptible in art.

One doctrine familiarly associated with the view of criticism as scrutiny was anti-intentionalism, *à la* Wimsatt and Beardsley. (This view will be discussed briefly in Chapter 11.) Their idea was that artists' intentions were not directly perceptible and, since the meanings of works of art were necessarily open to perception, intentions could have no bearings on such meanings. This argument has been widely attacked, for reasons which will appear later. But two of its features are of relevance here. First, it poses the question: 'Why shouldn't there be critically relevant "facts" or information which are not directly perceptible, however enlarged one's cognitive stock?'. Second, it makes one ask whether or not what is perceptible in a particular work is necessarily something that is recoverable from it (or from it alone).

To take those points in that order, consider the outcome in our discussion of the modest proposal to limit critically relevant information to

141

the directly perceptible: it was a failure – or, at least, no great success. There seemed no satisfactory rationale for the limitation in any form we considered it. And if critics were ever allowed to appeal to factors not directly perceptible, which we had accepted implicitly in allowing them 'general truths about the world and prevailing conventions of art', this restriction to the directly perceptible will certainly seem odd. But, that conclusion might at first glance seem decidedly out of place. How can criticism be a perceptual process if some critically relevant information is not directly perceptible? The answer lies in the second issue raised above. If we can have information perceptible in the work of art – if I already know it is there, or at least the sort of thing to look for – even if not directly recoverable from it in perception, the seeming contradiction disappears. The critic with the appropriate cognitive stock can indeed make his judgements on the basis of perception – so criticism is a perceptual process – and yet the passage of that cognitive stock into his understanding is not solely a matter of the perception of the particular work of art. This is the force of Wollheim's example about attributions mentioned earlier: critics can make attributions on the basis of certain features because they know what to look for, just as adults can find line drawings of animals in ways children may not. Or, again, it is that which allows Michael Fried to find, in the sculptures of Anthony Caro 'radicalness [which] enables them to achieve a body and a world of meaning and expression that belong essentially to sculpture' (Fried, 1974: p. 101). If Fried can see this and we cannot, then perhaps it is because he knows what to look for, or where to look. And he did not learn that solely by studying Caro.

Now we should take stock. Our search for an account of Wollheim's restrictive proviso has led us to recognize that an emphasis on the directly perceptible is misplaced, that any basis for the restriction be open to perception, but not necessarily directly. We noted that the simple restriction – that any interpretation will be answerable to the perceptible features of the work – was too simple. We there took as indicative of the problem of arbitrariness the charge of reading something into the work of art.

Arbitrariness and 'reading in'

Our discussion is advanced if we turn again to this notion of *reading in*, and here two points are crucial (see Cavell, 1981b: pp. 35–8). First, the notion of something as *read into* a work of art implies that there is something not read into the work, some meaning or interpretation (or

142

set of them) which can be contrasted with what is merely *read into* the work. But this contrast cannot usefully be maintained in the case of art works, at least, not once we have put aside any extreme claims, which can be dismissed as not answerable to the perceptible features of the work in question. That point is worth illustration. For example, a critic who urges that Alvin Ailey's *Adagio for a Dead Soldier* (1970) is a joyful piece, and yet accepts that neither movement nor music nor costume nor lighting supports this claim, might be said to be reading something into the dance: but it seems more accurate to say that he is just plain wrong! His interpretation is not responsive to the features of the dance.

Yet this way of categorically ruling out an interpretation cannot generally be done. Most interpretations are arguable in ways in which, as I set it up, this one was not. And if they are arguable, we cannot just rule them out of court. But then we see clearly why one cannot, in such cases, draw a general contrast between what is *read in* and what is *there*. For we have seen in Chapter 3 that to take an artistic interest in a dance is to see it as an interpreted object, an object for interpretation. And it is on the basis of such interpretation that one sorts out what is there in the dance one is watching, since the features of the dance (viewed as dance) are its aesthetic, or more exactly artistic, features. As Cavell puts it, referring to novels or films, which he treats as 'texts': 'you have to say what *is* there and it turns out to be nothing but a text. But in *that* sense you might just as well say that there is no dog in the text "Beware of the dog"' (Cavell, 1981b: p. 35). The dog is there in the sense in which an understanding of the text will make reference to a dog, real or imagined. And, while the case of art is more complex than this, in the same way it is the need to refer to features of a particular work of art in describing or appraising that work which establishes it as having those features – at least once the accuracy of one's description or appraisal is acknowledged by the Republic.

What we recognize, then, is that there is just a text to be interpreted, even if that text is a dance; this in turn does nothing to sanction the idea of some once-and-for-all interpretation (even some once-and-for-all set of such interpretations). One recognizes that what is there is arguable, a topic for rational debate within the critical tradition. Whatever line we take, on what is *there* and hence on what is *read in*, that line must be arguable in ways that people who discuss these matters would accept as an argument (Cavell, 1969: p. 92), although not necessarily as compelling. This is clearly the right response to this difficulty, but why? Complex theories of interpretation have been presented to make what we can see to be a very simple point. Of course, the issue of what is *there*, what is *read in*, turns on the meaning of the work of art, but this amounts to the kind of explanation of that work which is appropriate and acceptable. And we see that this is a matter for rational discussion. (Were it not tantamount to sacrilege, one would be tempted to conclude that a whole cloud of philosophy condenses in a drop of grammar [Wittgenstein, 1953: p. 222].) It suggests that any interpretation is acceptable, just in that case where informed critical theory or informed art theory of the time takes it to be acceptable. That is, it suggests a broadly institutional account of the kind developed in Chapter 3.

So when one thinks about *reading in*, it becomes clear (Cavell's first point) that one can only 'sort out' questions of *reading in* once one has a grasp of what is there – and that will involve reading the work in the light of informed critical theory or informed art theory of the time. So doesn't that grasp also *read in* something? Doesn't it import a set of contentious concepts? It is here that we might appeal to a complicated argument of Wittgenstein's, the so-called 'private language argument' (see Baker, 1981: pp. 31–71). Our answer (Cavell's second point) is that the concepts can never be that contentious, being based, as they are, on 'agreement not only in definitions but ... in judgements also' (Wittgenstein, 1953: section 242). The alternative (and mistaken) view is neatly captured by Baker and Hacker (1984b: p. 24): 'you know what "pain" or "looks real" means from your exemplar, just as I know from my exemplar. An evolution, or a good angel, has so arranged matters that our exemplars are qualitatively identical ... So thought and action rest firmly on the bedrock of the subjective'. Highlighting that false view brings out the relevance of this discussion to our question about arbitrariness, for surely this false view would generate two worries. First, how do we (or can we) *know* that our exemplars are qualitatively identical? Second, even if they are, isn't this just an accident, an uninteresting contingent truth? When Baker and Hacker speak of this view taking the subjective as 'bedrock', they are pointing up the major moral that, on such a view, perceptual judgement is at best accidentally non-arbitrary – which is the same thing as saying that it is arbitrary really! This misconception must be overcome both 'in the Large and in the Small' (see Baker and Hacker, 1980: pp. 334–5). One must consider both how it offers us a mistaken view of perception, through misrepresenting the role of concepts, and also how the place of those concepts within our 'form of representation' is also misrepresented.

As we saw Wittgenstein emphasizing in Chapter 5, the meaning of an expression is what is explained in an explanation of that meaning. Yet this harmless sounding truism compelled us to look, not to ephemeral meanings, but to the concrete, to our actual practice of explaining. And here the role of agreement was crucial. My use of an expression must be in accord with my explanation of what it means. Baker and Hacker make this point with one of Wittgenstein's examples, given previously: 'If I explain "red" by pointing at a sample, saying "This is red", then when I judge object A to be red, A must be *this* (pointing to the sample) colour' (Baker and Hacker, 1984b: p. 44). So what functions as an exemplar can also have the previously exemplified property ascribed to it (Baker and Hacker, 1980: pp. 284–96). It is the need for this sort of consistency in practice that Wittgenstein uses in the private language argument to register a central constraint on understanding: its use cannot be arbitrary, and hence must respect the distinction between the user *being* right and his merely *thinking* he is right. It must make sense to ask if he gives the correct answer, even in response to some self-directed question; and therefore this constraint applies to the intelligibility of his own words, meanings and so on.

The implication for perceptual judgements of this consideration are shown easily enough. Consider a term like 'red'. Since it will normally be learned in the context of red exemplars, the first phrases mastered (or at least logically prior ones [Hacker, 1976: pp. 23–46]) will be that something is red. Only later will one learn that something looks red (but perhaps is not), because looking red is, as Anscombe (1981, p. 14) puts it, 'looking as a thing which *is* red looks'. Here, in a simple case, we see the guarantee of the non-arbitrary character of perceptual judgements. They are not given by angels, but learned from exemplars.

To draw this phase of the argument together, let me point out how the private language argument meshes together with the institutional considerations from Chapter 3. When one learns about art, one does so from exemplars, together with informed discussion and the like. And here one learns how to explain art, how to discuss it; one learns how to go on in such discussions or arguments.[4]

Some criticisms of the view of criticism as noticing

Thus far, I have argued that the conclusion stated a long time ago, that perceptual judgements were necessarily non-arbitrary, could indeed be maintained; moreover, although this hasn't been stated too explicitly, that we could find grounds for a Wollheim-style restrictive proviso in the fact that one learns how to go on in the interpretation of art works. Thus far I have identified the inadequacies of a traditional view of criticism as implying rules, principles or criteria, and of the scrutiny view. Our objections to the scrutiny view (following Wollheim) led us to articulate a conception of criticism as a perceptual process, with an amplitive proviso to the effect that critical judgements must make us see something more in the work, or make us see the work in a different way, and with a restrictive proviso to the effect that not just any change in our seeing of the work would be an appropriate one. Here we parted company with Wollheim, urging that what was and what was not an appropriate critical remark would itself depend on the informed critical theory of the time. To this extent our judgement was an institutional one.

This concludes my exposition of the nature of criticism, in which I have urged that criticism should be modelled as a kind of noticing. Apart from specific criticisms of pieces of my argument, I foresee two general objections to this view of criticism, which I will take up here. Chapter 7, which employs this notion of criticism, should help both to elaborate and to elucidate how it can be that criticism is indeed a kind of noticing. The two objections I anticipate might both be phrased by claiming that what I interpret as the nature of criticism – that it is a perceptual process, a kind of noticing – is only one of the things criticism does. But that objection might amount to two different things. First, it might amount to saying that critics do things *other than* forward our understanding of works of art, in the ways that I have described. Or, second, it might urge that not all criticism can be comfortably modelled as a kind of noticing (Shusterman, 1981; Shusterman, 1984). I shall consider the objections in that order.

In response to the first kind of objection, I have two related comments. First, the variety of remarks that I have allowed within criticism – through the amplitive proviso that they be critically relevant – is wide and varied. So it seems to me that I have covered all the things that critics might be doing. But if someone wishes to insist that a critic typically, say, gives information about the history of works that is not critically relevant in this sense, but which still is the job of a critic, then I do not wish to strenuously disagree with this suggestion. Of course, the critic gives these remarks in order to produce changes in our understanding, in at least one of the two ways described under the amplitive proviso. But I see no reason to be unduly dogmatic on this point. I shall be happy if it is accepted that criticism is centrally or crucially a matter of the kind of noticing that changes our understanding. If it is sometimes other things, then I have nothing much to say.

On the second objection my response is a little more complicated. For writers on criticism who have argued in this way have typically wanted to model some criticism in ways other than as a perceptual process, thus arguing that more than one model for critical reasoning is required. Our response, if it were to be given in its full complexity,[5] would require a consideration of the other models to see if they are genuinely adequate. But briefly what I shall suggest here is that, when properly characterized, all the interesting things that critics do are subordinate to the one I have been describing; hence criticism can be completely modelled in this way, as a kind of noticing. But on one point in particular it is worth being very clear. My characterization earlier involved treating criticism as a species of noticing, rather than a matter of inferring. Given this characterization, an opponent might allege that this accepts or involves the view that criticism is not a rational procedure. The response here will be to remind such an objector of the extent to which stories and explanations of art have a role in justification and elucidation of perceptual judgements, as well as pointing out (again) the non-arbitrary character of such judgements. What is perceptual may also be rational (see McFee, 1985). This line of criticism should be seen as flawed by an over-emphasis on the persuasive, or public relations side of criticism. No doubt, as the institutional element noted in Chapter 3 makes plain, such a side exists and is important. But the real reason for accepting the judgement offered by a critic will be that the judgement is right or correct, that is to say, accords with how one sees the work and, given one's cognitive stock, what one sees in it. And this will involve an appraisal of the critic's reasons. It will bring his activities within the claims of rationality.

Recommended reading

Key texts here are Wittgenstein, 1953; Wollheim, 1980c; Danto, 1981: pp. 115–35; Danto, 1986: pp. 23–69. Shusterman, 1981, offers a useful background, but central is the picture of understanding in Cavell, 1969: pp. 73–97, pp. 180–237; Cavell, 1981b: pp. 1–42. An elementary discussion of the issue, leading to a similar resolution, is Ground, 1989: pp. 61–99.

7

Understanding, Experience and Criticism

In this chapter we will take up the second and third of the three issues identified in Chapter 6. Recall that the three were, first, the nature of criticism (dealt with in Chapter 6), second, the relevance of criticism to the understanding of dance, and third, the relevance of criticism to the experience of dance. If we have seen that criticism should be understood, or modelled, as a kind of noticing, what does that mean in detail for the relationship between understanding and experience in dance?

Certainly the remarks on criticism already made and the account of criticism developed in Chapter 6 might seem to have established the connection between criticism, as I understand it, and the understanding of works of art. Notice that this line of argument assumes that it makes sense to talk of understanding works of art, that works of art are fit objects for understanding. And I am willing to accept the charge of begging the question here, for when one thinks about criticism it does seem essential to establish the connection with understanding, and my opponents might think that I have merely assumed it. I hope that the argument of Chapter 5, together with this chapter, will silence that worry.

It may seem, at first glance, that the most important of our three questions – given my initial characterization of Chapter 6 and this chapter – is that concerning the effect on our experience of a particular dance of criticism of that dance. Those people who have said that criticism inhibits or destroys or distorts appreciation of the arts have tended to imagine that somehow it is their experience that was deformed or inhibited by such criticism. But in a fairly straightforward way this third topic can in fact be shown to be a not very relevant sub-category of the second.

There are two ways to establish the connection. The first is to return to the initial claim by opponents of the view to be defended here that criticism can inhibit appreciation. And what this means is that critical comment can interfere with, disturb one's experiences of the particular work of art in question (in our case, a particular dance). To spell that

148

out more elaborately (although here I may be merely repeating what is obvious) for this claim to make any sense, it must be possible for criticism to affect one's experience. That is, for changes in one's understanding to lead to changes in one's experience. So we needn't give too much attention to that experiential dimension, since it will be somehow dealt with or covered when we have a better understanding of the more general purposes of criticism.

That may seem a rather weak argument, but certainly there is another way in which the connection between the relevance of criticism to understanding dance, and its relevance to experiencing dance, can be brought out. And that is through the established thesis (mentioned in Chapter 1 and elsewhere) that perception is always concept-mediated, that (to put it roughly) what one can perceive – see, hear and so on – depends on what one knows. I cannot see a row of oak trees in front of me (to repeat one of Wollheim's examples) if I do not know what oak trees are (which means have the concept 'oak tree'). What I see depends on the concepts that I have, and that means that in the absence of any such concepts there is no interesting sense in which I am seeing at all. For what am I seeing? If I can answer that question, I can subsume my perception under some concept.

What this means is that the range and character of our experiences is partially determined by the concepts that we possess. Hence, if criticism can affect those concepts – which seems to be common ground amongst most views of criticism – it can affect the range and character of our experiences. Indeed, as we shall see, it is through its ability to affect our experiences, both in range and character, that dance establishes for itself a necessary place within the lives of human beings.

What I have urged then, is that the third of the three problems I identified in Chapter 6, that concerned with the relevance of criticism to experience, is one we can usefully and constructively see as part of a second problem: the relevance of criticism to understanding. But it should be recognized – and this is very important for the view of criticism employed throughout this work – that it makes criticism rather less of a detached, intellectual, 'cognitive' procedure than it is sometimes characterized as being.

Dance as an object of understanding

We now return to those three important questions (as identified initially). Our progress to date is as follows: we have discussed the first in Chapter 6, articulating an account of the character of criticism, and we've seen how the upshot of the third – regarding the experience of dance – in effect comes down to the second: the contribution of criticism to our understanding of dance. This remaining issue we will now consider.

Here I want to offer four thoughts, all fairly familiar by now. The first is that dance is a fit object for understanding. Certainly my conception of understanding is wider than that often employed, but nonetheless it seems correct to urge that dance has this status. That argument would be made out in two parts. One must identify how it is that other works of art are fit objects for the understanding, and then apply that conclusion directly to dance. But I will not here undertake the full argument. Much is implicit or explicit in what has been said in other chapters. For that rigorous account would develop in detail the notion of an interpretation of a work of art (begun in Chapter 4), arguing that all works of art are essentially interpretable objects (see Wollheim, 1980a: pp. 83–6), and then establish a link between such interpretations and 'what is expressed' by those works of art (see also Chapter 12). Here I will simply adopt another, more impressionistic, strategy consisting in reflection on the centrality, for the notion of art, of the idea of expression. In effect, this strategy amounts to offering a Humean challenge: would we be willing to accept as art something that neither we nor anyone else found expressive, something with *no* connection with the thoughts, feelings and ideas of humans? The implied answer, 'no', seems right, if only because asking someone what makes him think a particular object is a work of art (that is, asking for his reasons) invites him to appeal to the history and traditions of the art form in question, that is, to draw connections between the work under consideration and other works in the same art form (McFee, 1980b). The reasons one offers are drawn from such cases, although not of course by slavish adherence to their model.

And if one can provide such arguments, offering reasons and so on for one's conclusions, it surely seems right that these are conclusions which bear on one's understanding. As has been argued elsewhere (Cavell, 1969: p. 92; McFee, 1980a: pp. 220–2), the supposed parallel between one's admiration for wine and one's admiration for art breaks down at exactly this point. While we may agree that there is no recipe for a resolution in either case, for art there is genuine room for discussion; that is, there is room for the application of reasons. We recognize that certain considerations do bear on, say, the evaluation (the judgement) of a painting or a music performance or a dance performance; this fact distinguishes one's appreciation of art from one's *sensory preferences* in wine or food. Cavell (1969: pp. 91–2) brings this out neatly, modifying an example from Kant. Faced with a disagreement in our estimation of particular wine you can still insist that you like it even if I insist that it tastes like canary droppings and even if I have been rigorously schooling your palate. If you do so, I may doubt your judgement, but not your rationality. There is no price to be paid in my estimation of you even if, in the last analysis, you remain true to your claim to like that wine. In that sense, this should not be dismissed as a *retreat* into personal taste. Not so in a dispute about art forms such as dance, for there, when appropriate concepts are brought to bear, a framework for discourse comes with them. And, offered reasons of obvious relevance to the evaluation of a particular performance, to continue to offer a different evaluation without yourself offering any reasons in that opposed direction is to retreat into a personal judgement, that is, to retire from the appreciation of art into some subjective realm.

Notice the structure of the argument here. We are seeing how our finding a dance expressive involves us in making sense of that dance, which, of course, involves us in seeing the movement sequence as a piece of dance. The appreciation of dance brings with it a network of reasons; hence may with justice be said to necessarily involve the understanding.

But is all dance expressive? Again, no comprehensive answer can be offered. Yet, surely, if someone offered to us an example which they claimed was a genuinely non-expressive dance, we would want to reply, after the fashion of Cavell (1969: p. 253 and 253n), discussing intention, that what does not invoke expression must be thought of in contrast to expression, at the same level as expression, as a modification of human thought and feeling. And surely this idea has a great plausibility, for would we really be willing to acknowledge as art some object unrelated to human thoughts and feelings in these relevant ways?

Of course, this is not a complete argument to establish that works of art are fit objects for understanding. First, it is far too impressionistic, and second, it works through the intermediary of the notion of expression. But here one could add two supporting thoughts: first, if what was said earlier about the connection between experience and understanding is to be maintained, the notion of expression is a useful link to the idea of understanding; second, this connection between expression and understanding has been widely argued for in recent philosophical writing. For example, Scruton (1983: p. 77) says: 'It must be wrong to attempt to give a theory of musical expression which cannot

151

be re-written as a theory of musical understanding'. Or again, in a similar vein, Budd (1985: p. 151) urges: 'A theory of musical understanding should lie at the heart of a theory of musical value'. If these general points were accepted, one would be willing at least to consider works of art, in our case dances, as fit objects for the understanding.

The 'meaning' of dances identified with informed criticism

The second of the four thoughts mentioned earlier concerns what we constructively call the 'identity' of dances. Our thesis must be that the object as it is experienced, or as it is understood, is not straightforwardly identical with the physical or material event. That is to say, in the relevant case, what I see at some minimal level of perception is an agglomeration of bodies leaping this way and that way, a wash of movement. To take a parallel case, however, we can and must distinguish hearing a sequence of sounds from hearing a poem. So that, to return to an overworked example, a person who understands no French might be entranced by the flow of sounds upon hearing a recitation of some work in that language, but we would not think of that person as encountering fully the French poem. Indeed, to encounter the French poem one needs not merely a knowledge of French, but also a knowledge of poetry, its formal conventions and the like. To apply, the wash of movement must be seen as dance; it must be brought under appropriate aesthetic concepts. Only then are we genuinely confronting a dance. But if the object of understanding is the sequence of movements seen as a dance, then it is already seen in a way structured using the kinds of concepts central to criticism.

Here of course we are drawing on a connection made explicit in the remark on the nature of criticism quoted from Wollheim, who made no distinction between understanding the work and grasping its meaning. That is to say, meaning and understanding are correlative notions. So a discussion of the understanding of dance moves naturally to a discussion of the meaning of dances.

At this stage we might usefully remind ourselves of an assumption drawn from the philosophy of language, introduced in Chapter 5. As Wittgenstein repeatedly asserts, 'meaning is what explanation of meaning explains' (see Baker and Hacker, 1980: pp. 75–85). That is to say, that the meaning of an expression in language is what is explained in an explanation of that meaning. Within this harmless sounding truism, much is going on. It compels us to look, not to ephemeral 'meanings', but to the concrete – to our actual practice of explaining (see Baker and Hacker, 1984b: pp. 56–7, 111–15). And here the role of agreement is crucial. My use of an expression must be in accord with my explanation of what it means. I do not wish to elaborate this point (see Baker and Hacker, 1980: pp. 75–85; Baker and Hacker, 1985a: pp. 81–106), but if we accepted it, we would have an initial basis for explaining the connection between dance criticism and the under-standing of dance: it would be in such dance criticisms that our 'expla-nation of meaning' would be found. And here we will be building on a tradition of established work in criticism and, particularly, in meta-criticism; moreover, particularly in metacriticism from Europe, where it is urged that it is in terms of the critical discourse appropriate to a particular work of art that we are able to identify that work.[1]

To make these points more concretely, I shall continue to exemplify them primarily by reference to the work of one major contemporary dance critic, Marcia Siegel. But first, two points must be acknowledged, lest my view be misunderstood. I accept (what is obvious) the variety within critical discourse. So if we identify the meaning of a dance with informed critical discourse on it, we will have not one meaning, but many. My use of just one critic should not confuse on this point. As long as any critical interpretation of a particular dance is based on per-ceptible features of that dance, together with appropriate informed critical theory, it will be equally 'good'. But this does not lead to the 'anything goes' of subjectivism, for each interpretation will have a pub-licly available base, and any lacking this base will be plainly wrong (see Cavell, 1981b: pp. 35–8).

In the interests of clarity, I am making reference in this chapter to only one critic, and even here one must look closely to recognize the accuracy of my remarks, for the usual unit of dance criticism is the brief note that must identify and describe the work or works. That is, it must say quite a lot about what goes on in the performing area, in order to inform prospective patrons, and the like. As such, these notes often do not emphasize, for that dance 'what its extremities of beauty are in service of' (Cavell, 1979: p. xiv). At their best, and Marcia Siegel's are surely among the best, they can indeed pick out the meaning of a par-ticular dance, and how that meaning is achieved. For example, in *Untitled Solo* (1968):

Cunningham portrays the common man as hero, beset but indestruc-tible . . . he uses the persecuted, almost psychotic movements of fear. He focuses almost entirely on the area directly in front of him; he raises and lowers his gaze but doesn't glance behind or to the sides, as if he were afraid of taking his attention for a moment from the

153

main threat. His hands make nervous clenching movements... (Siegel, 1972: p. 235)

And so on. But if only the first sentence picks out the meaning of the
dance directly, we can see that those later remarks show us how to
interpret or understand that first sentence. So the point I draw is that
to be speaking of the meaning of, say, Cunningham's *Untitled Solo* is to
be referring to informed judgement of that work of a kind I am using
Siegel's writing to illustrate. Or, more exactly, to be referring to the
dance as seen through concepts supplied and clarified by the critical
discourse.

Interpretation and emotional education (I)

To summarize our argument so far in this chapter, we have urged, first,
that dances are essentially interpreted objects; second, that interpretation is done through what I am calling criticism, by which I mean that
interpretation is typically done in discussion of the arts, but that it is
best (or paradigmatically) done by established critics, since such critics
have access to, and an ability to mobilize, elaborate critical discourse. So
works of art are essentially interpreted objects, and that interpretation
takes place in criticism paradigmatically.

This leads us to the third thought, which builds on those developed
above: interpretation is important for roughly what we call 'what we
get out of' the work in question. So that, in the relevant case, if we ask
why people should take any interest in dance, then clearly we're going
to need an answer that appeals to intrinsic features of dance. It will not
do, for example, to appeal to spin-off features, or to say that dance is
enjoyable. All these things are true, no doubt, and important, but by
themselves they do not justify people taking an interest in dance; in
particular they do not justify them taking an interest in dance rather
than something else.

The element just mentioned brings us to some ground which I will
mention here briefly, and take up in Chapter 8 (see also McFee, 1984).
For our comments about the role of Wittgenstein's claim that 'meaning
is what explanation of meaning explains' allow the elaboration of a
rough model for the kind of enlightenment offered by the arts. We
should think of the arts as presenting to us articulated (if unsolicited)
explanations. That is, we should treat works of art, such as dances, as
if they were offering explanations (of rather a peculiar kind) of familiar
aspects of life, drawing 'new' conceptual connections for us, by making

us see that so-and-so, some previously 'grasped' concept, stands in need of explanation. And if so-and-so wants explaining for me, which I find in finding an explanation that works for me, it follows that I have learned something when, through my confrontation with the work, I now have that explanation. Of course, not in ways I could necessarily describe. For example, Siegel (1977: p. 199) comments:

> Graham's dances speak of the American temperament; of religion, right and atavism; of the anguish of artists and the obligation of kings; and of woman's struggle for dominance without guilt.

If this helps me make sense of, first, some of Martha Graham's dances (which it does) and, second, of elements of my own life, it does not do so in ways I could easily describe. And further enlightening remarks do not necessarily give me more to say. For example, Siegel had earlier remarked: 'Graham seems to start with the world's messages, then she states them in personal terms' (Siegel, 1977: p. 197). This is, of course, dead right if one thinks of, say, *Lamentation* (1930). And, as I will show presently, Siegel can bring out this connection for us. But if asked 'What precisely does this comment explain for you?', I would be at a loss to explain. As Best (1985: p. 175) puts it: 'The work of art casts a translucent light on the situation'. That is to say, the enlightenment need not be something I can easily say, at least not without sounding banal. Certainly the notion of explanation appears here at two different places. I have urged, earlier in this chapter (see pp. 152–4) as well as in Chapter 3, that our access to works of art themselves is through their meanings, and hence through our experience of them under concepts supplied by critical explanations of them. But also, works of art themselves function as if they were explanations of our 'life-issue' perplexities (Best, 1978a: p. 117). And these two are interwoven. Despite Siegel's rueful comment, 'I don't know whether the concrete experience or the evanescent metaphor is harder to capture' (Siegel, 1972: p. 5), she clearly captures both of these for the central figure of *Lamentation*; for example, when she says:

> It's a very ritualized, depersonalized kind of grief, one that allows the woman no real release. At two points in the dance, when she seems about to tip or pull herself off-balance entirely, she draws back into the stability of a symmetrical pose. She finds comfort in form and balance, not in letting go. She seems to be referring to heaven or to some cruel power outside herself as she rocks back and later stretches an arm high overhead. Now she is standing; now she puts one foot on

155

the bench, as if she would climb up and claw down the thing that is responsible for her condition. Again, no release. No jump, no explosion. (Siegel, 1979: p. 41)

If this way of looking at *Lamentation* informs me about the nature of grief, it is because this statement in 'personal terms' catches a nerve of the universal grief, one of 'the world's messages' (Siegel, 1977: p. 177, quoted earlier). Also, it is because I, its audience, have something to learn about grief.

As with any explanation, my confrontations with dances (indeed, with works of art generally) are useful and informative for me – I can learn from them – just in that case where they bear on questions or perplexities of mine. And of course one's encounters with art may reveal areas of perplexity of which one never dreamed. As perhaps through psychoanalysis, one may learn through confronting art that one's problems and views were not what one thought they were. But again, a model for this revelation is provided: in finding something is an explanation for me, I may learn those things in my understanding which needed (further) explaining (see McFee, 1984: p. 109). For instance, I might have thought I knew all I needed, or cared to know, about themes around notions of envy or power. But then I see José Limon's dances – for example, his *Emperor Jones* (1956). The central characters here are typical Limon heroes. As Siegel says:

They possess the world's powers and talents. They hold responsibility, often for the welfare of many other people – families, communities, kingdoms – and Limon shows them literally bearing the burdens on their backs, pulled between opposing loyalties. They are tormented by jealousy, tempted to folly, agonised by impossible choices. (Siegel, 1979: p. 310)

I feel, first, the inadequacy of my own ideas and conceptions and, with any luck, gradually I come to some new understanding. And then I find myself agreeing with Siegel (1979: p. 310) that 'Limon was elaborating on relationships that were conventionally shown in much cruder terms'.

Here my confrontation with art might be seen as simultaneously exposing a gap in my understanding and filling that gap, though a more accurate picture (as we will see) would make references to changes within my conceptual framework. (Notice too that I am here speaking of explanation; this relates my remarks to the context of understanding, for it is not true that anything which promotes understanding is an explanation [see Baker and Hacker, 1984b: pp. 118–19]. Hence we see why considerations irrelevant to the content of art as art – for example, some narrative elements – are irrelevant to what we learn from art, or how art changes our understanding. See McFee, 1984: p. 109ff.)

What I am urging in general is that art can show us the familiar anew (as Wisdom urged) because it can offer us explanations of the familiar that relate to problems or perplexities we did not feel until the work of art made them vivid for us. Thoughts of this kind run through much criticism. One clear statement occurs when Siegel (1977: p. xv) laments the passing of major dance pioneers:

> . . . their missionary dedication has been replaced by a more practical, competent professionalism: choreography (now) must be created to highlight a season, to feature dancers, to attract reviews, not to unearth mysteries.

Her diagnosis of what has gone wrong, then, will include this failure to seek 'to unearth mysteries'; that is to say, she associates a decline in dance with a loss of just the sort of elucidatory aims for which I have been arguing.

Interpretation and emotional education (II)

A more extensive treatment would give close attention to what I have been calling *the familiar* (see Chapter 8). People, actions, scenes, objects, values, ways of living – all may have aspects revealed through art, and the sort of 'revelations' can display considerable variety. But to give us some overview of the kinds of changes involved, and to relate those changes more directly to dance, we need to consider a general claim about the nature of dance which finds its most elaborate present-day articulation in the work of David Best. (We will consider it in more detail in Chapter 8.) This argument holds that the arts in general should be seen as providing a kind of 'emotional education'. Experience of the arts may allow us to experience finer shades of feeling, and it may do so because it may allow the refining of those concepts under which those feelings are experienced and under which those feelings are characterized. (Thus it is of a piece with our earlier remarks about the concept-mediated character of perception.) As Best (1978b: p. 76) puts it:

157

...a pre-condition for experiencing the subtle and finely discriminated feelings which are the province of art is that one should have acquired the imaginative ability to handle the appropriate concepts.

Now, one question must concern how this 'imaginative ability' is acquired. Certainly a part of the reply will emphasize the need to confront the works as art, and the general claim, then, is that one's contact with art may lead to a kind of conceptual 'refinement'. Hence the value of the arts is elucidated in terms of a refining of one's discrimination, and hence of one's capacity to experience finely discriminated feelings. This should be thought of as an enrichment of the person's conceptual range.

The point of Best's argument, and its clear relevance for us, has two dimensions. First, it fills out the connection already mentioned between (what I identified as the topic of this chapter) experience and understanding, which has a crucial importance. But, second, it identifies 'what is got out of' dance with some changes in discrimination and/or understanding to which confrontation with that dance gives rise. (Notice that I say here 'to that dance' rather than 'to that work of art' because the preceding arguments have established that only for that particular work of art, which in our case is a dance, will that particular something become available.) It is surely to catch this sense that Siegel entitled an article on Cunningham 'Human events', for among the things the article admires in Cunningham's work is the concern with human thoughts, ideas and feelings, even if treated in some abstract fashion:

We found our attention sharpened. We learned to appreciate changes rather than similarities, to keep readjusting our standards and finding new pleasures instead of trying to recapture old satisfactions, and most of all we came to value that very evanescence that is supposed to be dance's biggest liability. (Siegel, 1977: p. 278)

The claims for this dance, then, include a sharpening of our attitude to the flux of life, a new way of looking at our experiences. All this conforms well with the ideas articulated above.

In a sense, then, we have seen how changes in understanding and experience are related together. And once we add to that claim the one we have already developed, which relates the meaning of the dance to our explanation of that meaning and identifies that explanation with critical comments (both those we'd make and those we'd accept from others), we have, it seems to me, welded together the three thoughts offered so far in this chapter. Doing so, we have articulated to some degree a picture of the connection between criticism and understanding dance, for we have said that understanding dance involves the development or education of the feelings, that this education takes place through alterations in one's conceptual range (sometimes called one's 'cognitive stock' [Wollheim, 1980c: p. 194]), and that this kind of change might reasonably be expected to take place through the articulation or presentation of criticism.

The knowledge-base of criticism

Our fourth point, which relates of course to the last aspect of our third, is to comment on the need for 'professional' critics (although nothing is really being said about what people do for a living). The central thought here is one that Schoenberg[2] put most bluntly by saying 'If it's art, it's not for everyone. If it's for everyone, then it's not art'. This judgement has been dismissed as elitist. But before we concur with that judgement, that conclusion, I think we should distinguish between what one might call accidental or practical elitism and necessary elitism.

It is certainly the view of some theorists that art – and derivatively, art criticism – necessarily is some kind of elite activity. I can see no reason to agree with that view. And its exclusive tendencies must surely count against any uses that we might want to make of, for example, art in education. Such tendencies, if true, would equally count against general support – for example, public funding – for the arts, to mention two activities where one might think exclusivity was not the order of the day. So I think we have reason to believe, first, that we would be sad to find art to be necessarily elitist. But moreover, and second, I think we have reason to believe that it isn't.

If we consider the question of 'practical' elitism, we might better understand Schoenberg's comment. The point is simply this: that one needs to know certain things in order to appreciate certain works and that this knowledge takes time to acquire. And this is particularly true, of course, since one element of this knowledge is acquired only through direct experience. As a consequence, there is a serious difficulty about every single person acquiring a requisite amount of knowledge for all the arts. A parallel here might be with the sciences. It seems boringly true that we cannot all be nuclear physicists, or rather, that in order that we all be nuclear physicists then none of us could be biochemists or plant biologists or . . . (and so on).

So what we are urging here is that the kind of knowledge required in order to be a dance critic probably precludes one doing very much else, although working in another area of criticism, or working directly in the art, may seem less of a deviation from the task of criticism than, for example, endeavouring to be a farmer or, as John Stuart Mill[3] did, to work in the East India Company. Again, I mention Mill's example as something constructive. Mill did write profound criticism and meta-criticism, but then he was surely one of the greatest intellects ever to arise. We cannot all expect to compete in a set of areas simply because J. S. Mill succeeded.

I hope that that serves to distinguish what I have called the 'necessarily' elitist from the 'practically' elitist, and to urge that what is practically elitist – and here I would include dance criticism – is only just so because of the degree of knowledge and understanding that it requires. And our earlier remarks have clarified the logical position of that knowledge and understanding, for we have said that the experience of the arts takes place under concepts. We have not said, though it is implicit, that some of these concepts must be acquired or, certainly, are best acquired in connection with direct experience of the relevant art forms. And what this means in practise is that a great deal of knowledge is required in order to satisfactorily do criticism. Perhaps the nature of this knowledge can be misunderstood. It is not necessarily knowledge, let's say, of the particular art form, of its history, development and so on. Nor is it necessarily knowledge of the formal concepts the art form employs. Indeed, quite often profound criticism arises through the application of concepts appropriate to one form in the case of another form: as, for example, in Fried's use of the term 'syntax' to describe Caro's sculpture (Fried, 1977: p. 453). We can think of this as an invention of a new piece of critical jargon, where the context makes its use plain.

Conclusion

In this chapter it is argued that dance criticism has a crucial and central role within the understanding of dance, rather than a merely peripheral one. The reading of dance criticism is no longer something a dance student might do if he or she chooses, or equally, might decide not to do. Instead, I have argued that only the kind of informed confrontation with the dance that critical concepts entail will really be a confrontation with the work of art. The argument is made up of four elements, namely: that dance can be understood; that the meanings of dances are (roughly) the 'collected criticism' of them; that 'emotional education' is essentially a kind of conceptual change; and that genuine criticism is necessarily informed criticism. Each of these will be familiar to students of the literature; indeed, the whole is not particularly new. But from the perspective of our general picture of criticism as a kind of noticing, it becomes a powerful and unified account of the role of the dance critic.

Following Wollheim (1983), we took the central aim of criticism to be interpretation, that is, the business of making sense of art works such as dances, of rendering them coherent or intelligible. As we have seen through just one example, in successful criticism this aim is achieved by the placing of emphasis on 'this' aspect of the work rather than 'that' one, both by drawing connections within the work (between apparently disparate elements) and between this work and others, and by suggesting (perhaps better, 'unpacking') presuppositions and implications of the work when seen in this way. Notice two things: first, that this is essentially the recording of perceived connections; and second, that criticism on such a view seems amply fitted to the perceptual (or noticing) image. Moreover, it is clear why there are no eternally authoritative interpretations[4] or readings of works, for the contemporary force of a particular reading will depend on the concepts central to contemporary critical theory, and also the problems and perplexities within which the contemporary audience for art (and for criticism) finds itself. Such a view coheres well with my own general historicism about artistic meaning (see McFee, 1980b).

This view of dance criticism explains, as we have seen, the centrality of dance criticism within our understanding of dances. But more than that it explicates the two related facets of criticism, and hence allows us to return to the topic at which we began. We can see clearly the role of the knowledge-base of criticism (what might with justice be called its 'cognitive' element). Without appropriate knowledge – appropriate concepts under which his or her perceptions fall – a critic could not possibly do the noticing which, I have urged, is central; he or she could not make the fine discriminations from which we, later, can also learn about the work, and hence about ourselves. But also recognized is what may, with perhaps less justice, be called an 'affective' element to criticism. The critic's noticing is appropriately seen as an experience of his – an engagement of his feelings – although, of course, this is fully consistent with its being also an engagement with his rationality. As we have seen, confrontation with dance can result in types of emotional education, and can do so because dance criticism can bring about conceptual changes in those of us who read it, and hence can contribute (in the necessarily interlinked ways described above) to our cognitive and affective development.

UNDERSTANDING DANCE

For the discriminating and informed critics, what I have called affective and cognitive elements are necessarily harmoniously integrated. But what of others – say, beginners at art appreciation? Here it is easiest to think of poetry criticism, which many of us have had inflicted on us as children. And certainly the sorts of analysis it encourages can interfere with one's appreciation in so far as one is able to make the conceptual changes only in the cognitive dimension. The education of the emotions involves our being able to make use of the concepts we acquire, and that means, make use of them in experience! It is this that Wollheim (1986: p. 46) speaks of as the need to 'mobilize' our concepts. Of course there is a sizeable philosophical oddity: how can I both have a concept (cognitively) and not have it (affectively)? But this is just the problem about self-deception and about weakness of the will (see Davidson, 1969). Our model can explain both why the question of an antagonistic relationship between criticism and appreciation might have arisen, namely because the relevant concepts are sometimes not fully 'mobilizable', and also why there is no real question.

It may seem that I have now taken back something which I said initially, for did I not promise that authenticated cases of criticism interfering with the enjoyment of art would be impossible (following Pound)? And have I not just now recorded some situations in which criticism *could* interfere with our experience of art? Two points must be made here. The first is to emphasize that what I have said does indeed agree with Ezra Pound's comment. What it urges is that any genuine understanding of criticism – that is, one that allows the critical concepts to be mobilized – necessarily modifies our experience, and as such, cannot be thought of as interfering with it. (There is another point to be made here that we will confront in the next chapter, concerning the sense in which an experience of the arts is 'beneficial'.)

But the second point worth noting is that we must not think of these things in an 'all-or-nothing' way, for an ability to mobilize concepts in our experience may be a matter of degree. We cannot all be critics with the sensitivity of Marcia Siegel. But we will not really have learned from her words if we do not respond to the art in a way which moves us in the sorts of directions she indicates, even if the insights into life are not of the kind she makes. Yet, equally, we will not typically grasp the work as clearly (and hence as fully) as she does. And that is a central point: we cannot specify a sense of fully or completely understanding the work, for even Siegel's remarks might still be augmented. For example, we might return to the dance in question at a later date and still find the experience enlightening. To reiterate a point made first in Chapter 2, we cannot understand the idea of a complete answer here: only of

162

one that is complete relative to an issue or question. Hence there is nothing fixed or final here.

Finally, then, we have seen how our concerns with the notion of understanding lead us, first, into a rethink of the nature of criticism (Chapter 6), and second, to a reappraisal of such informed understanding in one's appreciation of dance. We have located the sorts of informed experience entailed by criticism at the heart of the understanding of dance. And that has involved a re-articulation of the nature and impact of the arts. An extension of this topic is the theme of the next chapter.

Recommended reading

The key general texts are those recommended for Chapter 6; together with Cavell, 1981a: pp. 108–17; Cavell, 1984: pp. 97–140. On the application of similar ideas to music, see Scruton, 1989.

8
The Point of Dance

My position on the point (or contribution) of dance to human life, thought and education may already be clear. I have urged (following Best) that dance, like the other arts, offers a kind of emotional education, and does so because it allows change in the concepts under which we experience the dances. Further, I have offered some vague comments, also following Best, about the connection between art and 'life issues' or 'life situations', to show how the conceptual changes in question should be thought of as educative or as bearing on human concerns. And if these claims are accepted, nothing is left to say about the point of dance. But what is missing is any convincing argument for these claims; the fuller articulation I give to the claims, and to their interrelation, should make the contours of such argument clear.

But, it might be thought, this whole topic is a red herring. Art has no point, or no point beyond enjoyment, or no point beyond itself. I cannot accept these answers since they represent different versions of the idea that artistic value is subjective, in the dismissive sense articulated in Chapter 1. Any account of aesthetics based on them must lapse into subjectivism, with any reaction to a particular work being of equal 'validity' with any other. Arriving at such a conclusion is, as we saw in Chapter 1, accepting that art is unimportant, for the kind of informed understanding at present characteristically associated with art critics (see Chapters 6 and 7) would be impossible; and so would aesthetic education, at least as anything more than a kind of 'light relief' to the other, more serious aspects of the curriculum. For this reason it is important to insist that *some* answer be given to questions about the point of art, by suggesting that all judgements of art do presuppose some general theory of the character of art, one which 'explains' the importance of art (Sparshott, 1963: pp. 10–15).

This chapter assumes that subjectivism is to be avoided, hence that a positive answer to questions about the point of art is to be sought. I shall argue, first, that art (more specifically dance) has a point, contrasting my position with (a) the view that art is pointless – an 'art for art's sake' thesis – and (b) the claim that art has some *purposive* (Beardsmore, 1971: pp. 6–21) dimension, for instance the inculcation of morality. Second, I will explore the nature of the emotional education which, as I have urged, is at the centre of the contribution of the arts to human life and understanding. Third, I will discuss the connection between the two elements identified in previous chapters: the conceptual change element and the life issues connection. Finally, I will further elucidate the idea of life issues through a discussion, applied to dance, of the idea of the familiar in the light of a thesis by John Wisdom that art reveals anew the familiar from life.

Purposive versus artistic justification

Chapter 1 introduced the idea that the general area of aesthetic judgement (the large concept) was to be distinguished from that of purposive judgement. Two of the major arguments are worth reiterating, here applied specifically to art (rather than to other aesthetic objects[1]). The point at issue is whether or not we should think of the outcome of art as an end at which we arrive by otherwise specifiable means. To employ a means/end distinction is to conceive of the means as separable from the end, as just one route to that end, among many. And this is not the way that we think about art works such as dances. Rather, we recognize that *only* this work of art is a 'means' to this particular 'end'. Thus we should not use the language of means and ends in talking about art. But how is this to be done?

To answer, we must backtrack a little. For purposive judgements it is possible to distinguish between means and ends, between what one intends to achieve and how one goes about achieving it. From this distinction it follows that the way one goes about doing something is merely one way selected from the possible ways, merely one means to that end. For the artist, this idea of 'alternative routes' is simply inapplicable. If we do not recognize this fact, we have failed to see why the artist bothers so much with the movements, words, lines or whatever of his work, why he troubles to get *just that* sequence of movements, form of words, lines or whatever. If the real importance resides in the end result, then the means (that is, the work) becomes virtually irrelevant. Such a situation fails to acknowledge that our attention (to a work of art) concentrates, or should concentrate, on that work itself, and not on some independently identifiable message or state of affairs: in effect, the 'meaning' of a work of art is uniquely identified by the work itself.

We can recognize another way in which the logic of purposive justifications differs from the logic of artistic justifications. If an activity is justified purposively, it follows that there can be features that cannot be specifically justified in this way, for example, the colour of the ink I have used in writing this chapter is not specifically justified. Black ink would flow as easily as blue. That is, there can be no purposive justification for choosing one rather than the other. But this is no criticism, for these details do not stand in need of justification: neither requires any additional expenditure of energy. In the arts, on the other hand, it must surely be a criticism of work, an aesthetic defect in that work, if certain of its features are irrelevant to its 'aim'; that is, if these features are not artistically justified (Beardsmore, 1971: pp. 8–9).

The only way in which all irrelevancies of this kind could be removed from purposive activity is by making the aim (the purpose) identical with the means of attaining it. But in such a situation we merely risk confusion by talking in purposive terms: in terms of means and ends. These two differences represent sufficient grounds for the conclusion that artistic justification is not purposive. But what follows from this?

Two distinct conclusions must be drawn. First, we have seen that the point of art is *not* to be explicated in a means/ends or purposive fashion. Second, the manner in which this point *is* to be articulated still needs to be elaborated. And to do so is, among other things, to rule out the idea that art is pointless (an 'art for art's sake' thesis).

The first step in implementing this second conclusion lies in seeing that, for any account of art worth the name, finding that art had no point is unsatisfactory. Although it is not the only interest of the topic of the point of art, consider the question of the educational impact of art. Here we see the need to explain or to justify an educational role for the arts in terms which, if not using, for example, the idea of life issues such as I employ, at least fulfil the same or a similar role. It may almost be plausible to dismiss the arts – to find no human role for them, or none beyond enjoyment – if one does not consider their educative role. However, might an opponent be satisfied to claim merely that art was pleasing or enjoyable? And hence to claim that art has an educational point without really having a point? To see that this will not do, three considerations are operative. And presenting these is the second step of the argument. We will look at each in turn.

First, the concept of the pleasing or the enjoyable is insufficient to characterize the difference between the impact of art and the impact of other things in which we take aesthetic pleasure. While we think of pleasure or enjoyment centrally in terms of an impact on our senses – a kind of 'buzz' in our feelings, operating at the level of, say, our central nervous systems – we cannot do justice to the pleasure of *art*. The object itself has disappeared from our consideration. Second, these

166

concepts (enjoyment, pleasure) are clearly not applied universally to art. There are 'objects' which, while uncontentiously art works, are none the less not pleasurable or enjoyable, at least as these terms are normally understood (see Chapter 1, where a similar point is made about beauty). Readers may supply their own examples, although students of mine have even suggested that they regard some seminal works by Martha Graham in exactly this way: undeniably important, but not as a source of pleasure when watched. As a more extreme case, there are some art works that explicitly deny the application of concepts such as 'pleasure', 'enjoyment': for example, the so-called *guerrilla dance* of Steve Paxton. Marcia Siegel (1972, p. 266) asks, 'Does anyone really like guerrilla dance?'. She is making two points: first, that many who profess admiration (and interest in) such dances could not honestly claim to like (or enjoy) them. This in itself shows the inadequacy of accounts of art that find art merely pleasing: there are art works that evade this categorization. But the second point is even more penetrating. Siegel's article is called 'Radicalising the Dance Audience', and the particular dance work at issue is called *Intraveneous Lecture*. It is accurately described (Siegel, 1972: p. 266) as an 'anti-performance': as something not designed to be liked. Yet if this is accepted as dance (the judgement of the Republic of Dance, and in particular of Siegal herself), then we have a dance form beyond the category of enjoyment. This is not to deny its importance. As Siegel (1972, p. 266) remarks, it 'raises some crucial questions about censorship and permissiveness in the arts'. Thus, this is explicitly non-enjoyable art.

If the first and second considerations were accepted, they would show the inadequacy of accounts of art in terms of enjoyment, both as insufficiently specific (because not relating to the object itself) and insufficiently general (in not applying to all art). The third consideration mentioned earlier is this: that to separate the understanding of art from the understanding of (the rest of) life, in the way an art for art's sake thesis must do, is to adopt a position roughly like the 'no cognitive stock' thesis discussed in Chapter 6. I urge that very idea of understanding art cannot be made sense of unless we connect art with life in ways which deny that art for art's sake thesis (Beardsmore, 1971: pp. 22–38). Such a thesis trades on the thought that we must understand the work of art in its own terms; we must read *its* meaning rather than reading something into it; our focus is on the work rather than on features extrinsic to it. But these are just different ways of drawing our attention to the character of our understanding, something we have already given due attention.

A key insight into the understanding of dance, by Peter Kivy (1975;

1978), is the idea that artistic judgement is *terminal*. As he remarks, 'To describe something in aesthetic terms *is* to *describe it*; but it is to savour it at the same time: to run it over your tongue and lick your lips; to "investigate" its pleasurable possibilities' (Kivy, 1975: p. 210). Thus, critical judgements, although presenting works to us and making them vivid for us, do not direct our attention from the work of art itself to some art-purposeful point. Of course, what Kivy claims here remains to be proved, and there is still room for elaboration of the thesis itself.

Emotional education and conceptual change

If, then, we conclude that it makes sense to speak of art as having a point without commiting ourselves to a means/end style of explanation of that point, how do we articulate such a 'point'? I begin by introducing what I shall call 'thesis A'. It concerns the way in which the impact of art is understood. If we ask what the arts have to offer, the answer (made famous by David Best) is that the arts provide us with a kind of emotional education. And they do so because they allow conceptual change in respect of the concepts under which, or through which, the works of art are experienced. More exactly, that experience of the arts allows us to experience finer shades of feeling, and may do so because it may allow the refining of those concepts under which those feelings are experienced, and under which those experiences are characterized.

A fairly simple case of a similar phenomenon may make this clearer (Savile, 1982: p. 92). Consider a boy who at age 15 wants to be a milkman. Suppose further that this boy stays at school and hence does not become a milkman. This course of events may result in his forming new wants and desires about his career; that is to say, he may then be able to formulate – which in context means 'to have' – wants and desires that were not available to him at the earlier time. Here he has clearly learned something. But, first, what he has learned could not easily be put into words and, second, it would not be expressible in terms available to that 15-year-old. He has learned not merely new ways of expressing his wants, but additionally he has learned to want or desire new things (see Chapter 2). This case provides a simple example of the way in which conceptual change – a change in the concepts available to a person – might change the range of desires open to him, and hence the range of experiences open to him. This, then, shows how a change in conceptual grasp and a change in feelings (in this case, wants) can go hand in hand. Thesis A may be roughly formulated in two parts:

...in exploring and learning new forms of expression, we are... gaining and refining the capacity for experiencing new feelings. (Best, 1974: p. 159)

...a pre-condition for experiencing the subtle and finely discriminated feelings which are the province of art is that one should have acquired the imaginative ability to handle the appropriate concepts. (Best, 1978b: p. 76)

The first part refers to the outcome of interaction with art, and the second to the *mechanism* of that interaction: namely, that it is conceptual change. This thesis is not without difficulties of interpretation.[2] However, the general conception here, that the value of the arts is elucidated in terms of a refining of one's discrimination, and hence of one's capacity to experience finely discriminated feelings, is what we wish to get out.

Such a picture may mislead in two ways which will tend to obscure the later argument. So, without discussing them in detail, let us record them, to put them aside. Both concern the scope of what I have called conceptual changes. The first asks whether all the changes brought about by the arts should genuinely be thought of as *conceptual* changes: the second urges that some of the changes in understanding brought about through the arts are of too small a scale to warrant being called conceptual change. The reply to both consists in recording how small a thing conceptual change (on my version) can be. If we think of a particular concept – say, 'love', to anticipate a later example – having a web of connections with other concepts, then the breaking or re-ordering of just one strand of that web will result in a new conception of love, by making what follows from the application of that concept just slightly different. And once we accept that all experience is concept-mediated, we see how such changes have this conceptual character. It is in this small-scale sense that I speak of art as bringing about conceptual change, and of such changes as resulting in a change in what can be experienced.

However, this powerful account of emotional education cannot completely answer our aesthetic needs. Even if thesis A can be accepted without requiring further elaboration, two major problems for the application of this thesis to aesthetics may arise. These problems are related. First, should the conceptual change central to thesis A be thought of as development or improvement, or should it be seen in some other way? Should it be thought of as implying some direction to the change, or should this be seen 'merely' as a change (for a change could be simply that, neither change for the better nor for the worse). Crucial to thesis A, if it is to be of any use in explaining the place of art in life – that is, in explaining the benefit of experience of the arts – must be that the conceptual change does indeed have a direction. And this is a problem, for how is such a direction to be guaranteed for conceptual changes? The second point builds on the first, for even if there is direction in the conceptual change, why should it be a change for the better, an improvement? So the second question is: to what extent do these conceptual changes constitute improvement (bearing in mind that we would characterize education very broadly in terms of some such improvement)?

Notice here that the manner of my exposition of this insight is not crucial. If we decided, for example, to drop the word 'development' and related expressions, we could still generate exactly these two problems for thesis A. Suppose instead that we spoke of the enlargement of one's cognitive stock. Well, in a similar way, one could ask, first, whether one could genuinely call this enlargement, whether it really is certain things remaining and others being added, rather than 'just change', where there is simply movement from one position to another. And had we decided that issue, we could go on to ask whether that enlargement was valuable, and if so why. I am suggesting, then, that the two questions I have raised in terms of my initial exposition of Best's thesis A – there in terms of conceptual development – could be raised in terms of any modified exposition of it.[3]

The two questions I have identified represent a major difficulty for any account of the value of art deriving from thesis A. There seems no straightforward way in which, on the basis of that thesis alone, we can guarantee the sense of development or progress required to answer the first question, nor any in which we can guarantee the sense of valuable progress required by the second question. All that thesis A can guarantee is conceptual *change*.

I shall not have much to say on the first topic here, and indeed those whose views about conceptual change differ from mine might think that it is something of a storm in a teacup. But the second issue – the *value* of any direction – is clearly an important one and, as I said, not solvable within the confines of the first thesis. Some other ideas are required, and to get them we turn to the second thesis. However, the first thesis itself requires more clarification, and to achieve this we must focus briefly on the nature of the relevant feelings or emotions.

The objects of emotions

This discussion takes us momentarily away from art; but our understanding is increased when we recognize the crucial role, in the characterization of any feeling, emotion or experience, of what writers have
called the *object* of that feeling or emotion. (Beardsmore, 1973;
Anscombe, 1981: pp. 3–20; Best, 1985: pp. 93–7). When I experience,
say, fear (to take a simple example) that is always necessarily fear of
something. To put that point into the jargon, the verb 'to fear' takes an
object. But, as this case shows, the object need not be very specific. The
fear need not be *of* any exactly specifiable list of things. When a creak
on the stairs at night turns me to a jelly of fear in my bed, I need not
be afraid of any particular thing. Or, rather, any number of appropriate
objects for my fear exist. Thus the escaped leopard, or the mad axeman
or the wandering ghoul . . . I am frightened of a whole host of things,
all of them and none of them, for my fear is not specific on that point.
In such a case the object of my fear will be characterized in this non-
specific way. Still, the fear has an object.

But if asked to describe the difference between that fear and some
other – the difference between the experiences, as it were – we eventually come back to the object of the emotion. Other bouts of fear might
have just the same intensity and duration, but what marks out that particular fear is its object – its fairly non-specific but still specifiable object
(Kenny, 1963: p. 61). For brevity, we might call this 'night-crawler' fear,
and we are distinguishing it both from a more specific fear – say, the
swimmer who becomes afraid when the music from *Jaws* reverberates
inside her head – and from the less specific, as with a generalized (and
we say 'nameless') dread. And so, asked to pick out *that* kind of fear,
I could reply 'It was night-crawler fear'. The point to recognize is that
characterizing an experience is, to some degree at least, characterizing
the object of that experience: a different object implies a different
experience.

Let us now apply that insight to the case of the experiencing of art
works. We have said that the character of fear is explicated by saying
what it is fear of, that is, in terms of the object of fear, of what is feared.
But, unlike the objects of fear, the objects of experiences of works of art
are never highly generalized. These experiences have a particular or
specific object: that object is the work of art itself – in our case, the
dance. To see this is to recognize something crucial about works of art.
If we give vague accounts of the feelings which relate to a work of art
('fear', 'man's inhumanity to man' . . .) these accounts fail to distinguish
our response to this particular work of art from our response to other

works. So that, for example, one might find man's inhumanity to man in Picasso's *Guernica* and in Alvin Ailey's *Adagio for a Dead Soldier* (1970). But that would not mean one thought these works were somehow 'equivalent'. It would not do to say to someone 'If you can't get to see *Guernica*, well, *Adagio for a Dead Soldier* will do just as well' (Beardsmore, 1971: pp. 17–18). Or rather, this would not be satisfactory if one's interest was in what made these objects works of art. Betty Redfern (1979, p. 18) brings out the absurdity clearly when she says:

There would be no need to see, for example, Martha Graham's *Night Journey*, since we could get the same experience by listening to Stravinsky's *Oedipus Rex*; and neither of them need really have bothered since Sophocles already "said" it all in *Oedipus Tyrannus* centuries before.

As this example illustrates, taking such an attitude to art works would make some of them expendable, being either superseded by later works, or rendered unnecessary by previous ones. That idea is nonsense.

Consider, then, some of the consequences of accepting that we could have the very same feeling (whatever that would mean) *vis-à-vis* two different works of art. What basis would we now have for urging that these were indeed two different or distinct works of art? Surely the fact that we had the very same feeling about each would lead us (using the language of Chapter 4) to argue that these works were actually tokens of the same type. Also, recall the idea that one's interpretations must be answerable to the perceptible features of the works in question. This surely applies to our experiences as much as to the interpretations they embody, and therefore one would expect two works with different perceptible characteristics to give rise to different experiences.

I conclude that we can only identify just that feeling by relating it to just that dance. It would simply be incoherent to suggest that we could refer to, or identify, the exact feeling expressed in a work of art apart from that particular expression of it: that is, apart from the work of art itself.

We have seen, then, how the work of art functions as the object of the experience of that work: and hence is crucial in explication of that experience. What must be added now is the thesis first introduced in Chapter 1 that all experience is concept-mediated. So that when we say that our experience of dance A differs from our experience of dance B, it follows that (at least some) different concepts are in play in the two cases. And so, if at one time I am only able to appreciate, enjoy, understand dance A (or, to make the example more realistic, dances of kind A, say classical ballet) and then, at some later time, I come to be able to appreciate, enjoy, understand dance B (or dances of kind B, say those employing Graham technique), I have learned to employ some concepts that I could not previously employ. To use a phrase of Wollheim's (Wollheim, 1986: p. 48; see Chapter 7), I am now able to mobilize these concepts. As a result, I am able to experience different things, that is, to have experiences mediated by these new concepts. Yet, typically, the difference here would not be expressed by saying that I learn a new concept, but that I learn a *nuance* of that concept. As we will see, this may be more than just a terminological dispute. Still, let us put the matter like this: in understanding new dances we may understand (and experience) new emotions, since those emotions have new and different objects. So any learning of new emotions by a confrontation with – in the relevant case – dances, will be learning of highly specific emotions, for these emotions will be characterized in highly specific terms, that is, in terms of the highly specific object that is the dance.[4]

Although highly particularized, the object of emotions involved in the performing arts allow greater flexibility than those involved in other kinds of art. What must be recalled (from Chapter 4) is that dances themselves are not fully determinate. Being performing arts, one performance may differ from another without thereby ceasing to be a performance of the same work, and for two reasons: either it may represent a different (performer's) interpretation, or the differences may be entirely due to specific features of tonight's performance. Thus, if asked 'Of what emotion is dance the object?', one's reply will (or at least might) present a much more general response relating to that dance in any (or many) instantiations: that is, any of a variety of tokens of this type might be the objects of such a response. Alternatively, the response might emphasize the highly individual character of a particular interpretation, perhaps even a particular performance. Thus, in coming to understand the character of the contribution of dance, one must recognize that this contribution may take either a specific or generalized form. (But, of course, even the generalized form still depends on a token of that type.)

Art and life issues

The second thesis, thesis B, also has David Best's writing as its direct ancestor. In his second book, Best (1978a: p. 115) says:

It is distinctive of any art form that its conventions allow for the possibility of the expression of a conception of life situations. Thus the arts are characteristically concerned with contemporary moral, social, political and emotional issues.

And he uses a similar form of words in his third book, where he says (Best, 1985: p. 159):

It is intrinsic to an art form that there should be the possibility of the expression of a conception of life issues.

Best uses this notion to rule out other candidates for 'arthood', such as sport.

I shall not be directly addressing the question of what Best means by the expression 'life issues' and 'life situations' (expressions he seems to use more or less synonymously). His own examples, as well as the characterization given earlier, ('contemporary moral, social, political and emotional issues'), manifestly do not deal with this problem (Best, 1985: p. 163n). But here it is sufficient to depend on some intuitive or pre-theoretical notion of life issues, and to consider thesis B in Best's exposition, as given earlier. (We return to this point later in the chapter.)

Indeed, one reason for introducing thesis B in this fashion, via quotation from Best, is to put aside temporarily the many difficulties of interpretation such a notion as life issues naturally generates. It is far from straightforward to put much more flesh on its bones. Certainly one part of the idea is to illustrate a connection between art and (the rest of) life. If the emotional experiences associated with life were (*per impossibile*) to have no connections with other experiences, one might wonder how they were to count as emotions (or thoughts or feelings) at all. That is, if the emotional experiences engendered in confrontation with works of art were so totally dissimilar from other emotional experiences, how are they to be recognized as experiences of, say, joy? But even if this point is granted, many questions remain. In particular, the idea of it as a *life* issue is something that cannot easily be further specified. The force of the phrase lies in its acknowledgement of the power and vitality of the matters on which works of art can bear, the profound effect typical of our confrontation with art. But naturally not all our experiences of art are of this sort (my relaxing with some favourite piece of music, for example). So the term 'life issues' can sound rather portentous. Yet the task assigned to it in my aesthetic is one best fulfilled by a notion that could be expanded in different ways in particular cases; here the examples (and the elaboration of the notion) given later may fill in some of the gaps deliberately left in this section.

Still, it is worth bringing out the sense in which value-commitments here might be thought of as general, hence as life issues, rather than just as issues specific to me personally. As in another work (McFee, 1978: pp. 154–8), I will approach this question via a discussion of objects which, although not art, might be thought to bear on one set of life issues. I refer, of course, to the pornographic. As many writers have urged (for example, Robinson, 1973: pp. 163–70), the problem of pornography is not centrally that it may cause depravity, but that it *is* depravity. Yet how is this to be shown? How are we to draw a line between (justified) explicitness and the pornographic? An historical aside has some relevance here. In a brief paper written in 1912 but not published until 1934, the distinguished British philosopher F. H. Bradley discusses 'the treatment of sexual detail in literature'. He there remarks that a great many studies – anatomy, physiology, medicine and so on – can touch on sexual matters without being 'libidinous' (Bradley, 1934: p. 621). He admits that such studies can, of course, be used in an improper way: for example, the titillatory use to which children (at least in films) regularly put biology books. But the very use of the word 'improper' makes our attitude here clear, in so far as they are used in these ways they have, as Bradley puts it, 'ceased to be scientific' (Bradley, 1934: p. 621).

Bradley next enquires about beauty in the pictorial arts. What, he asks, is characteristic of the proper treatment of beauty here? And this question is a crucial starting point, given the etymology of the word 'pornography': the representation of women as prostitutes. The case in point might be, say, a painted nude. Why is it beautiful and not pornographic? One important recognition here: if my interest in the painting were as pornography, it must centrally be *my* interest, based on my personal reactions to that painting. Bradley rightly concludes that artistic value is not subjective, that art is 'always outside of and above and beyond any mere personal feelings' (Bradley, 1934: p. 621). It follows, Bradley thinks and surely correctly, that any genuine (artistic) interest in beauty must prevent my concern, say, for this nude becoming a personal or private concern. And yet only through such a concern would the nude be considered pornographically. The essence of pornography is the private immediacy of its impact. Art, as Bradley says, leads us in another direction. But he recognizes that he is idealizing the situation, and comments:

There are times, we must admit, where at least in the case of certain persons art fails to achieve its end, and then may in consequence merely disturb and excite. Art again *can* even be intended to produce

175

this result. But here assuredly, so far and to this extent, we have not to do with genuine art. (Bradley, 1934: p. 621)

His point, of course, is that these persons are no longer able to take an artistic interest in the works.

Bradley seems to have his finger on exactly the right pulse. What he correctly infers from the possibility of pornography is a general constraint on art: it must be 'objective' in the sense that its problems are not purely mine. If I treat art in a way that lets these problems become purely mine, I am on a slippery slope which leads to sentimentalism, or to pornography, or... Anyway, away from art. Here is Bradley again, discussing our reaction to a poem by Tennyson:

But if your ideas and emotions stray beyond the vision of Fatima's passionate heart and burning flesh, if they begin to wander and turn to a mere something in yourself – it is because you have lost hold of the poetry. The beauty which transported you beyond your private being, and which held and purified your individual feelings, has vanished. (Bradley, 1934: p. 622–3)

The key thought here, then, is that art viewed as art cannot find a response in purely personal concerns.

If we ask 'Why not?', Bradley (1934: p. 623) again offers the right answer in a clear fashion: 'We have everywhere what we have called the impersonal direction and set of the interest. We are absorbed not in ourselves but by an object before our minds'. The central idea of course turns on the meaning of the term 'impersonal' in this context. Once we have accepted that the impact of art cannot be of a directly personal sort – for reasons Bradley outlined – we must see ourselves, first, as dealing with the work itself, and second, as involved with thoughts and feelings. Clearly if my appreciation of a dance must not depend on my specific relation to it – thereby ruling out, of course, say, my economic interest in it – then whatever reason I have for my appreciation must be generalizable. As Kant (1952: p. 51; see Guyer, 1979: p. 168n) put it, 'it must contain a ground of delight for everyone'. But the work of art obviously has some 'bite', some hold, on our attention, for otherwise why should we attend to it? Thus it connects with feelings, if not just with our personal ones. And certainly any account that allows art some point must concede here. And this amounts to treating the term 'impersonal' as meaning 'human': that is, about mankind, not just about me. The connection of art with the feelings is both intuitively plausible and a consequence of our discussion. This is the upshot of a (Humean) chal-

176

lenge repeated throughout this work: would we accept as art something with no connection with human thought and feeling? The answer 'no' is surely inevitable, not least, of course, for anyone interested in aesthetic education.

But what does this show? If art must in some way catch onto human thought and feeling, and if a thought and feeling cannot be mine alone (must be objective in the sense specified above), it is surely very plausible to describe these thoughts and feelings as dealing with life issues or life situations. These are issues or situations which arise for us because we are human beings, as we might say. In one sense, then, the argument has come full circle, for the whole of this work is predicated on the undeniable fact that human beings can find art moving or pleasurable, or some such: in short, they can find such objects meaningful (and expressive). The whole discussion of life issues or life situations in this chapter – together with much else in this work – is an attempt to clarify that rudimentary idea. Of course, we must recognize that the answers offered may seem unclear or imprecise. But the feeling of imprecision derives from a type of response that needs to be acknowledged.

However, there are two topics on which comment is required at this stage. First, it has been objected that this talk of life issues, and in particular its application to aesthetic education, is intended as a prescription of what 'ought' to go on in art, what art ought to be like. This I wish strenuously to deny. What is intended is just a characterization of what art is like, of the nature of art, and I take my dependence on the value, the 'validity' and the rationality of critical judgements (see Chapters 6 and 7) to illustrate that this view of art is not revisionary – at least, not radically revisionary.

The other topic concerns the range of art to which thesis B might be thought to apply, for it is often objected against an account of art of the sort given here that it cannot possibly deal with *abstract* art. I take the thought to be that what has no narrative or literal content cannot manifest a conception of life issues. This seems to me mistaken: once we recognize the profound effect of art, its capacity to modify human thought and feeling, it is absurd to deny that such art can bear on issues for us, that is, on life issues. And certainly such effects are at least as common with the abstract and non-literal in art as with other kinds. What is of course more difficult is to say what the effect is in a case of abstract art, to articulate what the issue is or was.

One revealing way in which this difficulty is sometimes overcome is by speaking of the works as 'celebrations' of something – colour, the body, the power of language, art itself. In fact, this connection between life issues may be seen as operating in two different versions. First, through a palliation of the unsatisfactory aspects – man's fallibility, inhumanity and the like – we come to understand (which is not to say excuse) these features in ourselves and others. And if we cannot improve our lot, at least we go through life humbler and wiser. But, second, there will be a celebration of the desirable aspects of human life experience – landscape, love and so on – and this duality of contributions reflects, of course, a paradox central to being human.

This is a rhetorical way of putting the matter, no doubt, but surely its point is to record that these are matters which can vividly alter or affect the quality of human life. And what makes that way of speaking a revealing one is that it suggests how life issues might be made out in the case of abstract art. But also it elucidates the notion of life issues: it may seem a little odd to call these 'life issues', but surely the oddity diminishes (if not vanishes) once we recognize that art itself is a part of human experience, a topic for such issues. What I am urging is that a more liberal understanding of what might count as a life issue allows abstract art to bear on life issues (see also Danto, 1981: pp. 84–5). To put the matter anecdotally, my own admiration for non-literal dance, the music of Schoenberg and the painting of Rothko does nothing to weaken my adherence to thesis B.

This sort of point is widely recognized by critics. And as usual Marcia Siegel (1972, p. 220) offers a clear case, commenting on the work of Alwin Nikolais:

> ...with "Somniloquy" and "Tent" Nikolais has reached the most impressive and meaningful realisation of his contention that man and his environment are inseparable. For some people this may mean that man is diminished. For me, *the human spirit* comes off immeasurably enriched.

Whether or not we see such 'enrichment of the human spirit' as a major aim of art, the point of course is that, in the eyes of one eminent critic at least, a work of abstract dance is none the less concerned with life issues. Siegel goes further, for she implies that Nikolais' greatness lies in his articulation or confronting of such life issues. As she puts it: 'Nikolais is a genius. Not because he is so clever with media, but because he can show us how closely related are the apparent polarities of the world' (Siegel, 1972: p. 222).

It may be worth stressing something of the pedigree of this sort of idea. Peter Fuller, for example, (1988b: p. 72) records Ruskin's hope that 'aided by scientific imagination, the painter would be able to see

THE POINT OF DANCE

and represent aspects of the Divine which had previously been hidden'. Collingwood (1964) is among those who have extracted such thoughts from Ruskin. My talk of life issues is a secularized version of this idea; my own interest in Collingwood may be one reason why these ideas seem to cohere so well with the insight of Wisdom's cited earlier (Wisdom, 1953: p. 224), that art can reveal anew the familiar from life (see Chapter 7). In sum, then, I have given examples of the sorts of connections between art and life which I wish to catch by using the expressions 'life issues', 'life situations'. We have seen both their varieties of scope and of directness of connection to human problems. Further, I have given reasons why nothing more specific could be said. Thus, even now, I am asking the reader for a 'pinch of salt' in the understanding, for my elaboration of the notion of life issues is not in any way proof against all objections. In the last analysis, then, this section takes for granted the idea of life issues (although the above comments and examples should elucidate it).

Art works and art forms

Even with this sizeable concession, the interpretation of thesis B is by no means plain sailing. What precisely is being said? What does it amount to for aesthetics? And what, if anything, would constitute a counter-case? Here we must recognize two major points of clarification: first, Best seeks to emphasize that this connection with life issues is a property of art *forms* rather than of art works, and second, all we are talking about is the 'possibility' of the expression of a conception of life issues or life situations. The difficulty posed, of course, is that – if the life issues connection is with forms – one cannot easily produce a counter-example to a claim about any art form, since then the fact that a particular work did not fit in with the characterization given would not be relevant, if the work were in a form that did fit in with that characterization. Moreover, since discussion focuses only on the possibility of such a relationship holding, there is, again, no suggestion that it holds in the case of every single work. Best puts the matter in this guarded fashion because he is trying to articulate a necessary condition for 'arthood'. With our rather different interests we can clarify his thesis by modifying it around these two points.

First let us specify one of these difficulties more exactly. Best's elucidation of his necessary condition for arthood locates any particular art work within the realm of art by relating that work to some art form: hence we are owed an account of what are and are not art forms.

179

Without such an account we will be unable to adjudicate on putative counter-examples. Suppose that it were established (or agreed) that all lyric poems, say, did not express a conception of life issues or life situations. This would still be no counter-case to thesis B if Best could respond that the art form in question was poetry, not lyric poetry; that is to say, the form (poetry) did allow for the expression of such a conception of life issues, as was manifest in, for example, the poetry of Wilfred Owen. Thus the form, poetry, fits in with Best's thesis B, even though particular poems don't. But then one poem that satisfies Best's condition allows all poems into the fold. Such an account seems generous to the point of vacuity.

Notice that my objection here is not that Best's account is somehow circular (or worse, viciously circular). The problem is not that his account of art depends on some prior notion of an art form. Indeed, I am willing to concede that he might deal with this unclarity by a complete enumeration of art forms, that is, that he might list all art forms without going on to say what they have in common, or what makes them art forms. Then we would be able to see what *scale* of notion he has in mind. Is it, for example, poetry, lyric poetry, Augustan lyric poetry or what? And, of course, with such a list we would be able to look for counter-examples. But while we operate at the abstract level of art forms – and while that notion remains unexplained – we cannot be sure that we are really saying anything.

In summary, then, the absence of such an account of art forms may leave one a little unsure what to make of this second thesis (thesis B) from David Best. I suggest a kind of modification that preserves what is best in this account and yet ties the thinking more closely to particular art works. To do so is to lose the sense of a necessary condition for art-hood, replacing it with a *defeasible* condition (to use a notion from Chapter 2). I am suggesting that it is distinctive of an art work that the conventions implicit in it allow for the expression of a conception of life issues. But I interpret this claim defeasibly. That is to say (to repeat from Chapter 2), I do not expect, in every single case, that art works will conform to the pattern I've laid down. But when they do not, it will be because they satisfy one of a number of recognized (if implicit) 'unless' clauses, the sorts of things anyone knowledgeable about works of that kind would recognize as part of an argument or critical consideration or excuse. This idea of defeasibility is indeed a technical one, but we are fairly familiar with its working. The crucial idea is just what we need, a relation which, while it does not hold in every case, nevertheless is guaranteed by satisfaction of certain conditions, and where recognized 'heads of exception' can be used to explain the defeating cases (Baker, 1977: pp. 52–3).

Notice that defeasible notions do involve an internal, 'logical' connection between whatever it is they relate. Thus my speaking of defeasible conditions as logical or 'internal' is not nonsense, for the satisfaction of certain conditions is a guarantee for there being, say, a contract between us. And yet this claim can be overthrown when one of the recognized heads of exception obtains. But this is a purely negative condition; given the satisfactions of the initial conditions it is not required that the one who insists that there is a contract between us should 'check up'. The onus of proof is on the one who denies that there is a contract. He must bring the disputed instance under a recognized head of exception, must show that one of the implicit 'unless' clauses is satisfied.

Notice too that my account, like Best's, is not intended to be a complete account of art. Certainly, experiences other than those of art can bring about conceptual changes which bear on life issues (as we will illustrate later in the chapter). So, at best, such a requirement for a life issues connection could only be used to rule out putative art forms, as Best does in the case of sport.

So my suggestion modifies thesis B by replacing Best's proposed necessary condition for arthood, based on the possibility of an art *form* expressing a conception of life issues, with the normally necessary condition (for arthood) that an art *work* expresses a conception of life issues. Moreover, whatever did not satisfy this condition should be treated as Stanley Cavell (1969: p. 253) treats intention in art: namely, that whatever work of art does not invoke a conception of life issues must be thought of in contrast to the invoking of such a conception, at the same level as it, as a modification of human thought and feeling. And the great plausibility of this idea, of course, is that we would surely be unwilling to acknowledge as art an object that was unrelated to human thoughts or feelings in some of the ways suggested under the general heading 'life issues' or 'life situations'.

My account of the life issues connection as being with works rather than forms will be an improvement[5] on Best's, if for no other reason than that it clarifies to which concept appeal is being made at any particular time. As I have tried to illustrate above, Best's own formulation will be uninformative in any case where it isn't clear whether (for the purposes of thesis B) a particular work belongs to the art form given by concept X – where a connection with life issues is obvious (my earlier example was poetry) – or by concept Y – where it is not (my earlier

181

example was lyric poetry). And this situation will be further complicated where Y is a sub-concept of X (as, for example, if Y were lyric poetry and X were poetry). As was said before, in the absence of a complete enumeration of art forms, Best's version of the life issues connection is always going to be susceptible to this line of criticism.

Two theses for an account of art

Thus far I have articulated the two theses whose interrelation I must now consider. First (thesis A), that what the arts have to offer, in general and in education, is a kind of emotional development based on conceptual change; and second (thesis B), that it is characteristic of art works that they allow the expression of a conception of life issues. What we must do now is to bring those two theses together, and see whether they will help us deal with the two questions mentioned towards the beginning of this chapter.

The difficulty, it will be remembered, was to describe why the conceptual change associated with confrontation with works of art should be thought of as educational, or more generally, beneficial. And I suggested that thesis A, the thesis about conceptual change, would not by itself answer that question for us. But if we add now thesis B, the modified thesis about life issues, there seems a fairly immediate kind of answer here. If it is confrontation with the conceptions of life issues inherent in works of art that brings about conceptual changes, those changes will be in the concepts relevant to such issues and situations, or so one might expect. That is to say, my view of what is going on around me will be modified as my understanding changes, as these concepts change. An example – one of my favourites (McFee, 1984: pp. 102–3) – explains: confronting a work of art such as Lawrence Durrell's *Alexandria Quartet* regularly 'does much to bring into order before the mind the many forms of love and their relation to what is not love' (as John Wisdom [1965: p. 144] said of Stendal's novel *De L'Amour*). *Alexandria Quartet* presents for us the nature and extent of certain interlocking 'loves'. So that one critic (Weigel, 1965: p. 99) offers a plot summary of the book as follows:

> Darley loves Justine, who loves Clea, Pursewarden, Nessim and Darley, Pursewarden loves Justine and Liza. Liza loves Pursewarden and Mountolive, who loves Liza – and Leila, who loves Mountolive. Nessim loves Justine and Melissa. Narouz loves Clea, who loves Justine, Amaril, and Darley.

But these loves, variously portrayed, show themselves to us as the characters in the novel confront each other and themselves. In their diversity, readers may discern the distinctive, individual character of each: we experience each differently. To rush ahead, we can imagine such experiences bringing about conceptual changes of roughly two sorts. First, established ideas of (in this case) love may be enriched, enlivened, augmented, so that we might say that we learn more about love. But, second, examples may force us to break away from traditional, familiar ways of looking at things. Through a case from the *Alexandria Quartet* – say, Justine's love for Darley and Pursewarden – we may come to think of our previous views of love as flawed, sentimentalized. (As our concept of adultery might be shattered by Christ's dictum that to look lustfully at a woman is to commit adultery.[6]) So here the conceptual change overturns some previous view, and in doing so, we now see the object or event differently, with different eyes as it were.

Now we see the force of Best's talk of 'the conception of life issues': confronting art forces us to attend to what are issues for us; and people, actions, scenes, objects, values, ways of living, all may have aspects revealed through art. And these sorts of revelation can display considerable variety. For instance, they can sometimes involve those conceptual changes where new concepts are applied in familiar situations (as when Impressionist ideas make us 'see' differently). Conceptual change may also lead us to pattern things in new ways, and this means seeing how the world appears when ordered or patterned in that way (see Savile, 1982: p. 106). Sometimes new conceptual connections will relate well-known objects or events previously thought of as disparate (Picasso's bull's head/bicycle parts) – which of course may involve our coming to use new words, but equally may not. Here, as John Wisdom remarks in 'The Virginia Lectures', we see the general in the particular. And there are many other kinds of cases which could be considered, but all of these might reasonably be spoken of as 'revealing anew the familiar from life' and treated in terms of conceptual change. (Of course this may put the matter over-emphatically, for we do not say that confrontation with the arts *will* bring about these conceptual changes, merely that it might.) So if I consider the idea of confronting certain issues – as David Best (1978a: p. 115) puts it, 'contemporary moral, social, political and emotional issues' – it is not hard to see how this could be conceived of as development; for it is through such confrontations that one develops one's own views and discriminations. As Stanley Cavell (1969: p. 85) expresses it in dealing with the arts 'one learns, so to speak, the hang of oneself, and mounts one's problems'.

Confrontation with objects that express a conception of life issues must be expected to lead me to re-evaluate my own conceptions of these matters. And that sort of development of independent thought is surely integral to any plausible conception of education, or of development more generally.

Nothing I have said bears on *how* this might be done in a practical situation. That is not centrally a philosophical issue. But it does seem that we have now an answer to our second question, as posed earlier. We wished to know whether we could describe the kinds of conceptual change possibly brought about by confrontation with art works as beneficial. We can see now that this would be appropriate, since those conceptual changes are in line with a re-evaluation of a conception of life issues or life situations. In that sense, we have used thesis B to answer one of our questions raised by the application of thesis A.

Can we say anything about the other question? Recall that the other question bore on this idea of whether there was mere change or whether there was a genuine direction to the conceptual change brought about by confrontation with the works of art. Again, we have an answer now, although to articulate it we must first put aside a mistaken picture of 'personal development'. It is not as though there is some person with fixed capabilities which could then be developed as one might develop muscles. Rather, the account of personal development we wish to differ is the simpler one, where a person lacking certain knowledge and experience at a particular time has that knowledge and/or experience at some later time. In this weaker sense of development, it is clear to see that the considerations already raised about progress answer the development question too. We can say that the person's confrontation with art has led him in such-and-such a direction, that he is now more critical and more discriminating than he had been. Of course, these judgements will have an historical character; they will need to be revised in the light of the purposes and interests of, roughly, informed critical judgement at any particular time. But that is true, after all, of any aesthetic judgements (McFee, 1980b).

One difficulty which might be raised here: for whom are these life issues actually issues? And here we see how this discussion might feed into discussion of the nature of criticism and critical reasoning. If we accept that works of art function as explanations for life issue perplexities (as I urge elsewhere [McFee, 1984]) and moreover that our confrontation with works of art is through their meanings, and hence our explanations of them, we have an answer. For such-and-such is an explanation for me only if it bears on perplexities of mine. But this issue is another huge one, too vast to be fully considered here (see Baker and

Hacker, 1980: pp. 72–9), although we will say a little more about it in the next section.

In summary, then, this chapter has therefore urged that we should think of art as bringing about conceptual change and as expressing a conception of life issues. And that these two theses, both drawn immediately from David Best, reinforce each other to explain the character of aesthetic education. The first relates to what are sometimes, and misleadingly, called 'cognitive' and 'affective' domains;[7] the second makes the value dimension explicit. If we combine the individual arguments for each of these theses with the argument, presented in this section, for their combination, we have one attractive picture of the value of the aesthetic. I have argued for the integrity, coherence and explanatory power of this picture applied to aesthetic education, or education in and through the arts (see Chapter 13). Of course, nothing I have said here proves that this is indeed the right picture, but at least by contemporary tests of theory construction, the considerations just mentioned – integrity, coherence and explanatory power – should weigh heavily with us.

Life issues and 'the familiar'

If that is our overall conclusion, the remaining debt to be discharged concerns the notion of life issues. On this topic no final account can be given, although a lot was included in earlier sections. However, a useful discussion begins by taking a step backwards, and thinking again about the relationship between art and life. Here it is worth reiterating (from Chapter 7 and earlier in this chapter) an insight from John Wisdom: art can reveal anew the familiar from life (Wisdom, 1953: p. 224). Our discussion will begin unfolding some aspects of this insight. I shall follow Wisdom in speaking about novels, but in ways which apply directly to dance.

There are two distinct dimensions of Wisdom's insight. The first concerns the connection between art and criticism on the one hand, and between art and life on the other. It amounts to an affirmation of the links between art and human values, conceptions of human harm and flourishing – in short, life issues again. Few would deny that art in some way connects with our values, that whatever lacked this connection would not be art. To any who disputed it, I would reply after the fashion of Savile (1972: p. 159): 'Very little can be said of a philosophical nature to prove that art may convey value. Anyone who cannot see that is blind'. Yet such connection only requires that art be valuable, not that

185

it bear on our values in other ways. In particular, it is not (yet) acknowledged that art informs our other value judgements. But it is for these value aspects, the interpersonal aspects of our lives (Cavell, 1984: pp. 97–105) that Wisdom's insight has most bite. That familiar aspect of our lives is both the most crucial and the most open to misunderstanding and failure to understand. But Wisdom's insight here lies in seeing that art can help us understand life; that art can contribute to our explanation of what is going on. And this is its second dimension.

Nor should one think that Wisdom is claiming too much here. Wisdom clearly says just that art may help us see the familiar anew, may bring to our attention important aspects of life previously before our eyes but not noticed, and so on. That is to say, he urges that this is one possible, and regularly neglected, function of art and of criticism. Aiming just to show that aspects of life can be revealed to us through art, even if this is no sort of necessary condition of art-hood, the most promising cases for analysis would seem to be those where moral, social and political questions seem obviously at the fore: for example, the range of inhumanity of which man is capable in Alvin Ailey's *Adagio for a Dead Soldier*; or equally in Picasso's *Guernica*; the nature of oppression in Athol Fugard's play *Sizwe Bansi is Dead*. In such cases the connection between the art work and the revelation of life seems almost a commonplace. (We have always known there are more interesting alternatives.) But, if the revelation of life by art were exhausted by these obvious cases, Wisdom's insight could scarcely be applied to the less obvious cases – say, to the lyrical in art, those works which are for many the antithesis of works such as *Adagio for a Dead Soldier*, *Guernica* and *Sizwe Bansi is Dead*.

Here one consideration that unfolds Wisdom's insight for us will be that raised early on in this chapter (pp. 165–8), warning us against 'aesthetic instrumentalism' (the view that art has some non-aesthetic 'point' or function [Beardsmore, 1971: pp. 6–21]). As the much-used comparison between valuing art and valuing friendship brings out, one does not value art – any more than one values a friend – for something that takes us outside the thing itself. Values such as friendship, generosity and benevolence are not valued *for* some otherwise specifiable aim.

We must recognize that, in discussing art, the reasons we give are not solely art reasons, and cannot be. The 'whole' of our 'story' with respect to work of art X will not be, say, that it has certain formal features. In the end, we will relate those features to others, to the sorts of things we find meaningful or important in our lives. How else could the works of art acquire the value they undoubtedly have for us? And it is important to see how that 'relating' comes about. If the same language were not used in the different activities in which a person engages, those activities could then have no bearing on one another. This means that the reasons I give when using the language of one realm of discourse may well have bearing on another realm, in our case the artistic. What one draws on, of course, is the 'agreement not only in definitions but also . . . in judgements' of speaker and listener (Wittgenstein, 1953: section 242; Baker and Hacker, 1985a: pp. 224–62). So our explanation cannot be exclusively couched in artistic terms if it is to do justice to our understanding of art viewed as art.

In seeking to explicate how it is that the familiar may reveal the new, Wisdom's way of treating the matter suggests an answer, and a familiar one: namely, through some kind of conceptual amplification or modification. When Wisdom (1965: p. 101) speaks of 'manifolds of understanding', he is suggesting that understanding which uses concept X is essentially a matter of fitting concept X into some sort of web of concepts and categories, into what Wittgenstein (1953: sections 50, 122) calls a 'form of representation'.[8] Hence any kind of conceptual augmentation, enrichment, or change must be seen as drawing additional 'threads' into the web, or cutting some previously used ones. Such changes could take place in one of two ways: either through the clarification of concepts (that is, through extant conceptual connections being made explicit), or through the construction of new concepts. Both would amount to the availability of a new web of concepts, categories and conceptual connections to provide reasons for a particular judgement. And of course, as we have said, the change need not be a very large one. In the context of aesthetics, this conceptual augmentation will amount to having available a new set of reasons for a particular judgement, and hence of making importantly different judgements.

Two considerations must be added to this picture, the first in supplementation, the second in qualification. First, the choice between the two ways of treating conceptual innovation is, for our purposes, spurious. From the point of view of the participant there will always be two kinds of feeling to be accommodated: the feeling of clarification of what one already knew, and the feeling of something new being revealed. So that even if one decided for theoretical reasons that all of these clarifications were in fact new conceptual connections, one would still have to acknowledge that, with respect to some of them, the conceptual innovation was barely noticeable. A second consideration is apposite here. For, drawing on work in language (Dummett, 1978: pp. 283–4), one must recognize that not all conceptual connections allow us to say something new. In mathematics, for example, one confronts the

187

situation where what one meant by the expression 'straight line' in Euclidean geometry is not expressible in the 'language' of Riemann geometry. Similar cases may strike us in respect of heavily theory-laden statements of, say, art critics (see Chapters 5 and 6).

The situation is further complicated because very often what one can say one has learned from a work of art is very uninformative. Here one familiar limitation on any presentation such as this must again be recorded and recognized. In traditional garb, it is the claim that no account of a work of art is ever equivalent to the work of art itself, that what a work of art means or says cannot be exhaustively stated in any way other than by the work of art itself. For us, more simply, it highlights the fact that any 'telling' of a work of art is a bald telling, and that baldly told, the power of a work of art may seem to amount to no more than a truism. Borrowing an example (and a discussion) from Beardsmore (1973: pp. 351–2) brings out this point clearly, as well as acknowledging the important conclusion that things other than works of art can cast light over aspects of life. For, if works are distinctive in changing our 'way of seeing' in a fashion related to our values, 'distinctive' here does not mean 'unique'. This role may be shared by non-art. Beardsmore quotes as an example the following from Orwell's presentation of a journalist's change of heart after seeing a dead soldier.

The Belgian had been broadcasting throughout the war for the European service of the BBC, and like nearly all Frenchmen or Belgians, he had a very much tougher attitude towards "the Bosch" than an Englishman or an American would have. All the main bridges of the town had been blown up, and we had to enter by a small footbridge which the Germans had evidently made efforts to defend. A dead German soldier was lying supine at the foot of the bridge. His face was a waxy yellow. On his breast someone had laid a bunch of lilac which was blooming everywhere.

The Belgian averted his face as we passed. When we were well over the bridge he confided that this was the first time he had seen a dead man... For several days after this, his attitude was quite different from what it had been earlier... His feelings, he told me, had undergone a change at the sight of "ce pauvre mort" beside the bridge. It had brought home to him the meaning of war. (Orwell [1945] 1968: pp. 3–6)

Orwell's journalist had learned something, though not anything he could necessarily describe. He feels rather as Alvarez (1971: p. 236) does after coming to value life through attempting suicide: 'It seems ludicrous now to have learned something so obvious in such a hard way'. There is no fact that this man learns that he did not already know, no new information that could be conveyed as more than a platitude. Yet his attitude has changed, his way of seeing is changed.

Recognizing that our topic is indeed such a change of view, attitude, perspective, we see why not just any interest in works of art is appropriate here. Cavell (1979: p. xiv) accurately characterizes a person with the right sort of interest in a work of art as someone who 'wishes to understand what its extremities of beauty are in service of'. We recognize why it would be simply irrelevant to consider, for example, novels where the narrative line carries the interesting ideas. If our interest were solely in the narrative, we would be blind to whatever that narrative was 'in service of'. So we see what is inappropriate about, for example, novels which offer us glorious utopian visions of what life might be. No doubt such utopian novels can teach us something, but not about aspects of life as lived now. George Orwell's 1984, by contrast, can enliven our view of the present state of things, but even then it is not irrelevant that Orwell originally wished to call that book 1948, the year of its composition. Yet if one goes beyond the narrative, and if one tries to articulate just what is learned from the novel, first, what one says may fail to distinguish one's 'learning from' this novel from reactions to others and, second, what one says may sound obvious, platitudinous.

So one can be struck by the apparent triviality of what can be said of the impact of a work of art such as the novel. However, as Phillips (1973: p. 52) argues, frustrations with such truisms must not lead us into importing into our discussion of the novel (or any other work of art) stylized and simplistic accounts of human life and flourishing and of morality; for if we do, those accounts will smother the insights of the novel.[9] If we do not, Wisdom (1965, p. 144) urges, a novel may help us to a new understanding of life, and perhaps a new understanding of understanding. And what is true of novels is, of course, true of dance. Indeed, we have seen, earlier in this chapter, Marcia Siegel finding just this sort of understanding in Nikolais and (to some degree) in Paxton. It is important to consider how.

The example given earlier concerned Durrell's Alexandria Quartet, with its multifaceted portrayal of love. Let us now reintroduce elements, from Chapters 5, 6, and 7, of our picture of the meaning of works of art, as found in explanations of that meaning. When we do so, a rough model for the kind of enlightenment offered by the arts suggests itself. We should think of works of art as presenting to us articulated (if unrequested) explanations. I am suggesting, as a key to

189

Wisdom's insight, this: that we should treat works of art as though they were offering explanations of those familiar aspects of life, drawing new conceptual connections for us by making us see that so-and-so (some previously grasped concept) stands in need of explanation. And if so-and-so works as an explanation for me, it follows that (in a sense) I lacked and needed such an explanation. If that need is now satisfied, then I have learned something through my confrontation with the art work: my 'form of representation' has changed.

But of course that change has not necessarily take place in ways I could describe. Suppose we are shown, for example, some facets of the concept 'love', as with the *Alexandria Quartet*. Here one would choose between the two forms of words: 'I learned more about the geometry of the concept "love"', and 'the geometry of the concept "love" became extended'. But, whichever were chosen, one recognizes that such alterations of understanding are only available to those who 'request' or perhaps need them. That is to say, they are not universally compelling. As with any explanation, they are useful and informative for me – I can learn from them – only when they have application to some puzzles, questions or perplexities of mine.

Of course, one's encounters with art may show that one had areas of perplexity of which one never dreamed. As one might through psychoanalysis, one may learn through confronting art that one's problems and views were not what one thought they were; we may begin to re-evaluate ourselves. But again, a model for this revelation is provided. In finding that something is an explanation for me, I learn those things in my understanding that needed (further) explaining. And because explanation relates to the content of understanding, since not anything that promotes understanding counts as an explanation (Baker and Hacker, 1980: p. 82), we see why considerations irrelevant to the content of art as art (for example, some narrative elements) are irrelevant to what we learn from art, or how art changes our understanding.

We see too why Wisdom is exactly right in what I have called his major insight. Art can show us the familiar anew because it can offer us explanations of the familiar that relate to problems or perplexities which we did not feel until the work of art made them vivid for us. For example, as a consequence of reading the *Alexandria Quartet*, one might become dissatisfied with one's complacent view of love, which before reading the novel had been a topic of little interest to one. In this way, one comes to understand love in a way that, previously, one had not. The familiar is revealed anew, in a way which bears directly on human thought and feeling (life issues).

Conclusion

Before drawing together the diffuse threads of this difficult chapter, it is important to bring three ideas to our attention. These are, first, the scope of these comments on life issues; second, their connection with the artistic/aesthetic contrast; third, some further reflections on the history of such ideas. When we have these ideas before the mind, we can see how they conclude our exposition of the nature of dance.

As we have seen, the expressions 'life issues', 'life situations' do not have a great deal of content here. They are not truly as grandiose as calling them 'LIFE ISSUES' might suggest: although they are not merely personal, and they are not all truly issues for human beings. Some are simply areas of celebration. My version (Best might disagree[10]) urges no more than that art works have an essential connection with human thoughts and/or feelings, although there may be exceptional cases where this is not so (but such cases are still explained in terms of human thoughts, feelings). It is this connection that allows us to see the possibility of conceptual change characteristic of the arts as beneficial; indeed, it explains why the arts are genuine objects of understanding. So what is urged here is not some mysterious version of the 'social benefit' of art (for example, some form of Socialist Realism[11]); still less the thesis that art is good in proportion to its comment on life issues or in proportion to the issues on which it comments. Rather, the claim here is the relatively weak one that art has that sort of connection with human thought and feelings which the term 'life issues' has been here used to suggest.

This thesis is better understood once its place in the picture of art is brought out. And to do so is to revisit the artistic/aesthetic distinction introduced in Chapter 1. As will be remembered, David Best uses two ideas to hold this contrast in place. Recall that the first is most easily seen through one of Best's own examples: attending a performance of the classical Indian dancer Ram Gopal, Best (1978a: p. 115) is 'enthralled by the exhilarating quality of his [Gopal's] movements'. But, as Best acknowledges, his appreciation was merely aesthetic, not artistic, because he (Best) did not understand Indian dance. Similar movements might also have been exhilarating, and so 'equivalent' for Best, but not for those in the audience taking an *artistic* interest. What is emphasized here is the importance of detail in relation to meaning/understanding. David Best does not understand Indian dance (of that style?) and hence is not appreciating it artistically, even though (a) he is enjoying/appreciating it and (b) it is indeed art. This picks out the sense in which a different kind of understanding is operative in the case of artistic interest from that which operates *vis-à-vis* aesthetic interest. The second idea is one concerned with life issues. It is this, for Best, that most truly marks the artistic from the aesthetic. But for our purposes in Chapter 1, it was sufficient if the distinction was accepted, and accepted as a difference in kinds of understanding, or, given the concept-mediated character of experience, as a difference in kinds of experience.

In fact, the whole idea of a life issues connection is really no more than a way of insisting on this important distinction: it is a way of showing how the understanding of art differs from (other) aesthetic understanding. Or, perhaps more exactly, how other aesthetic experience does not generate genuine understanding at all. It is this role for the arts, as an agency for understanding, which is centrally at issue here, and which this chapter has tried to elucidate and defend.

Further eludication can be found in reflections of the kind mentioned briefly earlier on in this chapter (see pp. 178–9). It is arguably (Fuller, 1988b: pp. 144–59) a characteristic of much British writing on art – Ruskin, Pater, Morris, Collingwood – that it has sought to emphasize a spiritual element in art as the key to art: one must distinguish the kind of moral perception of art from its (mere) sensuous enjoyment. (Ruskin called these *theoria* and *aesthesis* respectively [Fuller, 1988b: pp. 45–6].) A failure to do so reduces the impact of art on people to its impact on other members of the animal kingdom. And that denigrates art. As Ruskin put it, 'I take no notice of the feelings of the beautiful which we share with spiders and flies' (Fuller, 1988b: p. 49). Of course this position is complicated in two important ways. First, for Ruskin at least, there was an insight into the Divine to be got from art. Thus the term 'spiritual' was to be taken literally.[12] This thesis is no longer plausible. A secularized version is surely possible,[13] and will pay attention to the value aspects of human lives, hence the expression 'life issues'. Thus we find Collingwood (1938: p. 336) speaking about art as a remedy for the corruption of consciousness. The second complication is that, for Ruskin and Pater, the spirituality was also discernible in nature: nature was God's other book (Fuller, 1988b; p. 33). Again, the secularized version would reject this inference. If the 'handiwork' at issue is man's rather than God's, then the appropriate 'objects' for this interest will be man-made;[14] moreover they will be man-made under the aspect of the sorts of value-concerns discussed in this chapter.

The purpose of this historical reflection is to give a sense of background to the remarks about the nature of art developed here, to acknowledge intellectual debts not easily brought out by the sorts of philosophical reasoning of which this text consists. Further, it is designed to show that these are not just the ideas of an abstract theorist; they have a history, one in which the ideas are modified by changing circumstances and changing theoretical perspectives.

In this chapter I have completed the central discussion of this text by elaborating the conception of art on which it is founded. I have shown the connection between that conception of art and the understanding of art. That conception has at its heart the idea of art as offering conceptual change around life issues. I have given attention to the interrelation of these two theses, and to the idea of life issues. From this conception of art, and hence of dance, we can begin to understand the worth of art, and also its educative possibilities. It now remains, in Part Four, to consider some aesthetic (artistic) concepts with which the conception of art might be expanded and, in Part Five, to put aside the sorts of misapprehension and misconception with which this conception might be blighted.

Recommended reading

On the general value of the arts, see Bradley, 1934; Cavell, 1984: pp. 97–105; Scruton, 1989; also Best, 1985: pp. 153–94. A context for the discussion is provided by Wisdom, 1953: pp. 217–28; Beardsmore, 1971; McFee, 1984. For some implications for dance in education, see McFee, 1989a.

PART IV

Concepts for Understanding

9

Style and Technique

This chapter explores the connection between two key artistic concepts: (a) the idea of individual style for an artist (in our case, for the choreographer); and (b) the idea of the dance technique in which dances are constructed. My interest in these concepts is twofold. First, they serve as exemplars of aesthetic concepts, showing both what can and what cannot be achieved through discussion of them. But, second, they stand in a particularly central place for our understanding and appreciation of dance.

The notion of individual style

I begin with a discussion of individual style (drawing heavily on Wollheim, 1979; also Wollheim, 1987: pp. 26–36). To introduce that discussion, two points are required. First, we must recall that art has a constructed, conventional character; art is an *intentional* activity. This means that one makes art deliberately and not accidentally, even when chance is used as a compositional tool, as is widely recognized. For example, Marcia Siegel (1979: p. 293) comments: 'Many people mistakenly believe a dance created by chance operations is improvised or haphazard. Actually, just the opposite is true. Chance is one of the most concrete and objective procedures by which art can be created'. One must recognize, as it were, that the choreographer chooses a great many of the elements, even when such a procedure is used. Indeed, he chooses to use the procedure! What is less commonly recognized is that it follows that judgements of works of art, too, have a learned character: my appreciation of a work of art *as* art requires that I see it as art. And this of course repeats in another form the distinction between artistic appreciation and aesthetic appreciation, articulated earlier. This point has been put (Wollheim, 1983: p. 102) by saying that an artist requires that his work 'carry meaning': this is an aim implicit (where not explicit) in the procedure which, when discussing the institutional theory of art in Chapter 3, we spoke of as the 'self-election' of the artist. So that first point reminds us of both the aesthetic/artistic contrast and of the institutional account that we are giving of art.

The second introductory point concerns the term 'style' itself. The word can be and is used in a number of different senses when talking about works of art, and in particular when talking about dances. For example, one speaks of a particular performer 'having style'; one speaks of the 'style' of a particular period; or one speaks (in grander or more universal terms) of certain categories of style, for example, the classical style. Without spending too much time on this point, I want to employ a formulation *vis-à-vis* our interest in style, drawing heavily on Wollheim (1979) who urges that speaking about the individual style of an artist (think of him as artist A) is employing forms of words such as 'the style of A' for works *by* A: that is to say, works within A's corpus. (This last qualification is introduced because we might refer to 'the style of Giotto' speaking not of Giotto, but of some Giotto-esque painter [Wollheim, 1979: p. 131].) So this is individual style for artists. And I have emphasized the need to distinguish that interest of style from the many other uses that the word 'style' might have.[1]

There is an additional qualification that I shall mention but that I wish to ignore. Wollheim insists that his remarks are about *pictorial* style, that is to say, style in painting. It is his view (Wollheim, 1979: p. 131) that:

... the function, and the importance – possibly even the nature – of individual style are things that differ as we move from one art to another. The relevant factors here, differentiating the arts, include the role of the medium within that art, the degree of apprenticeship required to be a practitioner of the art, the significance of tradition, the involvement of bodily techniques, the character of the structural or compositional principles employed.

Clearly it would be a mistake to override these features or minimize their importance. Yet we should hope that within all arts, individual style has some role, and that the features offered in discussion of it have some place in any art; moreover, that our earlier discussion should help to tailor our remarks to the discussion of dance. With this note of caution, then, I shall drop the qualification 'pictorial'.

Two characteristics of style

I turn now to a brief presentation concerning the nature of style. Here I employ some of Wollheim's arguments, and I begin with his example:

198

painting. In what paintings is it plausible for us to take an artistic interest? We may be interested in many different kinds of painting – for example, the paintings of chimpanzees – but clearly this is not an artistic interest. Nor, we might say, is our interest in the paintings of children or famous men. Moreover, we cannot conclude that this fact is explained by the superiority of the paintings in which we do take an artistic interest, over those in which we do not. The judgement of worth – of better or worse – is not in itself independent of the judgement that a particular painting is an appropriate one in which to take an artistic interest, meaning it is an appropriate one for the application of artistic concepts. We will reinterpret a work if, having thought it the work of person A, we then learn it is a work by another artist, B. What might be called the *canons* and *resources* of A and B will, at least usually, differ. And here we will characteristically be raising or lowering our judgement of a work. So, for example, if we find that in order to utilize 'classical perspective', a painter had to invent or rediscover it, we should regard his work differently from that of a painter within whose tradition such perspective was commonplace. Learning that the work is indeed the work of a chimpanzee, or a famous person, or one of our children, leaves us unsure what to make of it. We have no canons of criticism to bring to bear, no idea of the resources (practical and theoretical) of the maker of this painting. Nothing has the status of a reason for judging this work. Or rather, as part of our hypothesis, we know that this person has neither artistic canons nor practical resources, for we have identified the author of this work as someone not part of an artistic tradition. Thus, in Wollheim's words (1979: p. 133), this alters our judgement of the work by 'knocking it sideways'. What this shows, Wollheim thinks and rightly, is that to be an artist is, for this purpose, to be one whose work is 'decipherable' (Wollheim, 1979: p. 133).

The reason we only take an artistic interest in the paintings of painters is that only they are decipherable for us: they are the only ones we can make sense of. It is only through them that we can (in principle) have any grasp of the canons or resources which they are employing. It is only for them that artistic concepts can be applied. So it is a precondition of artistic interest, then, that the paintings in which we take such an interest are the works of painters. But what is it to be 'a painter' in this sense? And, following Wollheim, I shall suggest that to be a painter just is to have a formed style.

Nothing in this argument strictly turns on our choosing painting as the example. Exactly the same point could be made about dance. We could ask: 'In which dances do we take an artistic interest?'; and reply: 'In the dances created by artists (choreographers)'. The argument would go through in just the same way. What makes the painting case clearer is simply that we can imagine paintings being done by non-painters much more easily than we can imagine dances being made by non-choreographers. Although, of course, some of the constructions of children and of other societies certainly should give us pause for thought here. This argument relates the analysis of style to the idea of decipherability. What we have argued so far (Wollheim's first characteristic [1979: p. 133]) is that decipherability is a precondition of aesthetic interest; further, that decipherability in turn rests on the having of a formed style, for that is what it means to be an artist in this sense.

Wollheim also suggests that decipherability in this sense is also a precondition of expressiveness (second characteristic [Wollheim, 1979: p. 133]). It is a truism that one would only take work X to be expressive if one can interpret or decipher it in such ways as to make it expressive, and that one approaches a work of art with just that expectation. Naturally, what one can decipher depends on what concepts one has available to one, and what is possible for one. But it also depends on attempting to interpret the work, itself a necessity if one is to confront the work of art, given that this interest must be what we have earlier characterized as an artistic interest.

This point is most clearly seen when decipherability becomes strained, when one is at a loss when considering how to interpret certain works. David Best (1974: p. 169) takes as examples cases of dancing robots, or parrots reciting poetry. At first glance these seem unintelligible to us as examples of the expressive, for robots cannot have emotions (that is part of our hypothesis): and so it might seem that their 'actions' cannot be expressive. Yet we accept such possibilities as expressive just in that case where we are able to interpret them. I do not say for a moment that we would be able to do so; but certainly *if* we could find them decipherable, then we would be able to find them expressive. Both of these cases would depend on logically prior cases of human dancers or poets, whose feelings really were expressed through the medium of dance or poetry. In this way, perhaps, we could decipher the problem cases, and hence see them as expressive.

This reiterates, with a different inflection, a point made in Chapter 3: understanding works is, among others things, making sense of them in their style and their technique, and this can sometimes become very explicit. Understanding part of London Contemporary's Dance Theatre's *Class* (1975) depends, in a clear way, on the previous effort *Acrobats of God* (1960), which, like *Class*, displays the practical preparation of a dancer. Like Graham's later *Acts of Light* (1981), *Acrobats of God* and *Class* are composed of 'the elements we use technically in our school, and it is composed of these to show in some way the eagerness and vitality and the beautiful awesomeness of youth'.[2] Of course, the differences are important too: London Contemporary Dance Theatre's production is more 'realistic' to the actual class. It lacks, for example, the whip-carrying taskmaster. Yet both fit Don McDonagh's (1973: p. 259) description: 'a serious exposition of the difficulties in the lives of the creative and the interpretive artist'. Also, both are comic. But what is brought out, of course, is that the influence of the style of one work on the understanding of the other carries over to the ways in which we understand the second dance via our understanding of the first.

The place of technique (I)

Thus far, I have articulated two of Wollheim's three conditions of individual style. Wollheim calls these two 'external' characteristics of style, in that they locate style in the web of artistic concepts, rather than telling us anything in particular about the notion of style itself. Wollheim's third characteristic of individual style – that style has psychological reality – is something he describes as an 'internal' characteristic of style, something he takes to tell us something fundamental about style, rather than locating it in the web of aesthetic concepts. I shall come to that idea of Wollheim's later on, since I am in sizeable disagreement with it; moreover it sheds some interesting light on the aesthetics of dance. However at this stage I wish to move from Wollheim's exposition of the concept of style, with which I am so far largely in agreement, to make some remarks about technique.

My claim will be that technique is a precondition of style. With reference to dance, the term 'technique' is here employed as it would be when one speaks of 'Graham technique', 'Cunningham technique', 'classical ballet technique'. Such examples must serve by way of explanation here, for I do not believe that any concise and yet comprehensive account of technique in this sense is possible.[3] Very roughly, technique (on this conception) is bodily training for a dancer, inculcating certain fairly specific sets of bodily skills. And then my claim is (roughly) that individual style for a choreographer is possible only against the background of such technique in dancers. Of course, I cannot argue straightforwardly that technique is a precondition of style. Rather, I shall make use of the equivalence between the having of a style and decipherability developed in the earlier discussion of style.

Where have we arrived thus far? First, we have recognized that our artistic interest is primarily in those works which are decipherable for us: that is, those with a formed style. And second, this emphasis on decipherability of dance is of a piece with earlier remarks on the need to find movement understandable when seeing it as dance. That is to say, when seeing it as dance rather than mere movement, which amounts to being able to apply artistic concepts to it. Now the last step is in sight. We need only ask if decipherability with respect to dance has any preconditions other than a formed style for the creator; or rather, if the possession of a formed style in this case (at least) has any preconditions. We will see (for dance) that technique is a precondition for style.

We must ask whether or not, in dance at least, one's work can be decipherable unless the technical resources one exploits are decipherable; that is, to ask 'Can I have a formed style in the absence of a formed technique?'. Let it be granted that this question is problematic in a 'chicken and egg' fashion, a point that must be recorded again.

Once more a comparison and contrast with painting is informative here. Representational painting might be thought to be intelligible in the absence of conventions of representation. That is, we know that a certain two-dimensional design is a representation (a picture) of a fish without benefit of knowledge of any conventions of representation. This way of picturing fish might be taken as natural. But this is wrong. In art, there is no 'natural', only the more or less familiar; and that particular way may be an extremely familiar way of representing a fish, even though it is not the only way. In dance, there are no such familiar ways, if only because we have become used to two-dimensional representations of fish, for example, on food packages, while there is no comparable place to learn the expressive potentials, the 'language', of dance. (In Chapter 12 I shall say a little more about the difference in our interest in dance and our interest in other movements which we sometimes describe as 'expressive'.)

The point we are making here indicates two uses of the term 'technique' as articulated by Marcia Siegel (1972: p. 106): 'Technique in dance is two things, really. It's a method of training the body to achieve specific movement tasks . . . But technique is also a systematic approach to the whole process of moving'. Thus we should think of technique not merely in terms of bodily conditioning, but also as having aesthetic or expressive consequences. Siegel (1972: p. 106) notes this point by contrasting 'the mechanical aspects of technique' with its 'aesthetic implications'. Later she refers to the second of these in a revealing way: as 'technique-as-aesthetic' (Siegel, 1972: p. 107). Of course, we would call the implications at issue artistic, since they are characteristic of art works. This is a way of saying that works of art are typically in a *medium*, and further that this medium is integral to our understanding of the work. For a medium isn't just a material. For sculpture, the medium isn't marble, for that is merely the material; a medium is 'material-in-certain-characteristic-applications' (Cavell, 1969: p. 221). Now, we can see how such an idea might have application for arts like painting and sculpture, where the materials can be marble, tempera, gouache, oil and so on. As Cavell (1969: p. 221) puts it: 'The home of the idea of a *medium* lies in the visual arts'.

How is this to apply to dance, if at all? What this idea of a medium emphasizes is the set of characteristic possibilities, the 'applied range of handling and result' (Cavell, 1969: p. 221), which grows from the practice of art within that medium. The parallel for dance, then, is just that picked out by Siegel (1972: p. 107) when she speaks of 'technique-as-aesthetic'. The expressive potentials of the technique arise in just this way: Graham technique typically involves not just a way of handling movement in dance, but also a way of understanding movement. Certain features of the movements in a dance have the status of reasons for any judgement that we make of that dance, and they acquire that status, as we saw in Chapter 3, from the history and traditions of the art form. In this case, that really means from the master works which exploit the same technical resources.

This point comes out clearly if we consider a case where the technical accomplishment of the dancer (however great) is simply inappropriate: the technique implicit in the choreography is not realized in the performance. An example is provided by Marcia Siegel writing about the casting of Graham's *Night Journey* (1944): 'Rudolf Nureyev made his celebrated debut as Oedipus in the winter 1975 season, and proved at best a curiosity compared with the men in the Graham company' (Siegel, 1979: p. 202). But why should this be? Why should the movement of this gifted dancer fail to integrate into the dance? Siegel's answer is that Nureyev did not 'understand the balanced interrelationship of movement, acting and staging in which the works are forged' (Siegel, 1979: p. 202). That is to say, the technique was integral to the dance, and not merely antecedent to it. It was this aspect that Nureyev's performance did not accommodate. A similar point is made by Arlene Croce (1978: p. 162) of another occasion. 'It wasn't good Graham dancing, but it was good Nureyev'. What is admired here, of course, might also be called style, but that is not our topic, not the individual style of the choreographer. And it is this individual style which has the connection with decipherability.

203

Four notes of caution

At this point, four issues deserve mention. First, I shall shy away from talking about the notion of 'language of dance' in any detail. (I have said something about it in Chapter 5.) But this much seems right in the analogy between dance and language: if I do not know the particular 'language' in which a dance is constructed, I will not be able to understand the dance. This should be a familiar point from our discussion of categories of art: say, serial music (Walton, 1978: p. 103). But, second, as perhaps in the music case, there is no one language here, any more than there is only one two-dimensional representation of a fish. In the dance case, there isn't even a *predominant* language, that is to say, there isn't just one technical resource on which a choreographer could draw in expression of, say, grief. Rather, there is a mêlée of techniques.

To put the matter more clearly: I am saying that, in order that a dance be intelligible to me (decipherable, as I put it), I must be able to make sense of the technical resources employed in the dance; for the expression (obviously) employs or utilizes those resources. If this is right, we can see the sense in which technique is a precondition of style: to have a style is for one's work to be decipherable, and this requires a form and a technique for one's dances. This point takes us back to remarks (earlier in this chapter, but also Chapter 1) about seeing dance as an 'intentional' activity, that is, as deliberate rather than accidental. For one source of, at least, my dissatisfaction with one piece by a particular Graham-orientated children's dance group (whose work I greatly admire) is just this: there are some resources of the 'language' – that is, of the technique – which I cannot credit them with employing. Roughly, I cannot credit them with those intentions.[4] The raw sexuality, which is always a possibility within Graham technique, is not something that could be manifest in these children's movements. This is to say that their movements do not carry conviction – they appear like robots or puppets. Just those movements, but on the bodies of adult dancers, might be a very different matter indeed. Of course, it is possible that I could be convinced that the effect was deliberate, reflecting a subtlety I had not noticed – say, a kind of 'innocence and experience' motif. Yet even if this example is not persuasive, surely the point it makes is. One cannot separate what is expressed from how it is expressed. And an element of that 'how' is that its technical resources become part of the dance in a way that does carry just this conviction.

This point leads to the third word of caution. In requiring that resources of a technique be intelligible, I am not urging that one be able to say what they are. Consonant with points made in Chapter 1, the ability to recognize the technique – to understand it when one sees it – may be quite sufficient. But since I am not requiring that one be able to say what the resources of the technique are, it follows that I do not require that all those resources be known, whatever that can mean. Rather, one needs to know enough, as it were, and we cannot generally say what would count as enough.

This leads me to the fourth and final note of caution. Dance techniques are often brought about by the very process of choreography (McDonagh, 1973: p. 168), so one cannot, strictly, be said to grasp the technique first and then to understand the dance: these may happen together.[5] Three considerations make this less than a crucial difficulty: (a) this happens in, for example, painting too. So either it is not a worry, or it is a general worry. In any case, it is not a worry specific to dance. The contemporary conventions of any art form must always be created with reference to (although not necessarily with obedience to) the traditions and past conventions of that art form. And that means that one constructs the new conventions by constructing new works. Also (b) the newly constructed pieces of technique should be seen as depending on other technical resources, even those *within the technique* (if other bits of it exist) or in other techniques. Thus, the evolution of Cunningham technique owes a debt to Graham technique. People who understand Graham technique could then be taught either to do or to understand Cunningham technique. Finally (c) the appropriate unit here is the whole dance, and so, bearing in mind the point just made, each piece of a technique might be seen as supporting other pieces. Then, if one can 'attach' a particular dance to the familiar in that technique or others at some points – say, through established techniques or familiar patterns of movement response within our culture or society – we may be able to render the whole intelligible.

Outcomes of the style/technique connection

Suppose that all this is right. What does it tell us? I will mention three things. First, it puts pressure on any attempt to construct a 'technique-free' dance, by suggesting that such dance would be necessarily style-free and hence necessarily beyond the scope of intelligibility. One may use many techniques, or vary or develop them, but one cannot use none, for what is necessarily not intelligible is, by that token, not dance. Artistic concepts characteristically entail the idea of intelligibility. Second, we see something about what techniques in dance (for example, Graham skills) are for: we see how they make a contribution to the formal resources of the work of art, and how in doing so, they make a major contribution towards expressiveness. Thus these are not, as it were, circus tricks. Indeed, the criticism that ballet was too 'technical' at some historical periods really describes a decline in the technique, such that it became a matter of the ability to perform certain 'circus tricks' (such as a large number of *fouettés*) and hence, lost its connection with expressiveness.

Third, and perhaps as a consequence of the others, we see what happens if one expects the creation of dances from those who lack these resources. Again, a linguistic parallel makes the point: giving someone sounds and hoping for him (or even expecting him) to make sentences. We know, first, that the building block of the sentence is the word, not the sound. And, also, that words only have a meaning in the context of a whole language (or at least, some substantial fragment of a language). I am suggesting that seeing technique as a precondition of style for dance gives us glimmerings of how to apply this knowledge to dance.

There is a further point, sometimes puzzling in the analysis of dances, on which these remarks have a substantial bearing. It is sometimes puzzling, in discussing the question of individual style for choreographers, to recognize the way in which the works of some choreographers are heavily dependent on the works of others. How do these stand relative to individual style? For example, one might think of Robert Cohan, of London Contemporary Dance Theatre, as not having a formed style, but as simply being a Graham-esque artist (as a painter might be 'Giotto-esque'). While not wishing to comment on individual cases, we can see now how the lines between choreographers can be drawn, as it were, in two dimensions. First, there are those with different styles but employing the same techniques. Thus, Graham's dances might resemble Cohan's, because they were exploiting the same technique, and hence exploiting certain ranges of expressive potential. Then we might distinguish between choreographers using different techniques, that is to say, we might contrast Graham technique with Cunningham technique. Then the distinction between Graham and Cunningham would be, perhaps, in two dimensions, whereas the distinction between Graham and Cohan will be simply in one. Once one recognizes that whether the difference was in one or two dimensions was not in itself a qualitative comparison, one has a set of ways of describing differences amongst choreographers.

As in many other cases, one wishes to pay special tribute to the creators of techniques. Thus, to take a musical parallel, Schoenberg is of value both for his music and as the primary creator of the twelve-tone technique – even by those who prefer the compositions of his friends and pupils Berg and Webern. To apply: preferring certain works by Graham's successors to works by the inventor of the Graham technique is not taking anything away from one's admiration of Graham as the creator of that technique. Indeed, this way of speaking allows us to distinguish our admiration of the technique from our admiration of the dances.

Later, this chapter will explore Wollheim's proposed third characteristic of style – that style has psychological reality – and we shall see that it connects up again with the notion of technique. Before doing so, however, I want to put aside some objections that might be raised against my remarks so far in this chapter. It might seem that my concentration on the choeographer has undervalued the dancer. The reply is that I have been concentrating on the choreographer at this stage, but that my remarks about technique identify a key role for the dancer, and indeed, a variety of roles for different dancers. One may find certain parts or aspects of the technique 'happier' than others. A good discussion of this process is to be found in Richard Austin's (1976: p. 115) description of the choreographing by Christopher Bruce of *Black Angels* (1976) with respect to the dancer Lucy Burge: he records Bruce attempting to make use of her 'richer, more sensual way of movement' and calls her 'the dancer of the earth'. (The contrast is with other dancers in the company, especially 'the dancer of the air', Catherine Becque). Further, the general misunderstanding of the role of the performer in the performing arts is discussed in Chapter 12.

This connection between style (and, associatedly, technique) and being able to 'say' something in one's dance makes the concept 'style' such a crucial one for the aesthetics of dance. If style is related to the possibility of expression in the ways suggested here, or in any fairly similar ways, the lack of such an individual style would lead to the derivativeness of school style, and ultimately to emptiness in dances. This conclusion is exactly that reached (though by a different route) by many critical writers on dance. As usual, Marcia Siegel provides a clear example, when she laments the passing of the genius of dance pioneers such as Graham and Cunningham:

> ... their missionary zeal (the dance pioneers) has been replaced with a more practical, competent professionalism: choreography must be created to highlight a season, to feature dancers, to attract reviewers, not to unearth mysteries. Dancers can do everything from a contraction to a split-jump, and they want to display their skills; it seems

unfair to them not to be allowed to point their feet and look beautiful. (Siegel, 1977: p. xv).

First, Siegel diagnoses what is wrong by reference to loss (for dance) of aims of the elucidation of what we call 'life issues' (see Chapter 8). On this view, the situation is blighted because dancers do not seek 'to unearth mysteries', but merely seek to please or to display talents and skills. Second, she comments on the way in which technical virtuosity can replace individual style. The implication, of course, is that such a route leads to a decline in dance. And this is just what we could expect if individual style were related to expression (and intelligibility) in ways described here.

Moreover, Siegel accurately diagnoses the 'longevity' of Graham's works (and others) by emphasizing how the technical resources they exploit have become formalized or conventionalized (see Chapter 3) to a degree where they are readily understood by others. As Siegel (1972: p. 177) puts the point, 'Some modern dance, principally that of Martha Graham, became almost as formal in technique and as pronounced in style as ballet itself – and thereby lasted longest'. What we see here is an example of the articulation of a technique and of a style, and their connection with the 'decipherability' of the works in that style and technique.

Condition three: psychological reality

I turn now to the third characteristic which Wollheim (1979: p. 134) identifies for individual style, namely, that style has 'psychological reality'. It is clear that any characterization of individual style for any art form must do justice to what we would intuitively, or pre-theoretically, understand by the expression 'psychological reality' here: a work of art by an artist in his style must be somehow based on and true to his own ideas. As this formulation makes clear, there is something misleading about my speaking of individual style for an artist as though artists had only one style, for, clearly, some artists (though not all) work in a number of different styles, all of which are recognizably theirs. But with this qualification noted, I shall revert to speaking as though artists had but one style.

To talk of psychological reality may give the impression that what is meant is that certain thoughts or ideas pass through the mind of such-and-such a particular person at a particular time. Then for a work to have psychological reality would be for it to depend on or be true to those thoughts or ideas. If this were what was meant, there would be real content in calling an explanation based on those thoughts or ideas 'psychological', although the picture of thought employed would be an extremely crude one. But, as Wollheim (1979: p. 135) makes plain, these can be implicit thoughts or ideas: they may be the sorts of thing the person might have thought if, for example, he had taken the trouble to articulate a position on this matter; or if certain resources for articulation had been at his disposal; or, perhaps, if the question had been put to him. To put that another way, these are things it was possible for him to have thought. Again, they may be unconscious thoughts which a proper (modern?) psychology could make explicit. The problem with such an account is that the feature that made his explanation of style seem psychological in a strong sense has now disappeared. We no longer are seeing the matter in terms of a discussion of thoughts or ideas which the man himself consciously had and could affirm for us. At best, we seem to be interpreting his behaviour and the like: offering explanations which are psychological in some weak or attenuated sense.

The worry here, then, is a familiar one (see especially Chapter 6): that our understanding of a particular work of art might read in to that work certain features or properties not actually there. In this case, that our attribution of thoughts, ideas or whatever (that is, our attribution of psychological reality) to the work might fail to do justice to what the artist actually thought, and hence read in meanings not actually available. One part of the worry here is generated by a mistaken view of what it is to have thoughts and feelings, for once we realize that thoughts and feelings are not private objects in the head of some person at some particular time, we avoid many tempting errors in aesthetics (McFee, 1982; Best, 1985: pp. 122–5). For example, as we shall see in Chapter 11, the role of the artist's intentions in understanding the work or in the work's meaning can be misunderstood in two ways. First, using the picture of thoughts and so on presented here and considering intentions to be relevant, we may bewail the fact that so few statements of these intentions are actually available to us. Or, second, taking this view of intention and not wishing to employ in criticism (or appreciation) things not available to us, we may urge that intention of the artist has no critical relevance.

Both these positions are mistaken. And both depend for their mistake on the shared view of thoughts, feelings and the like. Clearly it is important to do justice to the connection between a work of art and its creator. Given that our interest in the work of art is an artistic interest, what is really missing from our interpretation of the work of art if it makes no reference to private thoughts in the artist's head? Certainly, the details of the origin of a work of art should not be forgotten. But what other requirements for the adequacy of an interpretation (in this respect) can there be? The artist's intentions are not, or not necessarily, things he actually or explicitly thought or intended: that is to say, the implicit intentions, thoughts, ideas (or the unconscious ones) must be respected. Thus we return to questions of decipherability, for making sense of a work is, at least in part, making sense of the intentions of that work. As we saw initially, works of art are intentional in just this sense. A choreographer does not make a particular work of art in a particular style, choosing from the range of 'all possible styles' (if such a notion makes sense); rather, he selects from, as it were, his own alternatives. What each choreographer could do is constrained by who and where each is, both in place and in history. Moreover, the requirement of decipherability may involve us in seeing certain works as unintelligible if taken as the work of painter X, say Giotto; but they are perfectly decipherable on the assumption of a quite different authorship, say Seurat. Perhaps even more clearly, finding the equivalent of a tone-row in Mozart amounts to something different from finding one in Webern, where tone-rows are a compositional tool. The alternatives are different, so one work is decipherable in those terms, the other not. Such points apply directly to dance. And in saying we cannot make sense of the work on these particular assumptions of different 'authorship', we are saying that we cannot attribute certain intentions to certain 'authors'. (And this is a point that I have made earlier in respect of a children's dance group.)

To anticipate Chapter 11, 'what the artist intended', once properly understood, is criterial of the meaning of the work of art; or, better, of an adequate interpretation of that work. But this is not to be explained in terms of some entailment relation between interpretation and intention. The difficulty, then, lies simply in taking the expression 'what the artist intended' correctly. This requires making sense of the artist doing one thing (making this particular work of art) in terms of other things (perhaps all other things) that this artist does, including what she says and writes. Such a procedure may be viewed as preserving the artist's psychology. Thus it is in terms of these elements that I would give an account of the psychological reality of style.

Viewing the artist's intentions in this way leaves the interpretation of what she intended liable to alteration in two ways. First, we may later acquire evidence that was not available to us at an earlier time. We then conclude we were wrong or mistaken in our interpretation; that is to say, an interpretation which held good before no longer does so. But, second, sets of interpretations may become available to us: a new theoretical perspective may provide a new way of viewing, for example, the artist's intentions or actions. This might be brought about by theoretical changes, say, in psychology, or motivated by changes in artistic practice which generate new theoretical perspectives in an 'internal' way. In such a case, it is not necessarily true that one interpretation will supersede the other, for they may coexist; that is to say, either interpretation may be maintained, or both. That there might be two interpretations of a work of art, both of which were psychological (in this sense of being based on what the artist intended), may be repugnant to some of our intuitions. We tend to think that, if only we could get to it, one of the interpretations must be true, the other false; unless both are false. To deal with this problem is, I suggest, not to search for one (the 'real') psychological interpretation of the work of art, but rather to cultivate a view of the psychological in which what seemed problematic is recognized not to be so.

Notice that this account of the psychological arrives, by referring to what the artist intended, at the same place as our earlier remarks in Chapter 1: judgements of art might allow for a variety of acceptable answers, without thereby becoming merely subjective. We are beginning to see here how reference to the psychological, to what the artist intended, could still be based on and answerable to observable features of the work itself. This conception will be expanded in Chapter 11, when we look at the idea of the artist's intention.

The place of technique (II)

I want now to elaborate the connection between the point just made about style and the notion of technique. We have said that even the psychological reality of style can be understood in terms of perceptible features of the work of art. This has important bearings on criticism of performances in dance as 'technical'. A simplistic way of understanding such a criticism would be to say that the performances simply employ the technique (bodily training for the dancer, teaching a fairly specific set of bodily skills) rather than engaging the thoughts or feelings of the dancers. On this conception, the difference between a technical and a non-technical performance lies in what the dancer thinks, rather than in what he does. But our understanding of the psychological reality of style can now be applied to the question of technique. Just as the psychological reality of style was not dependent on private, internal

211

events in the artist (now explained in terms of them) but, rather, on features of his public creations, so the differences between the technical
and non-technical will be differences in the performance. (This was
mentioned briefly in Chapter 2.) This point is sometimes mistakenly put
by saying that the difference between a merely technical performance
and one which is not just technical is an imperceptible difference, but
this is exactly the opposite of the truth! We have succeeded in perceiving the difference, and that is what allows us to classify this performance as 'technical', that one as 'expressive'. The expressive
potentials are built into the technique, not into the dancers! Moreover,
those potentials are exploited by the artist, and this means that the
psychological reality of his style is invested in that work itself.

However, it would be a mistake to treat the psychological reality of
style in too individualistic a fashion. Certainly a work by a choreographer and in his own style will be true to his ideas. But those ideas will
be shaped by, for example, the style of production, performance,
characteristic of that time (Kivy, 1988: p. 223). The artist shapes his
ideas in terms of the conventions of his day, but as we have seen,
without necessarily acquiescing in all of them. Indeed, his practice may
well shape contemporary (and future) practice. So that, for example,
Glenn Tetley's influence on Christopher Bruce (Austin, 1976: pp. 47–8)
was certainly technical, and shaped the characteristic themes of his
work; but the impact of Tetley can also be seen in the staging and the
production values of Bruce's work – what Siegel (1977: p. 177) speaks
of as 'a gloss of seriousness'. Still, the outcome is a characteristic Bruce
style, true to his ideas.

Thus far I have explored the twin conceptions of style and technique
for dance, taking Wollheim's provocative comments on individual style
as a guide. The outcome is not a neat, pretty picture. But the complex
connections between style, technique and decipherability (the possibility of understanding) for dance should by now be clearer.

Conclusion

There is a great deal more that needs to be said here, if one is to convince a sceptic that talking about psychological aspects of a dance – its
moods, the feelings it expresses and so on – is a way of talking about
the dance, and not, for example, talking about the thoughts or feelings
of the audience of that dance. Still less is it talking about some private
or inaccessible thoughts and feelings since, first (as Wittgenstein's
private language argument shows[6]), thoughts and feelings are not in

general logically private; and second, the expressiveness of the dance is an outcome of the style of the dance and of the technique of the dance, and these are both perfectly public, shareable phenomena. We will return to some of these vexed questions about the place of psychological value when, in Chapter 11, we consider the role of the choreographer's intention in our understanding of the dance.

Recommended reading

The general background is provided by Wollheim, 1979. For consideration of issues, see Sirridge and Armelagos, 1977; Goodman, 1978: pp. 23–40; Danto, 1981: pp. 165–208; Armelagos and Sirridge, 1984; Margolis, 1984. Another version is found in Wollheim, 1987: pp. 26–36.

10
Imagination and Understanding

The two concepts, imagination and intention, are linked in this chapter and the next for a significant reason. Once we see, negatively, what the problem of imagination is, then we will be in a position to put aside certain misconceptions regarding the role (in artistic explanation) of the choreographer's intention in our understanding of the dance itself. In that sense, both the notions dealt with in these chapters operate in a negative way: we learn what it is sensible to say – and as usual, that roughly corresponds to what we say anyway – and we learn various ways in which those sayings might be misrepresented or misunderstood.

There is a perfectly good sense of the term 'imagination' that applies to the creation of art works, but this is really just equivalent to the idea of art creation. Consider, for example, extreme cases (in dance Cunningham; in visual art Rothko) where the philistine says (perhaps rightly) 'a child could do that'. But what the child lacks is, for example Rothko's imagination. This remark says no more than that Rothko is, and the child is not, an artist (see Chapters 3 and 5). And similar things could be said of our dance case. Our interest is in the role, if any, of imagination in the understanding/appreciation of art works.[1] This means that the key term for aesthetics is 'imagination' and not 'imagined', or 'imaginary'.

The relation of imagination to our understanding of art, and the role of imagination in our perception of art remain vexed issues, even when one has cleared away the mass of confusions associated with mistaken understandings of imagination. These include (1) the opposition between imaginary and real for objects; (2) the question of the necessity of imaging or of mental imagery; (3) obfuscating notions, for example the 'imaginal'. I shall return to these ideas at the end of this chapter. The point I am urging is this: perception of art works does not, in any interesting sense, typically employ the imagination.[2] So, first, perception in art is like perception of other things; that is, the difference is only a matter of degree at best. And second, the difference lies in the

214

concepts under which the perception takes place. Nor is this an original idea. At root, Wollheim (1986: pp. 45–6) articulates this same conception when he remarks:

... if we exclude the vapid sense of imagination in which it means no more than the opposite of narrowmindedness ... imagination has no necessary part to play in the perception of what is represented. Imagination may put us in the right frame of mind for such perception, but it does not have to be a constituent of the perception itself.

Imagination and perception

A central thought here is that the appreciation or perception or understanding at issue is of the object, of the work of art in question. So it will be important to avoid assigning too great a role here to the spectators or audience, for if they contribute too much, first, we may have doubts about the extent to which their appreciation is of the object, and second, dangers of subjectivism loom. And this thought is central, just because all the participants in debates around this issue should be true to it.

A valuable step forward is to recognize the sense in which the spectator makes 'a contribution' in ordinary cases of perception – my seeing the trees, hearing the birdsong and so on – for that case is widely supposed to differ in crucial respects from the situation obtaining when we confront works of art. It is assumed that imagination typically has no role in this ordinary case of perception. Indeed, this must be so if, as its proponents claim, there is to be an intelligible contrast between perception that does involve imagination – 'aesthetic perception' – and what I am calling 'ordinary perception' (although I of course accept its variety, complexity and the many ways in which it is interesting, and therefore not ordinary).

Notice, first, that if we decide that – as I shall argue is so – aesthetic perception is just a species of this 'ordinary' perception, we will be obliged to treat both as typically not involving imagination. Certainly, there are theoretical accounts of ordinary perception without imagination being invoked. (I shall not question their completeness or adequacy [see Hacker, 1987].) But now, second, recognize the contribution of the spectator in ordinary perception: he supplies the concepts under which the perception takes place – for all perception is concept-mediated – and this means that there is a clear sense in which two people standing in the same room, looking in the same direction, could

215

see different things. For example, I see (undiscriminated) trees, while you see oaks, elms and ashes; or you see a cathode ray oscilliscope while I see a funny sort of TV set; or, again, you see internal organs portrayed in an X-ray, while I struggle even to make out the ribs (Polanyi, 1973: p. 101). The difference here lies in the concepts each of us brings to bear, and as these concepts become more finely discriminated, so our experiences too become more finely discriminated. So we should see perception as involving not only the possession of concepts, but also their mobilization (in Wollheim's phrase [1986: p. 48]), although of course these aren't so much two processes as two things, either of which could backfire or go wrong.

What I am urging is that the perception of art works is typically of exactly this structure, although of course the concepts under which the objects are perceived are concepts appropriate to art in general, and art in the appropriate form or 'category' (Walton, 1978) in particular. Indeed, it is just this which allows us to be seeing art at all: that is, to be seeing art rather than a pleasing wash of colour, sound, movement or whatever (see Chapter 1).

Any brief detour to expand this point will draw attention, again, to the distinction between artistic appreciation and aesthetic appreciation: that is to say, between our appreciation, judgement and so on of works of art on the one hand, and, on the other, our judgement and appreciation of other aesthetic objects, for example, sunsets, mountains, fountains and firework displays (see Chapter 1). The point I am trying to bring before the mind is simply that the perception of art brings with it a batch of characteristic concepts (what Best [1978a] calls 'artistic concepts'). This is of relevance in my discussion of imagination because, as I urged earlier, my claim is that in this perception no recourse need be made, in typical cases, to the notion of imagination.

Two considerations weigh heavily here. The first, due directly to Wollheim, is that our ordinary perception, say our perception of trees, may become augmented in just the way that our perception of painting can be augmented, and both seem appropriately described as changes in the concepts under which the objects are perceived. That is to say, no additional mechanisms or factors need to be postulated. Wollheim (1986: p. 49) displays the structure of this augmentation, in the case of a painting, with the following example:

A spectator looks at Manet's "Execution of Maximillian", and at first he sees in it three figures facing a group of men, holding objects parallel to the ground. As his understanding of the represented scene increases, he will perceive it, or parts of it, under such concepts as

216

"riflemen", "firing squad", "emperor and his two generals", "sombrero", "kepi", and so on. These concepts are foregrounded. However, what justifies the spectator in subsuming the represented scene under these concepts, is a body of beliefs which he has about such matters as the Mexican expedition, the involvement of Napoleon III, the Juarist uprising and its outcome, the sympathies of liberal Parisians at the time, the uniforms of the two sides, the conventions of military executions, and so on. These beliefs are backgrounded. Periodically, as the spectator attempts to deepen his understanding of the picture, further concepts will be plucked out of his background beliefs and be foregrounded: each time this happens, how he sees the picture shifts somewhat. His perception expands.

Wollheim's example, though concerned primarily with pictorial representation, illustrates how a perceptual model can account for our experience of art. It shows how a change in one's concerns or one's knowledge can result in a change in what is foregrounded or backgrounded in one's experience of the work of art. Indeed, this is just the sort of change we should expect if, following Chapter 6, we model art criticism as a kind of noticing.

A lengthier exposition would draw attention to the variety of things which function in approximately the way Wollheim here describes. The concepts which move from the backgrounded position to the foregrounded position in Wollheim's example are, one might think, of a fairly traditional kind: they are the sorts of concepts one might have independently of one's confrontation of art works. But a similar movement might take place in one's understanding of formal concepts, when one sees concepts that have application, for example, for one kind of art work (say classical ballet), and which are therefore backgrounded in one's understanding of another kind of art form (say, dances employing Graham technique[3]), moving from background into foreground.

As the second consideration – perhaps also due to Wollheim (1973: p. 190; see also Wollheim, 1983: p. 555) but now indirectly – let us consider, for example, the case of line drawings with animals 'hidden' in the trees, where adults can typically see the animals but children cannot. Here, it seems to me, the concepts are not fully mobilizable by the children; they have not yet learned that way of seeing. But this is still a case of ordinary perception. And, in this respect, the difference between the adult and the child is closely analogous to that between expert and beginner in art appreciation. The one can see certain features of the work in the work, the other cannot, but typically he can be brought to do so. In both these situations there is a strong parallel between the case of ordinary perception and the case of artistic perception. These convince me that ordinary perception is indeed an appropriate model for artistic appreciation, at least when perception is treated in a rich, rather than an impoverished, fashion. And, to repeat, I am talking about what artistic perception typically is like, not what it always is like. So, it seems to me that appeal to imagination at this stage is unnecessary and likely to confuse (compare Wollheim, [1986]; Savile [1986]).

Wollheim (1986: p. 46; also 1987: pp. 46–7) raises a further consideration here: that the understanding of pictorial art manifests 'twofoldness'. By this he means that, in seeing a painting of a horse, one sees both the horse (in the painting) and the painted surface. Applied to dance, this would amount to recognizing the expression in the movement, but also seeing the movement as – conventionally (see Chapter 3) – part of a dance. In particular, these are two things one sees; one does not infer or imagine or interpret one of them. If this idea is acknowledged, it identifies yet another feature in which the perception of art is like ordinary perception, and in which imagination (as normally understood) has no role.

Some objections considered

I foresee three main objections to the picture of understanding art prescribed here. The first is that my account does explicitly employ the idea of imagination. Witness my use of a quotation from David Best (Chapters 7, 8 and elsewhere) which speaks of an 'imaginative ability' required for the understanding of art (Best, 1978b: p. 76). But this objection is not conclusive: (a) I deliberately use quotation marks when discussing this idea. It does seem to me there is something well-caught by the word 'imaginative' about the appreciation of art, but which has really little to do with the imagination. So what does this 'imaginative ability' to apply concepts really amount to? It amounts to being able to see the objects as works of art (in ways the Republic of Art acknowledges), and to talk of this as an 'imaginative ability' will be misleading if we assume that such imaginative abilities have anything in common with imagination more generally conceived. So (b), like Wittgenstein (1953: p. 207), I do not intend the word 'imaginative' to have much force here – it applies simply to mark out the point about mobilizing concepts. That is to say, a spectator may have sufficient understanding perhaps to describe a concept which he cannot then mobilize in his own experience. But this ability seems to me to have little or nothing in common with what we would usually describe as imagination.

The second objection is that I import the idea of the imaginative in requiring that works of art be perceived under aesthetic (better, artistic) concepts. Certainly this will be true if the use of artistic concepts, artistic perception, implies the imaginative – but that is just the point at issue. And notice that my view makes use of fewer explanatory notions: why invoke extra faculties if we can explain the phenomenon without them? Certainly, I require the use of artistic concepts in perception, but there seems to me nothing in them which inherently demands appeal to the imagination.

The third objection might be that my view, particularly my 'thick' account of perception makes, say, the lightness of a dancer – which is perceived lightness – a property of the dancer (or perhaps of the dance); and yet we know that the dancer weighs nine stone. There is some incoherence here. That is to say, my view makes what can otherwise be thought of as imaginary properties of the dance into real properties. But to this objection three related replies are important. First, tertiary qualities/properties are indeed properties. The liquidity of water is emergent on its molecular properties: there are no liquid molecules, but that is not to say that liquidity is not a genuine property (Searle, 1984: p. 22). Similar things could be said about more human properties (Scruton, 1983: p. 87). Second, identifying the movement in question as, say, dance and not something else is a way of ignoring certain physical properties of the event, and emphasizing others. This is just what it means to say that artistic concepts are employed in that perception. So, for our purposes, that is to say, in describing the dance, the weight of the dancer at nine stone is irrelevant, or perhaps even false. Third, the alternative may be to locate the lightness 'in the perception' or, worse, 'in the spectator' – two obviously absurd and also demeaning views. And that can be seen from their subjectivism. I conclude that my view of the perceived qualities of a dance as real is defensible.

Notice that I am not saying that the imagination never enters into artistic perception – indeed, I can mention a few works where it seems to me it necessarily has a place.[4] But the point is that *typically* it has no place, and certainly no necessary place, any more than the fact that lambs or fish function occasionally as Christian symbols in paintings shows (what is false) that all painting is symbolic. Notice too that if another account of perception were employed – say, one which involved imaging – my point here could still be made. For my point is just that whatever account is given for 'ordinary' perception, that same

219

account will typically do for artistic perception, once we are mobilizing artistic concepts in that perception.[5]

Three other ideas of the imaginary

Thus far I have shown how the notion of imagination has little or no role in artistic perception in standard cases. I must still discharge my debts in the other senses of the term 'imaginary' and its cognates, initially rejected as irrelevant. The rationale for the exclusions was that many appeals to the imagination are simply excuses for woolly-mindedness or mystification. Consider an example from visual art, for which there is no parallel for dance: an example where, let us suppose (what I don't actually accept) technique isn't important – for example, Rothko. Suppose we read that what distinguishes Rothko's work from a child's (or a chimp's) is his imagination. Well, as it stands, this isn't philosophy, it is criticism. So we need to demystify the claim. First, what is important is Rothko's ideas as part of artistic traditions, even when/if he is reacting against such traditions. That is, Rothko is making art, an intentional activity. It is his vision which allows him to see this activity as art, but the term 'vision' is here used metaphorically. Second, and minimally, the use of the term 'imagination' in the original does not commit one to other claims: for example, of the role of imaging, of the object in question as 'not real'. Hence it is not clear what is really being said. Third, and stronger, there is a real difference here between the use of imagination (that is, the imaginative, for want of a better word) and the imaginary. So that if art involves the imagination, even in the example we are giving, that does not make art in any sense imaginary.

It is now appropriate briefly to make good my claims as to the irrelevance of the three uses of the term 'imaginary' noted initially. The first sense of the term contrasted it with 'real' for objects. There seem, in fact, to be two elements in this. The first is the way in which a unicorn is an imaginary animal, rather than a real one; the second, the way the lion I hallucinate is an imaginary lion, in contrast to the real lions in the London Zoo, or in which a child's imaginary friends might be contrasted with his real friends. For most of us, art works are not imaginary in either of these senses. There really are art works: they are neither non-existent nor hallucinatory. Even those who agree that dances are abstract objects (Chapter 4) are not thereby committed to thinking that these are somehow imaginary or not real. Indeed, one might think of the dance itself as only instantiated in the performance, and yet acknowledge that it is instantiated there, and hence that these moving bodies really are the dance. Even those like Collingwood (1938: pp. 140–1) and Wollheim (1980a, sections 40–2: pp. 91–8), who argue that the work is only encountered when one confronts it with artistic concepts, are not really claiming that the art work is non-existent or hallucinated. At best (in spite of what they say) they are arguing that it is only instantiated when it is perceived; that even then, it *is* perceived, and hence it is rooted in what is real. I conclude that there is no useful talk of imagination here.

The second matter concerned the role of *imaging*, or of mental imagery. The point to be made here is just that we do not need to discuss mental imagery or imaging in our account of art. This point is widely accepted and argued for in different ways. As Wollheim has argued in many places (for example, *Painting as an Art*, 1987: p. 19), any account of a painting must involve reference to the physical medium, to marks on canvas and so on. Hence a mental image of an art work is much less than a blueprint for that work, and is certainly not the work itself: any mention of mental images would be at best a very inadequate account of that work. And here, what is true of painting is true of other arts also. This point is well put by the novelist John Fowles. Considering the case of people claiming to imagine art but not produce it, he remarks (1977: p. 5) on 'that bizarre face of the imagination that seems to be more like a failure to remember the already existent than what it really is – a failure to evoke the non-existent'. Of course, I have not proved that this conception of imagination or imagery is mistaken, but at least the idea of the error is clear here. As Mallarmé put it, responding to a comment about the difficulty of writing even when one is never at a loss for ideas, 'you can't make a poem with ideas ... you make it with words'.[6] A concrete example from the world of dance can be found in David Bintley,[7] discussing the composition of his *Gallantries* (1986): 'It's rather like I can see the whole thing almost from a distance, so you can't see the particular movements, just a kind of overall view of the atmosphere that I want to evoke'. In this case, does Bintley have an 'image' of the dance? We might conclude that he does; but certaintly it is not the complete dance 'in his head'. Rather, he has some vague ideas which he has attempted to make into the dance by making the steps. He is in that process evoking the non-existent (in Fowles' words): that is, he is bringing the work into being, from non-existence. Bintley's own word for what he had before, 'atmosphere', seems exactly right here. The point to emphasize is that this is not an example of the dance work complete as a mental image, which is then

221

transferred to movement. The medium, the body in motion, is involved as soon as anything recognizable as a dance exists.

But in fact the argument against the relevance of imaging is even stronger. Scruton (1974: p. 93) accurately summarizes the defects in an appeal to imagery to explain perception as follows: 'it fails to distinguish imagery from sensation (Ryle, Sartre); it does not account for the intentionality of imagery (Husserl, Sartre); it makes the image into a private object about which nothing can be said (Ryle, Wittgenstein)'. He comments, 'Each of these arguments are conclusive'. At the very least, it cannot be essential to make reference in any special way to mental imagery when one speaks about art, for any role attributed to mental imagery in perception in general will apply equally to art: equally, but not more so.

Finally, it is appropriate to put aside talk of the imaginal.[8] To explain this idea of imaginal experience, Elliott (1973: p. 89) says: 'When contemplating Chagall's picture *The Falling Angel*, the observer places himself in the time of the represented world at the moment depicted, retaining in memory some part of the angel's descent and anticipating its imminent future. In this mode of imaginal attention he relates himself to the depicted angel very much as he would to a bird or aeroplane which he saw falling in real life'. Quite what he means here remains unclear. I shall attempt to simplify around its major elements before going on to discuss its general relevance to artistic appreciation. Certainly Elliott's method of clarifying his position is not helpful. I do not in general 'enter into' the world of a falling bird or aeroplane in any sense that is relevant. I certainly don't try to imagine what it would be like to be falling (Nagel, 1979: p. 169). More importantly, Elliott certainly doesn't think that we achieve imaginal experience of art by trying; rather it is a feature of our sensitivity to art works that we find ourselves experiencing them in this way (to the degree that we do). It is, to use Elliott's phrase, 'involuntary imagining' (Elliott, 1973: p. 90).

On this second point Elliott is clearly right: I do not (typically) choose to experience a work of art in one way, I am just struck by it in that way. A partial parallel might be with one's reaction to a joke: one just finds it funny. In the case of art, my experience can be altered and sharpened, for example by reading criticism, discussing the work with others, or even by exposure to other works, but it is still *my* experience that is at issue. So on the question of its involuntary character, Elliott is certainly right, although the word 'involuntary' is perhaps not one I would have chosen. But what about the idea of involuntary imagination? What role has been ascribed to imagination here?

Now it is certainly true that we can be struck by art works in this way, that we can be 'caught up' by them, that we can find ourselves 'in their world' and so on. But these are all metaphorical descriptions of what we could only otherwise describe as experiencing art. Since we do not really or actually walk about in a painting, any sense in which we might speak of ourselves as 'stepping into' a Breugel, say (or even speak of the painting as a 'window into the world') is bound to be indirect in some way. To elaborate here, we might see the central question being posed in the following way. We do not really go into Breugel's painting, so how do we go there? Answer: in the imagination. It is this sense of imaginative participation which is the root of Elliott's idea of imaginal experience of art.

A moment's reflection shows that the answer given above to the question about entering Breugel's painting is the wrong one. The fact is, we do not enter the painting at all. A parallel question: how did I climb Everest when I merely dreamt I climbed it? Parallel answer: I climbed it in my dream! In fact, I haven't climbed it at all. And the key here lies in the point accepted earlier about the involuntary character of artistic experience. Speaking metaphorically, I might say that I just find myself in the world of Breugel. But even when that metaphor is cashed out, my role in it will still be a largely passive one. It is not that I imagine that world, as I might (on command) imagine a horse in a field. Rather, it is a little more like the pink elephant imagined by the alcoholic (that is, hallucinated). The point I am making is that Elliott's imaginal experience of art (as I understand it) is not usefully modelled on imagination more generally. And can usefully be ignored in our discussion of the place of *imagination* in the understanding of art works.

This is another place where Wollheim's (1986: p. 46) idea of two-foldness might be invoked, for, crucially, one recognizes *both* the landscape and the painted surface. Hence it makes no sense to talk of just imagining the world of Breugel. That ignores the fact that my 'imagining' is constrained by Breugel's canvas, for I am also aware of that canvas. To apply, the experience of dance does not consist in confusing the movements of the dancer with those of a 'real' human being. To be thus confused is to be like the apocryphal Eskimos who leap onto the stage to stop Othello strangling Desdemona. Their perception lacks twofoldness. But we recognize *both* dancer and the dance. And that distinguishes 'our' world from the 'world' of the dance.

That point can be clarified by a rather different example. Consider almost any of M. C. Escher's wonderful etchings: it is sometimes thought that these represent 'logically impossible worlds' or 'logically impossible objects'. The idea seems to be that we could imagine finding ourselves in such a world, that this is within our power. It is this sense of the imagination as 'within our power' that is important to contest, for one can only imagine what can be described in a consistent fashion. This is a point shared with, for example, Russell (1921: pp. 159–60). But, like many analytical philosophers, Russell would interpret the 'consistent fashion' in terms of asserting without self-contradiction. Yet the constraints to be recognized here will actually be more strict than merely those of self-contradiction. The contours of the relevant concepts must be respected if we are to make sense of what is imagined. And this, as we might say, is what the Escher etchings fail to do. Or, more precisely, what they play against. In fact, these are '"logically impossible pictures", i.e. pictures which violate the "logical syntax" of pictorial representation, and so make no "pictorial sense"' (Hacker, 1976: p. 24). How we experience them depends on the concepts available to us, and hence is not really 'within our power', for we cannot change all such concepts at will. But if (some of) the constraints on 'entering' Escher's 'world' are given by conventions of pictorial representation, the same is surely true of Breugel's world and, with suitable adjustments, for any 'imaginal' involvement with any art work. So part of the topic for study, if one wished to pursue the idea of the imaginal experience of art, would be the concepts under which the art works in question were experienced. The degree to which art works can be 'entered into' will be constrained in that way. Thus one is left with a set of questions, by the idea of imaginal involvement, rather than with a tool for answering questions. No doubt it is worth stressing that these are questions for the aesthetician. No doubt some writers have forgotten or ignored or denied them. But they are questions about the nature of artistic experience, not a way of connecting artistic experience with imagination.

Two further issues about the imaginal. First, one might also note how infrequently such experience occurs. Thus if one's interest were in 'typical' artistic experience, imaginal involvements would not be one's major concern. The second point turns on my reaction to the notion of the imaginal: I called it obfuscating. I intended this as a remark about its wider application. Whatever one thinks of this notion in the hands of its creator, R. K. Elliott – and I find his descriptions evocative – at the least one must concede that it has not been clearly used by his followers. It is easy to see how such ideas might reintroduce the thought of (mental) imagery, or contravene the constraints laid down by the private language argument (Hacker, 1986: pp. 245–75), for it invites us to talk in terms of an 'inner' world, without making plain that world's connection to the real world.

Conclusion

This discussion of imagination and the understanding of art has focused on the irrelevance of the idea of imagination to standard cases of perception of works of art. It is argued that artistic perception is just that: a species of perception, and hence not typically understood as involving imagination. Of course, the complexity of the idea of perception must certainly be acknowledged by anyone taking such a route. It would be a mistake to reduce it, as some psychological writing does, to a property of rods, cones and the like (see Hacker, 1987: pp. 48–9). Perception is done by people (see Chapter 13), and it is just a catch-all name for the operation of the five senses. The discussion here further constrains the idea of artistic experience, by saying a little more about the concepts under which art works are experienced (and made). In particular, it has emphasized the public character of the experience of art, and has rejected the appeals to mental images and other offshoots of psychologism (Baker, 1988: pp. 171, 267).

Recommended reading

The context of the discussion is set by Wollheim, 1986. Scruton, 1974 provides a difficult (yet classic) discussion. The required Wittgenstein scholarship begins (as implied in Chapter 10, note 5) from the works of Baker and Hacker. Best, 1985: pp. 84–6, 178–9 offers a related discussion.

11
Intention and Understanding

The upshot of Chapters 6, 7, 8 and 9 has been to emphasize the import-ance of the concept 'art'. We recognized (in Chapter 9) that saying an object, for example a dance, was expressive is really no more than saying the object in question succeeds in being a work of art. To put that another way, it is constructed, or intended, under artistic concepts (and of course, other-acclaimed by the Republic). We might easily express this point by talking about artistic purpose or artistic intention. But this way of speaking, while very natural, is fraught with dangers. It can look like an invitation to understand the dance in terms of some events 'in the head' of the choreographer, and this would reinstate the kind of psychologism we criticized in Chapter 9.

The aim of this chapter is to bring us to the point where we can put aside certain misconceptions regarding the role (in artistic explanation) of the choreographer's intention in our understanding of the dance itself. In that sense, this chapter (like the previous one) operates in a negative way: we learn what it is sensible to say (as usual, that roughly corresponds to what we say anyway) and we learn various ways in which those sayings might be misrepresented or misunderstood. We must proceed slowly, for there is a large and complex literature on the place and role of the artist's intention in our understanding or appreci-ation of his artwork,[1] in which two views in particular hold sway. Both are mistaken, and mistaken in closely similar ways, or so I shall argue. I will first of all identify the issue a little more fully, then sketch both of the opposing views, highlighting the deficiencies of each. Then I will show how both represent a mistaken view of intention, and relatedly, a mistaken conception of how we recognize authorial intentions, in the case of art works such as dances.

Intentionalist and anti-intentionalist positions

At its most general, the issue about the intention of the artist is this: how, if at all, is the meaning of the work of art related to the intentions, purposes and so on of its creator? To what extent is it legitimate to use

226

information about the creator (for example, biographical information) in understanding or appreciating his works? This issue arises for two reasons. First, we have a natural tendency to talk as though what was in dispute about art works is, for example, what Christopher Bruce intended in *Ghost Dances* (1981) or *Black Angels* (1976), as if we would be better able to understand or to appreciate the dance in question if we knew this. Second, as we have recognized, to make a work of art is, at least to some degree, to intend to do so. The making of artworks only takes place when the object is made under artistic concepts (see Chapter 1 and elsewhere).

Of course, neither of these reasons, of itself, gives us any fixed answer to the two questions posed above. While we may speak about 'what Christopher Bruce intended', we might decide not to expand or elucidate such remarks by reference to Bruce's life, work, biography or psychology. And we might feel that the context of the creation of the dance gave us a sufficient warrant for its being created under artistic concepts. To provide a clear response to this issue, we must explore the reasons which might be offered to lead in one direction rather than another. To move on here we must consider the two kinds of views mentioned above.

On the one hand an *intentionalist* view would claim that, when we are uncertain as to the interpretation of a work of art, our puzzlement can always be resolved by discovering the artist's intentions. Two main thoughts support this position. The first is simply that the artist knows what he is doing, that he is an authority on his own activities. And this is sometimes offered as a general 'fact' about human beings. The second thought is more specific. If we do not know to what *category* of art a work belongs, we can mis-perceive it (as we saw in Chapter 6 and elsewhere), so it is important to identify the category of art. Further, we may misunderstand works if we describe their features inappropriately. An example from painting: an artist may intend certain brushstrokes, and the outcome of those brushstrokes may look like the Tower of London, without the artist intending that they look like the Tower of London. The action is not intentional *under the description* (see Chapter 2) 'Tower of London painting', but we might mistake it for a painting of the Tower of London. Only an appeal to the artist's intention will rule out such a misunderstanding. Or so it seems.

There is clearly something right about such a view. It seems to represent the actual practice of critical writing, for critics often mention biographical facts about the artist in question as a way of justifying aspects of their interpretation. (As I will later urge, it actually does so.) For example, to decide whether or not a certain passage was ironic, one might comment on the likelihood of such irony, given the prevailing facts of the author's life at that time.[2] And the widespread use, in critical discussions, of choreographers' own descriptions of their works coheres with this view. Thus, for example, Susan Leigh Foster's discussion of Yvonne Rainer's *Trio A* (Foster, 1986: pp. 174–6) includes a passage where Rainer herself discusses the dance. It is natural to take Rainer's comments here as *authoritative*: but should we do so? What counter-arguments might be raised?

To answer these questions is to approach the opposing, or *anti-intentionalist* view. Like intentionalism, the anti-intentionalist view has been most extensively articulated for the art form of literature. Some of its major proponents are already familiar to us as the scrutiny theorists on the nature of criticism (see Chapter 6). In essence, they wish to make two related points. The first is that if reference to intention were required in order to understand or appreciate art works, then many art works would not be open to criticism, understanding or appreciation. If the artist is dead, or unknown, or uncommunicative, one simply would not be able to find out the intention. Or, to put that the other way around, if we can sometimes get by in understanding art works without appealing to intention, then we can always do so. Notice two features of this point. First, it assumes that what is sometimes required is always required, that is, it employs a certain conception of the completeness of the understanding of art works. This is an idea intentionalist and anti-intentionalist share. The thought is that a complete interpretation (or a complete understanding) of the art work will always either have (for the intentionalist) or not have (for the anti-intentionalist) a reference to the artist's intention. It would be a criticism of any interpretation to find that it was not complete in this sense. Or so the position assumes. Second, it begins to bring out how appeal to intention is conceived of on this view: that is, conceived of, as I put it earlier, as requiring that one look 'inside the head' of the artist.

The second point made by the anti-intentionalist is well captured by Cavell (1969: p. 181) when he says 'it no more counts towards the success or failure of a work of art that the artist intended something other than is *there*, than it counts, when the referee is counting over a boxer, that the boxer had intended to duck'. The thought is that what the boxer intended is irrelevant if it differs from what he did: he intended to duck, but he failed to duck, so the bare intention can be ignored. If we are interested in those intentions, for example if he had actually ducked, then we can concentrate on what he did. We do not need to look to his thoughts or ideas. These points carry over to our discussion of the artist's intentions. If what he intended is something other than is there – something other than what he achieved – it is his (artistic) achievements that are our interest. That is to say, we must judge the work itself, what is there, and not appeal to what is external or extrinsic to that work. As will be recalled from Chapter 6, a big difficulty here revolves around making out this extrinsic/intrinsic contrast. One cannot decide on such questions independently of interpreting the actual work of art in question. Yet such interpretation presupposes the appropriateness of certain concepts and categories. Suppose, for example, that we feel that 'the depth of Graham's choreographic achievement has everything to do with her longevity as a performer. She created roles from the inside, with her own huge dimension; ultimately, she had to dance them' (Siegel, 1977: p. 236). One might take such a 'fact' – Graham's longevity as a performer – as crucial to the understanding of some of her work: for example, *Appalachian Spring* (1944). At first glance, this might seem to be a fact quite external to the movements and so on that comprise *Appalachian Spring*: but where does this view of Graham arise from? What is it that makes this a fact at all? The answer, of course, is that it arises from the understanding of the dances of Graham, and in particular, *Appalachian Spring*. So that this is true (if it is) is not independent of the way we understand the dances; hence it is not external at all. However, the anti-intentionalist point is clear, and the simplest way to put this point is as follows: that anti-intentionalists conceive of intentions as something antecedent to the work of art in question, connected with it at best *causally*. Hence, for them, to look to the intention (or in Graham's case, the biography) is to look, as it were, away from the work of art itself.

There is something importantly right about the thought behind such anti-intentionalism. If we are to appreciate art on the basis of what the artist intended other than what he did, we are on a slippery slope towards sentimentalism. Dances which are only appealing because, for example, one is touched by their subject – say, the death of a beloved pet – would be central cases here. No doubt the artist intended something great and profound but (as much student choreography shows) the outcome can still be trite or meaningless. Attention to the work itself is an appropriate antidote here.

One way to proceed would be to interrogate in detail both the intentionalist and anti-intentionalist positions. But, for our purposes, such an investigation is unnecessary, for both positions are deeply flawed, and in similar ways, as I will go on to show. Our needs will be satisfied if we can expose these flaws and, as a result, arrive at a plausible account of the role of intention that does justice to the insights of both positions. (As we will see, this will be, roughly, intentionalism constructed out of anti-intentionalist materials).

There are two main flaws shared by both intentionalist and anti-intentionalist theorists. The first, comparatively minor, is that both urge that intention is either always relevant, or it never is. That is, they both assume that the point at issue is whether or not reference to the artist's intention is a necessary condition for the adequacy of an interpretation. Thus one group claims that, because we can sometimes understand works without appeal to intention, intention cannot be such a necessary condition. The other group urges that, since reference to intention is sometimes helpful in understanding art works, that it is a necesary condition for the acceptability of any interpretation (for its adequacy). But suppose we are no longer bound by the need to deal in necessary conditions. Suppose we do not think of logical or internal connections in this way (that is, in terms of necessary and sufficient conditions[3]). Now we will no longer be impressed by an argument that moves from 'sometimes X' to 'always X', or from 'sometimes not Y' to 'never Y'. And we will have such an attitude if we accept the possibility of a defeasible logical relation of a kind described throughout this work.

The second flawed area shared both by intentionalist and anti-intentionalist concerns the nature of intention itself. Both adopt an essentially dualist (Best, 1985: pp. 122–5) conception of intention, with the intention itself as a piece of prior planning, antecedent to and, at best, causally connected with the work of art. As Wollheim (1971: p. 186) puts it: 'Both these two doctrines share a common assumption: that there exist inner states of a certain kind – states which occur frequently in the process of making – and which can be understood independently of the product in which they issue'. Then the intentionalists – who find reference to intention useful – are obliged to say how such an antecedent event is nevertheless important; while the anti-intentionalists – who recognize that to look to antecedent events is to look away from the work itself – urge that intention can play no role in (legitimate) criticism or appreciation. The answer to both positions lies in rejecting such a dualistic conception of intention.

In fact there are two importantly related dimensions here. The first involves recognizing that we must think of intentions, not as something prior to activity, but rather as inherently involved in what the activity is. This means, secondly, that the intention and the action which fulfils it are logically related, that not any action would count as fulfilling that intention. Hence the action is more than just a sign of an intention. To put the point simply, the intention to dig is not a private mental event that just happens before one (or worse, one's body) starts digging. By the first point, since the intention is the intention to dig (and perhaps to dig in a certain place and in a certain way), that intention would only be satisfied by that digging: this is a feature of the intention. But if intentions have public dimensions of this sort, in particular ones that relate to the outcome of the intention, it is clearly mistaken to see intentions and their outcomes as importantly different in kind.

By the second point, we must recognize that the fact that one is digging is, other things being equal, a proof that one intended to dig. Of course, this proof operates defeasibly: if someone doubts that I intended to dig, when he sees me digging, he must show that there is something unusual in the situation. What this means of course (and to repeat) is that the activity of digging is more than just a sign of the intention to dig. Rather, it is something logically or internally connected with the intention to dig. David Carr (1987: p. 352) made exactly this point applied to dance: 'the purposes and intentions whereby the physical performance is invested with meaning are related not causally or productively to the movement, but *logically* or *internally*: the purposes are *inherent* in the movement rather than *antecedent* to it'. Carr is emphasizing two major points: that what we see is, other things being equal, the choreographer's intention (which, of course, he can deny by, say, complaining about the performance or voicing his dissatisfaction); and that seeing the activity in this way, we are seeing it as meaningful action (not as mere movement: see Chapter 2).

So the idea of intention that is to be rejected is that talk of the artist's intention is no more than talk of his inner state, and not, centrally, of the work of art. On such a view, the truth of a statement ascribing intentions to some artist would depend on that inner state, and as such would be only contingently[4] related to the work of art. Roughly then, the thesis shared by intentionalist (view A) and anti-intentionalist (view B) amounts to this: *that there was some one thing which went through the artist's mind when he made work X, and this determines the truth-value of statements ascribing intention to him. It is to this 'something' that we would be appealing if we appealed to the artist's intention.* Of course, view A concludes that we must appeal to it; view B that we cannot, do not, or should not. On view B it follows that, since we can indeed find out the meaning of a work of art (but not the something that went on in the artist's head) the intention of the artist cannot be relevant to the determination of meaning. On view A, it follows that only when we can find out what the artist intended (really) can we be sure what the work means; since this is not the usual situation, we will not usually know (really know) the work's meaning.

The public character of intention

We have seen the incoherent outcomes of both the intentionalist and anti-intentionalist views. But with what can we replace them? We have seen what our view will not be. But what will it be? The first step must be to recognize the public character of intention, in particular, of the criteria for the ascription of intention. Moreover, to ascribe intentions in general is a matter of interpretation. Consider a case where a person we have known for some time then acts (as we think) extremely uncharacteristically. In such a case, we will seek to interpret his behaviour so as to make sense of this new behaviour. Searching for an explanation of his present behaviour may cast light over his past behaviour. We may even come to make sense of this present behaviour by changing our view of his *past* behaviour; so that we modify our previous interpretation, or understanding. His intentions, we may come to think, were not what we thought they were, and any such interpretations of a man's intentions will make reference to the context of his action, for that is implicit in treating it as action (see Chapter 2). As Wittgenstein (1953, section 337) pointed out, an intention is always embedded in a situation.

Also important here is the recognition that self-ascription of intention is equally a matter of interpretation, that our searching for an explanation of a person's present behaviour may cast light over his past behaviour *for him*. That is, he may see that his intentions were not what he thought they were. He is not the person he thought he was. And here we should recall Freudian methods in psychology as bringing the patient to accept another interpretation of his past behaviour.

All of these are remarks about intention in general, but a key thought here is that the artist's intentions operate in a way not dissimilar from intentions more generally. To apply these remarks: understanding an artist's intention in this work may require us to consider both his other work and his life – although this may not be a hard and fast divide, especially if his life is also relevant to understanding of his other work. That is, our interpretation of his life comes at two points.[5] For example, in her discussion of Graham's *Appalachian Spring*, some of which was quoted earlier, Siegel (1977: p. 236) refers implicitly to other major female roles that Graham created towards the end of her own performing career. We can imagine that a consideration of the female roles in these other works may help us to understand this one: they may help us to see its formal qualities and its significance. But Siegel (1977: p. 236) also remarks that Graham 'made herself a bride at fifty – in *Appalachian Spring* – because she was a bride then'. Yet we can imagine this fact (of Graham's marriage) being relevant to the interpretation of the other roles also.

How then are the artist's intentions to be explicated? An account of the artist's intentions for a particular action (a particular art work) cannot be separated from an interpretation of that artist's life and work, and this conforms to how we treat intentions more generally. In judging a man's intentions, we relate what he is doing to the wider context, his past intentions and the like. Certainly a criterion for one's intention is what one actually does. What others say of your intentions must generally agree with what you say. Why? Because it is in relation to what others say that you learn to characterize both your intentions and your behaviour as intended. To deny this connection in a particular case is to deny an almost universal generalization: namely, that guaranteed through the defeasibility of the relation between an intention and the action which fulfils it (Hacker, 1990: pp. 358–9).

Thus far I have urged, first, that the (general) ascription of intention does not normally work in quite the way philosophers have described; and second, ascription of the artist's intention (specifically, the choreographer's intention) is almost exactly like the ascription of ordinary, everyday intention, the only difference residing in the fact that the art work is now criterial of what is intended in ways that an action might be for an ordinary intention. This second point is important because it locates the burden of proof just where our analysis, employing the notion of defeasibility, places it: on the objector. And it is recognized to do so, for we typically explain action by a reference to the agent's intentions. As Wollheim (1987: p. 37) puts it in the case of painting:

> ... the burden of proof would seem to fall upon those who think that the perspective of the artist, which in effect means seeing the art and the artist's activity in the light of his intentions, is not the proper starting point for any attempt to understand painting. For it is they who break with the standard pattern of explanation in which understanding is preserved.

The point, of course, is that we have a right to expect the artist's intentions to cohere with interpretation of his work; the case where it does not will be the exception (and itself open to explanation).

What this means, of course, is that discussion of the artist's intention (specifically, the choreographer's intention) will not resemble the discussion of intention imagined by either intentionalists or anti-intentionalists.[6] To augment this point, we will consider briefly a concrete description of a choreographer at work, and see how these remarks show the artist's intention. But before that, some remarks which clarify our 'commitment' to the importance of the artist's intention and so on. There is another way in which the artist's biography might be brought to bear on an interpretation of a work of art: namely, that the way in which the work comes into being – what I shall call the history of production of the work of art – is always relevant to its identity. A powerful argument for this contention is to be found in Wollheim's work (Wollheim, 1978). If this argument is accepted, the importance of who the artist is to the identity of his work, and hence to its appreciation, is established, and with it, some of the claims of intentionalism.

Wollheim's argument is elegant, simple and persuasive. It assumes, reasonably enough, that when an artist makes any work of art, he does so in terms of a conception of the appropriate art form. Indeed, this is the point we made earlier (Chapter 1 and following) in claiming that works of art were in a category and were to be seen (and hence made) under artistic concepts. Clearly, we will understand the work better if we understand this conception of art, which Wollheim calls the 'artist's theory'. No doubt, the content of such a theory will be heavily sociologically and historically determined. But Wollheim argues that this 'theory' or conception of art contains reference to the history of production of the work of art in question, and he motivates this contention in the following way: he points out that an artist thinks of a work as 'his own. He has made it; he is responsible for it, if it expresses anything, it expresses him; it can be properly understood and appreciated only in the light of his having made it' (Wollheim, 1978: p. 37). But, as Wollheim notes, any artist recognizes that nothing in the work will be uniquely his. The particular movements a choreographer employs will typically have appeared in other dances, especially if the choreographer is working with an established technique, such as Graham technique. The movements themselves are not his; and even if he invented them (as Martha Graham, perhaps, did) they are still not his unique property. They can still be employed by others without plagiarism. Indeed, the very idea of a technique, especially of the creation of a technique, shows us this. Techniques are made (both conceptually and historically [see McDonagh, 1973: p. 168]) by taking elements from one dance and employing them (perhaps suitably modified) in some later work. For a novelist (Wollheim's example), neither words, phrases, sentences or even paragraphs are uniquely his. As Wollheim (1978: p. 37) says, 'all these belong to the language. What he thinks of as his is the novel: and this must show that, for the novelist, "the novel" is not what might be called a "macro grammatical" concept'. That is to say, one cannot think

234

of the novel as simply a collection of grammatical components: words, phrases and so on. There are two elements in his view here. Wollheim (1978: p. 37) again: 'the thought that what he has made is *his* and the thought that what he has made is a novel'. For the artist, this amounts to a consideration of the history of production in his work. Any orthographically indistinguishable work – that is, one containing the same words in the same order – will not be his novel, unless its history of production coincides with that of his novel: that is, unless he made it. This is surely sufficient argument to show that *what* work of art we have does indeed depend on its history of production.

Applied to dance, it would go like this: only certain combinations of movements count as his dance (if Chapter 4 is right, then those which conform to the thesis of notationality). But that is not enough to guarantee that a dance is his. None of the movement elements is his unique property. Suppose we imagine a case where a dance is performed from a notated score. Now the dance must not simply conform to the score, but must do so because of the score. The score in such a case is what establishes the connection of the performance and its creator, the choreographer. It would not be his dance without that connection. If a dance is performed on the basis of recollections of previous performers (see Chapter 4) the same point still applies. If it is to be his dance, those recollections must eventually lead us back to him, to the artist's hand.

What this means is that, without such a connection to a history of production (perhaps, better, history of construction), it would not be the dance it is. And we have argued that interpretations of each work are unique (non-transferable). Thus a different history of production would entail differences of interpretation. We might even find an explanation of the importance of the history of production here, by showing how such differences of history of production do make different sets of reasons open to us. An example may illustrate. Borges (1962), in his story *Pierre Menard, Author of Don Quixote,* imagines a man in the twentieth century coming to compose a word-perfect text of (parts of) Cervantes' masterpiece. This composition is made, as it were, in isolation from *Don Quixote,* so it is not merely copying.[7] But Borges urges that Pierre Menard's text, though containing exactly the same words, is actually more beautiful, rich and complex than Cervantes'. The same words have a different force because different sets of reasons for their employment are available. In a fairly clear way, their employment is an additional decision on the part of Menard, one for which he would be additionally responsible, if only because his alternatives were different. He has consciously decided to use a foreign language, and one of a

235

different period, for example. Cervantes simply uses his own language. Thus the history of production, the temporal location of authorship in particular, allows us to find Menard's work more consciously mannered than that of Cervantes.

The upshot, then, is an artificial case where the history of production is crucial; but it illustrates the more general relevance of the history of production both to what we can say about the work and to what work it is. This point is often missed. For example, Wallace (1987: p. 359) says: 'if all I want to say is that it is . . . well painted, it does not matter who painted it'. This cannot be right as it stands. For in Chapter 9, in a discussion of style in relation to intention, we have already seen something very different: finding that a painting previously thought to be the work of painter A was in fact the work of painter B would make us reinterpret the painting; indeed, that it would typically modify our judgement of it. It would do so because A and B would stand in different traditions – or in different places in the same tradition – and this would mean that what could be expected of them would be different. Further, it would typically mean that what counted as 'well painted' for each would be different. So deciding what was and what was not well painted would be no small matter. It would refer to the category in which the work was rightly seen, and this would make reference to the temporal (and possibly spatial) location of composition. Further, in identifying the object in question as *that* painting, it would refer, perhaps implicitly, to the history of production of the painting.

Similar points could be made for dances. What is unintelligible when conceived as a romantic ballet may become perfectly comprehensible when seen as involving 'radical "deviation"' from the norms of classical ballet (Levin, 1983: p. 94). Equally, a dance thought incomprehensible as Ballanchine might make perfectly good sense when seen as employing Cunningham technique. Viewed that way, its expressive potentials are 'decipherable' (see Chapter 9), so that one could then see in it typical romantic themes: 'the intersection of joy and sorrow' (Siegel, 1979: p. 325). That description of Cunningham's *Septet* (1953) could equally be applied to *Swan Lake* (1895). But what could be seen in a particular work depends on us recognizing it as of a particular kind, in a particular category. Further, it is important that the work in question really is Cunningham's *Septet* and not something we mistake for *Septet*, otherwise, we will not know how to see the dance aright. That condition makes implicit reference to the history of production: that it comes, as it were, from Cunningham's hand.

This point suggests that one might identify successful or appropriate ways of seeing the art work with the way the artist saw it: with the

236

artist's fulfilled intentions. Thus Wollheim (1987: p. 86) speaks of 'the fulfilled intention of the artist' as offering a means of distinguishing (in principle) a right and a wrong way to look at art: 'the right way ensures an experience of art that concurs with the fulfilled intention of the artist'. Of course, our interpretation of this idea may differ from Wollheim's, but this much seems correct in it: that one locates the fulfilled intention of the artist by looking at the work itself. Only when we have a reason to doubt an interpretation of a work do we raise the question of whether or not it reflects the fulfilled intention of the artist. It is not the case that one must know these intentions in order to interpret the work; rather, any interpretation which is answerable to the perceptible features of the work, seen appropriately, is an account of the artist's intention, but defeasibly. One way of rejecting the interpretation would be to dispute its right to be regarded as representing the artist's intentions. But to do this is, in ways we have seen, likely also to lead us to doubt the category allocation of the work, and hence the appropriateness of our perception of it.

So my aim in this section is to reject some misconceptions about appealing to the intention of the choreographer, and to reinforce the idea that such appeal is not a way of looking away from the dance, but a method of looking into it.

Choreographer's intention and *Black Angels*

To make this discussion slightly more concrete, I will conclude this chapter with a case study. One way forward would be to look in detail at the way dance critics use (or don't use) reference to choreographer's intention. This will clearly augment the remarks quoted earlier from critics in other art forms. But we are fortunate to have, in the literature on dance, a document which offers another source of insight into choreography: Richard Austin's description of Christopher Bruce's *Black Angels* in his book *Birth of a Ballet* (Austin, 1976). In this work we have description of the design, lighting and music, as well as a day-by-day account of its choreography. For our purpose we can see it as describing what Bruce said, what he did, and to some degree what he thought. Further, Austin observed this process, and his observations may stand for an audience's reaction to the proceeding.

Though the whole text is relevant, I have selected a few typical passages from the account of the early sections of the choreography. It must be remembered that the question here concerns the relevance of these remarks to our understanding of the dance: do we need to know the choreographer's intention in order to understand the work? (That is, do they set a standard for the correctness of the interpretation of the work?) I urge that Austin's description does reveal Bruce's intentions to us, and in ways that our analysis had predicted.

Austin's comments are of many different sorts. So we should consider some typical examples of each, and see how they fit together. First, a general description of the work at its inception, which can serve as an overall account of the dance: 'It is to be a work in which the eternal struggle between light and darkness is to end on a note of hope, the triumph of good over evil' (Austin, 1976: p. 95). If we suppose that this represents (some part of) Bruce's intention, where is the evidence for it? The expectation, based on our analysis of the idea of intention, would be that this general conception would be supported by reference to actual features of the dance. What actually happens next? 'At this stage, the dancers do not listen to the music, but immediately begin work on the first section... At once the choreographer crystallises his ballet around three opening images' (Austin, 1976: p. 95). Yet these images take the form of elements of movement; that is to say, they are not (in any interesting sense) in the head of the choreographer, so that the locating of such intentions on the choreographer's part is indeed available to the audience.

> As the dancers run onto the stage, flung from heaven on the shuddering flight of the music, the first pose is a fall on the right shoulder, the legs hooked grotesquely in the air as if they clutched it for support; they lurch upright in an image of terrible lamentation. They crawl forwards as if swimming through the lake of fire, the heads then raised to gasp at the cool air. One couple cling to each other in their grief; a man stoops while the girl leans backwards across his body, then to be flung from him in a wide-angled leap. (Austin, 1976: p. 95)

These images from the dance then are the sorts of things an observer can understand, say, if he or she were to see the finished dance. A feature of the interpretation here (as typically) is that it relates the understanding of this piece of the dance to a view of the work of the whole; that is, to the general interpretation noted earlier. Austin (1976: p. 97) comments:

> There is, in this first section of the choreography, no sense of the once bright angels of God; these are debased beneath the human, so that

they can only crawl on their bellies like maimed animals through the atrocious fire.

The relevance of this, of course, is that even at this stage the intentions of the choreographer are to be understood in terms of making sense of the movements: they are a matter for interpretation. And the base of that interpretation, as we predicted, lies in the informed perception *of the movements*.

Austin's description of the intentions in the dance typically make this point, connecting behaviour and emotional content. For example, on the next day he comments: 'He (the dancer) looks dazed, even demented, head lolling, eyes sightless and mouth agape. "At this moment" Christopher Bruce tells him, "I want you almost insane, with an empty grin on your face". To Sylvia Yamada he says "I want your body twisted, as if drawn on a rack"' (Austin, 1976: p. 99). Clearly, Austin's interpretation of the dance at this point will be based on what Bruce said and did. But what do we as audience need know to attribute such intentions to the choreographer? The answer is given in a revealing way by Austin. He comments that the dancers 'seem to feel in their limbs the flame of their damnation, sinking and rising again in the lake of fire' (Austin, 1976: p. 99). Again, in this description, once the movements are seen under the characterization supplied by our general view of the work, we are able to interpret (or understand) them. In the relevant case, this means that Austin 'sees' the interpretation in the movements of the dancers, and that interpretation makes implicit reference to what Bruce wants or intends, or how Bruce conceives of the dance. Thus it seems right to characterize it, as we have been doing, in terms of the choreographer's intentions.

Sometimes our access to what Christopher Bruce does is presented in a more direct way. For example, we are told (Austin, 1976: p. 100) that Bruce:

> ... makes the opening statement in three connected images: the first a loping run for all the dancers diagonally across the stage, the little skip after the first five paces; this leads into a defiant stamping dance which Bruce describes as the devil's dance, and this is followed by a groteque little sequence like a drunken tap dance.

Clearly this represents what Bruce intended the dancers to actually do. Do we need to know this? Again, the answer seems to be that knowing it could help us to understand the dance. But equally, this is not achieved by looking into Bruce's head. As before, we can get the relevant knowledge from looking at the movement of the dancers, at least, if our scrutiny is informed by a general understanding of the appropriate dance forms. Moreover, the meaning or impact of these movements is accessible in the same way. Yet again, Austin makes the relevant points here. Talking of 'the range of emotion compressed into these three short sections' (Austin, 1976: p. 100), he refers to this as something the audience can *see* (Austin's word, p. 100). The implication is that we see in these movement sequences 'the running of whipped curs, broken and defeated; then there is this thrust of arrogance, the first assumption of diabolic pride, followed at once by the little jigging dance which is a kind of mockery of simple human joys, now beyond their reach or their understanding' (Austin, 1976: p. 100). Of course it is right to regard these as statements of Bruce's (fulfilled) intentions, for what justifies our use of them is reference to movements of the dancers, rather than to what is 'going on' in Bruce's head.

As will be remembered from Chapter 4, Marcia Siegel (1972: p. 178) makes the following remark: 'It seems absurd to be talking of trailing after the artist, gathering up dances as if they were crumpled memos he'd made to himself and then discarded'. Of course, she is commenting partly on the absence of a satisfactory notation for many dances of the past. But this is also a remark about the role of the choreographer's intention: that one can make sense of dances without such a procedure, and that to do so is *not* to reject the idea of intention. Rather, it is to see one's understanding of the artist's intention as based on the things that he does: in particular, the dance that he makes using the performance styles and the techniques that he sees fit to employ.

Earlier I characterized my view as 'intentionalism made from anti-intentionist materials'. I hope that the justice of that description is apparent by now, for I can imagine the anti-intentionalist – noticing that I have relied on features of the dances themselves, on facts about their history and about the style of dance and dance presentation current at certain times – claiming that I am no intentionalist at all. 'Where', he might ask, 'is the reference to what went on in the artist's head?'. My reply of course is that it is *there* in the discussion of – as we might say, following Kivy (1988: p. 223) – the public documentation of his intentions, of which such things as the features of dances, styles of performance and history of production are parts.

The effect of this brief survey of some of the material on the choreographing of *Black Angels* is to reinforce the position to which theory has led us: that an appeal to intention is not to be a matter for the psychoanalytic couch, but for the informed observer of the dance.

Recommended reading

An insightful yet elementary discussion of this issue is Ground, 1989: pp. 31–60; a clear, if complex view is Wollheim, 1983. Useful, although indirectly, is Danto, 1981: pp. 1–53. The whole context of this chapter is provided by discussion of the 'intentional fallacy' (see Chapter 11, note 1), in a context raised in Chapter 6. Hence the readings for Chapter 6 are also relevant.

12

Expression in Dance

It seems to me inevitable that aestheticians will continue to 'consider the vicissitudes of expressiveness as a constituent of the concept of art' (Wollheim, 1973: p. 116). Hence it seems inevitable that there will be continued discussion of the expressiveness of dance. This is unfortunate for, as this chapter will show, the notion of expressiveness takes us no further in the understanding of art – although discussion of it may suggest other metaphors or images which do take us further. If this is indeed progress, it is because the notion of understanding looms large, a feature typically ignored in accounts of expression (for example, Osborne [1982]). If we add this feature it transfers our interest from expression to understanding.

The argument of this chapter is fairly straightforward. I will state it here, and then go on to elucidate (and demonstrate) each of its premises: (a) the expressiveness of dance is like the expressiveness of the other arts, *not* like expression in movement; (b) therefore, expression in dance must be characterized using what David Best calls 'artistic' rather than 'aesthetic' concepts, and hence, the reasons employed in the discussion of the expressiveness of dance are dance reasons; (c) therefore, dance must be found to be expressive – which means it must be understood; (d) such understanding is conventional and therefore learned, hence a crucial notion will be understanding (what Wollheim (1979) calls decipherability). Finally, in the light of these claims, the chapter will consider two crucial questions. First, is all dance expressive? Second, expressive of what?

Expressiveness in dance versus expressiveness in movement

The first thing to be urged is that the problem of expression in dance is just a specific case of the general problem of expression for works of art. That is to say, the question to be answered is, 'How can the thought, feeling or whatever be *in* the object, action and so on?' How can a dance be happy, sad? Expressiveness is regularly, and surely rightly, taken as a feature of works of art, and hence as integral to the concept of art. It is unsurprising that the question of its character arises for the art form dance. That is to say, we are concerned with a sort of expressiveness characteristic of art. Let us consider a particular example. In discussing one of Rothko's *Four Seasons* canvases, Wollheim (1973: p. 128) says:

> The greatness of Rothko's painting lies ultimately in its expressive quality, and if we wanted to characterise this quality – it would be a crude characterisation – we would talk of a form of suffering and sorrow, and somehow barely or fragilely contained.

It is to similar sorts of remarks, but for dance, that we are referring in speaking of accounts of the expressiveness or expressive qualities of dance.[1] And here, of course, it is relevant that we do not care whether or not our dancers are themselves sad. Their states of mind are as irrelevant as the absence of any state of mind – because of the absence of any mind – in the painting Wollheim discusses. But recognizing that this is indeed our topic, when we consider expression in dance, is actually a large step forward, for it means that questions of expression in dance are not assimilated to more general questions concerning the expressiveness of *movement*.

To clarify this matter we can draw on a distinction constructed by David Best (1978a: pp. 138–62), for the notion of 'communication'. Best's point is that the term 'communication' is popularly used in two quite different ways, and to conflate these two uses is to mislead oneself. We can say that the term 'expression' has two similar uses. For the purposes of clarity, Best proposes to mark the difference in an explicit way: that is, by contrasting *lingcomm* with *percomm* (although later acknowledging that it may be better not to use the term 'communication' at all where the percomm sense is the appropriate one). The fundamental difference is between cases where the *intention* to transmit information is embodied (lingcomm) and those where it is not (percomm). As Best (1978a: pp. 139–40) notes, one may learn much about a person from things that he does in situations where he does not intend that one learn anything (from the way he walks or wears his hat, or whatever). But these cases differ crucially from cases where it is his intention that one learn from those things. For example, if bored at a meeting you might yawn. Another person, seeing this (perfectly natural) yawn might infer that you were bored. This would be percomm in Best's terminology, because although one person's behaviour allowed another to find out something about him, it was not something the yawner intended; indeed, it might be something he profoundly wished to conceal.

That this situation is importantly structured by the percomm character of the learning can be brought out (as Best does [1978a: p. 140]) by considering the case where the same basic behaviour appears as lingcomm, or communication manifesting the intention to communicate. At the boring meeting, you catch the eye of a friend and then yawn elaborately. Here you are intending that he notice and trying to tell him how boring you find the meeting. If he does not take this into account, if he mistakes this yawn for a natural yawn, he will not understand what is going on. In order to characterize what went on, then, one must distinguish the lingcomm yawn from the percomm one. Failure to do so will lead one to a misunderstanding or mischaracterization of the situation.

Best's point about communication is that it is a mistake to run together these two kinds of case – as is often done in using the expression 'non-verbal communication'. As the example above shows, what is non-verbal may none the less be of either sort. (This point, if accepted, should count heavily against those who treat disparate cases in the same way: for example, the deaf sign language, which is lingcomm, and the positions of the body of candidates at interviews, which is at best percomm.) So one must be very careful, in thinking about communication, to distinguish communication of the sort embodying the intention to communicate from those situations where this intention is absent, but where one person can still learn about another.

Best's examples clearly demonstrate the existence of this distinction: a similar distinction can be drawn within our normal uses of the term 'expression' for human movements. Sometimes, in using that word – calling a particular movement 'expressive' – we mean simply to imply that feelings or ideas can be gleaned from that movement. Here we have a parallel for Best's percomm: there is no intention to be expressive 'behind' the movement. It is at this point the contrast between expressiveness in dance and expressiveness in movement becomes central. In the case of art forms such as dance the intention to be expressive is built into the activity. Objects constructed under concepts appropriate to dance, viewed as art, will have this explicitly expressive dimension, as we shall see. That is to say, anything put forward under the general category of art is put forward as expressive, or as communicative (a point to be reconsidered and modified later).

Thus, even if we do speak of the expression of thoughts or feelings in senses roughly analogous to both lingcomm and percomm senses, it is clear that the lingcomm sense is the crucial one for us. To be expressive is to be seen under concepts appropriate to expressiveness, and these import the intention to express. Since the problem of expression for dance is just a special case of the general problem of artistic

244

expression, we have a reason for paying attention to the arts in general, not just dance; from there we will come to understand artistic expression.

From the fact that expressiveness in dance is a specific case of expression in the arts in general, one might conclude that expressiveness in dance depends on works being constructed (or perceived) under concepts appropriate to art. This is surely right. Yet such a view will still be vitiated by misconceived ideas of what it is to *express* something. We shall consider two such misconceptions at the end of the chapter.

Expression and artistic concepts

If we are to follow up the idea that expressiveness in dance is a species of expressiveness in the arts in general, we will need to improve our understanding of what it is to confront art as art. The crucial distinction here is between 'artistic' judgement and appreciation (our judgement of works of art) and 'aesthetic' judgement and appreciation (our judgement of natural beauty, of fountains and firework displays, perhaps better called 'merely aesthetic' judgement). It must also be remembered (from Chapter 1) that these different kinds of judgement and appreciation could equally be spoken of as different experiences, for all experience is concept-mediated: it takes place under concepts. As the concepts under which an object is experienced change, so the experiences might be thought of as different. (Indeed, this is pretty much the only sense which could be given to the idea of 'different experiences'.)

But what are the crucial artistic concepts? Certainly no complete list can be given; and for each, an analysis of the different uses to which that concept can be put is needed. (Wollheim [1979] has begun this task for the concept 'style', and we have used that work in Chapter 9.) But typical concepts here would be 'form', 'style', 'unity', 'beauty', and also some which bear on what Cavell (1979: p. xiv) speaks of as 'what its extremities of beauty are in service of'.

How are such concepts learned? The answer seems fairly clear. We learn to use them by seeing them used in other cases, in other works of art. (Note the way in which art appreciation courses typically operate by studying works which function as exemplars[2] in categories of art, or of typical artistic concepts.) So our understanding of the functioning of these concepts depends on their operation in earlier works of art. In this respect, our employment of any of these concepts in appreciation of a particular work of art relates that work to the history of art, and to the history of that art form. Obviously a key artistic concept will be expression.

We have concluded thus far, first, that artistic concepts must be brought to bear if one is to see a sequence of movement as dance and, second, that any account of the expressiveness of dance must do justice to the intention to express. There is something very natural about that second conclusion, if one reflects on the way the artist is responsible (in both senses of the word) for his art work. But this is not to say that every feature of every object which is art is intentional, nor even that all art is straightforwardly intentional. Readymades[3] provide a clear counter-example to such a claim. And one might wonder about aleatory (chance) compositional methods (but see Chapter 9 [Siegel, 1979: p. 193]). So what is to be our response? Consider in this context two remarks by Cavell (1969: p. 235 and p. 235n):

I do not wish to claim that everything we find in a work of art is something that we have to be prepared to say that the artist intended to put there. But I am claiming that our not being so prepared *must* be exceptional.

Our concept of a work of art is such that what is not intended in it has to be thought of, or explained, in contrast to intention, at the same level as intention, as the qualification of a human action...

This seems to me exactly right. Here, as often, we are reminded that our understanding of, and our judgement of, works of art in general – in our particular case, works of dance – is answerable to reasons in the last analysis. One can explain why dance A is more interesting, powerful than dance B. Perhaps I who make the judgement am not able to do this explaining myself, but at least I will recognize an answer that satisfies me, and perhaps a host of unsatisfactory answers that will both prompt me to search my own answer and suggest materials to me. As Cavell points out, these answers assume the art work is intentionally created, and when that assumption is defeated in a particular case, that fact too must be explicable.

In trying to understand the various dances, then, I make the assumption that their creators intended them as expressive objects, objects open to interpretation. The role and importance of expression comes out clearly if we consider the aesthetically (artistically) central notion 'style' and in particular if we consider this notion in the fashion of Wollheim. Wollheim's work on individual style brings out clearly that commitment to intention (that is, an instantiation of the intention to

246

express) which the comparison with communication also brought out. Style is a precondition of expressiveness because the assumption of intention logically precedes finding the work expressive. But, as we have seen (Chapter 9), not merely is style a precondition of expressiveness; style also has *psychological reality* (Wollheim, 1979: p. 134). This means that the author's commitment to expression is quite explicit. To say of a work by a particular artist that it is in the style of that artist is to say, roughly that it is true to (and based on) his thoughts, ideas and feelings and so on.

Yet what does this commitment bring with it? What can we learn from it about understanding dance? The crucial point is that we can only take a particular dance this way, seeing it as expressive, by bringing to bear on it concepts used in finding other dances expressive. This means (again) that it is a prerequisite for understanding works of art that the traditions and conventions of the particular art form are brought to bear: in our case, we must view the object both as dance, and as dance of a certain sort, utilizing a particular technique and particular expressive resources.

Before further elaborating this idea of intelligibility, we must recognize that, in finding dances intelligible, we must appeal to reasons – not, perhaps, reasons we could give if asked, but reasons we would accept if they were offered by someone else (say, a critic). In finding the dance expressive, indeed, in confronting the movement as dance, we in effect point to features of what is going on that we see as important or valuable (or, equally, harmful) to the performance of whatever it is. To put that another way, certain things have the status of reasons for any judgement that we make; we would justify those judgements in terms of those reasons.

But what sorts of thing can acquire the status of reasons, what sorts of features are valuable? In answering this question we must bear in mind that we are talking of artistic or dance value here, so to present features as, say, of biomechanical value would be beside the point (see Chapter 2). The reasons we give must be dance or artistic reasons. Now if we ask how any fact can acquire the status of a dance reason, the reply must be that it acquires this status by reference to what has gone before in dance, that is, to the practice of dance, dance theory and dance criticism. Not that slavish adherence to the practices of the past is prescribed by this recognition. It may seem that, in order to be intelligible, works must be like those of the past. This may seem to rule out innovation. But this is not so. The ideas of a revolutionary are dependent on those of the society (or whatever) against which he is rebelling: his ideas are only intelligible in terms of theirs (see Scruton, 1983: pp.

22–4). Yet his ideas can and, doubtless, will be radically different. In a similar way, the behaviour of dancers is only intelligible to us as dance, and as expressive, if its concepts connect with concepts familiar to us – and in speaking of 'its concepts' I intend both what it expresses and (more importantly) how. Thus the question, 'Is this movement sequence a part of dance?', is answered by reference to what has gone before in dance. It is because this is so that we can, in general, rule out my carrying my philosophy books to the library as a dance sequence. So the reasons operating here must be dance reasons. Indeed, this is what it means to see the movement as dance, or to apply artistic concepts to it.

We have also recognized a constraint on this procedure: not just any-thing would count as dance movement, although the differences between what was and what was not dance movement might well have nothing to do with the bodily movements in question and rather a lot to do with the context within which they take place. Thus, while the possibilities of a medium are not 'givens' (having to be invented or dis-covered) they are not infinite in number. Not just anything counts as a work in that medium. It is not a case of 'anything goes'; nor of what is dance in my opinion as opposed to what is dance in your opinion. As we have seen (Chapter 1), to dismiss the issue as 'subjective' is to fail to grasp certain important features of reasoning and of rationality (see McFee, 1984: pp. 106–12).

Let us recap our progress to this point. Having decided to treat the problem of expression in dance as one case of the general problem of artistic expression, we found that assumption imported the (justified) dependence of artistic expression on the intention to express. And we saw how the intention to express brought with it, first, the requirement that expression be intelligible and, second (as a consequence), reference to the traditions and conventions of that art form.

Expression and understanding

Since we have already accepted the key point that one learns to use the concept 'expression', like other artistic concepts, it follows that only when I can employ that concept (when I can *find* the work expressive) will it be expressive. This means that I must be able to do what Wollheim (1979: p. 133) speaks of as 'deciphering' the work of art, for this is just what it means to be able to apply these concepts.

To better understand this point we should approach it indirectly, via an important question about the nature of expression: namely, what is

the mechanism of expression, or how can works of art be expressive?
First, as Bouwsma (1965) makes clear, works of art are not sad in the
way that, say, humans are. We can understand a sad person who didn't
look sad, but a sad work of art is one which looks (or sounds) sad: there
is nothing other than that. Still, the manifestations here are not like
those of humans either. To put it figuratively, art works don't cry. But
this might be a more difficult point to accept for dance than for the other
arts. With dance we are confronted with the human body, the very
same body that does laugh, wave and so on. The antidote here lies in
remembering the point made initially: that we are considering artistic
expression in all cases. Equally, the representation of crying is insufficient to make a painting sad. Goodman (1978: p. 23) offers, as a useful
oversimplification, the thought that *content* is what a work of art says,
while *style* is how it is said. In terms of such a contrast, we could say
that expression is a stylistic feature. By contrast, representational
characteristics, such as the representation of crying, belong to the
'content' aspects of the work, rather than the 'expressive' or 'stylistic'
aspects. Nor can we glibly assume that sad works of art symbolize
sadness. Symbolic theories of meaning are too suspect for that (Best,
1978a: pp. 123–37; also Chapter 5). Such works certainly do not stand
for sadness; rather, they are sad.

This might be put by saying that expressive properties are 'tertiary'
or 'emergent' properties (Pole, 1983: pp. 105–9; Scruton, 1983: pp.
28–31): not something subjective, of course, but that sort of feature of
a system the recognition of which requires human understanding. But
the expressive qualities of dances are not merely emergent, or tertiary:
as we have seen (Chapter 3), they are also conventional. One learns to
find certain forms and combinations of forms expressive. If this answer
were right, it would explain why so little useful material has been developed on the 'mechanism' of expression, as I am calling it. There simply
is no answer as such to how works of art are expressive. One simply
learns to find them so. Like discussions of 'aesthetic attitudes',
discussion of expressiveness is the end of the line, something about
which nothing can usefully be said (see Wollheim, 1980a: p. 111).

However, it seems to me that two important conclusions for
aesthetics can be drawn from this discussion. First, and explicitly, we
see the general unhelpfulness of the notion of expression (in itself). The
expression that interested us was the peculiar expressiveness of works
of art, and we see why little of interest could be said about that. But
second, and implicitly, our consideration of expression throws us time
and time again into discussion of notions such as decipherability, intelligibility or understanding. The conclusion I offer, although not fully

argued here, is that aestheticians' time would be better spent confronting such notions directly, rather than reaching them mediated by the notion of expression (Beardsmore, 1973: pp. 23–46).

To develop this point, let us consider again one final question: is all art expressive?, or for our purposes, is all dance expressive? Such a question could never be answered in the affirmative directly, for one would need a transcendental argument to show that art *must* be expressive. Instead, one might adopt one of two strategies – although these may come to the same thing if we both follow Wollheim (1979: p. 133) in taking 'expressive' here to mean decipherable (as we have), and accept that to be decipherable is to be subject to acceptable interpretations. The more impressionistic strategy – the one mentioned in Chapter 7 – consists in reflecting on the centrality of the idea of expression for the notion of art. As we saw, this strategy amounts to offering a Humean challenge: would we be willing to accept as art something which neither we nor anyone else found expressive? But when we ask someone what makes him think a particular object is a work of art, his answer involves, perhaps tacitly, an appeal to the history and traditions of the art form in question. In offering reasons for the judgement, we draw connections between the work under consideration and other works in the same art form. Art works of the past are taken as bearing on the lives of people, as modifying their thoughts or feelings, as making them see or understand differently, or some such. That is to say, those works are taken as expressive. So we would expect any justification of the art status of a particular object to at least make reference to such expressiveness.

However, a second more rigorous strategy is also open to us. Having accepted that works of art such as dances are essentially interpreted objects, we need only develop the notion of an interpretation, establishing a link with 'what is expressed' in the dances, to demonstrate at least the plausibility of urging that all dance is expressive. And this strategy will connect with the one described above, for both will emphasize how giving reasons for judgements or interpretations connects the understanding of a particular work with the understanding of other works. Moreover, much of the material necessary for such a discussion of interpretation is already at hand (from Chapters 4 and 6), so I will present it here briefly and dogmatically. Certainly, we must consider what, in Chapter 4, was called the critic's interpretation: not what the performer does to turn the type into a performance, but what the critic or observer does in making sense of a particular performance. Speaking of the work as expressive directs our attention to those who find it expressive: its audience. But the critic's interpretation of a particular dance is not just a string of words; it explains the meaning of a dance to me (Chapter 5). In doing so, it brings the dance to me, for I understand the dance more, as it were, through the interpretation. So that when Marcia Siegel's (1977: pp. 205–6) discussion of *Seraphic Dialogue* (1955) (quoted in Chapter 6) gives me an understanding of the dance, it does so by changing my experience of the dance. And, if I am able to 'find in myself' the sorts of problems to which it offers an answer (Chapters 7 and 8), then it can alter my understanding by bringing about conceptual changes (Chapter 8 and elsewhere). These conceptual changes will typically be in relation to that heterogeneous conglomeration that we spoke of as 'life issues' or 'life situations'. But the changes thus brought about are not merely changes of the understanding, not merely what we sometimes call cognitive changes. Rather, since I am able to mobilize these new concepts in my experience, they modify how I see some issue (the example used in Chapter 8 was the concept 'love', drawing on Durrell's *Alexandria Quartet*) and hence how I experience both the art work and the world.

Thus far I have articulated the conception of critic's interpretation that we have been building up in this text. But why should this picture lead one to think that all dances were expressive? To answer, we must return to the idea of life issues or life situations, an idea central to the account of interpretation just stated. In Chapter 8, I spoke of the life issues connection as operating in two different ways: 'through a palliation of the unsatisfactory aspects: man's fallibility, inhumanity, and the like'; but also through 'a *celebration* of the desirable aspects of human life and experience: landscape, love and so on'. I quote these ideas again here because they so obviously pick out the sorts of things art works are typically thought to express. Recall Wollheim (1973: p. 128, quoted earlier), speaking of Rothko in terms of 'a form of suffering and of sorrow, and somehow barely or fragilely contained'. What he is doing here is bringing out for us how the work in question is expressive, and of what. That expressiveness is of a piece with what we have been speaking of as 'a conception of life issues or life situations', for it is what the work of art expresses not least because it also describes the outcome of our confrontation with the work itself – what, if we were clear that this was not cause/effect language, we could speak of as the effect of the work on us.

Has this discussion really connected the interpretation of dance to 'what is expressed' in dances? We can see it has by considering two additional facts. First, we have seen that the meaning of the dance is

251

given through explanation of the dance. Such explanation (a) is done by critics' interpretations and (b) typically contains references to expressiveness or expressive qualities, or to something as expressed. To repeat one example, Marcia Siegel (1979: p. 41, quoted in Chapter 7) speaks of 'a very ritualised depersonalised kind of grief' in *Lamentation* (1930). So theory tells us that the claims of critics, once properly understood, make plain the meaning of the dance. And those comments typically make reference to expression. But – the second fact – these critics' interpretations operate on us in such a way as to change our experience of the dance (by changing the concepts under which we experience it). Hence they change not merely what we think about the dances, but what we feel about them, and this is what is usually meant by 'what the dance expresses'. Thus we have indeed connected interpretation and expression.

There is, of course, much more to the story, only some of which is crucial now. We must say a little more about how the critic's interpretation is formed; about its roots, as we might say. Clearly the practicalities are roughly as described in Chapter 1: the critic merely looks and sees. But his seeing is shaped by artistic concepts. When he comes to make sense of a particular dance he again brings these concepts to bear. Yet where does this understanding of these concepts come from? Again, practically, the answer might be 'from his training or apprenticeship in criticism'. Applied to the audience more generally, this amounts to saying that it comes from their experience of dance, and of viewing dance. But this just means that we are drawing connections, perhaps implicit ones, to what we have previously learned of dances: the concepts to apply to them, the way to see them and so on. In short, we are drawing on the history and tradition of the art form in question.

This is of importance for two related reasons. First, only in this way can the critic make sense of the dance; only in this way can he find the dance intelligible. Second, it is only in this way that he can view it as dance at all, rather than, say, as just a sequence of movement. Finding the dance intelligible amounts to finding it expressive. But this is not easy to show. In the first instance, this is perhaps most easily seen from the point of view of the artist, although of course the intelligibility requirement applies everywhere (not only to those performing or constructing the work). Here things work out in practice just as theory predicts. In the learning of technique and of specific dances, dancers and choreographers acquire a grasp of what Noel Carroll (1981: p. 102) rightly calls 'the repertory of traditional choices'. This knowledge provides the basis for their consideration of dances. As Carroll (1981: p. 102) continues: 'When the dancers become choreographers, they can mine this vast reservoir of information intuitively'. And in this context, the word 'intuitively' means just that the choreographers can do it without there necessarily being a path of reasoning which they would avow.

But what makes these traditional choices important is that we have learned to understand them: we can make sense of them. This allows us to find them expressive. And anything that is to be intelligible to us must depend in this way on what we have learned to understand. Only in that case do we have the relevant concepts, the appropriate cognitive stock.

The context of Carroll's discussion, of course, is those 'non-literal' dances where the choreographer insists that the dance does not express anything. Again, similar sorts of claims have been made by creators in other art forms. Naturally, one doesn't want to take these artists' word for it. Rather the plausibility of their claim must be analysed.

As Carroll's discussion shows, two things must be recognized here. The first is the essentially polemical nature of this stance: the artists in question are trying to make a point about the fundamental nature of their respective art forms. Perhaps the strongest parallel for dance is with music, where an answer given to questions about the nature of music was that music was sound, nothing but sound. Similarly, non-literal choreographers might be taken as saying that movement was the medium of dance, and this amounts to claiming that dance was 'just' movement. The outcome of any discussion here is to relate this polemical answer to previous answers (or at least to previous questions). For the response 'movement', as an answer to questions about the nature of dance is not so much wrong as it is incorrectly formulated. The medium of dance is not just any movement, it is dance movement (which is the same as saying that dance reasons must explain it). What makes the answer 'movement' a polemical answer is the extent to which those who would give it would also distinguish sharply between what they do under the title 'dance' and what has been done before. Thus we see why their claims about the non-expressiveness of dance must be taken with a pinch of salt, for these claims are intended polemically.

The second point about the nature of expression connects with the one just developed: that, as Paul Ziff (1981: p. 107) said in discussion of Carroll's paper, we are becoming clear of the sense 'in which expressing nothing was to express something, and that is inevitable in the context of the dance'. Once we accept the dependence on previous works in the form, first, of our understanding of a movement sequence as a piece of dance and, second, of our deciphering of it, and once we see those previous works being treated as expressive, it will be difficult to put something into that same context without finding it expressive too. Difficult, but perhaps not impossible. Yet if someone offered me what they claimed was a genuinely non-expressive dance, I would want to reply after the fashion of Cavell, quoted earlier, on intention: that what does not invoke expression in art must be thought of in contrast to expression, at the same level as expression, as a modification of human thought and feeling. So I am suggesting that works of art will typically be thought or found to be expressive, but that this is a defeasible condition: that it may not hold in every case (Baker, 1977). Still, we must expect that any dance that was not straightforwardly expressive none the less did make contact with human thoughts or feelings or emotions, or some such. To repeat the Humean challenge, what motive could one have for taking a movement sequence to be art (that is, to be dance) if it lacked this contact with the human, particularly since works of art typically make this contact?

In this context, then, I am offering the guarded answer that all dance will be found to be expressive, for the reasons given above. But notice how little that actually says. What it really means is that dance will be taken to be a suitable object for understanding, and found decipherable. Saying this is again highlighting that it is understanding that is the central topic of aesthetics. Recall that Scruton (1983: p. 77) urged this point for musical aesthetics by saying 'it must be wrong to attempt to give a theory of musical expression which cannot be rewritten as a theory of musical understanding'. My aim in this chapter has been to make a similar plea for attention to the understanding of dance.

Expressive of what?

To conclude the chapter, I want to fill in my account by raising one further point, and this makes good an earlier promise. It might be asked *what* works of art, such as dances, express. I prefer to remain silent on this question, giving the following two reasons for doing so. First, and most simply, however one responds there is inevitably something left out. Peter Strawson (1974: p. 185) remarks, on the description of works of art:

The only method of describing a work of art, which . . . is entirely adequate for the purpose of aesthetic appraisal . . . is to say "It goes like this" – and then reproduce it. And, of course, this is not a method of describing it at all.

Similarly, one might speak of a particular work of art, say, Picasso's *Guernica* or Christopher Bruce's *Black Angels* (1976), as an expression of man's inhumanity to man, or of human frailty. Yet of course this would not distinguish either of these works from numerous other works. Moreover, the description could certainly be augmented to distinguish any particular work from any particular other, but the point is rather that any such augmentation would not finally distinguish the work in question from *all* others. Unlike reports of, say, car accidents, exact equivalents of works of art (not themselves merely tokens of the same type) cannot be constructed: not in ordinary language, and not in the form of other works of art in the same or in a different medium. To think otherwise amounts to urging that, as Betty Redfern (1979: p. 18, a passage quoted in Chapter 8) notes:

> There would be no need to see, for example, Martha Graham's *Night Journey* since we could get at the same experience by listening to Stravinski's *Oedipus Rex*; and neither of them need really have bothered since Sophocles had already "said" it all in *Oedipus Tyrannus* centuries before.

The conclusion to be drawn here is that no satisfactory unitary account of what is expressed can be given.

The second reason for refusing to be drawn on what is expressed is really a generalization of the first. Even if (like me) one is impressed with the idea that, say, all art forms allow for the possibility of the expression of a conception of life issues (see Chapter 8), this is centrally a generalization from the specific expressiveness of specific works of art. At this point it may useful to record Wittgenstein's (1958: p. 160; Wollheim, 1980a: section 41, pp. 93–6) distinction between transitive and intransitive uses of a particular term. When I say of someone that he has a peculiar walk, I may be going on to discuss or to describe the walk (transitive use of 'peculiar'), or I may simply have said all that I have to say in pointing out its peculiarity (intransitive use of 'peculiar'). In this second case, one would say that the whole walk was peculiar: it all contributed to the peculiarity. Clearly (Wollheim, 1980a: section 41, pp. 93–6; Scruton, 1983: p. 50) the term 'expression' has both transitive and intransitive uses. But equally clearly, talk of expression in dance tends to use the term intransitively: we do not intend the further question 'expressive of what?'. When, as in Wollheim's judgement of Rothko (quoted earlier) we offer *an* answer – speaking of the work as expressing a 'barely or fragilely contained' sorrow – our remarks can never be made fully specific, so that they apply only to that work and to no others. There is always *something* to be said about the expressiveness of works of art, but never *everything*.

Two misconceived ideas of what it is to express something typically further confuse this vexed issue. The first of these assumes that what is expressed by a dance is some thought or feeling on the part of the dancer. Or, in some versions, on the part of the choreographer. Such a view should be dismissed as unacceptably dualistic (Best, 1974: pp. 153–72), because either it takes those thoughts or feelings to be the logically private property of dancer or choreographer or, if it doesn't do that, it lacks substance. To see what is wrong with the first option, we need to rehearse again Wittgenstein's argument against the possibility of a private language.

This argument could be presented in many forms,[4] but at its simplest it comes down to this: suppose that words and feelings were given their meanings in some logically private way, such that the giver could not be wrong in his use of them and no one else could know these meanings. In this situation the 'giver' would be unable even in his own case to, as Putnam (1982: p. 122) put it:

... [make] sense of the distinction between *being right* and *thinking* he is right; and that means that there is, in the end, no distinction between *asserting* or *thinking* on the one hand, and *making noises* (or producing mental images) on the other. But this means that (on this conception) I am not a *thinker* at all but a *mere* animal. To hold such a view is to commit a sort of mental suicide.

As Putnam says, only when it is possible to maintain the distinction between thinking one is right and actually being right can one understand even one's own words (Wittgenstein, 1953: section 258), even in one's own 'sayings in the head'. (Wittgenstein makes the point eloquently about *belief* and about *memory* [1953, sections 260 and 271].) In order that feeling words be meaningful, they must have connection with other language uses, and that means with other language users! The 'privacy' doctrine is untenable.

The other alternative here would be to concede that the thoughts or feeling as expressed by the dance were indeed publicly available, shareable. Then the force of insisting that they were nevertheless the thoughts or feelings of a particular dancer or choreographer disappears. So, on either alternative, this view of expression is misconceived.

A second misconception about expression is best introduced by an example. It is often assumed that a work that presents or discusses, say, grief is a work that expresses grief. This is clearly wrong, if one reflects on certain simple examples. One might, for instance, take all paintings of the Crucifixion to have the same 'story', but some are expressive of the (religious) glory of the event, others of pain, and so on. What I am urging then is that the expression of any work of art, in our case a dance, should not be identified with the subject of that work. This means that, for expository purposes, there is a useful (if tendentious) distinction – previously mentioned and due to Goodman – to be drawn between the content and the expression of that work of art. For example, discussion of a feature film might bring up a question about the 'world' or 'values' of that particular piece. Such a concern might be countered in either of two ways. It might ask no more than the nature of the values portrayed or presented in the film, or again it might ask about the values expressed (where these are not necessarily the same). To see the difference, we might say that the first were (roughly) the values of the characters or the society portrayed, while the second were (roughly) the artist's values, the ones which 'come through' the film. Although such a contrast is an oversimplification, it will serve to locate the expressive features of a work of art within the stylistic features.

Lest it be thought that these two misconceptions of expression never appear in discussion of dance, both can be found in one chapter of a book which, while no longer new, is still widely read: namely H'Doubler's *Dance: A Creative Art Experience* (1940). She speaks of one of the 'problems of obtaining sincerity of feeling and clarity of communication [as] . . . that of conveying the emotion that is central to the dance' (H'Doubler, 1940: p. 85). As the context makes plain, she thinks of this emotion to be conveyed as the private (she says 'invisible' and 'mental') property of the dancer – which is the first misconception. Later she is critical of 'conscious imitation as blind copying' (H'Doubler, 1940: p. 97), but has already made clear that, in her view, expression in dance consists in the presentation of movements characteristic of certain thoughts and feelings. She comments: 'Every emotion has its appropriate and peculiar movement. There is a movement of joy, rage, excitement, peace, fear, devotion, and so on through the list of feeling states' (H'Doubler, 1940: pp. 88–9). But thinking of expression in this fashion is misconceiving it in the second way highlighted above. A presentation of any of these emotions in a dance will not necessarily result in the dance being expressive of the emotion in question.

To put the matter the other way around, consider the following from Marcia Siegel (1977: p. 199):

Graham's dances speak of the American temperament; of religion, of rite and atavism; of the anguish of artists and the obligation of kings; and of women's struggle for dominance without guilt.

This seems to me a superb account of the expressiveness of the dances under discussion. But how is it to be understood? The worry here is that an interpreter who takes Siegel either to be discussing Graham's private thoughts (since she calls Graham's work 'personal' [Siegel, 1977: p. 199]) or just presenting the story of the pieces: that is to say, this critical comment might be read – misread – in terms of either of the two misconceptions highlighted above. While Siegel says neither of these things, those interpretations will only become unavailable if one recognizes these misconceptions.

In fact, both kinds of misconception actually turn on the same point (see Wollheim, 1973: pp. 85–9). In both cases what is expressed is being seen as independent of the particular work in question: specifically, independent of the medium of expression. The first misconception seeks to divorce the work from the expression by locating the expression in the private, subjective domain of a particular person; hence it seeks to separate the expression from the actual work of art. The second misconception works in the opposite direction. It finds the expression on the surface of the work, in a way which ignores the 'how' of the production. If we accepted Goodman's oversimplification (mentioned earlier), then content would be what a work of art says, style how it is said. In terms of such a contrast, expression would indeed be a stylistic feature. Nor should that be a surprising conclusion, at least for those of us who accept Wollheim's account of individual style for artists (see Chapter 9), for, as we have seen, he urges that style is a precondition of expressiveness.

So we have identified three misconceptions to be avoided. First, there is no useful general account of what is expressed. Second, it is a mistake to think of the expressiveness of dance in terms of the expression of emotions of dancers, audience or choreographers. Finally, we must not equate expressiveness with any 'content' feature of the work. In general, these points again reinforce the overall contention that analysis of the concept of expression is not a fruitful way forward for aesthetics.

Conclusion

The outcome of this chapter, as identified initially, is chiefly negative. It directs attention away from the concept of expression, and towards the idea of understanding, for we saw that finding dances expressive presupposed some sense of understanding them. The bulk of the chapter has concerned itself with elaborating and elucidating the connection between understanding and expressiveness. The final conclusion applies to dance an idea which Scruton (1983: p. 77, in a passage already quoted) articulates for music: any theory of expression could be rewritten as a theory of understanding. The outcome, of course, is a re-direction of our studies in aesthetics towards such a theory of understanding. In *this* sense, the chapter has a positive dimension.

Recommended reading

Key texts here are Wollheim, 1973: pp. 84–100; Carroll, 1981; Danto, 1981: pp. 165–208; Scruton, 1983: pp. 49–62, 77–100. A neat summary is Sparshott, 1988: pp. 348–50.

PART V

Applications and Implications

13
Aesthetic Education

Some Myths

This chapter presents some material of a very broadly negative character, in an attempt to eradicate a number of major misconceptions which relate to aesthetic education in dance. It might be urged that a great number of myths of aesthetic education have already been exposed, and that, in so far as the aim of dance study is *aesthetic* education (in so far as the aim of dance is an *artistic* aim), exposing myths about dance follows as a consequence of that other work. Such objections would be further strengthened when it is understood that this chapter simply draws together arguments and conclusions from other sources. But I offer two replies. First, and minimally, it is useful to have the arguments (with a commentary) in one place, together with references to their original appearances. This may be particularly useful in a book used for beginners in aesthetics. Second, clarity may be gained from reframing, using dance examples, some arguments originally cast in terms of painting or drama (Eisner, 1974; Bolton, 1981). A third and more powerful speculation would be that this process of drawing together and reframing allows something unforeseen to appear; this speculation is especially plausible, given our earlier remarks (for example, in Chapter 4) on the performing art status of dance.

In discussing these myths, the aim is to free the aesthetic educator from misconceptions about the nature of the goals or aims appropriate to dance. There is little worse for the development of a coherent and plausible account of aesthetic education than approaching it with one's vision clouded by unreasonably romantic conceptions of children, of creativity and of aesthetic activity. The need for a clear view requires the combination of a number of strategies, in addition to the one employed here. First, one requires general remarks on the character of dance in education. Some of these can be found implicitly or explicitly in Chapter 8 (see also McFee, 1989a). But the literature offers us a number of more elaborate, if less closely argued, expositions of this theme (for example, Redfern, 1983; Redfern, 1986). A second strategy requires a lucid account of aesthetic assessment and its educational relevance: for example, of the kind given by Aspin (1981). Some of this material is implicit in earlier comments; in particular, those on subjectivity in Chapter 1.

The very idea of a kinaesthetic sense

The topic of kinaesthesis, or of a kinaesthetic sense, haunts the aesthetics of dance. Some writers speak as though it were obvious that we have a kinaesthetic sense (see Arnold, 1979: p. 90); others as though the notion of kinaesthesis were merely a convenient layman's expression for a set of mechanisms best thought of via the technical terms of science (see Dickenson, 1974). But, at least if the notion is to have an interesting use for us in our thoughts about the aesthetics of dance, it must make some contribution to the meaning and/or understanding of dance (or of dances). But it is sometimes thought to do just that: 'the felt tension evokes a kinaesthetic response that makes possible the perception of meaning in the work of art'.[1]

My discussion[2] asks if it makes sense to talk of a 'kinaesthetic sense'; and to what extent our understanding of dance can be modelled on, or seen as involving (or some such) a contribution from a kinaesthetic sense. Clearly the second issue is the more important for the understanding of dance. To summarize my position; the notion of a kinaesthetic sensory modality is counter-productive. If we think of it as a sense (to be understood in terms of, and modelled on, the other sensory modalities) it is a fraud. There is no such sense. If we think of it in some other way, it is far from clear what can be made of 'a kinaesthetic sense'. Other art forms depend only in a very roundabout way on the specific details of specific sensory modalities. I for one should be horrified to think that dance, an art form I greatly admire and to which I have given much of my time, should enjoy that kind of unique notoriety. So here it is argued, first, that one does best not to think of a kinaesthetic sensory modality; and, second, that such a thought (if entertained) still has nothing to do with the understanding of dance.

To clarify this matter, two discussions must be undertaken. First, we must consider a few general things about sensory modalities: that is, about sense perception. Second, we need to review the relation of such modalities to understanding. Let us undertake the discussions in that order. When one thinks about the senses in this context, the following question arises: 'Why does one think that we have only five senses?'.

The answer is that I (at least) don't, necessarily. Rather, I would coun-tenance a sixth sense – for example, the one that we now, and misleadingly, call extrasensory perception (ESP), telepathy, or indeed any other 'sixth sense' – just in that case in which it satisfies two con-ditions. First, it becomes as well established and 'documented' as the other five; second, it meets the conditions (drawn from those other five) for being a sensory modality at all. These, then, are the constraints for there being a kinaesthetic sense. The second point is important, for we often talk loosely of 'a sense of X', 'the sense of X', without really intending that this X be thought of as some kind of sensory modality. This is a familiar point from the literature (Parry, 1976). For example, although we speak of 'the moral sense' or 'a sense of direction', nobody seriously thinks of the sense of direction as a sensory modality. Thus one could talk of 'a kinaesthetic sense' without believing in a kinaesthetic *sense*.

What is involved in being a sensory modality? One should be aware of a limitation on the answer here. One cannot expect to list all the rel-evant features, for two reasons. First, in line with Chapter 1, we do not expect some precise definition here. The second remark is more com-plex, for our question parallels one given concrete form in Lawrence Durrell's *The Revolt of Aphrodite* (1970: p. 245 ff.). There, an android is constructed which looks and acts like a woman in all the situations that its creators devise. But will 'she' always act like a person? What behav-iour *now* would guarantee her person-like behaviour in the future? Without an answer to such questions, we cannot decide whether or not this is indeed a (constructed) person. We may think that some list of characteristics picks out persons from other things; then, if Aphrodite had those characteristics, she would be a person; and if not, she would not! But further reflection disabuses us of this simplistic idea. We can recognize persons all right, but our basis is the diffuse knowledge that we have of other persons. What is required of a person is just that it behave 'like a person', and we cannot be sure just what that amounts to when what is in front of us lacks other features of persons – for example, their biological origins (Wiggins, 1980: pp. 121–3; 177–88).

To apply, when we ask 'What is involved in being a sensory modal-ity?', we are requesting generalizations from the acknowledged sensory modalities, the five senses. We can understand the idea of a sensory modality only in those terms. Anything else that counts as a sense does so in terms of features drawn from these other five. Well, what can be learned by looking at such sensory modalities? Two points seem imme-diately obvious. First, sensory modalities typically depend on organs of sensation. One sees with one's eyes, hears with one's ears, and so on.

Second, for sensory modalities, typically (perhaps even always) it is the *person* who does the sensing, does the perceiving. This means that the word 'perception' is just a catch-all term for the sensory modalities – made up of hearing, seeing, touching, tasting, smelling – together with any later discoveries! Further, the person does the perceiving. So although one sees through one's eyes, perception is not done by the eyes, nor by the rods and cones; in particular, perception is not done by the brain, but rather by the person. Thus it is misleading to say: 'The sense with which movement is felt is the kinaesthetic sense which relays muscular tension to the brain which, in turn, tells the mover what parts of the body have moved, where they have moved to, and gives an image of the position they have attained' (Preston-Dunlop, 1963: p. 3). This is misleading, of course, because such a description would be inappropriate when applied to any sense. Whatever the mechanical story that explains perceptual understanding, the relevant consideration here is what the *person* makes of what is seen, tasted, and so on. To apply, the mere fact that we have ganglia in the joints (or whatever) does not show that we have a kinaesthetic sense. This point is widely recognized (Gibson, 1978: p. 74). With this in mind, we will not mistakenly infer from the existence of sensors to the existence of a sensory modality. There is a reason to suggest that sensory modalities require organs of sense, not least because our understanding of what it is to be a sensory modality is based on the original five – and these typically do have organs. This point will clearly count against the idea of a kinaesthetic sense.

The argument thus far shows that we do not have a kinaesthetic sense. But this is not the crucial segment of the argument. Even if we have a kinaesthetic sense there is still room to question the place of such a sensory modality in our understanding of the aesthetic aspects of dance. Here, there is something relevant to be learned from the relation between the arts and perception. It is no accident that the sensory modalities primarily used for the arts are *projective* modalities: that is to say, sight and hearing. These allow, as it were, a *gap* between the percipient and the object of perception, between me and the thing that I sense. By contrast, I can only taste and touch those things that are contiguous. (Smell, of course, begins to seem a little more like hearing.) So we have art works constructed to employ the projective modalities (seeing and hearing) and virtually none in the localized, contiguous modalities, touch and taste.

A qualification must be added here: there are some instances of works of art constructed for touch, for example, art for the blind. But such cases will be few and far between. They do not constitute a sufficient case for the postulation of tactile art. Speaking of tactile qualities (for example, of paintings and sculptures) does not in general imply that they will be touched; indeed most galleries forbid this! Using the expression 'tactile' refers to a touching in the imagination, as it were, not to a sensory modality. If any sensory modality is at work here, it is visual perception.

This is an important idea when thinking about kinaesthesis. Even if there were a kinaesthetic sense, since it could not be projective, its use (in explanation) would resemble the ascription of tactile qualities to works of art. We are not suggesting that we know what it feels like to touch that thing; contrary to popular opinion, the tactile sense is not operative here. Similarly, the ascription of kinaesthetic qualities to dances cannot require appeal to a kinaesthetic sense. The argument can be briefly stated. Sensory modalities are of two kinds, the projective and the contiguous; they must be seen in the context of the crucial role of an audience for works of art, as described earlier. We can usefully repeat Cavell's (1969: p. xxvii) articulation of this point: 'It is tautological that art has, is made to have, an audience, however small and special. The ways in which it sometimes hides from its audience, or baffles it, only confirms this'. Thus this central role of the notion of an audience for art implies that the fulfilment of the place of an audience for art requires just the kind of projection that the projective modalities imply. So, as far as works of art go (at least in general), only projective sensory modalities can play a central role. And kinaesthesis cannot be one such.

In this light, one thinks again to think about the very idea of kinaesthesis: what can be meant here? Roughly, the idea is that one knows where the bits of one's body are without appeal to other sensory modalities. That is to say, I do not need to see or touch those bits of my body in order to know where in space they are, what position they are in, etc.; one just knows – as philosophers have said – non-inferentially (Dilman, 1975: p. 91). That is to say, one does not know this by or through knowing something else. One just knows. And this is a power which, at least, humans have.

I shall not argue that all knowledge from sensory modalities is of this kind (although some discussion on this point is implicit in the remarks on subjectivity in Chapter 1). Our point is more localised. The mistake here would involve thinking that one inferred where the bits of that person were from how one felt – a clear mistake. If there is any non-inferential knowledge, this is an example of it. Lest that be disputed, we can establish it quickly, drawing on the work of Elizabeth Anscombe (1981). Suppose that one did assume that clues (say, from one's senses) were needed as to the present spatial organization of one's body parts

267

(say, whether or not one's legs were presently crossed). As Anscombe points out, such a view is inherently self-refuting, for one must appeal to the position of one's body parts in order to understand what it is about, that is to say, in order to make out this view. She comments:

> ... if one ever did have to use the feelings of resistance on the upper leg and the weight and pressure in the lower leg as clues going by which one judged that one's legs were crossed, one would also need assurance that the sensations of pressure, weight, and the resistance were produced in one leg by the other, and not by some quite different bodies. *Ex hypothesi*, knowledge of the position of one's legs could not itself supply that assurance. (Ascombe, 1981: p. 71)

What is urged, and surely correctly, is that the feeling that one's legs were crossed must, if it is to be evidence that one's legs were crossed, originate from the fact that one's legs were crossed. This cannot be guaranteed, without already introducing what one is aiming to prove. Thus it must be accepted that knowing the spatial orientation or position of one's body parts is (at least generally) non-inferential.

There might seem to be an argument here for the existence of a kinaesthetic sense. Given that one just knows where the bits of one's body are, one might ask 'How does one know?'; there is a temptation at this point to invoke a sensory modality with which one knows. We have suggested that the senses do provide non-inferential knowledge of approximately the requisite kind. Thus, one might postulate a kinaesthetic sense. Yet there are two problems here. First, a general problem about the relation between sensory modalities and knowledge, concerning whether the need to explain one's knowledge is any reason for creating or postulating a new 'sense'. There are general doubts as to whether our existing five senses give us knowledge. But suppose we put these worries aside. The second difficulty is more specific and more crucial. One needs to distinguish, as I did earlier, between appeals to a sensory modality and appeals to something metaphorically called a 'sense'. Can we do that reliably here? Just as I am fairly good at knowing where the bits of my body are, I am fairly good at knowing where I am in relation to other places; that is to say, I know how to get from here to there. I have a pretty good sense of direction. But in this case the expression 'sense of' is clearly metaphorical. So the very best that one could argue for, with respect to a kinaesthetic sense, is the same situation. At best, this case would support the claims to a metaphorical use of the phrase 'kinaesthetic sense'. But that would not support the claims of a kinaesthetic *sense*!

Given that sensory modalities share an interesting and distinctive character, the addition of other things lacking in important elements of that character (say, lacking organs of sensation) can only lead to a confusion. This is a good reason for arguing that the kinaesthetic sense should not be added to our present catalogue of senses. Also, the putative kinaesthetic sense is, in the last analysis, a subordinate sense. If I say that I know where my arm is, I can tell by touch or by looking whether or not I am right; hence that I am wrong on some occasions. Moreover, since sight is projective, and both sight and touch very public, *you* could also tell that I was wrong, in such a case. It is clear that I can be wrong in respect of my kinaesthesis, and not just in unfavourable situations, but even in the most favoured situations. That is to say, the tests of where my arm is never appeal to kinaesthetic information; rather, I refer to my seeing or touching. Thus the idea of kinaesthesis is appropriately downgraded in our explanatory hierarchy.

Moreover, even acknowledging a kinaesthetic 'sense', as thus far described, leaves unclear its possible relation to the meaning of dances. Since our knowledge of meaning for art works depends centrally on the recognition of formal significance for features of those works – and hence on the recognition of the features *as* formal features (as well as the location of the work within its category) – one might well wonder if a kinaesthetic sense, once established, could make much of a contribution to our knowledge or understanding of meaning for dances. The significance of such formal features is something that one learns and recognizes, and that means through our projective sensory modalities. One recognizes features as formal in the context of the whole entity, or at least some significant part of it; an observed feature of a system cannot be derived solely from the properties attributed to its constituents. Thus, for example, the fluidity of water is not at issue, although none of its molecules are liquid in this way. Yet kinaesthesis could not offer the perception of such 'emergent' features, for emergent properties are the domain of the projective sensory modalities. Only when this 'projectedness' is a possibility can one ascertain in perception more than the immediate sensory inputs. The contiguous modalities, then, offer at best narrowly sensory experience. As such, these lack, among other things, any *temporal* dimension, and that is crucial to the character of appreciation or understanding of any performing art such as dance (Urmson, 1976).

Discussion of kinaesthesis sometimes employs the unfortunate form of words of 'knowing what it feels like', for example, for one's arm to be in such and such a position. This mistaken idea has already been dealt with in one of its dimensions, namely, the idea that one 'infers'

269

the location of one's body parts from 'clues'. Another and related area lies in the implicit suggestion that there is some *way* that it feels to be in such and such a position. This idea is surely misguided (Dilman, 1975). More importantly, consider the contribution of the supposed sense. What I know is where my arm is, not what it feels like for my arm to be there. Kinaesthesis, at best, provides me with information about me: that is the best this putative sensory modality offers. Again this is crucial, for appeal to the kinaesthetic in relation to dance very often involves the thought of it as somehow projective, or empathetic; that is to say, not primarily kinaesthesis on the part of the dance, but rather some kind of kinaesthetic awareness of the dancer by other people, so that others might be kinaesthetically aware of the dancer's position or movement. The suggestion is that kinaesthesis somehow reaches out, is a projective modality as distinguished earlier on. What is projected are the feelings of some other person! This is clearly false. To repeat, if there is a kinaesthetic sense at all, it allows me to know where the bits of *my* body are. Here the parallel with the tactile is useful. When I see a painting or sculpture, I may be inclined to remark on its 'tactile' qualities, but these are qualities presented to me in the imagination (see Chapter 10), and not through the senses. Or, more exactly, through the senses in so far as I see such qualities, but not through the tactile sense!

We must also distinguish between the *sensuous* and the *sensory*. Certainly a painting or sculpture may have a profound appeal, which it seems right to describe as sensuous, as 'conjuring up and catching' one's senses. But that is not (or not centrally) the application or operation of a sensory modality. So the sensory modalities are to be distinguished (at least crudely) into the projective and the non-projective; if there were a kinaesthetic sense, it would fall into the projective side, although many discussions of it and its relation to dance suggest (mistakenly!) that it is projective.

There is an additional point here. Someone might say that, while kinaesthesis plays no part in our audience-style understanding of dance, surely it plays a part in the dancer's understanding of the dance. Here two comments are apposite. First, the role of the dancer's feelings, in general (the role of information the dancer receives through his senses as a part of that) is simply irrelevant to the meaning of the dance and the understanding of the dance. That much is clear, at least when we construe dance as an art form. If the dancer is miserable, or if the dancer *feels* (kinaesthetically) that a bit of his body is in the wrong place, these are simply irrelevant. What is relevant is, in the first case, whether or not it is a miserable dance (or perhaps, when the dancer's feelings

270

cause him to perform the dance rather badly); in the second case, whether or not that particular bit of his body *is* in the wrong place. He may surely think that it is and be mistaken. Of course, if the dancer says his body part is in the wrong place, he has a good chance of being right, for he is well used to making such judgements; it is a criticism of the performance that this bit of his body is in the *wrong* place, so the question will be an important one. But its centrality depends not on what the dancer feels, but on his body part being in the wrong place. That is a matter on which the audience may have at least as good a say as the dancer himself. After all, he may feel that the body part is in the right place, but if it is not, that is still a criticism of the dance (perhaps of the performance). So, first, what the dancer thinks or feels is not part of the meaning of the dance. Second, it is not clear what the force of an appeal to the dancer's kinaesthetic responses would be. By and large, if there were some kinaesthetic sense (consisting in knowing where the bits of you are), or some kinaesthetic possibility of knowing where the bits of you are, then dancers don't so much use *it* as have *grooved-in* where the bits of them are going to be; that is, where the arms, legs, torso are going to go. In an ideal situation they do not actually know where the bits of them are any more than one thinks what one is doing when one changes gear while driving; rather, one simply responds to, say, the sound of the engine. So there is no kinaesthesis here.

One might draw a contrast in visual perception between *seeing* and *noticing*, such that looking at a crowd of people that contains Uncle Charley, one sees Uncle Charley. But, since one might not know that he was there, one did not notice him. Of course this is a highly artificial contrast, not conforming to ordinary language. But it makes a useful point, so let us apply it. The point is this: dancers do not kinaesthetically notice where the bits of them are, even if they kinaesthetically see where the bits of them are. When one reflects on the relation between perception and knowledge, it is clearly the noticing aspect which provides knowledge, if any does. The role of the putative 'kinaesthetic sense' in our understanding of dance is thus, at best, a very limited one. It does not give the dances meaning; it plays no part in the communication of that meaning; and it is misleading to think of it as the source of the dancer's knowledge of the spatial positions of his body parts. In light of all this, one might well reject the explanatory value of talk of a kinaesthetic sense, identifying kinaesthesis as a myth.

Finally, then, it might be argued that central to the meaning of a dance is some kind of kinaesthetic 'empathy'. On this topic I have nothing to add to David Best's (1974) discussion, but it may be useful to briefly summarize his arguments and conclusions. He points out how unsatisfactory it would be to urge that only those who have performed movement X can understand the meaning of movement X as it occurs in a dance. It would be, he says (Best, 1974: p. 142), like arguing that only violinists can understand violin music, and that in order to understand orchestral music one would need, not only to have played all the instruments in the orchestra, but also to know what it feels like to play them all simultaneously! On such absurdities this view founders. It might be thought that such a view could be saved by urging that all that is required is kinaesthetic empathy, such that 'the kinaesthetic sensations of the dancer are communicated by causing empathetic feeling in the spectator' (Best, 1974: p. 144). In this case one does not actually employ the kinaesthetic sense, but somehow one's own kinaesthetic sense is triggered by one's observation of the movements of the dancers, each somehow responsive to his kinaesthetic experiences. Against this line, Best points out the inadequacies of any explanation of meaning in terms of what caused one to think of that. The meaning of a dance does not depend on what is caused or brought to mind in a particular case. Rather, the claim to understanding should be rejected whenever the 'brought to mind' response does not coincide with the meaning. As Best (1974: p. 147) points out, such misunderstandings have dogged the philosophy of language. So that, for example, a broadly Lockean view of language explains the meaning of a word in terms of whatever it 'suggests' to the hearer, or 'brings to mind'. The absurdity of such a view is made clear in Sterne's novel *Tristram Shandy*, where the sentence 'My young master . . . is dead' brings to the hearer's mind his mother's well-washed nightdress. But it is clear that the sentence 'My young master . . . is dead' does *not mean* a nightdress, whatever it means. The theory of language that gives rise to such a view is clearly mistaken, and it is equally mistaken applied to the meaning of dances.

These considerations reinforce, as well as complement, points made earlier in this section. One cannot adequately account for aesthetic understanding in terms of a kinaesthetic sense. Indeed, even if there were a kinaesthetic sense, it could have nothing to do with the understanding of art, any more than we aestheticians can learn much of interest about the understanding of painting by studying visual perception.[3]

This section has urged, first, that we have good reasons to reject the idea of a kinaesthetic sensory modality, even if we wish to preserve the expression 'a kinaesthetic sense'; second, that even if there were a kinaesthetic sense, it could have no part to play in the explication or understanding of dances, since (a) the non-projective or contiguous modalities have little aesthetic role, and (b) the focus on the performer is not appropriate to an art form such as dance.

The importance of performance

This myth has two dimensions. It is easy for writers of aesthetic education in dance either to underrate or overrate performance. Each tendency leads to a corresponding overreaction. For example, undue emphasis on dance performance in some early writers on dance in education (H'Doubler, 1940) provoked a discussion which emphasized the role of the audience. This discussion in turn has been criticized for doing no justice to the point of view of those with a 'practical involvement' (Hamby, 1984: p. 34) in dance, either as dancers or choreographers. This criticism in its turn failed to acknowledge that the writers who were its targets[4] did not really think that dance performance was of no importance, but rather that its importance was logically secondary. If one had to choose a viewpoint for aesthetic appreciation, it would necessarily be the viewpoint of the spectator. Aesthetic appreciation (better, artistic appreciation) is first and foremost of the creations of others. But, of course, one does not in general need to make such a choice.

To avoid any misunderstanding, one point is crucial: that dance, as a performing art, is only confronted or encountered when one encounters or confronts a performance of it (Urmson, 1976). This point was elaborated in Chapter 4. Notated scores may offer insight, but, as with a musical score, encounters with the score are not in themselves encounters with the work of art. Indeed, it is arguable that viewing the dance on film, TV, or video is equally not encountering the work of art itself, for then our experience of the dance is mediated by the interpretive impact from the particular recording medium. But I shall not here assess that point. The crucial recognition is that, contrary to what Hamby says, nothing follows from this sort of importance for performers. Since both performers and spectators must confront the work in performance, the point may be used to sustain either of the two myths identified above – either to underrrate or overrate performance – and also must be accepted by any myth-free view!

We must recognize that the overrating of performance has two main sources. Some writers have wished to do justice to some kinaesthetic sense. That idea has been thoroughly discussed in the preceding section. Other writers wish simply to say that the child's participation in dance was central to the use of dance in education. This seems unexceptionable. But it was often expressed by claiming that one could not understand dances unless one performed them, or at least unless one had performed them. There seems no warrant for such a claim; indeed, reflection on corresponding claims should make that apparent. Many who said *that* would also have encouraged their students to use (and hence, one imagines, to have understood) music without the parallel requirement that they must make the music themselves. No doubt such music-making was seen as desirable, but it was not seen, as performance in dance *was* seen, as essential. Again, taken to its extreme, the parallel claim would be that one could not understand orchestral music unless one had played all the instruments, and simultaneously at that! We have already remarked on the absurdity of such a claim.

Moreover, the importance of the spectator role for any art form, such as dance, was often ignored. Children were thought of as dancing for themselves; this seemed to withdraw the requirement for an audience. But it did not do so, for two reasons. First, the general requirement for the possibility of appreciation by others is implicit in notions that were still applied (by such theorists) to these dances: notions such as expression and communication. Second, the fact that on a particular occasion the dancing child did not have an audience does nothing to remove this requirement. We need only ask 'In whose eyes was this child's dance a work of art?' to clarify the issue. Since the child would not be in the best position to see what actually happened, as opposed to what he thought happened, his own view of the matter cannot be the final arbiter. So another viewpoint is necessarily invoked. The need for a spectator viewpoint is established, and this does something to justify the requirement for an audience articulated in the previous section through quotation from Cavell.

A more complete account would draw on Wittgenstein's so-called 'private language' considerations at this point (Baker and Hacker, 1984b). That is, it would remind us of a general requirement or understanding to the effect that whatever can be said to be understood by anyone could in principle be understood by more than one person; that is to say, there are no logically private objects of understanding. As we have seen in earlier chapters, Wittgenstein (1953) argues for this conclusion by emphasizing the importance within our concept of knowledge and understanding of the distinction between being right and thinking one is right. To lose such a distinction is to make matters arbitrary. Wittgenstein asks rhetorically, 'What value can one give to the word "right" if *whatever* I say is right automatically is – that is, if I can't be wrong?'. Clearly the answer here is that no value can be given to the word 'right': we see this by noting that no value can be given to the word 'wrong' either (Hacker, 1990: pp. 15–30).

To apply, it is sometimes thought that the child could be dancing for himself alone. This might be practically true, in a particular case, but it cannot in general be true. If the child gets something from the dance, then that 'something' is, in principle, shareable. To think otherwise is to commit what, as we have seen, Putnam (1982: p. 122) aptly called 'a sort of mental suicide' (see Chapter 12). To speak of the child gaining something, feeling something, learning something, and yet deny the possibility of someone else coming to understand what the child gained, felt, learned is to rob the words 'feel', 'learn' of their meanings. How are we to distinguish the child genuinely feeling something from his thinking that he felt it, and so on? Such a picture of understanding has as a consequence that the child could never understand his own feelings. This brings out the aptness of the expression 'a sort of mental suicide'. As a consequence, this view of understanding must be given up, as has been suggested a number of times in this text.

Notice that little has been said about why the child must perform the dance. We have taken it for granted that there is some educational objective that this performance fulfils. But we have not yet produced one, and certainly not yet found one which is within the ambit of aesthetic education. This point is relevant, of course, because we will need to look to just such an explanation in order to give due weight to the performance (that is, to combat its overrating or underrating). Without the explanation, we cannot estimate the appropriateness of any weight placed on performance. Our route is somewhat indirect. First we need to be clearer about the general importance or value of dance in education: and, of course, I mean its intrinsic importance or what is attached to it by virtue of its being the art form dance. So I am not concerned with any claims of spin-offs for dance, such as physical fitness or social development, no matter how important these may be. Clearly the appropriate answer here is that already articulated in Chapter 8: that the arts in general should be seen as providing a kind of emotional education. Experience of the arts may allow us to experience finer shades of feeling; and it may do so because it may allow the refining of the concepts under which those feelings are experienced and under which the experiences are characterized (Best, 1978b). Moreover, these concepts must be mobilized (Wollheim, 1986: p. 48) in our experience. We have already offered some remarks in Chapter 8 as to why this is educational, and as to how it supports the place of all art forms in education, rather than merely some.

Now our question becomes, 'How is the ability to mobilize such concepts acquired?'. A part of the reply will emphasize the need to confront the works as art, which is centrally to confront them as a spectator. But fundamental to the concepts one must learn to handle is the concept of 'medium' (see Chapter 9), in the sense in which that term is used by Cavell (1969: p. 221):

> The home of the idea of a *medium* lies in the visual arts, and it used to be informative to know that a given medium is oil or gouache or tempera or dry-point... because each of these media had characteristic possibilities, an implied range of handling and result. The idea of a medium is not simply that of a physical material, but of a material-in-certain-characteristic-applications.

Applied to the case of dance, we might think of the medium of dance as movement, or as a particular technique (say, Graham technique), or as a range of such techniques. Whichever answer was given would be a polemical answer (McFee, 1977: p. 56), just because whatever answer one gave would entail 'an implied range of handling and result' (Cavell, 1969: p. 221); which is to say, characteristic sets of expressive potentials. The argument here, of course, is that given in Chapter 9, relating style, technique and decipherability. If this point is granted, one is led to ask how children might acquire an understanding of the 'characteristic applications' central to the idea of a medium (in this sense). It is not a direct consequence of these considerations that they must do so by the manipulation of that medium; but such a route seems both obvious and direct. (Manipulation of the medium in the case of dance requires at least performance and/or choreography.)

To sum up: if one is to give performance due weight, one must look for an explanation of its educational role. One aspect of a kind of conceptual refinement central to experience of art is the variety of changes in understanding brought about through the manipulation of an artistic medium (in Cavell's sense). This locates the place of performance within artistic education, and because such an account emphasizes the manipulation of that medium, it serves to combat the underrating of the performance. In addition, I have tried to show the need for a spectator viewpoint, which should counteract the overrating of performance.

The 'creative process'

Three issues are addressed here. The first concerns the understanding of the term 'creativity': in particular, the need to understand this matter in a non-technical fashion. The second concerns the account of creative processes typically invoked in discussing creativity in education (a topic widely considered by other writers [Best, 1985: pp. 64–89]). Finally, we consider the relationship between so-called 'products' and so-called 'processes' – which has implications both for our theorizing about creativity and for questions to do with teaching. It is important to discuss creativity, not least because for some theorists aesthetic education is best understood in terms of the development or the exercise of some creative process. I shall argue that this is an unduly romantic conception of the nature of persons, and also a misconception of the role of mental processes.

The place to begin consideration of the nature of creativity, and of the usefulness of the notion of creativity in educational theory, is with common sense. The notion of creativity is, in one fairly clear way, a common-sense, everyday notion. What then can we learn by considering the common-sensical? There are three main points.

First, we notice that creativity is indeed an everyday idea; the word 'creative' and its cognates are in the vocabulary of most people, even if it is not a word that trips regularly from their tongues. So we do have a lot of information about creativity, a lot of cases of the uncontentiously creative. And this point is important, because it gives us a standard by which to test theories of creativity. We all have a stock of recognized examples of the uncontentiously creative, which must turn out to be creative on any theory of creativity which is to be acceptable. So that, for example, if a theory of creativity led us to conclude that one of these recognized cases of the uncontentiously creative (let us use Beethoven as an example) was not creative, the theory would thereby be cast into disrepute. It would have failed to fit our data about creativity.

This point has far-reaching consequences. Some psychologists attempt to give what they call 'operational definitions' of terms like 'creativity'. That is, they say something like 'to be creative is to perform at or to such-and-such a level on such-and-such a test'. But is that the topic we wanted to know about? Does their operational definition tell us about creativity? We will need to be convinced on this point. Our concern was creativity – of the kind manifest in our recognized examples – not whatever is tested by these tests. Here we see the irrelevance of this whole procedure. As we said, finding Beethoven 'bad' at such tests, we would not conclude that he was not creative after all, but rather, that the tests were not tests for creativity. This shows more than just the strength of our uncontentious examples. It also shows the irrelevance of such tests. Beethoven's performance at, say, open-ended tests (or any other tests) is simply beside the point. However he does at these tests cannot affect our judgement of him as creative. Indeed, the only thing that might affect that judgement would be a radical rethinking of our attitude to Beethoven – but that would still leave us with other uncontentious examples.

A second point from common sense is this: the term 'creative' applies over some range of activities, or part of one's life (usually) in general. One is a creative painter: not, or not usually, a creative person. People are not in general creative in the whole of their lives, but rather over some specifiable range. If there are some creative people, such as Picasso, for whom this range is very large, none the less it is finite. Indeed, there are some things people do – for example, spelling – where creativity would be out of place. The mistake here is like that made when, say, eminent scientists are asked their views on art or religion: their eminence in one field is thought, mistakenly, to guarantee eminence in another. There is really no reason to think this.

Yet this mistake is informative for us, for it emphasizes that creativity is essentially linked to certain 'media' (including thought, of course), and hence makes no sense in a vacuum. But when we ask what the creative painter or poet does, we find that they produce things of a certain sort – paintings or poems, in this example – which are then thought meritable. We explain the person's creativity in terms of such products; creativity makes sense only in those terms.

Third, we realize that creativity is not equivalent to the mere production of novelty. Something can be new but uninteresting, or trivial. The term 'creative' carries with it an implication of rightness, which mere novelty does not guarantee. Moreover, the creative need not be novel. Any innovation must be intelligible, and that may limit the novelty which can be brought to bear. This requirement will make connections between the creative new thing and other things in a similar tradition. Both will be understood, or made sense of, using similar concepts. Thus, for example, one might recognize novelty in the use of avocado paste to clean green shoes (an idea suggested on a London radio station). What makes this a joke is the inappropriateness. But suppose we decided that this was indeed a useful or intelligible idea. Now we would be treating avocado paste in the way in which we treated other shoe-cleaning materials – we would understand it in those terms.

The outcome of reflecting on our common sense understanding of creativity is to make us see that much investigation of so-called 'creativity' – for example, by some psychologists – is bound to be beside the point for educationalists. Whatever it tells us about, it does not tell us about creativity. Best (1985: p. 76) makes this point by urging

278

that 'there is something necessarily inexplicable about [creativity] so that even those who are most creative are at a loss to explain it'.

To make the most of this set of points, we should see how they undermine the idea of the creative process: the myth that there is some one unique 'process' common to all creative people, or perhaps that one goes through in the creation of creative artefacts. There is much wrong with such an idea, but before we criticize it, let us note some oddities inherent in this belief in a unique creative process. The account of processes given by adherents of this view – which take processes to be logically private occurrences in the minds of individuals – makes problematic any theorizing about such processes. If they are indeed inaccessible, how is the theory to be rooted in an empirical grasp of them? How can these theorists know that they are right? A further oddity is that this view seems to contradict our experience of the creative: for what, except a prior belief in such a process, could lead us to say that there must be something in common among the diverse creative activities that make up, say, the arts? Painting seems to be very much one thing, composing dances another, and writing poetry yet another; why must there be something in common? Further, why must that thing reflect creativity? These questions are difficult to answer.

Our criticism of the myth of the creative process has two prongs. The first attacks the implied contrast between process and product, a contrast implicit in such phrases (found in 'educational' writings) as 'attend to the process, not to the product'. How are we to locate the process? As noted above, those who believe that this is the right way to characterize such matters treat processes in ways that render them inaccessible, for they treat them as logically private occurrences in the minds of particular individuals. To understand the misconception inherent here one needs only ask how one attends to the process. What one attends to is what the person says and does. For those who work with a firm distinction between process and product, these will be examples of what they will call 'products'. But clearly, these are all we can ever encounter. At the root of this mistake, of course, is a rather confused, dualistic and simplistic account of the mind and human action (Best, 1974: pp. 5–14). It is right that we *see* anger, fear, depression; not merely that we see the products of anger, fear (or more exactly, to say that we typically see both of these things). Of course, what we actually see is a person who is angry, afraid and so on. This point can be made succinctly by returning to the idea of creativity. We identified Beethoven as a creative artist by attending to his achievements, his work. In so far as we pay attention to creativity and the like in aesthetic education, reflection on this case should make us attend

279

to the product, without giving a hang about any (possibly mythical) processes.

Such a conclusion goes too quickly, for two reasons. First, it mistakenly employs the traditional version of the process/product dichotomy. We need to undermine such a contrast. As we shall see, the point is not to deny creativity, nor to deny a creative process in some sense. Either of these positions would be crazy. Rather, it is to properly understand what it means to speak of creativity here. Second, we do not want a return to some search for achievement in dance, if this means simply, for example, the number of *fouettés* accomplished, or something like that. Belinda Quirey (1976: p. 122) makes this point with the following note on the *Rose Adagio*:

> *Rose Adagio*: a famous dance in the first act of Petipa's ballet The Sleeping Beauty, where the ballerina is partnered by four princely suitors. Each in turn supports her and lets her go while she holds (or fails to hold) an attitude, standing on the pointe of one foot. The audience meanwhile holds its breath until the feat is concluded. Next to the thirty-two fouettes in the third act of Swan Lake, this is one of the worst circus tricks in the whole ballet repertoire . . .

The last thing wanted for dance in education would be such 'circus tricks'. But attending to the product is not necessarily aiming for something like this. Rather, we are looking for the sorts of product which display aesthetic sensitivity and understanding. Recognizing these in, say, the dance of children – both their choreography and their performance – is a matter for the sensitive and knowledgeable eye. But that eye is attending to the products, the dances, and not to something else.

Consider also the idea of 'attending to the process' in the context of a teacher working through some choreographic ideas with the class. The class may have much input into this process; we can imagine it taking place over a considerable number of weeks, resulting in, say, a performance in week ten. On a simplistic view, to attend to the product would be simply to look at that performance, while attending to the process would be something other than that. What is really required in this case is attending to what the children have done in the various weeks leading up to that final performance. No doubt one could think of this as attending to the process, but it also involves attending to what the children say and do in those weeks, which, on the traditional view, would amount to attending to a series of products.

The outcome of this discussion, then, is that we recognize creativity in terms of certain kinds of products, which means (in effect) that the term 'creative' is only indirectly applicable to a person. Rather, a creative artist is (roughly) one who is responsible for products like that. Here we see that the idea of a creative process is theoretically redundant, at best. All that can usefully be said about creativity can usefully be said of the products, although this does not mean only, as it were, the final products. Even if one accepts the process/product distinction, one sees that interest lies in the object – the product – no doubt seen in relation to its creator, and no doubt (when a part of education) valued for its contribution to the development of the creator, to the changes in his understanding.

I was once asked, when discussing these matters, what Picasso was 'doing' when creating a masterpiece such as *Guernica*. The questioner hoped that I would discuss the 'mainsprings of the creative process', but the most honest and truthful answer I could have given would have been to mime the application of paint with a brush! That is what Picasso was *doing*; to discuss the 'creative process' here would be, at best, to discuss the various versions through which the *Guernica* canvas changed, in an attempt to understand how succeeding versions constituted improvements. As this examples illustrates, we could think of ourselves as discussing the creative process, but doing so would be looking at tangible objects, public objects.

As a second prong of our attack on the myth of the creative process, compare doing something creatively with doing something slowly. When I speak of doing something slowly, the implication is that I might, if more skilful, have done it faster – the very same thing, but done quickly rather than slowly. So one might say that the word 'slowly' here refers to the process of doing whatever it is. But doing something creatively is not like that at all. I could not do that very same thing, either with the creative process (creatively), or without the creative process (not creatively). If I do just that thing – write that poem, make that dance – then I am bound to be doing it creatively. For example, given that a particular dance is a piece of creative art, then anyone composing that dance would be acting creatively. The creativity is dependent on the dance, not what the person does or feels. Again, there is no useful place for a 'creative process' in our discussion of creativity. That leaves us with one of two options. Either we agree that the notion has no value, is a myth, and simply drop it, or we continue to employ it, while accepting that it has no explanatory value. (Note that this is not to cease to talk of creativity, but merely to cease to characterize it in terms of some unique process.[5])

The very idea of an aesthetic education

The three views discussed above are centrally matters on which aesthetic educators writing about dance go awry. They can slip into mistaken discussions of the kinaesthetic sense, misjudging the importance of performance, or misconceiving creativity. As such, the previous sections may serve a counter-balancing role. One last issue, although rather parochial, sheds light on the account of aesthetic education centrally employed here. I imagine an objection being raised which challenges fundamental assumptions of my whole procedure in this chapter, drawing on a paper of David Best's entitled 'The dangers of "aesthetic education"' (1984).

In this paper, the objection might run, Best expresses his dissatisfactions with the whole idea of aesthetic education; and hence a discussion like mine, which is about aesthetic education, must – by Best's light – be fundamentally misconceived. This will clearly be a substantial blow if the argument itself is based, as mine obviously is, on Best's ideas, as is especially clear from Chapter 8. I might reply that this objection is not strictly relevant. The ideas of David Best used elsewhere might be logically independent of the ideas which give rise to his 'dangers of "aesthetic education"' paper. Neither I nor the imaginary objector have shown, as yet, whether or not they are. Some support for the objector's case would come from Best's use of his account of the importance of life issues against the idea of aesthetic education. Or so it seems. But I do not propose to take this line. It seems to me that this whole objection is based on an important and revealing misreading of Best (which is why I have chosen to consider it).

To defuse the objection, one needs first to understand the character of Best's condemnation of the phrase 'aesthetic education'. In essence, that condemnation stems from the familiar distinction between, on the one hand, aesthetic judgement and appreciation (typically, natural beauty, graceful movement, 'fountains and firework displays', as I called it elsewhere [McFee, 1978: p. 84]) and, on the other hand, artistic judgement and appreciation – that is to say, the appreciation of works of art. Best argues for this distinction in many places, and, as noted earlier, he takes this idea of a life issues connection to provide one important distinguishing feature of artistic from (merely) aesthetic appreciation. This distinction is obviously right, and obviously important, but one must avoid being misled by *mere* words here. David Best objects to the confusion that results from thinking of aesthetic education in terms of (his phrase) aesthetic judgement and appreciation: that is, treating aesthetic education as involving, or being importantly similar to, our appreciation of natural beauty, graceful movement and so on. And it is not. In terms of Best's distinction, it is clear that the area is more properly called artistic education; or, if that sounds inappropriate, education in and through the arts. Indeed, aesthetic education is typically conducted in just that way: through dance, drama, visual art, music.

So where have we arrived? I have conceded that what I have throughout called 'aesthetic education' should more properly, if one used Best's distinction, be called 'artistic education'. But that is just the point: most writers and thinkers don't use or understand this crucial distinction. This means that expressions 'artistic education' and 'education in and through the arts' are likely to be misleading just when we are using them to gain clarity. The point, which Best accepted,[6] is that we should not conceive of judgements central to our aesthetic education as being importantly similar to judgements of what Best terms 'the aesthetic'. If we avoid that misconception, it does not matter what words we use. So, in effect, I believe in aesthetic education (as does David Best), although we agree that the term aesthetic education is potentially misleading. Thus there is no dispute here; and no objection to my line in the body of this chapter. What discussion of this objection reveals, of course, is the centrality for aesthetic education of the artistic/aesthetic contrast.

Recommended reading

The clearest texts are those cited in the chapter: Eisner, 1974; Bolton, 1981; Aspin, 1981; Best, 1984; Best, 1985: pp. 64–89; Redfern, 1986. For an overview of the implications for dance in education (and of the view of education presupposed) see McFee, 1989a.

283

14

Dance and Society

In this chapter I argue that certain ideas sometimes thought to be central to the study of dance – in particular, ideas that relate dance to the general condition of society, or to forces of production and the like – are of little or no relevance to our enquiry; at best, they offer insight into society, but not into dance (Marx and Engels, [1846] 1970: p. 150). Thus much work done as 'sociology of dance', 'anthropology of dance' and so on may be inherently mistaken or misguided. It is certainly not, as its practitioners often claim, relevant to us. Yet one criticism of the aesthetics of dance that might be raised by sociologists of dance is at least partly justified, although it can also be met within the traditions of the aesthetics of dance anyway. That idea concerns the need for (what I shall call) a sense of history.

The meaning of the word 'dance'

It is sometimes urged – particularly by anthropologists of dance – that dance has many different functions, and that these differences reflect, in some (interesting?) ways, on the various societies within which the dances take place. It is sometimes even urged that dance occurs in all societies, that 'to dance is human' (Hanna, 1979). Such claims are extremely dubious, and it is revealing to review in what ways, for they represent one direction in which criticism of the work of this text – perhaps of the aesthetics of dance as traditionally done – could take place.

It might be thought that the approach of this text cannot take account of these 'anthropological' or 'social' facts, and hence is irreducibly bound up with one culture: roughly, a certain period of Western European and American culture. For ease of reference for the reader, (most of) the examples in this section are drawn from one of the best modern collections of anthropological writing (Spencer, 1985), and for two reasons. First, it represents an accessible place for further elaboration of the examples quoted or cited. Second, in it we see more of the virtues and fewer of the vices which, I shall argue, traditionally infect

284

this sort of discussion of dance. The problems encountered in Spencer's book are typical of (at least) the best anthropological writing on dance.

Let us review such claims. It might seem that the major difficulty lies in proving that, for example, dance takes place in all societies, in finding out enough about societies to decide whether or not there is dance in them all, or whether or not the dance does have various functions, or whatever. It might be accepted that this is a very difficult task, calling for intensive field work in the various societies in question. Now this is a good point. It is certainly difficult to prove claims such as these. But that is not the key difficulty. The key difficulty comes, as we might say, prior to that investigation. In order to conduct such an investigation, I must be able to identify dance: to sort out what are and what are not examples of dance, distinguishing dance from dance-like activities. It makes no sense, for example, to speak of there being dance in all societies if, by this, is meant simply that in all societies there are movement sequences which could be mistaken for dance. This is indeed an error: it does not support the claim being made (Bambrough, 1968: pp. 146–7).

Of course, not all anthropologists of dance make this sort of mistake. Indeed, it is explicit anathema to the best of them – Kaeppler, Youngerman, Williams for example – as the collection under discussion makes clear. As Adrienne Kaeppler (1985: p. 92) comments: 'In many societies . . . there is no indigenous concept that could adequately be translated "dance"'. As a result she does not write about dance as such, preferring to consider the 'movement dimension of separate activities' (p. 92) within the society. However, the point Kaeppler rejects is regularly urged by critics writing on the anthropology of dance. Consider two simple examples. It is sometimes said[1] that in 500 BC Greece, 'To sing well and to dance well is to be well educated'. To decide on the truth of this claim, we must be sure that the Greek word here translated 'dance' (orcheisthai) does indeed mean dance, for if it does not, then the claim as quoted above is not, despite its appearance, a claim about dance at all. An investigation would show that the word translated 'dance' here referred to drama and to graceful movement more generally, even to movement in religious ceremonies. Well, is that dance? Is that what those writers who use the claim were meaning when they spoke about dance? These questions really ask us if we understand the activity better once we have called it 'dance'. It is clear that this is not so. Putting the point in this way, as a point about language, helps clarify it. It may be that no better English word can be found here instead of the word 'dance'; we may be obliged to use the word 'dance' here. Were that the case, writers on dance would simply not draw any implications from the use of that word in reference to ancient Greek activities. Like the word 'bank', the word 'dance' would, in such a situation, be equivocal.

Again consider a case where a certain pattern of movement was only used in some religious ceremony. For example, suppose we discover a 'dance' which 'shows the... spirit of the deceased that it has no further place within the settlement' (Middleton, 1985: p. 170). To be clear, this is not merely a depiction, or portrayal, or presentation of that fact but, as it were, an actual order given to the spirit – as we might show the card shark that he has no place in our poker game (and our showing would amount to an order to the card shark to 'never darken our door again'). Any argument we could produce to show that the movement sequence in question was indeed a command to a spirit would, simultaneously, be an argument against this movement sequence being *dance*. Or suppose that we establish that the Ghost Dance of North American Indians has 'the very specific... purpose of restoring lost lands and tradition' (Spencer, 1985: p. 2). Again, this sort of aspiration is clearly not within the compass of dance: that is, dance as we understand it. Certain dances might, for example, express a yearning or longing for lands and traditions. Indeed I suspect that this is the right way to understand certain contemporary choreographic efforts; perhaps, for example, some of Pina Bausch (see Copeland, 1990). A dance might even 'stir up' a revolution which reinstated those lost lands. But that is not the interesting case: we do not think of *the dance itself* as bringing about the restoration of the lands. At best, it might be instrumental in precipitating the revolution. The success (or otherwise) of that revolution would be a further matter. Rather, the case to be considered is one where the dance itself is supposed to bring about the desired outcome. Here the point is that already recorded: anything that could achieve this end would not be dance. And any argument that suggested that the movement activity aimed at this outcome would, at the same time, be an argument that this activity was not dance.

The word 'dance' might be used of these activities, but is the activity really dance? If we are not sure, any understanding of the activity that we gain by calling it 'dance' will be ill-founded. How can we be sure that it is dance? To what features of the activity will we pay attention in order to decide? I suggest that the fact that, in each case, the activity in question is used only in the ritualistic way described above should, at the least, give us cause to doubt that it is really dance.

So, to summarize, I am urging that we must know whether or not a particular activity is dance before we can start analysing the place of dance in that society. Finding activities with a very different use from that in our society – a very different function – must make us wary of thinking of them as dance at all.

The relevant thought here (from Chapters 2 and 3) is that whether or not movement sequence X is indeed dance depends, roughly, on whether or not it is called 'dance' by the society which gives rise to it. Of course, care is needed in employing such a thought. For example, *figurative* uses of the term must be avoided: dancing with joy isn't dancing. But at least we then have a way of sharpening the questions to be asked by the anthropologist of dance (also the historian of dance). They must ask if the society in question really calls the activity dance; and not, for example, if the best word we can come up with for the activity is the word 'dance'. We have already seen this point to some degree. Another example may sharpen it still further, showing how a point about language can generate a substantial (and not merely verbal) conclusion: I am reliably informed that the Japanese word *giri* is regularly translated – say, in novels – by the term 'duty'. But suppose we find the concept *giri* used in those novels to explain, say, one person beheading another after the second had committed ritual suicide. I take it to be clear that such an action goes beyond what could be required by one's duty as *we* understand duty. Thus any argument to show that *giri* was indeed the correct explanation of the behaviour in question would simultaneously be an argument against the translation by the word 'duty'. That is far more than duty: the two concepts are recognizably not co-extensive. Of course, there may be no other suitable word. But, to the extent that this is true, English speakers would not be able (fully) to understand the Japanese texts in question. Aspects of them will be opaque to us. This is not a dance example; still, it illustrates the importance of discerning what is and what is not dance, as opposed to just the verbal question of what word is used.

The requirement articulated here is not for a check-list (or worse, 'criteria') for distinguishing dance from non-dance. The requisite ability to distinguish one from the other could be recognitional. Indeed, the discussions in Chapters 1 to 4 suggest that there will be a recognition ability at work here. So the question is not whether we can in practice distinguish dance from non-dance: it is not a question about the practicalities at all. We cannot say what would and what would not be relevant even in our own case. And yet we can identify dances.

Yet notice three things from our earlier analysis. First, if that analysis is right, whether or not a particular movement sequence is dance or not depends centrally on the *context* of the performance: knowing the movement description alone will not answer the question. One must know the *action-description* (Chapter 2). Second, finding the correct action-description is an institutional matter, handled through the Republic of Dance. This requirement is not clear: we have no close specification of the membership of the Republic of Dance; nor can we expect a completely unified answer from the Republic, once we have located it. Still, the right answer here is an institutional one (Chapter 3). Third, our concern is with dance as an art: that is, with those bits of the field of dance where it is true that dance is an art form. This qualification was introduced initially, both by using the artistic/aesthetic contrast (Chapter 1) and by looking at the point of dance (Chapter 8). These three facts amount to a specification of what is meant by the term 'dance' in my discussion. Anything which deviates from this specification is not dance, or anyway, we would need a long story to show that it is dance after all. To return to one of the examples given earlier, it tells us why it is a mistake to use the word 'dance' of the ancient Greek activity under discussion. Notice that this is indeed a point about the nature of society. It tells us that, on the understanding of dance that we are using, there was no dance in ancient Greece.

These points are not exclusively the concern of writers on dance. They apply to the other arts. So that, for example, the account of art given here means that the cave paintings in Lascaux are not art; or, anyway, that a long discussion (by the Republic of Art) will be needed to show that they are. But these points are of more central relevance to dance theorists than to theorists in the other arts, just because some major element of the study of dance as done at present does focus exclusively, or primarily, on activities which, if the considerations raised here were accepted, would not be dance at all.

The points offered here are not unknown to the writers quoted or cited. But they feel able to dismiss them. For example, when commenting on the Warranunga fire ceremony in Australia, Paul Spencer (1985: p. 1) remarks:

Here dancing merged into leaping, prancing, singing, yelling, shouting, taunting, practical joking, processing, mock attacks with blazing torches, and ultimately a mêlée among the flying sparks and embers: there was moreover a highly utilitarian purpose – to patch up old quarrels and live in peace.

This account certainly identifies sets of (non-aesthetic) goals for the physical activity. But are they properties of dance, even if we agree with the account? Two considerations suggest that, at best, this is not clear. First, notice that this is described in terms of dance 'merging' into these things; that is, they are not (all) dance. The second point is that, in this description, the idea is of the *whole* as having this purpose. It does not attribute the goal to just some parts of it. But suppose we wished to do so. Well, which parts? We cannot say, and therefore cannot (or not necessarily) identify those parts which *are* dance. The overall outcome is that, in this case, we can speak with confidence neither about what is and is not dance nor whether the functions of the activity are functions of its dance element.

Again, Judith Hanna (1979: pp. 18–19) records Richard Waterman (1962: p. 47) as reporting of the Australian Aborigines, 'the term that comes closest to the word for "dance" – the word "bongol" – has . . . both a larger and a smaller reference than our term "dance"'. *Bongol* includes music as well as dancing, and at the same time it does not include the pattern steps or bodily movements included in some of the sacred ceremonies or certain activities of a children's age group that we would certainly characterize as 'dancing'. Implicitly, this discussion recognizes that members of such a society do not dance; rather, they *bongol*, and this is not dance because the contours of the two concepts differ radically.

In spite of these recognitions, writers in their tradition have still treated dance as a unitary concept, regarding the activities of certain societies as examples of dance. In part, then, the problem has been recognized, but the typical response has been simply to regard our account of dance as somehow arbitrary or *ad hoc*. Indeed, the claim is often directed at the definition of the term 'dance', as though that were the point at issue. For example, Spencer (1985: p. 38) urges, 'dance may be identified in whatever way seems most appropriate to the study of any specific situation or society'. But this cannot be the case if one's interest lies in studying dance, for then whether one is actually studying *dance* (and not something else) will be one of the points at issue. Of course, as Spencer (1985: p. 38) continues: 'Dance is not an entity in itself but belongs to the wider context'. But accepting this claim will not commit us to his conclusion: 'the wider context of ritual action'. Claiming that dance is a kind of ritual action is offering (the beginnings of) an account of dance. Of course, Spencer might mean that dance is a kind of action that can be understood and misunderstood. If so, he has expressed his point very inexactly. First, we have a clearer way of saying that dance is meaningful or meaning-bearing – namely, using those expressions. Second, one can to some degree study other meaningful or meaning-bearing areas, for example language, without committing oneself to the view that language is 'an entity' or to the reification of language. But, again, study of language could not begin from whatever definitions of the term 'language' 'seem most appropriate to the study of any specific situation or society'. Rather, it must begin from the account of language which does justice to what is already claimed for it: its meaningful character!

At this stage, if not sooner, an accusation will be levelled against the remarks in this section, and it will take one of two forms. Either it will claim that my discussion focuses in an unacceptable way on our society or our culture – that it needs to be cross-cultural – or it will urge that I am defining the word 'dance' so as to make my claims about it true. These amount to the same accusation: in both, the objection is that I am being unduly or inappropriately *specific*. But, for ease of reply, I shall treat them separately. The first version of the objection implies that the word 'dance' has a cross-cultural sense. It is this sense that I am supposed to be ignoring by focusing on our society. But this is just the point at issue, for I deny this idea of a clear cross-cultural sense of the term 'dance'. My position, unlike my opponents', is supported by an argument about the nature of concepts or the nature of understanding. I have asked how we understand the term 'dance', and I have articulated a number of conditions for what we mean by the word 'dance'. Now I claim, quite simply, that whatever does not fulfil those conditions is not dance, and this followed from the basis of our understanding of the term 'dance'. (This sort of point is elaborated in the section on relativism later in this chapter.)

The second objection might continue from here. It might say, even in our culture or society there are perfectly good activities rightly called 'dance' which I have excluded: for example, what is sometimes (and misleadingly) called 'social dance'. By this term is meant disco dancing, ballroom, tap and the like. It is certainly true that I excluded them, but my response is twofold. First, I have explained and justified this exclusion: it coheres with the general impression we have that these activities are dance 'in a different sense' or 'in a different way' than the dance that is art. Indeed, the rough-and-ready distinction between theatre dance and social dance (Quirey, 1976) makes just this point. They are different, and our concern is with only one of them. I am not saying that the other things are not dance, but that they are not dance in the relevant sense (McFee, 1989a). Notice too that this objection is raised, in a particular context, by writers who wish to apply what they have learned about dance in one sense to what they have learned about dance in another – to what they think of as 'dance generally'. But I agree with them that social forces shape phenomena. For me, this means that an activity which is radically different, where different social forces operate, is not dance! And not dance *for that reason*.

The second aspect of my response is more concessive. Suppose I now expand my accounts of dance to include the kinds of dance at issue – in this case, 'social dance'. The problem remains: for my account would still centrally be based on Western European and American forms. It still excludes 'dances' used in worshipping tree gods and the like. The important point here is that one cannot simply identify dance in some abstract way – or, worse (see Chapter 2), in terms of its movements – and then ask questions about its place and function in society. Only once one has sorted out some questions about its place and function society can one identify it as dance!

That rather abstract way of putting the point is easily clarified. No doubt the focus here is very narrow, concentrating solely on dance that is art. And this has meant concentrating on dance for which artistic judgements are appropriately made: which is appropriately experience through what, in Chapter 1, were called artistic concepts. Even with this narrower focus, we could not specify what was a dance as such: anything appropriately seen using such concepts was a dance, and then discussion elaborated what it was to be appropriate here, and what such concepts were like. To repeat, what makes a movement sequence a piece of dance rather than something else depends on the context, and the context involves, for example, the use to which that activity is put in society. Although I have concentrated on dance as art, that point is equally true for all dance – indeed, for all action (see Chapter 2).

Even if I consider more examples of kinds of dance, a crucial feature which identifies those kinds will be certain functions, or certain places and uses in society. Then my account cannot accommodate more functions without, simultaneously, accommodating more kinds of dance. But what is wrong with that? Why shouldn't there be a huge number of kinds or forms of dance? Before answering, it is important to clarify that I am talking here of different kinds of dance in relation to their social use or social place. Hence classical ballet and modern dance, elsewhere called two forms of dance, are for these purposes just one form of dance. So why should one not have as many kinds of dance as one wishes? The answer lies in the usefulness of calling all these disparate activities by the same word, 'dance': when I group activities under a common heading, I do so because (for some purpose of mine) it is useful to think of this as like that in some respect. The point can be presented quite abstractly. The danger (see Chapter 1) for this kind of procedure is that A may be like B in some respects – so that A(s) and B(s) can both be called X(s) – and B may be like C in some respects – and hence C be called an X too – without A and C having anything in common. Of course this danger can be overcome by careful handling of the concepts. This would mean that, although we use the same word for A and for C, we think of them as essentially different: points we have learned from A cannot, without further argument, be applied to C, and so on. In such a context, calling both A and C by the one word 'X' is likely to be confusing. At the least, it is not helpful.

So, to apply, there is no added clarity in saying that all these activities are dance, yet of totally different sorts. Saying they are different sorts amounts, in this context, to saying that what we have learned about one will not necessarily transfer to the others. Further, we are likely to confuse ourselves, for we will be running together activities that their proponents think of as different in kind. If they see these activities as different, how can we insist on seeing them as importantly the same?

In conclusion, then, I have met the objections to my procedure. And where does that leave us? It leaves us with the need to be wary about undue generalizations concerning dance as such, and hence with strong reservations about the claims made for dance in the anthropological literature.

Dance as 'natural'

Of course, we should not underestimate the role of the social. As the institutional idea of the Republic of Art illustrates, the concept of art articulated here does have a social dimension. An emphasis on the idea of what is 'natural' or 'instinctive' for human beings will be hugely misleading. The implicit contrast has three elements. We contrast what is instinctive (or natural) with what is trained, and also with what is learned. But, for human beings, almost nothing will be genuinely instinctive: everything has been overlaid with the social. As Betty Redfern (1979: p. 17) puts it, 'What is "natural" in the case of human beings, apart from certain biological features and processes, is always apt to be problematic . . .'. If we consider something with an instinctive base (as we might think) it involves learned (or trained) behaviours; so that what is instinctual – sexual drive, say – manifests itself in behaviours which are learned. Many actions which, as we might say, we do automatically, equally have a learned dimension. For example, we change gear automatically when driving a car; we don't have to think about it. Yet this is obviously learned. Even if we accepted that the urge to stop when someone steps out in front of one's car is, in some way, instinctive, we must still concede that the mechanism for the emergency stop is learned.

We can see that our reactions to art works such as dances manifest

292

similar learned or trained responses. This is not to deny that the *capacity* to appreciate art may be (perhaps must be) natural for human beings. But this is really just like saying that the capacity for language is natural for human beings. Yet one cannot simply speak *language*; one can only speak a particular language. The capacity must be actualized in a particular social context; hence, as a particular language, or set of them. In a similar way, how we react to art, and also what we react to, is learned, but typically in that particular way in which first languages are learned – 'with one's mother's milk', as it is sometimes put. What goes for appreciating/understanding art, goes equally for making it, not least because art-making itself involves such critical processes (see Chapters 6 and 7).

This discussion undermines any suggestion that dance is 'inherited from brutish ancestors'.[2] Such theorizing persists, although it has been thoroughly criticized by Suzanne Youngerman (1974), Joanna Kealiinohomoku (1983) and by Drid Williams (1976/7). The view really has two dimensions: the equation of human with animal behaviour and the subsequent claim about the 'naturalness' for humans of dance. The second of these is effectively ruled out by the argument of the previous section: the variety of distinct uses of the term 'dance' shows that one can only make such a generalized claim about the naturalness of dance by running over these various distinctions. The other mistake is easily brought out by asking about the intellectual leap from the behaviour of stilt birds in Australia to *Swan Lake*: surely it is too huge to be plausible (Wiggins, 1987: p. 100). And it won't be minimized by inserting a few 'intermediate' cases: for example, apes. Roughly, we understand our behaviour in terms of that of animals to the extent we attribute to the animals the sorts of motives we find in ourselves. Thus behaviour of some creatures, for example those 'that are conscious, can rest without sleeping, can adjust the end to the means as well as the means to the end' (Wiggins, 1987: p. 100), more closely resembles ours. For this reason, it seems right to find 'important differences between the life of the cannibalistic blindworms . . . and the life of (say) a basking seal or a dolphin at play' (Wiggins, 1987: p. 100); also to see our behaviour as more like the second group. But this is not all, for such creatures are not persons in the relevant sense, nor do their behaviours constitute actions. Thus there is 'a different difference, between the life of seal or dolphins and the life of human beings living in communities with a history' (Wiggins, 1987: p. 100).

One aspect of this difference is that animals are not even potential art-makers: their behaviour is not intentional in the relevant sense. We explain the behaviour of even those animals as 'natural'. To reduce art

293

to a series of natural impulses is to denigrate art. Thus, we must see the events in question as actions (Chapter 2), and that involves seeing them as dealing with the intentional actions of persons, as has been recognized (to some degree) by writers on this area. For example, Roderyk Lange (1975: p. 48): 'Perhaps many of the older stories concerning animals quoted in literature must be dismissed as anthropomorphisms and classed along with the fables'. To this extent he is not happy with the move from animal evidence to claims about human activity. But he continues, 'this cannot be done with all of them'. It might be thought that the arguments here refute such ethological claims. But a weaker conclusion is all we need: at least, such claims will not inform us about the nature of dance.

Indeed, their position is almost as silly as the account of dance given by the *Encyclopaedia Britannica* of 1908, which claimed that dance resulted from overheating the brain! If true, this position reduces dances to a mechanical or movement phenomenon rather than an intentional or action-based one. No one who valued dance could urge that it is simply a product of our animal nature, or of some other mechanical cause. Indeed, the outcome of the discussion (in Chapter 12) was to think of the expression in dance not in terms of expression in (other) human action, but rather as an artistic activity.

The point to be extracted from this discussion is that it is a mistake to see dance as other than a social activity, a human activity. It is not *natural*; rather, it is the product of human intentions and interests, and intelligible using concepts in the history of that art form. We may like to say that the capacity to appreciate art is natural, but this is to say no more than that humans can do it.

An 'art-shaped hole' in the theory

One area of dispute between typical aestheticians and typical sociologists of art has been the degree to which each deals with the phenomenon *art*: each group has argued that, at the least, the other leaves out something important. This is the topic of this section and the next. It is largely constructed in terms of art in general since the extant discussion is not specifically about dance.

The first question is whether or not the sociologist of art can indeed deal with questions raised by the existence of art. If he can, aesthetic enquiry will look superfluous. Here we should not limit our sociologist to the sociology of artistic consumption. In the case of books, this might include 'how books are published, the social composition of their authors and audience, levels of literacy, the social determinants of "taste"' (Eagleton, 1976: p. 2). It is ground common to the aesthetician and the sociologist of art that their exercise must not degenerate into a mere counting of heads. (Contrast Judith Hanna [1983: p. 144] where she does seem to go for such counting; where, as she puts it, the matter is treated 'quantitatively', at least in theory.) But where does this concession leave us?

A useful guide is Peter Fuller (1980), who remarks on the way art criticism in the 1970s left an 'art-shaped' hole: it spoke of many things which related to art, which were important to art, but (as we might say) were not about art itself. The same seems to be true of much sociological writing about art in general and about dance in particular. Although such writing succeeds in characterizing certain features of the condition of art, it leaves obscure what makes the object in question art and not something else; it ignores (or leaves out) the aesthetic – the artistic – dimension. Is this really an omission? The theorists in question would say not. But they are demonstrably wrong. To understand this claim consider, as Fuller (1980: p. 236) does, a work of art made collectively. To see this case at its clearest, consider a piece of architectual sculpture: my favourite here is the Caryatids, or Doorway of the Maidens, on the Acropolis.[3] Anyone who has studied the Caryatids (even in a photograph) will have recognized that they are not equally well crafted: some of the statues of the virgins are more expressive than others. The difference is centrally one of the sculptor's handling of his material. Fuller (1980: p. 236) makes a similar point about the Parthenon frieze: 'Some [sculptors] . . . depicted folds in robes or drapery through rigid slots, dug into the marble like someone furrowing the surface of a cheese with a tea-spoon. Others worked their material in such a way that their representations seemed to have lightness, movement and translucence: the stone breathes and floats for them'. In other words, some of the artisans at work were also artists: they were making art. Their fellows were not. There is, one might say, a difference in sensibility. This difference is clearly manifest in what each does – it is a perfectly public, shareable, noticeable difference, even if it is not one we could describe in a neutral way. So talking about 'sensibility' here is not taking us away from the (material) conditions of the marble: not luring us into subjectivisim. But, as Fuller (1980: p. 236) continues, 'All the Parthenon craftsmen originally worked under *identical* ideological, social and cultural conditions'. Or, even if in fact they did not, we can assume that they did. Such an assumption is not fanciful. This means, of course, that reference to 'ideological, social, and cultural conditions' could never explain the differences described above. So we have identified a difference in

295

the properties of the work of art in question: its elements are of different artistic value. This difference is a perfectly recognizable, 'material' one. Yet this difference cannot be explained in those terms available to our typical sociologist of art. Having talked about 'ideological, social and cultural conditions', he has exhausted his brief.[4] If this point is accepted, we see why – as I claimed earlier – there is typically an omission from the sociology of art: Fuller's 'art-shaped hole'.

We need, of course, to ask the nature of this omission. Fuller (1980: p. 13) again gives a clear answer: 'I would stare into that hole, and faces like that of Vermeer's *Unknown Woman* would be gazing back at me'. That is to say, what remains unexplained is a characteristic experience of works of art; in particular, works of art which move us. This amounts to saying that, at root, artistic value eludes such analyses, and, of course, this study is centrally concerned with just such artistic value. That is, I urge for dance what Wollheim (1987: p. 249) says about painting: 'a real distinction, or a distinction in the nature of things, between what a painting means and what falls outside that meaning'. What falls outside its meaning for me, as for Wollheim, concerns the interrelation between art works (what might be called, inexactly, 'the relation between the art work and society'). Thus, for example, it will not do to treat ballet as a form of ethnic dance (Kealiinohomoku, 1983) for reasons which relate this section to the first in this chapter: to see ballet in this way ignores, or puts aside, what makes it art. Then, however well one discusses its social position, one is ignoring what makes it ballet. Indeed, the object of one's study is no longer ballet at all, for a key feature of ballet, its art status, is not part of one's investigation. Indeed, as Wollheim (1987: p. 359) points out: 'The case against the social explanation of art ... is brought home very forcibly when we turn our attention from works of art to artefacts that do indeed have a social function, and we observe how powerful a method social explanation becomes in such cases'. Having accepted the power and vigour of social explanation for some objects,[5] its comparative fragility for art will suggest that perhaps the wrong questions are being asked; this form of explanation has failed to catch the value of art.

For such points to be accepted, one must demonstrate that art works have such a value: one must explain the nature of artistic value. Some of that argumentation comes later in the chapter, where I demonstrate that my view can do justice to the historical character of art, and that it does not collapse into an unacceptable relativism. Moreover, since texts such as this one are centrally concerned with artistic value, the whole body of this work needs to be considered, not least the claims it develops about the relationship between art and education. To do more, and briefly, would involve discussion of the persistence of art, and in particular, the persistence of interest in art works of the past. This is one variant of the problem for Marx noted earlier: how to explain the persistence of interest in art, when the ideology which gave rise to it has withered away, along with the attendant mode of production (Marx, 1973: pp. 110–11). The answer must lie in some enduring capacity to find such things valuable (Wollheim, 1987: p. 357), for we find art work of the past intelligible, and hence valuable. Of course, this argument goes too quickly, and leaves unanswered questions about whether or not the art works are understood in the same way now as earlier. So these considerations do not, of themselves, decide on whether or not the appeal to art is in any sense permanent or eternal, contrary to claims by, for example, Janet Wolff (1983: p. 46).

Again, the conclusion of this section is well put by Peter Fuller (1980: p. 277): 'I am not advocating that the social and ideological analysis of art should be abandoned as a futile pursuit'. Rather, we must recognize that this is not all there is to the study of art. With such a conclusion in mind, we can turn to an objection that both expands and defends this reply.

A sense of history

It is often urged that aesthetics can do no justice to the relation between art and society because it lacks a sense of history. In a sense, I accept this criticism of much theorizing in aesthetics. The objection here, as in previous sections, is against the thought that aesthetics concerns itself with eternal verities, whereas in fact all that is available to us is the historical and contingent phenomenon of art. It is important not to misunderstand this point, for our interest typically lies in the significance for this day and age of the works of art, not (usually) their past significance. Our interest more closely resembles that of a theoretically inclined critic than that of an art historian (as traditionally conceived). Our interest is in artistic value, as we have seen. To have a sense of history here is just to recognize that our judgements are not more absolute than those of any past or future era, but since they are the judgements that concern us, they are the ones that we must treat as permanent, paradigmatic and so on. So here, recognizing historical forces does not send us looking at history at all. A sense of history recognizes the functional irrelevance of much of the past (and, obviously, the future). Past events can only be of relevance if they bear on the contemporary understanding of the particular work of art, and then it seems equally

297

appropriate to characterize them as present. Baker and Hacker (1984c: p. 4) bring this point out clearly:

Although we know the Impressionists were outrageous revolutionaries in the theory and practice of painting, we can no longer *see* them as outrageous. Because we know what Mozart made of Haydn's novel musical forms, we cannot hear Haydn's works as his audience was meant to, and did, hear them. We cannot return the apples from the Tree of Knowledge and History. The shifting viewpoint of successive generations renders the object of study essentially inconstant to view.

Certainly we bring the concepts that we have to our understanding of, in this example, the Impressionists. And we did not typically invent these concepts; rather, we were, in Cavell's (1984: p. 64) phrase 'born into' them. This means that our contemporary theorizing about art is already permeated by the ideas created by, and in response to, theorists of Impressionism. I may have seemed to imply one could study history, or the past, as such, but this study too must be saturated with a sense of history: it is our reconstruction of the past that we are investigating, yet this is no flaw in our procedure. Our reconstruction is the target, and what others (posterity) might do in the way of reconstruction is also functionally irrelevant.

Clearly what is required here is an understanding that does justice to the historical character of art: and that means more than just understanding it as an historical phenomenon. We need to locate artistic value within such a picture, and this is not easily done. In this sense, Marcuse (1978: p. 15) is right to comment that 'Marxist aesthetics has yet to ask: what are the qualities of art which transcend the specific social context and form, and give art universality?'. Even if we reject one sense of the term 'universality', we know exactly what is meant; and that takes us back to Fuller's 'art-shaped hole' in much theorizing.

Further, there is of course nothing inherently romantic in the position of the aesthetician. It may be true that many aestheticians do adopt a view of art and artists which makes it entirely dependent on the individual drives, decisions and so on of a unique genius, whose actions are understood as springing solely from his psyche. But there is no reason why they are obliged to. Two factors are of special relevance here. First, any variant of the institutional theory of art (see Chapter 3) will militate against such romanticism. Indeed, a notable critic of institutional theories explicitly attributes this criticism of them to 'the quasi-Romantic view of art that I cling to' (Beardsley, 1976: p. 20). The second consideration is slightly less direct. One explanation for the sociologist of art finding romanticism in the writing of aestheticians is that those writings do emphasize the role of individual artists for reasons made plain in the previous section of this chapter. So the aestheticians seem to be emphasizing the role of persons as agents, at the expense, one might say, of the role of social structures.

But some recent writing on the nature of social theory – most especially that of Anthony Giddens – has emphasized the connection between *structure* and *agency* (Giddens, 1979; Giddens, 1984). As Giddens (1987: p. 18) put it, 'the subjects of study in the social sciences and humanities are concept-using beings, whose concepts of their actions enter in a constitutive manner into what those actions are'. I do not wish to insist, of course, that social theory must be done in the ways Giddens suggests. My point is simply that giving a role to agency is not tantamount to rejecting the explanatory force of the concept of social structure. Indeed, it is arguable that only by giving a role to agency can one do justice to the complexity of social forces. As Raymond Williams (1974: p. 120) remarks, 'what this question has excluded is *intention*, and therefore all real social and cultural processes'.

Some philosophers, in rightly emphasizing artistic value, have 'seemed' to go overboard in rejecting social influences and the like. (I say seemed because this is a doubtful way of reading most of the writing, but it is current enough to be worth consideration.) A suitable example is Wollheim's criticism of externalist views of art. He is discussing painting: 'the theory gives an externalist answer to the question, what makes a painting a work of art? In other words, it answers the question by picking out a property of the painting that has nothing to do with its being a painting, with its paintingness' (Wollheim, 1987: p. 15). Of course, this simply raises the question of what does, and what does not, have to do with an object's being the kind of art work it is. Still, it is a criticism of any theory that its truth would detach questions about the nature of art from properties of art forms. Yet two comments are crucial here. First, we are reiterating points recognized in the previous section: if we locate the character of art outside art itself (outside questions of artistic value) we will be re-instantiating the 'art-shaped hole' in our theory. Second, one should not conclude from Wollheim's insistence on the importance of the properties of the work of art that social processes are thereby excluded. Wollheim (in common with most aestheticians) certainly does not do that! Certainly he wishes to comment on the artist's psychology, but any modern account of the philosophy of mind must do justice to the consideration generally known as Wittgenstein's private language argument. Filtered through such considerations, the public character of psychological phenomena is clear (Hacker, 1986: pp. 245–75).

One important aspect for aesthetics is the recognition of a genuine role in our understanding for the traditions of the art form, and in particular how those traditions import an historical dimension to our understanding Roger Scruton (1983: p. 24) makes this point by bringing out the historical nature of the grounds of such judgement. He asks us to contrast what we might say of Wagner with what his contemporaries might say:

> To Wagner, it would have seemed only that he was stretching to its limits something already there in the tradition of Romantic music. To us, looking backwards, *Tristan* seems to mark not a limit, but an intermediate step between Mozart and Schoenberg. We now see Wagner's chromaticism not as the extreme point of attenuation of a practice that preceded it, but rather as one step in the logical development that made it possible. Just as we could read that tradition forwards from Wagner to Schoenberg, so we read it backwards from Wagner to Mozart... no contemporary of Mozart could have found those qualities, but that does not make it wrong for us to look for them and to value them. In other words, tradition always makes its object present. It aligns itself with the past only to redeem that past for our present feelings.

Two objections must be met here. First, that this sense of history as I have been describing it is a recipe for conformity. Second, that it overemphasizes the contemporary, elevating it to an unwarranted 'necessity'.

Let us consider these two objections. First, accepting the possibility of future reversal yet concentrating on the contemporary may seem to dictate conformity to contemporary views. But it does not: it merely informs us that the stating of alternatives (call them revolutionary) is not by itself enough. One must find a place for these within the Republic of Art. To find such a place is, in part, a public relations exercise of the kind undertaken by Ruskin on Turner's behalf, and no less important for that (Chapter 3). Yet a constraint on that exercise is also apparent. What can intelligibly be made sense of, understood, as part of that exercise, must have connections with what the Republic of Art previously understood, for it is in terms of past doings and sayings that present doings and sayings are rendered intelligible. The aspiration to make all things new simultaneously is, as previously noted, an incoherent aspiration. Second, the question of the 'contingency' of the

300

present views: what must be asked is, 'What is the alternative?'. Those who bemoan the contingent character of much of contemporary aesthetics, and urge that my emphasis elevates those views to unwarranted necessity, have in mind some alternative conception of objectivity, or necessity, in thought and reason. But that cannot withstand the demands of a sense of history. History makes us work in a structured way towards goals specified by the discipline itself, which means, in effect, by the past and present practitioners of that discipline. This is what it means to speak of 'historical logic' (Thompson, 1978: pp. 229–42): the historical facts are *real* facts, but that does not exempt them from being seen 'under the aspect of history', as one might say. To think otherwise is to engage in a futile and scientistic search, 'the search for universal commensuration in a final vocabulary', as Richard Rorty (1979: p. 368) put it. It is to search for necessities beyond those given by our human understanding, for there is no 'God's-eye view' of events in terms of which a human account of them could be judged true or false. Or rather, such a view must necessarily be unintelligible to humans.

Aesthetics can lack this sense of history, but only when it is not well done. Or, more exactly, to do aesthetics lacking a sense of history is for that reason to do it badly (Shusterman, 1989). It should be noted that what is needed is not social history as such. Aestheticians were right on that score, for the historical forces to be recognized in acquiring a sense of history revolve around our own position in history. Thus 'informal ethnographies' generated by self-aware reflection are to the point. Here the historical character of art is recognized when we accept that the meaning or significance of particular works of art is not a timeless matter,[6] but neither is it a subjective one (or one where anything goes).

In this section and the previous one I have discussed a variety of ways in which, when done properly, aesthetics does not need to be augmented by the sociology of art, and in which aesthetics can genuinely be said to be discussing art and society. This did not require the aesthetician to ignore social processes, but it clarified his interest in art around the concept of aesthetic value, as well as clarifying this concept. Yet mention of artistic value raises again the spectre of relativism: for is not artistic value just a culture-relative phenomenon?

Relativism and understanding

Throughout this chapter we have considered the relation between dance and society. The final question is this: are judgements of the arts somehow relative to some particular society or culture? The relevance of this question lies in the differing conceptions of aesthetic (artistic) value generated by any answers. In particular, if we wish to understand the sense in which art works are products of particular societies or cultures, we must give due weight to the idea of artistic value as specific to that society or culture. But the implication of such weight is yet to be explored. A key question here: does our attitude generate *relativism*?

To begin, we require a brief account of relativism, and a brief account of what is at issue.[7] Consider a case of disagreement, where I say that X is true and you say that X is false (or that some contrasting statement Y is true). Now, it seems that one of us is right, the other wrong, unless we are both wrong. However, a relativist answer here allows that we are both right, and those two characteristics – one asserting what the other denies, and both being right – define relativism for us. The varieties of relativism result from the various explanations of how it is possible for us both to be right. For example, if X were true from the perspective of one culture and false from the perspective of another, we should have cultural relativism.

Three important qualifications are needed. First, we are not merely talking about the effect of what philosophers call 'indexicals'[8] such as 'here', 'I', and so on. Of course we can both be telling the truth when you say 'It's raining here', and I say 'It is not raining here', if you are in Blackpool and I am in Brighton. But this is not a case of location-relativism. We are not contradicting each other. Second, you must be asserting what I am denying, or whatever. If you say there is no money in the bank, and I say there is money in the bank – but you mean the bank of the river when I mean the Bank of England – then there is again no relativism: for we are not in fact disagreeing. The third qualification is that we are not just talking about our beliefs. If you say that you believe it is raining in London, and I say that I do not believe it is raining in London, we are (again) not disagreeing. It may be true that you believe that it is raining (that is a fact about you, as one might say), and true that I do not believe that it is raining (or that I believe that it is not raining), but there is no disagreement, we are just reporting our beliefs on the matter. Now there are certain matters – for example, whether it is presently raining in Brighton – for which a relativist account would be decidedly odd. No doubt there are theorists who might argue for it, but we will not consider such views here. Our concern is with claims for the relativity of cultural judgements, of a kind which should become clearer as we continue (Winch, 1987: Best, 1986).

With these qualifications, what is the issue? Why do we care about relativism? The answer, of course, concerns the sense in which claims about the nature of art in general – and dance in particular – can really be true. If we have a relativist view of these matters, it will be apparent that no real sense can be given to the idea of truth here: all we can have is truth relative to X, for some X. So, for example, it might be thought that certain tribal 'dances' were indeed dance from the perspective of a relevant tribesman: it was true for them that these were dances, even though these were not dances for us, or not dances from our perspective. And what works for the idea of truth here works equally for the idea of value. We might think that a certain dance was good for them (that is, the sort of thing they would find valuable, or see value in) and not good for us (not the kind of thing that we would see value in).

However, consider one simple case to clarify the issue, before applying our results to dance. It is sometimes urged that in fifth century BC Sparta theft was not wrong, the evidence being that young men of the period were kept short of food and thereby encouraged to steal it. (This was thought to breed self-reliance.) Thus we can imagine a Spartan of this period asserting 'theft is not wrong', and a Victorian Englishman declaiming 'theft is wrong'. Now the relativist would urge that each is right relative to his own time or society, and, by implication, there can be no more general ways in which one can be right.

A moment's reflection shows us two possible theses here, not one: *relativism* and *incommensurability*. As well as a relativist claim that there is something that one asserts and the other denies (both being right), we might also encounter an incommensuralist's claim that the two remarks do not really contradict one another: that they pass one another by. (It is important to draw this distinction since some of the arguments traditionally deployed against relativists are actually considerations of incommensurability theses.) Let us consider relativism first.

The chief arguments deployed in support of relativist positions are those deriving from the multiplicity of value: the different practices which are or have been valued in cultures at various times and places. It is thought to follow that each of these practices was indeed valuable at that time or in that place, but since they are not valuable here and now, it follows that values are culturally relative. Three related considerations show the incoherence of this position. The first is most simply put by those who reply to relativists: 'Well, relativism is not true for me'. That is to say, there is implicit within relativism a claim for at least one transcultural truth – namely, the truth of relativism itself. If we cannot just dismiss relativism as just 'not true for me', it must be because the relativist thesis (at least in its full generality) is false. So there is a deep incoherence in relativism. It wishes to employ the notion of a (general) truth, and simultaneously to deny such a notion.

The second consideration turns on the connection between relativism (as I use the term) and subjectivism. If it were true that truth is culture-relative, we would require an account of what were and what were not 'cultures', for example, of how big a culture was. Are all inhabitants of the UK part of one culture? If not, are all inhabitants of Scotland? All women? The only satisfactory stopping point – at least if the idea of a subculture, and a sub-subculture, is accepted – seems to be with a 'culture' of one; and that is subjectivism. We have been at pains to expose the incoherence of such a position. As we have seen (Chapters 1 and 3), if we ask 'Is X really a work of art?', 'Is this movement sequence really a dance?', this can't be just a matter of opinion, where one can say what one likes. An object may interpreted in various ways, but this fact does not count against its art status. Further, one can be wrong in claiming that X is a work of art. Yet this reply depends – one might think – on agreement about what art is; or, as it might be put, on the definition of the term 'art'. But, as we say in the first section of this chapter, that is an impossible requirement. Nevertheless, accepting that the term 'art' cannot be defined still allows that not all objects are art, still limits what objects are art (and also what I can make sense of as art, for these two ideas are not necessarily co-extensive).

What this comparison in particular shows is the connection between relativist views and subjectivist ones. Faced with that conclusion, one may lurch towards the opposite of relativism, a kind of *absolutism* (or 'realism') in which there is just one way to view art works. As we have seen (Chapter 1 and elsewhere), this is not a plausible view, given the variety of ways art is – as a matter of fact – seen, for example by critics.

We make progress by addressing the third consideration of relativism, that concerned with understanding. As we saw earlier in this chapter (pp. 286–7), it is crucial that we really mean *dance* by the word 'dance' – for example, when translating from a foreign tongue or a different time. The Japanese word *giri* was used earlier to illustrate this point. We may have to translate it as the term 'duty', but to do so is, or may be, radically misleading. This insight applies directly to the case of relativism. Recall that my characterization of the truth of relativism required that there be some thesis asserted by one party, denied by another, and yet both were right. But now we can see how problematic this will be. Any argument that suggests that both speaker A and speaker B were correct in their assertions will, for that reason, be an argument against their talking about the same thing. Thus, when our fictional Spartan says 'Theft is not wrong', we might feel that something was amiss in our translation. Surely theft or stealing is something characterized or picked out as wrong. Hence we should treat this not as a case of relativism but, at best, as a case of incommensurability.

So the three considerations from relativism lead us towards discussion of the other position mentioned earlier: the incommensuralist one. It may help to clarify this position, which is neatly characterized by Kuhn (1976: pp. 190–1) as follows:

In applying the term "incommensurability" to theories, I'd intended only to insist that there was no common language within which both could be fully expressed and which could therefore be used in a point-by-point comparison between them.

What is denied is the possibility of a point-by-point comparison of two ways of looking at the world, not the possibility of any comparison. Such a view, then, offers an alternative to relativism – we do not have two views in disagreement, with both correct – but without lapsing into the absolutism of only one right view. If we are dissatisfied with absolutism – perhaps because we can't make much sense of the idea of genuine reality, of which other accounts are partial reflections – we need to locate a viable alternative. While our rejection of both relativism and absolutism may lead in that direction, a positive argument would be advantageous here.

The outline of such an argument can be seen if we confront a counter-argument, one often, and mistakenly, directed against relativism. The counter-argument is this: that incommensurability means that only those who believe in something can understand it, and that this conclusion is incoherent. Hence the incommensurability thesis is incoherent. Let us examine the moves this argument makes, returning to our Spartan example. The idea is that what we mean by the word 'theft' is not what the Spartan means by the term we have (mis-)translated as 'theft'. But what does he mean by his term? There is no concept in our cognitive stock which corresponds to, or has the same connections as, his. Like *giri*, what the Spartan means by 'theft' is unavailable to us. Yet of course it is available to other Spartans. They share his values (some of what philosophers call his 'beliefs'), therefore they can understand what he means. The only way we could understand would be to become Spartans – and we would be able to understand to the extent to which we achieved this. Generalizing, this means that one could only understand from within the paradigm[9] to which one belongs. And to belong is to share certain beliefs. Thus, for example, Newtonian scientists would be incomprehensible to Einsteinians, at least to the degree to which their 'beliefs' differ. Only when the beliefs are shared can there be understanding. This seems to render the position immune to criticism, for why should those who believe in it criticize it? Thus, it is argued, the whole idea of incommensurability is incoherent, since it renders informed criticism impossible: and this is absurd.[10]

Before responding directly to this argument, it is worth reminding ourselves that the conclusion reached is perhaps less absurd than is proposed. As we saw in Chapter 5, to understand a statement in mathematics, it is necessary to learn (at least some) mathematics. One cannot understand a certain operation in mathematics – say, differential calculus – unless one understands mathematics. To that extent, one must become a mathematician in order to discuss or criticize mathematics. And yet discussion and criticism are possible. Here we see one aspect of the key to the whole position: that to share certain understandings is not, or not necessarily, to share certain beliefs; it only appears to be because philosophers play fast and loose with the idea of belief. As Winch (1987: p. 196) has pointed out, when you assert that John is in pain and I deny it, the theorists in question would urge that the content of our belief is the same – namely, John's pain. There is a clear sense in which, if we do not both understand the concept 'pain', we cannot disagree about it. But when we do understand it, disagreement is still possible. So the supposed conclusion does not follow in any straightforward way. As for the mathematicians, a common understanding does not automatically lead to a common conclusion. Thus the need to understand is misinterpreted in the counter-argument. There is more to be said, for not all areas of our understanding are even of this kind: asserting incommensurability in one area of our thought does not require incommensurability in all. Thus theorists such as Winch (1987: pp. 189–92) emphasize the heterogeneity of thought and culture – neither is a seamless web – and are recognized to do so.

Two further points central to the incommensuralist position must be recognized. First, one should expect incommensurability to be a rare event rather than a common one (Feyerabend, 1987: p. 272). Most of the time, when two people are content to discuss a particular topic, they do so from within a paradigm (as we have said): they share concepts and cultures sufficiently for informed discussion. This is why we expect a person with an avowed love of classical music to admire some of the canon: Bach, Mozart, Beethoven, Mahler. Without such common ground, we would not accept that person's claim to love classical music. And within the common ground, we know how to go on. Evaluations of, say, dance performances are *'arguable*, in ways that anyone who knows about such things will know how to pursue' (Cavell, 1969: p. 92). The explanation here is given by Wittgenstein (1969: section 298, p. 38): 'We belong to a community which is bound together by science and education'. We have been brought up to understand, using concepts we did not invent.

The second point is a further complication. There is one question for the philosopher here, a different one for the critic. Even in science, as Feyerabend (1987: p. 272) puts it: 'incommensurability is a difficulty for philosophers, not for scientists'. From the philosopher's perspective, the view of an earlier group of scientists may be incommensurable with those of a later group; but from the scientist's perspective, the views of the later group are right and those of the earlier group are wong; and this is quite correct, for at any time one's judgements are made from within one's paradigm. Only the philosopher needs to recognize the temporal location this implies.

We are compelled to take a fish-eye view of art (as of everything else): to see ourselves and our judgements as part of the passage of a process. Thus *our* judgements are the ones that typically concern us. In summary, when such judgements differ from those of past theorists, those past theorists will look wrong; and will be wrong. The term 'wrong' here is founded on the historical character of the judgement. We could equally say that future generations may (or will) find our best judgements wrong. But that should simply be read as an expression of humility before the fact of history. It should not be seen as taking seriously the thought that our 'best shot' is mistaken. In particular, it should not be seen as a ground for present doubt, or present scepticism. Doubt needs a specific ground, and here there is none.

So what Feyerabend says for the scientist can also be true for the dance critic: the views of an earlier time will often be false, and that means 'false when understood as they now are'. But this is the only way the critic presently needs to understand them. The important historical dimension of understanding is reinforced. A specifically aesthetic thesis follows from this for, paradoxically, accepting that art has an historical character justifies a certain kind of ahistorical judgement: what we *presently* say about art works is then true of them. It must be, because we are in the flow of history. But nothing is unalterably fixed: any aspect of taste could be changed (although not all at once).

This then is my vision of the understanding of art, which integrates it into a more general web of human normative activities (and practices) and which emphasizes its historical character. And that view is essentially an incommensuralist one. The illusion that the incommensuralist conception of truth and so on is weaker (or weirder) than it is may be fostered by the sort of diagram or model used to present it. We are asked to think of a series of unrelated views, say, portrayed as a series of circles on the page. Yet this model in fact concedes the absolutist's point, for it gives us a 'God's-eye-view' of the incommensurable 'systems'. What is needed is something more like a fish-eye view. We are within one of the circles, on such a diagram; there is no external position. Of course, seen from our position, certain other views are false or crazy, as the Einsteinian physicist sees the work of both Aristotle and Newton as misconceived in one way or another. Once we recognize this, we will be less inclined to dismiss the incommensuralist perspective.

What is right, of course, is that any grasp of the concepts 'art' or 'dance' depends on the understanding that we have of the practices in question: both 'we' and 'the practice' are in a particular cultural context. This is just to deny two things: first, that there is one standard across the huge diversity of activities mentioned earlier in this chapter. Second, that there is some neutral position from which our judgements are not contestable. Neither of these claims could be defended, for both assume that the conceptual questions are straightforward: that *our* concepts, and in particular 'dance', have an obvious application in all these different cultures. Writing in a similar vein, Best (1986: p. 89) remarked on the 'crucial point ... that one should be very careful not to assume that cultural practices which bear some immediate resemblance to practices in our culture are the same and have the same values applied to them'. A further point is of considerable importance. My aim here is to defend our everyday understanding, and our understanding of that understanding (see Putnam, 1987: p. 17): that, against the more general relativist, there really are tables, ice cubes and rainbows – and dances – in the world, hence that there are things true of them, including value things (Bambrough, 1979: pp. 11–34). But such a thought will run counter to some versions of absolutism/objectivism/realism, for although the official position is of a world independent of any view of it, that can easily be identified with a view given by the natural sciences, and especially physics. And, as the work of others (Stebbing, 1937: pp. 15–20) has shown, such a perspective can seem decidedly odd. For example, it can deny the reality of tables on the grounds that tables are solid objects and, as particle physics shows us, the things we call 'tables' are in fact largely spaces with just a few solids: that is, the molecules/particles. If we were to see this as the absolutist alternative, it would surely strengthen the appeal of my incommensuralist picture.

But is it in fact the right way to see the absolutist/objectivist? One problem for the exposition of his view suggests that perhaps it is. How is the absolutist to describe the absolute reality of how things really are? To put that in a certain way, what language is he going to use? And that question is difficult. He cannot consistently mention a particular 'language',[11] for that seems to bring with it a perspective or way of looking (at least if we focus on topics of interest to us). Equally, he cannot use no language if (a) he wants his claim to be understood and (b) he claims to be really saying anything. Faced with such a choice, many an absolutist has chosen a neutral language for his account of reality, and that neutral language has been the one provided by natural science. For this reason, then, it seems fair to see many absolutists as embracing the 'description' given by science, with the consequences outlined in the paragraph above.

The interest of this possibility is that one part of any defence of the incommensuralist position would turn on showing how its opponents can do no better in answering the key difficulties: in particular, that realism is – as Putnam (1987) urges – the kind of seducer from a B movie who promises much to the innocent maiden but cannot deliver. If this point were accepted (and the lure of 'one right answer' correspondingly reduced) a plausible non-relativist (but incommensuralist) alternative might be found.

Conclusion

This chapter has defended an account of art (and the understanding of art) which is incommensuralist without being relativist; which accepts the historical character of art without turning into social history; and which locates the aesthetics of dance into the 'art-shaped hole' left by the sociology of dance. Of course, all of this is done schematically, but if it is accepted, my general account of dance, founded on the account of understanding dance, will be located as a foundational element in dance studies.

Recommended reading

Two useful anthologies are Copeland and Cohen, 1983, and Spencer, 1985. On relativism in general, see Winch, 1987: pp. 194–208; and Putnam, 1990: pp. 3–42. On cultural relativism, an introductory discussion is Best, 1986. Applied to dance, see Sparshott, 1988: pp. 210–30, 271–88.

Conclusion

This work has articulated an account of dance which makes plain that dance is an intentional, valuable human activity, of a kind suitable to have a place in formal and informal education. At the same time, it has sought (a) to avoid undue emphasis on the (easily misunderstood) *intentions* of its creators or performers; (b) to steer clear of wild claims (for example, that to dance is human) while explaining why they are wild; (c) to show why the value question is neither financial nor instrumental in some other way. Each of these points has its own importance. But perhaps the most crucial comes from combining the *value* of dance (as an art form) with its *human* (or intended) quality, for these amount to the understanding of dance being 'objective humanly speaking' (an apt expression Putnam [1990: pp. xix, 210] attributes to David Wiggins).

At the centre of the account of dance is the picture of the meaning of dances as related to the *explanations* given of them, a relationship drawn via a slogan from Wittgenstein. This account is defended in Chapters 6 and 7, and employed throughout the text. Such an emphasis makes the *meaning* of dance works (and also the *understanding* of them) a public process: the sort of thing which can be learned, discussed, and itself understood. Further, the connection between art and life issues, explored in Chapter 8, means that dance has a generally enhancing impact; that it can lead to forms of personal development.

A necessary limitation on the presentation

If this is so, why is the developmental quality of dance (which I urge is so important) never stated more explicitly in the text? Three factors militate against a concise characterization of the personal impact of dance: it is an individual process; it is not a once and for all process; one sees it always with hindsight. Let us elaborate each of these points in turn.

● It is an individual process. The sorts of (conceptual) change brought about for me by confrontation with dance will typically differ from

310

those brought about for you. To use a metaphor introduced earlier (Chapter 9), what I learn depends on my puzzles and perplexities, and these will typically be different from yours. Notice, though, that there is nothing subjective involved here.

- It is not a once and for all process. We return to the same works of art time and time again, and this is especially true of works we consider 'great'. On the image of a well, we might say that such works are inexhaustible. Whatever this really amounts to, it clearly means that we cannot characterize one unique, once and for all outcome of (even) my interaction with an art work. So the individualized point recorded above is further inflected with an historical dimension.
- One sees the case with hindsight. Here the problem is a familiar one: after a conceptual change, one may be unable to describe accurately the impact on one's pre-change concepts. So that, for example, adopting a conception of straight lines drawn from Riemann geometry leaves one with no way of describing what one meant by the expression 'straight line' when one's geometry was Euclidian (Dummett, 1978: p. 284).

However, each of these factors is explicitly explored in the text. The individual character of the impact of dance does not lead to subjectivism; the possibility of further insight does not make one's initial insight incomplete or partial; the need for historical specificity too does not render contemporary judgement uncertain or tentative. Subjectivism of the sort described in Chapter 1 (contrast Wiggins, 1987: pp. 185–214) must be rejected if the value traditionally ascribed to the arts can be maintained. Luckily for those of us who admire the arts, this can be done, and the kind of historicizing and institutionalizing which I have urged are important gives us a humanly developed account of the arts.

Methods and a key assumption of the text

The point just made about the human scale of the account of dance being defended is also reflected in a philosophical commitment throughout this work: although that is perhaps less than fully articulated. The commitment in question requires bringing to philosophy a robust sense of constructivity,[1] on a parallel with Russell's talk[2] of 'a robust sense of reality'. In practice, this will mean limiting our claims and our cases to the realm of what is possible for humans to understand. And hence that our claims to understanding cannot outstrip our

311

capacity for getting evidence for those claims. Moreover, we should not automatically assume that we can, say, imagine such-and-such simply because we can make a sentence without obvious self-contradiction which seems to assert such-and-such (Hacker, 1976: p. 24). Of course, this is not the place to pursue such abstract discussions; but I hope the commitment to a robust sense of constructivity has been apparent throughout the argument.

Of course, I am thinking here not of detailed argument in philosophy so much as the kind of pictures which support it. Wittgenstein makes the point clearly, when asked whether his aim is to drive thinkers from a paradise created by contemporary theorizing. He remarks (Wittgenstein, 1975: p. 103):

I would try to do something quite different: I would try to show you that it is not a paradise – so that you'll leave of your own accord. I would say, 'You're welcome to this; just look about you'.

In this vein, my aim throughout has been to characterize a commonly held view of dance, as a way of leading those in dance studies out of that 'paradise'. Here, of course, there is another picture in the background. Much contemporary philosophical thought has concerned itself with the nature of truth and understanding. Russell thought himself to be standing up for a very common-sense, everyday picture of the world, of truths about the world, and of understanding about those truths (see Passmore, 1968: pp. 203, 226). That sort of account seems to me largely mistaken. I view the world, truth, and understanding in a different fashion. At first it may appear more complex, but it comprises one complex idea initially, leading in a fairly straightforward way to a straightforward conclusion. Views such as Russell's, which appear simple at first, require so much augmentation 'further down the road' to maintain plausibility that they end up at least as complex as the view I espouse (Baker and Hacker, 1984a: pp. 386–9).

Applied to aesthetics, the central idea is that the limits of art-critical or aesthetic concern are roughly continuous with the limits of possible human knowledge and understanding. That is to say, there are no works of art which are in principle beyond the scope of human interest in a direct – that is, perceptual – fashion. Of course, there may be one or two peculiar or extreme or imaginary examples which challenge such a claim. But the general point is that aesthetic relevance cannot be sought for objects beyond human powers in these ways. This will count against Aesthetic Platonism[3] and other such claims. This point warrants further explanation. It amounts to this: believing in the truth of claims about aesthetic value is not tantamount to believing in eternal,

Platonic 'ideas', which are the 'objects' of such judgements. A useful comparison here might be with the philosophy of mathematics. We believe in numbers and in, as we might say, the realm of numbers – constructing a new method for solving simultaneous equations is a creation in the realm of numbers – without needing to believe in numbers as perpetual or eternal, abstract 'somethings'. This is having a robust sense of constructivity with respect to mathematics. Believing in the objectivity of numbers does not, by itself, require that we take numbers to be anything other than within the scope of human knowledge and understanding, the sort of things people can (and do) understand (Dummett, 1978: p. xxii). A robust sense of constructivity is required if one is to deal appropriately with aesthetic matters, just as it is if one is to deal appropriately with numerical matters.

These points amount, in concrete terms, to a view of aesthetic matters giving due weight to human powers and capacities; doing so is acknowledging the etymology of the word 'aesthetic', from the Greek word for sense perception. Of course, a great deal of aesthetic water has passed under the bridge since that time: we would certainly wish to deny the Greeks' contrast between matters of sense perception and matters of understanding or reason (see Chapter 6). But finding an appropriate place for such theses within philosophy requires more extensive discussion (some perhaps quite technical) of the philosophy of understanding and the philosophy of mind. (These are topics for a later text.)

Two fundamental principles of aesthetics

The Introduction identified a number of key themes for the text, and two principles in particular. As well as its commitment to rigour, it aimed to defend (a) the *autonomy* of judgements of art (artistic judgements were not to be subsumed under some non-artistic heads) and (b) the genuinely *explanatory* nature of such judgements, both on a parallel with jurisprudence (see Baker, 1977: p. 26). These promises are fulfilled throughout the text. We have seen (in Chapter 5) how the explanations of critics comprise the meanings of dances, for they are the explanations which explain meaning: they constitute acts of understanding dance. So the explanations are genuine, and integral to the idea of dances as meaningful or meaning-bearing. Further, they are not reducible to non-artistic explanations, for two reasons. First, one only sees dance (rather than, say, mere movement) when one brings to bear action-concepts appropriate to the art form of dance. Any non-artistic explanations would not involve seeing the dance *as dance* at all. Second, the

313

explanation of dance as dance depends on the conventions and traditions of dance: on its history, as we might say. Again, any explanation lacking this relation would, for that reason, fail to be an explanation of dance. (As we saw in Chapter 3 and elsewhere, having such a relation is not equivalent to making explicit mention, nor to conformity.) So our two fundamental principles are defended.

Dance in education

This text is about the understanding of dance; but it has an eye on the place of dance in society, in particular, the role of dance in education. This is a topic on which I hope to write extensively in the near future (see also McFee, 1989a). But it is worth sketching explicitly how some of the theses elaborated here might comprise an attractive picture of the nature of dance in education: what I call 'the artistic approach' (because it emphasizes seeing dance as an art form). If the arts in general have the potential for positive impact on human life (which the life issues connection guarantees), it follows that dance, when viewed as an art form, has this same potential. Further, the meanings of dances are, on the view developed here, in principle publicly available for discussion: they can be found in the explanations offered (or accepted) of dances. So this account replaces a mysterious 'process' with something perfectly public: the practice of discussion and explanation. Such a tendency would maintain the objectivity of dance study but – because it emphasizes both the mobilization in perception of concepts and the experience required for such mobilization – the informed observer will be central, rather than the test or check-list. This account of dance seems to me realistic and practical, although it may run counter to some current educational thinking in the United Kingdom. Still, it gives due weight to dance as an object of understanding and as a human activity.

Recommended reading

As implied throughout, the way forward will involve a discussion of the philosophy of understanding: Dummett, 1978; Baker and Hacker, 1984a; Blackburn, 1984. It should also involve a discussion of Wittgenstein's work: Baker and Hacker, 1980; Baker and Hacker, 1984b; Baker and Hacker, 1985a; Hacker, 1990. Further, it may be important to consider the nature of philosophy: Baker, 1986. As noted initially, the only sustained philosophical account of dance is Sparshott, 1988. This is difficult and, as its sub-title implies, merely 'first steps'.

314

Notes

A general comment:

My own feelings on the currently vexed topic of the use of gendered examples and pronouns in writing generally, and in scholarly writing particularly, are well captured by J. O. Urmson (1988). I employ the style he describes more or less consistently throughout this text, and can do no better than to quote him directly, and with approval, to explain:

> The author has followed the ancient literary use of "man" as a noun of common gender and the convention that the pronoun "he" refers to persons of both sexes in the absence of contrary indications. He has not the literary skill to write otherwise without intolerable clumsiness of diction. In adopting this style he intends no offence to anyone and hopes that none will be taken.

Introduction

1   For our purposes, *aesthetics* is that part of philosophy which deals with art, beauty and the like. So it is centrally part of (the academic discipline of) philosophy. Its exact boundaries are a matter of dispute: for some key issues see Ground, 1989. One of the most comprehensive accounts of aesthetics is Sparshott, 1963.

2   Ludwig Wittgenstein (1889–1951) was an Austrian who became Professor of Philosophy at Cambridge. An elementary but trustworthy introduction to his work is Kenny, 1973; a more detailed account is Hacker, 1986. Various memoirs of his fascinating life exist: for example, Malcolm, 1966; Rhees, 1984; Redpath, 1990. The first part of an authoritative biography is McGuinness, 1988. Any thorough study must begin with the Baker and Hacker commentary on Wittgenstein's major work, *Philosophical Investigations* (1953): see any of Baker and Hacker, 1980; Baker and Hacker, 1985a; Hacker, 1990. For a discussion of Wittgenstein's papers, see Von Wright, 1982, pp. 35–62; Kenny, 1984: pp. 24–60; Hilmy, 1987: pp. 1–39. Of particular relevance here is the discussion of explanation, Baker and Hacker, 1980: pp. 69–85; also of the project of philosophy, Baker and Hacker, 1980: pp. 531–45.

3   The expression 'logically equivalent' is a technical one in philosophy. Roughly, two terms are logically equivalent if they can be substituted for one another in a statement without changing the meaning of that statement. So that if, say, 'cat' and 'feline' were logically equivalent, then 'the cat sat on the mat' should mean exactly the same thing as 'the feline sat on the mat'. One test for logical equivalence here might be whether the first

statement could be true and yet the second false. If so, the two terms are *not* logically equivalent. See, for example, the 'definition' given in Carruthers, 1986: p. 257.

1 Basic Concepts for Aesthetics

1 A vivid illustration of this point comes from the film *Kotch* in which the Walter Matthau character, completing a Rorschach (ink-blot) test, learns that the tester thinks his answers too literal. Faced with the next ink-blot, he says it looks like a lonely spermatozoa asking the way to the nearest fallopian tube. It is difficult to see how one can specify in advance what ways of seeing a design are impossible, once such a degree of inventiveness is acknowledged.
2 This classification, and much else in the chapter, owes a debt to the lecture 'Accountability and Aesthetic Education', which David Best delivered at Brighton Polytechnic in 1987 (here cited as Best, 1987).
3 For a discussion of these issues, see Chalmers, 1982, under 'rationalism', 'objectivism'. A typical author would be Winterbourne, 1981.
4 In the 1930s, the philosopher Carnap 'invented' a character who took such a God's-eye-view, knowing absolutely everything. He was called 'Logically Omniscient Jones', or 'LOJ'. So the perspective here is that of LOJ. See Putnam, 1990: p. 5.
5 As is obvious, this work owes a considerable debt to the works of David Best, but also to his lectures and private communications. In fact, many of the theses originate in authors admired by Best and myself (for example, Wittgenstein). But Best's exposition of them is typically the most suitable for a beginner.

2 Dance as Action

1 This exact way of putting the point derives from correspondence with David Carr.
2 This task was undertaken by Drid Williams, in her PhD thesis (unpublished, University of Oxford 1976).

3 Dance as Art

1 As Terry Diffey made clear in conversation (see also Diffey, 1985: pp. 147–53), Tolstoy's work could be seen as an attack on artifice in art. But then one must distinguish artifice – the excessive, as it were – from conventionality. And Tolstoy does not do this. So, at best, it might be urged that Tolstoy is less ideal an example than Beardsmore finds him to be.
2 The quotation is from *The Martha Graham Dance Company*, BBC 2 Television (10 October 1987).

3 The word 'institutional' has two fairly distinct uses in philosophy. The first, in moral philosophy, has a class of institutional facts, which depend for their truth on human practices (see Anscombe, 1968: pp. 71–5). The other, used here in connection with art, is stronger in urging the necessity for an 'authoritative body' – the Republic of Art (see Baker and Hacker, 1984a: pp. 272–3).

4 The topic of the relationship between claims to art status and to artistic value is discussed in McFee, 1989b. There is also a general point here, encapsulated in the contrast between 'thick' and 'thin' value-predicates: see Putnam, 1990: p. 166.

5 The aesthetic attitude has been variously characterized in philosophy. See, for example, Beardsley, 1958; Sparshott, 1963: pp. 212–13; Saw, 1972: pp. 51–75. For some criticisms, see Dickie, 1974: pp. 90–146. As well as Beardsley, Elliott (1973, 1978) might be thought an aesthetic attitude theorist.

6 See also Wollheim's discussion of Rothko: Wollheim, 1973: p. 128; and my comments: McFee, 1985.

7 *Adagio for a Dead Soldier* was premiered by the Alvin Ailey American Dance Theatre at Sadler's Wells, London, on 25 November 1970. The playbill attributes the choreography to one of the dancers, Geoffrey Holder, but in discussion Ailey remarked on the collaborative nature of the choreography within his company. Therefore I shall attribue the dance to Ailey, really meaning the company.

8 See, especially, Baker and Hacker, 1984a; also McFee, 1982. The central thought here is that the philosophy of language should maintain 'a robust sense of constructivity' (see the Conclusion of this text). More generally, see Baker, 1986.

9 For example, in my PhD thesis 'The Historical Character of Art' (unpublished, University College, London, 1982).

10 As noted previously, the concept 'art', and other institutional concepts, are more like concepts as envisaged under the community analysis. See Kuhn, 1969: pp. 176–90; Kuhn, 1977: pp. 340–51.

4 Dance as a Performing Art

1 For a brief characterization of identity questions, see Shoemaker, 1963: pp. 2–3. For its application to persons, see Perry, 1975: pp. 3–30. In general, see Wiggins, 1980.

2 It is worth stressing that we invoke the type/token contrast only for those works of art that are multiples; we do *not* use it for those works that are particular objects. So that, at present, reproductions of the *Mona Lisa* are not 'examples' of that art work at all. If they become tokens of a type, then the reproductions and the paint and canvas version would be in the same position.

3 This objection was suggested by Myrene McFee.

4 See Pater, 1974: p. 55. The point was suggested by Richard Wollheim in a lecture at University College, London, in 1978. See also Wollheim, 1973: pp. 258–9.

5   Contrast Sharpe, 1979, which argues that, if the token is the performance, the type must be the performer's interpretation. The status of the work itself is left unclear. (This is a very suitable article for a beginner, showing what could be achieved through one good example, thoroughly discussed.)

6   Literary works differ from the performing arts on this point. Omitting one comma from *Ulysses* may well make no aesthetic (artistic) difference, hence require no explanation. But, first, such a difference is to be expected, given the 'anomalous nature' of literature: see Shusterman, 1978. Second, no such point could apply for, say, a very short poem. There every feature is crucial.

7   One topic that might be explored here would be Aesthetic Platonism. See Levinson, 1980; Kivy, 1983; Kivy, 1987. Discussion here should reflect modern thought on Platonism in the philosophy of mathematics: see Dummett, 1978: pp. 202–47.

8   I owe this point to Kivy's paper, 'Aesthetic Platonism in Music: another kind of defence', read to British Society of Aesthetics National Conference, September, 1986. However, the discussion does not appear in the amended published version (Kivy, 1987).

5   Dance as an Object of Understanding

1   See, for example, Dummett, 1975: pp. 99–102; Baker and Hacker, 1980: pp. 81–5. Applied to music, see Scruton, 1989: p. 85.

2   The phrase is from Wittgenstein, 1974: p. 59, p. 69. For discussion, see Baker and Hacker, 1976: p. 274 ff; Baker and Hacker, 1980: pp. 68–85. This point is a key insight of this whole text.

3   See Wittgenstein, 'Big Typescript' (TS 213) p. 11. For discussion, see Baker and Hacker, 1980: p. 82. For details of this unpublished material, see Von Wright, 1982: pp. 55, 58–9. See Hilmy, 1987: pp. 25–39 for scholarly reflection on the importance (and difficulty) of this text.

4   The view is more regularly assumed than stated: for discussion in the case of Tolstoy, see Diffey, 1985: pp. 22–5; the view has been attributed to Langer. For discussion, see Budd, 1985: pp. 106–20. A brief but helpful discussion may be found in Sparshott, 1963: pp. 264–6; also Bouwsma, 1965: pp. 21–50. On the general issue, see Putnam, 1990: pp. 144–50.

5   There is a whole debate in aesthetics concerned with the 'heresy of paraphrase'. It is confused by two main features. First, that one side claims that there is a heresy that one can give paraphrases, the other a heresy that one cannot; second, what is at issue between the disputants is often not clear. For example, Cavell (1969: pp. 78–9) argues that there can be paraphrases but that they would include expressions like 'and so on'. For Beardsmore (1971: pp. 15–18), the need for an 'and so on' rider shows that there is no paraphrase here. See also Strawson, 1974: p. 185; McFee, 1978: pp. 129–31.

6   Winch (1987: pp. 194–207) develops the general connection between language, understanding, and relativism in ways central to this text. See also Winch, 1973: pp. 8–49; and Winch, 1987: pp. 33–53; pp. 140–53.

7   For a more complete (and critical) discussion of the application of the ideas from structural linguistics in philosophy, see Baker and Hacker, 1984a.

318

8 See Travis, 1981: pp. 143–55; Travis, 1984; also Travis, 1989: pp. 17–35. Travis's important work on the nature of meaning and understanding is central to much of the thinking in this text. For a different way of presenting a similar phenomenon, see Baker and Hacker, 1985a: pp. 218–28.
9 *Indexicals* are expressions such as 'here', 'now', 'you', 'me', etc. So that I use the word 'here' for where I am, and 'me' of myself, and you do the same about yourself. Hence if you say, 'It is raining here' and I say 'It is not raining here' we are not in disagreement if your here differs from mine. For discussion, see Notes to Chapter 14; also Rundle, 1979; pp. 43–51.

6 Understanding and Dance Criticism

1 See, for example, Lyons, 1970: pp. 84–90; Baker and Hacker, 1984a: pp. 281–3, pp. 311–12; Putnam, 1990: pp. 35–6.
2 This view has a considerable recent history. For attribution of it to Gilbert Ryle, see O'Hear, 1984: p. 203 n; for Wollheim's views, see Wollheim, 1980c: pp. 197–8; see also Baker, 1981. My remarks here and elsewhere in this chapter are due, in part, to Richard Wollheim's remarks on an earlier draft of this material.
3 This is Wollheim's word, from a presentation to the British Society of Aesthetics National Conference, September 1982. The published version (Wollheim, 1983) does not contain the precise expression.
4 Cavell brings this point out powerfully, both generally in a modified Kantian example (Cavell, 1969: p. 92) and specifically in the case of Tolstoy's weird account of art (Cavell, 1969: p. 193).
5 The contrary view is put by Shusterman, 1981. For discussion of the idea, see McFee, 1990; also McFee, forthcoming.

7 Understanding, Experience and Criticism

1 A post-structuralist critic such as Paul de Man (1979) might acknowledge just such a dependence of the meaning of a particular work on an artistic (including critical) tradition. This is not to deny fundamental errors in post-structuralist thinking: see Scruton, 1981: pp. 31–49; Baker and Hacker, 1984a: pp. 316–19.
2 See Machlis, 1961: p. 334, where it is translated 'If it is art, it is not for all, and if it is for all, it is not art'. The idea is central to Schoenberg's Society for the Private Performance of Music (Rosen, 1975: pp. 72–8). If justice is to be done to music, it requires adequate rehearsal time, but also an informed and knowledgeable audience.
3 John Stuart Mill was a major British philosopher of the nineteenth century, and a polymath, making contributions to mathematics, economics and literary criticism as well as to all branches of philosophy. See Mill [1873] 1964; Schneewind, 1968: pp. ix–xvi.
4 Contrast Savile, 1982: pp. 60–6 on 'canonical interpretation'.

8 The Point of Dance

1 This is just a way of re-affirming the commitment to the artistic/aesthetic distinction drawn in Chapter 1. See Best, 1978a: pp. 113–22; Best, 1985: pp. 153–68.

2 For discussion of the imaginative, see Wollheim, 1986; also Chapter 10.

3 The answer cannot be merely an evolutionary one. We should be wary of any facile equation of change with progress. For example, Holland (1984: p. 180) notes: 'As H. G. Wells' projection of our future in *The Time Machine* argues, an evolutionary process is not by itself any guarantee of progress or improvement'.

4 Best (1981: pp. 350, 357) has urged that we see the emotions as ranged on a spectrum, from those with highly particularized objects to those with highly generalized objects. Both art and other aspects of life may have the highly particularized sort. He takes this to be a criticism of Beardsmore (1973), yet both agree that the arts represent highly particularized objects of emotion.

5 In correspondence, David Best raised the question of whether or not my version of the requirement that (roughly) art reflects life issues was indeed a development of his; whether or not, in his words, 'it moved the discussion any further'. It seems to me that mine is certainly a clearer view, and, I hope, at least equally defensible.

6 John Wisdom discusses this point on p. 94 of his lectures on 'Proof and Explanation', given at the University of Virginia in 1957, and hence called 'The Virginia Lectures'. They remain unpublished, but have circulated in typescript since their delivery. As they have this public existence, I cite and quote them here. The substance of these lectures may be gleaned from Yaldon-Thomson, 1974; see also McFee, 1978: pp. 35–58.

7 The contrast between cognitive and affective domains has a long history in philosophy and in views of the mind, but it distinguishes thought and feeling in an appropriate way. The inappropriateness of such a contrast – given that thought and feeling are vast areas, not isolated instances in the mind – is the topic of Best, 1985. In conversation, Best remarked that calling this book *Feeling AND Reason . . .* tended to mislead, and to perpetuate the myth.

8 The idea of a 'form of representation' is a complex one. See Wittgenstein, 1953: sections 50, 122; Baker and Hacker, 1980: pp. 297–300, pp. 531–45, pp. 546–8. However, the images in the text should be suggestive of the right way to treat it. See also Baker and Hacker, 1984a: pp. 379–86. A roughly parallel notion is Collingwood's idea of 'absolute presupposition': see Collingwood, 1940: pp. 44–9, especially pp. 48, 66.

9 It is easy to find a superficial reading of the *Alexandria Quartet*; for example, to see it as an English version of the Rashomon Gate story, where events are successively retold from different perspectives. Such a misconception appears to be supported by aspects of the text.

10 It is unclear whether, for Best, the answer here is that these works, while not themselves expressing a conception of life issues, are simply in an art form where such expression is possible.

11 Socialist Realism is the most extreme form of the thesis of the social benefit of art: see Fischer, 1963: pp. 107–8; Arvon, 1973: pp. 83–99; Laing, 1978:

pp. 36–45. All of these texts discuss other versions of a similar thesis. See also Wolff, 1983.

12 See Fuller, 1988b: p. 72. Ruskin's hope was that: 'Aided by scientific imagination, the painter would be able to see and represent aspects of the Divine which had previously remained hidden.' The importance of Fuller's reading of Ruskin, and of Fuller's works more generally, cannot be over-stressed.

13 Roger Scruton seems to have doubts about this possibility. His most explicit presentation of these doubts was in his paper 'Aesthetic Experience and Culture', read to the International Conference on Aesthetics, Nottingham (August 1988), unpublished to date. See also Scruton, 1983: pp. 138–52.

14 There is, of course, the question of 'found objects'. See Dickie, 1974: p. 25 for one way of discussing such cases; see McFee, 1978: pp. 60–4 for another way; also Ground, 1989: pp. 24–6.

9 Style and Technique

1 It is important to make this qualification, as there are so many other uses of the word 'style' in the offing. For example, to refer to a dancer as having style (or even a style) is simply beside the point here.

2 The quotation is from *The Martha Graham Dance Company*, BBC2 TV, 10 October 1987, which includes discussion with Graham and with Robert Cohan.

3 As Mollie Davis noted, on this point, technique is just one way of distinguishing between kinds of dances; both Graham technique and Cunningham technique might generate modern dance. Such modern dance might be contrasted with classical ballet, but in its British versions this might be ISTD, or Ceccheti and so on.

4 This was the Harehills and Carnegie Dance Group, an excellent children's group in the 1970s. The technique level of this group was very high: some of its ex-members founded Phoenix Dance Company. My reservations about some of the dances they performed derived from the fact that while they appeared able to do the movement, it lacked its usual expressive power. So there is a subtle perceptible difference here; but it may have much to do with the contextualization of the movement as action (see Chapter 2). For discussion of intention in this sense, see Chapter 11.

5 In a programme titled *Bob Fosse's Steam Heat* shown on Los Angeles television Channel 28, on 10 August 1990 (as part of the *Dance in America* series) Bob Fosse claimed that many of the characteristic moves and positions in his choreography resulted from characteristics of his own physique: in particular, hunched shoulders and an inability to achieve the turnout required by classical ballet. As this case indicates, the relationship between technique and choreography can be very complex. (I owe this example to Myrene McFee.)

6 The fullest exposition of Wittgenstein's private language argument in this text occurs in Chapter 12. For more complete treatment, see Baker, 1981; Baker and Hacker, 1984b; Hacker, 1986: pp. 245–306; Hacker, 1990: pp. 15–286. The original location is Wittgenstein, 1953: section 243ff. A simplified version may be found in Best, 1974.

10 Imagination and Understanding

1 This chapter owes a considerable debt to Wollheim (1986), only some of which is apparent from the discussion here. A fuller treatment would give much more time to his notion of 'twofoldness': see also Wollheim, 1987: pp. 46–7, 72–5.

2 Also of interest (but too difficult to treat here) is Scruton's (1974) account of imagination. We should recognize two crucial aspects: (a) a picture of mind and meaning to allow *supposal* – the entertaining of unasserted 'propositions'; (b) a picture of aesthetic perception via *aspectual seeing* or 'seeing as . . .'. These two are related to cases like 'to think of X as Y': see Diffey, 1977. The first of these aspects will be rejected if we do not adopt its account of meaning (for reasons, see Baker and Hacker, 1984a); the second if we recognize that aspectual seeing is not a model for perception more generally, while perception of art works is, in the relevant respects, like ordinary 'perception'.

3 Mollie Davis remarked that there was a difference in kind here, that the parallel for classical ballet should be, say, modern dance. Graham technique produced a different genre only. This is a complex point. Certainly the (relative) unity of classical ballet is only mirrored by selecting modern dances based on one (or a few related) techniques. Just why this should be is, of course, an interesting question – but one for another occasion. Wollheim (1987: pp. 26–36) offers thoughts, in the case of painting, which may be a helpful beginning.

4 See also Wollheim, 1986 on *internal spectators*; also Wollheim, 1987: pp. 102–40, 160–85.

5 Those familiar with the literature on the perception of art and its relation to imagination might expect a discussion of *aspectual seeing* or 'seeing as'. See Aldrich, 1963; Scruton, 1974. To do justice to this topic would require, first, a long digression from the main argument and, second, some Wittgenstein scholarship, since Wittgenstein introduced the idea of aspectual seeing into philosophy. Briefly, my view is that there are three cases to be considered. The first is the standard case of the perception of art works: in so far as this connects with the aspectual, that connection is explored by Wollheim's notion of *seeing in* (Wollheim, 1980d). The second case is genuine aspectual seeing: seeing this *as* that. Yet, as Wittgenstein (1953: p. 197) remarks: 'Seeing as . . . is not part of perception'. So that if our concern is with the perceptual, 'seeing as' will have little or no part to play (see Baker and Hacker, 1980: p. 365). The third case is one Wittgenstein (1953: p. 207) explicitly contrasts with the seeing as cases. For example, the 'bare triangle' figure is not merely seen as an object that has fallen over. The additional step required is translated by Anscombe as requiring '*imagination*'. This case is problematic in a number of ways. Are we convinced that *imagination* is the best translation here? Is this the kind of imagination germane to discussion of the arts? At bottom, though, this case describes a very rare kind of experience, and hence is not a suitable model for perception of the arts.

6 The quotation from Mallarmé is given in Copeland and Cohen, 1983: p. 103.

7 The quotation is from *Bintley's Mozart*, BBC2 TV, 31 December 1987.

8   Although he has not published many papers, R. K. Elliott has been influential through his teaching; he is clearly a major figure in aesthetics (see Savile, 1986: pp. 29–31). Because of his formal connection with the philosophy of education, Elliott's work has been particularly adopted by educationalists with a concern for aesthetics. Most do not employ his ideas as successfully, or as subtly, as Elliott himself. See, for example, Curl, 1983. For elaboration of the ideas, see Elliott, 1978.

11   Intention and Understanding

1   There is an extensive literature on the place of the artist's intention in the appreciation of art works. Key texts will be Hirsch, 1967; Cioffi, 1978; Wimsatt and Beardsley, 1978. An overview is provided by Ravel, 1981; and an elementary exposition by Ground, 1989: pp. 31–60. See also Wollheim, 1987: pp. 17–19, 37–9.
2   See, for example, Alvarez (1971: pp. 138, 141) on John Donne: the poem 'Nocturne upon St. Lucy's Day' is discussed in terms of Donne's life and health, and of his work on his book on suicide, *Biathanatos*.
3   To understand the (technical) ideas of necessary and sufficient conditions, consider the case of a triangle from Chapter 1. Triangles are (a) plane figures, (b) with three straight sides, (c) completely bounded by those sides. Each of these conditions is necessary, in that, say, if condition (a) fails, the figure is three dimensional; if condition (b) fails, the figure could be a square or some such. Without satisfying condition (c), the figure might be a kind of open box. So a figure lacking any of these conditions is definitely not a triangle. Equally, the conditions jointly are sufficient: any figure which fulfils all three conditions is definitely a triangle. Taken together, therefore, necessary and sufficient conditions comprise a definition.
4   Contingent connections are those which simply occur, either as a result of coincidence or as a result of the laws of physics and so on. So that if, for example, Ann and Beth regularly go to college together, one might, seeing Ann, infer that Beth was there too. But there is no guarantee here. The connection is just *contingent*. Equally, if I discover eating a certain mushroom brings me out in red spots, the connection between spots and mushrooms is just a contingent connection, even though it follows from scientific laws.
5   Our interpretation of the artist's life comes in at two points when, for example, the women with their faces covered with cloths in other works by Magritte help us understand *The Lovers*, say, by helping us see the formal features of the work, but also when we learn that Magritte's mother was drowned and found with an apron on her face.
6   It has been objected that this discussion misses the point of the traditional debate around the so-called 'intentional fallacy': that it should be discussing the relation between the causal or productive role of the artist and the understanding of his work. But this is mistaken for three reasons: (a) the role of the artist *for understanding* is not just a causal one; indeed, when our focus is on understanding, it is not causal at all (see McFee, 1991); (b) the issue here (as argued in Chapter 6) is what cognitive stock a legitimate

critic is allowed, and my aim is to avoid an unnecessary restriction of cognitive stock; (c) ascription of intention in art works may begin from the artist's life (or his other works) but the question of their truth depends on features of the work under consideration.

7   In contrast to the interpretation here, Wollheim (1978: p. 34) takes the Borges story to be nothing but the production of another token of the type provided by *Don Quixote*.

12   Expression in Dance

1   This text contains many such examples, chiefly from the pen of Marcia Siegel. The most taxing case here is perhaps her account of William Dunas' work (Siegel, 1977: pp. 313–15) discussed in Chapter 3.

2   The idea here is that exemplars function (albeit temporarily) as standards after the fashion of the standard metre. For discussion of this point, see Baker and Hacker, 1980: pp. 284–96; Baker and Hacker, 1984b: pp. 44–6.

3   Readymades, for example the winerack Marcel Duchamp exhibited in 1914, are everyday objects treated as art: a kind of 'found art' (*objet trouvé*). For discussion of the idea, see Wollheim, 1973: pp. 101–11, esp. pp. 105–8.

4   The private language argument (the argument against the possibility of a private language) describes a constraint on intelligibility: that is, what must be the case in order that something be a fit subject for understanding, whether that something is a word, a feeling, a work of art, a symbol . . . The argument includes the familiar point that, if meanings were not public, they could not be understood by others. This alone shows the untenability of dualist positions (see Best, 1974: pp. 1–14). But the centre of the argument consists in showing that, if meanings were logically private – that is, available only to one person of necessity – even that person would not be able to understand them. Hence the supposition of meanings which are logically private is an incoherent one. It follows that meanings must be public; but how? Hacker (1990: pp. 5–6) notes the requirement for 'independent justification for the use of a word' in order to maintain the crucial 'distinction between correct application [of the word] and an application that only seems correct'. He remarks that this is found in the connection between words and the actions which 'satisfy' them. So that expecting it to snow tomorrow is appropriately accompanied by getting one's rubber boots ready for use, but not by, say, putting them on today, nor by laying out one's bikini (at least, other things equal). Speaking of words ('expressions'), Hacker (1986: p. 250) comments:

A rule for the use of an expression and the acts which accord with it are not independent of each other but are two sides of the same coin, two aspects of a *practice* . . .

Since the locus of this argument is Wittgenstein (1953), just how it is to be understood (and whether, as I have urged, it is a powerful and important argument) is clouded by questions of Wittgenstein scholarship. The best texts on the private language argument are those which most closely follow

Wittgenstein: they are by Baker and Hacker (references given in Chapter 9, note 6). But all relatively elementary books on the philosophy of mind contain elementary expositions. See, for example, Carruthers, 1986: pp. 163–71; Brown, 1989: pp. 39–52. What the argument establishes, at best, is the unintelligibility of a picture of understanding. As such, it establishes that there is a logical bar to knowing the thoughts and feelings of others (see Chapter 1). As Dilman (1975: p. 211) puts it:

> The real obstacle to knowledge of another person's feelings and thoughts is his unwillingness to let me near him, perhaps his unfriendliness and suspicion, his reluctance to let me see him as he really is.

13 Aesthetic Education: Some Myths

1 This idea was attributed to Alma Hawkins; I have been unable to discover any source. However, it represents the kind of thing regularly said by dancers and (some) dance educators.
2 This discussion owes a debt to Parry, 1976; as well as inspiration, that article also provides some of the material quoted here.
3 The term 'aesthesis' in Greek originally referred to sense-perception, contrasted with 'noeta': a contrast between the sensory and the intellectual. Our word 'aesthetic' has little or nothing directly to do with the Greek word since Baumgarten began using the term in the philosophy of art, of beauty and so on. See Bosanquet, 1904: pp. 1–3.
4 The villains in Hamby's essay are called 'philosophers': I take it (from conversation) that I am one of those intended. See, for example, McFee, 1989a.
5 This is not, of course, a comment about how these matters should be taught: see Best, 1985: pp. 65–6, which accurately diagnoses a root of the idea of free expression in the desire for a less restrictive pedagogy. But that could be achieved from within the aims of previous theory. For discussion here see Bolton, 1981; Eisner, 1974.
6 As David Best made plain in correspondence on this point, his objection is to some misleading implications which might be drawn from the expression 'aesthetic education'. If these are avoided, there is no real dispute. Our difference is whether continuing to use the expression 'aesthetic education' makes this more or less likely.

14 Dance and Society

1 This is (roughly) from Plato's The Laws, 1970: p. 87: 'the well-educated man will be able both to sing well and to dance well'. For discussion of the Greek words involved, see Lawler, 1964: p. 124. The point is not simply one about translation: see Putnam, 1990: pp. 212–13.
2 The quotation, from Curt Sachs (infamous) World History of the Dance (1937: p. 12), appears with approval in Blacking, 1985: p. 68.
3 This example imports, for the sake of clarity, three disputable assumptions: (a) that classical Greek works are art; (b) that this architectural work is an

example of such art; (c) that what is said about it can be applied unprob-
lematically to dance. If the example were rejected, one might still have the
point clear.

4 For a discussion in this specific context, see Fuller, 1988a: pp. 13–96.

5 This is not to deny the power and interest of the concern with popular culture, but rather to dispute its relevance to understanding dance viewed as
dance. See McFee, 1989a: pp. 23–5. For some elementary elaboration of the
concern with popular culture, see Gibson, 1984: pp. 61–7; Gibson, 1986:
pp. 72–9. A key text will be Williams, 1965; see also Williams, 1980.

6 The complex idea of the historical character of art receives some treatment
in McFee, 1980b, although much of that paper is no longer exactly what I
would say now. It also receives some discussion in the next section of this
chapter. The thought is, roughly, that the meaning of a work of art (with
the usual qualifications around the word 'meaning') could change at some
later time; even that the object might become art, or cease to be art, at some
later time.

7 The word 'relativism' has, unfortunately, a variety of uses in philosophy.
See, for example, Feyerabend, 1987: pp. 19–89; see also Wiggins, 1990: pp.
72–5. The account here should be taken to define relativism for the purposes of this text. (However, I would argue that it represents the central,
interesting, sense of the term 'relativism'.)

8 As recorded in the notes to Chapter 5, indexicals are terms such as 'you',
'me', 'here', 'now'. They fix people, places or times by reference to the
person, place or time of the speaking. See Rundle, 1979: pp. 43–51. Two
speakers will be saying different things if the indexicals fix different objects.
So that 'I am taller than John', said by James, might be true (state the truth),
while 'I am not taller than John', said by Bill, might also be true. But since
they say different things, this is not a case where relativism is at issue.

9 The idea of a paradigm in this sense was introduced into the literature by
T. S. Kuhn. It is built on accepted good practice of the past, and serves as
a standard in terms of which practitioners 'know how to go on'. So for
example, Newtonian science provides a paradigm for scientific activity at a
certain time. Kuhn (1969: p. 189) speaks of it as 'a time-tested and group-
licensed way of seeing'. The work of a scientist working within such a paradigm – what Kuhn calls doing 'normal science' – is 'firmly based upon one
or more past scientific achievements, achievements that *some particular scientific community* acknowledges *for a time* as supplying the foundations for its
future practice' (Kuhn, 1969: p. 10, italics added). As the emphasized passages make plain, this is an institutional account of science. It should not be
taken as a general picture of knowledge. However, it may have direct
application in the case of art, if 'art' too is an institutional concept. On
paradigms, see Kuhn, 1977: pp. 293–319; for discussion, Toulmin, 1972:
pp. 107–17.

10 This form of argument, called *reductio ad absurdum* (or *reductio* for short), is
an important one in philosophy. It consists in assuming a position, and
showing how that assumption leads to self-contradiction or absurdity. In
either of these cases, one is then justified in denying the position initially
assumed. See Shaw, 1981: pp. 189ff.

11 There are three important points to notice: first, this insight is really most
easily recognized by thinking about (so-called) natural languages like

English and French. No doubt one could have spoken in French or English or German, but any speaking must be in *a* language from such a list. Second, the connection between thought and language, or 'ways of seeing', is well discussed. See, for example, Winch, 1987: pp. 18–32, 194–201. Third, to assume some neutral standpoint here is indeed to be committed to the sort of 'God's-eye-view' position rejected throughout the text. See Putnam, 1990: pp. 5–18.

Conclusion

1   The central idea of constructivism here, drawn from work in the philosophy of mathematics (Dummett, 1978: pp. 163–4, 180–5, 208–9), is that what can be *true* depends on what can be *proved* (or known). Applied to aesthetics, it amounts to claiming that the limits of artistic truth are circumscribed by the possibilities of human knowledge. So, to retain a robust sense of constructivity is to insist strenuously on the philosophical justification for limiting one's aesthetic claims to the realm of (possible) artistic knowledge. My earlier view (McFee, 1980b) required a formalized constructivist logic and theory of meaning (see also Baker, 1977: pp. 50–7). However, I now see that commitment as misguided. But the lesson for philosophy involves the maintaining of the robust sense of constructivity. See also Baker and Hacker, 1984c: pp. 3–5; Baker, 1986; Baker, 1988: pp. xii–xvii.
2   Russell (1919: p. 170): 'A robust sense of reality is very necessary in framing a correct analysis of propositions about unicorns, golden mountains, round squares, and other such pseudo-objects.' As Russell explains, 'The sense of reality is vital in logic, and whoever juggles with it by pretending that Hamlet has another kind of reality is doing a disservice to thought'.
3   For Aesthetic Platonism, see Levinson, 1980; Kivy, 1983; Kivy, 1987. My key thought is that *if* Platonism can be avoided for mathematics – which deals with genuine abstract objects (numbers) – it should be more easily avoidable for aesthetics: art works are either physical objects or have physical instantiations (as movement, sound and so on).

Bibliography

Aldrich, V. (1963) *Philosophy of Art* (Englewood Cliffs, NJ: Prentice-Hall).
Alvarez, A. (1971), *The Savage God* (London: Weidenfeld & Nicolson).
Anscombe, G. E. M. (1986), 'On brute facts', reprinted in J. J. Thomson and G. Dworkin (eds), *Ethics* (New York: Harper & Row), pp. 71–5.
Anscombe, G. E. M. (1981), *Metaphysics and the Philosophy of Mind (Collected Philosophical Papers Vol. 2)* (Oxford: Blackwell).
Armelagos, A. and Sirridge, M. (1984), 'Personal style and performance prerogatives', in M. Sheets-Johnstone (ed.), *Illuminating Dance: Philosophical Explorations* (Cranbury, NJ: Associated University Presses), pp. 85–100.
Arnold, P. (1979), *Meaning in Movement, Sport and Physical Education* (London: Heinemann).
Arvon, H. (1973), *Marxist Esthetics* (trans. H. Lane) (Ithaca, NY: Cornell University Press).
Aspin, D (1981), 'Assessment and education in the arts', in M. Ross (ed.) *The Aesthetic Imperative* (Oxford: Pergamon), pp. 25–52.
Austin, J. L. (1970), *Philosophical Papers* (Second Edition) (Oxford: Oxford University Press).
Austin, R. (1976), *Birth of a Ballet* (London: Vision Press).

Baker, G. P. (1977), 'Defeasibility and meaning', in P. M. S. Hacker and J. Raz (eds), *Law, Morality and Society* (Oxford: Clarendon Press), pp. 26–57.
Baker, G. P. (1981), 'Following Wittgenstein: some signposts for *Philosophical Investigations* 143–242', in S. Holtzman and C. Leich (eds) *Wittgenstein: To Follow a Rule* (London: Routledge & Kegan Paul), pp. 31–71.
Baker, G. P. (1986). φιλοσοφία: εἰκὼν καί εἶδος [Philosophy: Simulacrum and Form], in S. G. Shanker (ed.), *Philosophy in Britain Today* (London: Croom Helm), pp. 1–57.
Baker, G. P. (1988), *Wittgenstein, Frege and the Vienna Circle* (Oxford: Blackwell).
Baker, G. P. and Hacker, P. M. S. (1976), 'Critical notice: Wittgenstein *Philosophical Grammar*', *Mind* vol. 85, pp. 269–94.
Baker, G. P. and Hacker, P. M. S. (1980), *Wittgenstein: Understanding and Meaning* (Oxford: Blackwell).
Baker, G. P. and Hacker, P. M. S. (1984a), *Language, Sense and Nonsense* (Oxford: Blackwell).
Baker, G. P. and Hacker, P. M. S. (1984b), *Scepticism, Rules and Language* (Oxford: Blackwell).
Baker, G. P. and Hacker, P. M. S. (1984c), *Frege: Logical Excavations* (Oxford: Blackwell).
Baker, G. P. and Hacker, P. M. S. (1985a), *Wittgenstein: Rules, Grammar and Necessity* (Oxford: Blackwell).

BIBLIOGRAPHY

Baker, G. P. and Hacker, P. M. S. (1985b), 'Wittgenstein and the Vienna Circle: the exaltation and deposition of ostensive definition', *Teoria* vol. 2, pp. 5–33.
Bambrough, R. (1968), *Reason, Truth and God* (London: Methuen).
Bambrough, R. (1979), *Moral Scepticism and Moral Knowledge* (London: Routledge & Kegan Paul).
Beardsley, M. (1958), *Aesthetics: Problems in the Philosophy of Criticism* (New York: Harcourt Brace Jovanovich).
Beardsley, M. (1970), *The Possibility of Criticism* (Philadelphia: Wayne State University Press).
Beardsley, M. (1976), 'Is art essentially institutional?', in L. Aagaard-Mogensen (ed.), *Culture and Art* (Atlantic Highlands, NJ: Humanities Press), pp. 194–209.
Beardsmore, R. W. (1971), *Art and Morality* (London: Macmillan).
Beardsmore, R. W. (1973), 'Two trends in contemporary aesthetics', *British Journal of Aesthetics*, vol. 13, no. 4, (Autumn), pp. 346–66.
Best, D. N. (1974), *Expression in Movement and the Arts* (London: Lepus Books).
Best, D. N. (1978a), *Philosophy and Human Movement* (London: George Allen & Unwin).
Best, D. N. (1978b), 'Emotional education through the arts', *Journal of Aesthetic Education*, vol. 12, pp. 71–84.
Best, D. N. (1981), 'Intentionality and art', *Philosophy*, vol. 56, no. 3, pp. 349–63.
Best, D. N. (1983), 'A reply to my critics', *British Journal of Aesthetics*, vol. 23, no. 2 (Spring), pp. 148–63.
Best, D. N. (1984), 'The dangers of "aesthetic education"', *Oxford Review of Education*, vol. 10, no. 2, pp. 157–67.
Best, D. N. (1985), *Feeling and Reason in the Arts* (London: George Allen & Unwin).
Best, D. N. (1986), 'Culture-consciousness: understanding the arts of other cultures', in J. Adshead (ed.), *Dance – a Multicultural Perspective* (Second Edition) (National Resource Centre for Dance), pp. 86–96.
Best, D. N. (1987), 'Accountability and aesthetic education', lecture delivered at Brighton Polytechnic, unpublished.
Blackburn, S. (1984), *Spreading the Word* (Oxford: Oxford University Press).
Blacking, J. (1985), 'Movement, dance, music, and the Venda girls' initiation', in P. Spencer (ed.), *Society and the Dance* (Cambridge: Cambridge University Press), pp. 64–91.
Bolton, G. (1981), 'Drama in education – a reappraisal', in N. McCaslin (ed.), *Children and Drama* (Second Edition) (London: Longman), pp. 178–91.
Borges, J. L. (1962), *Fictions* (trans. A. Kerrigan) (New York: Grove Press).
Bosanquet, B. (1904), *A History of Aesthetic* (Second Edition) (London: George Allen & Unwin).
Bouwsma, O. K. (1965), *Philosophical Essays* (Lincoln: University of Nebraska Press).
Bradley, F. H. (1934), 'On the treatment of sexual detail in literature', in F. H. Bradley, *Collected Essays*, Vol. 2 (Oxford: Clarendon Press), pp. 618–27.
Brinson, P. and Crisp, C. (1980), *Ballet and Dance: a Guide to the Repertory* (Newton Abbot: David & Charles).
Brown, G. (1989), *Minds, Brains and Machines* (Bristol: Bristol Classical Press).
Budd, M. (1985), *Music and the Emotions* (London: Routledge & Kegan Paul).

Carr, D. (1984), 'Education, skill and behavioural objectives', *Journal of Aesthetic Education*, vol. 18, no. 4 (Winter) pp. 67–76.

Carr, D. (1987), 'Thought and action in the art of dance', *British Journal of Aesthetics*, vol. 27, no. 4 (Autumn), pp. 345–57.

Carroll, Lewis ([1894] 1973), 'What the tortoise said to Achilles', in *The Complete Works* (London: The Nonesuch Press), pp. 1104–8.

Carroll, N. (1981), 'Post-modern dance and expression', in G. Fancher and G. Myers (eds), *Philosophical Essays on Dance* (New York: American Dance Festival), pp. 95–104.

Carruthers, P. (1986), *Introducing Persons* (London: Croom Helm).

Cavell, S. (1969), *Must We Mean What We Say?* (New York: Charles Scribner's Sons).

Cavell, S. (1979), *The World Viewed* (Enlarged Edition) (Cambridge, Mass: Harvard University Press).

Cavell, S. (1981a), *The Senses of Walden* (An Expanded Edition) (San Francisco: North Point Press).

Cavell, S. (1981b), *Pursuits of Happiness* (Cambridge, Mass: Harvard University Press).

Cavell, S. (1984), *Themes Out of School* (San Francisco: North Point Press).

Chalmers, A. F. (1982), *What Is This Thing Called Science?* Second Edition (Milton Keynes: Open University Press).

Chapman, J. (1984), 'XXX and the changing ballet aesthetic: 1828–32', *Dance Research*, vol. 2, no. 1 (Spring), pp. 35–47.

Cioffi, F. (1978), 'Intention and interpretation in criticism', in J. Margolis (ed.), *Philosophy Looks at the Arts* Second Edition (Philadelphia: Temple University Press).

Collingwood, R. G. (1938), *The Principles of Art* (Oxford: Clarendon Press).

Collingwood, R. G. (1940), *An Essay on Metaphysics* (Oxford: Clarendon Press).

Collingwood, R. G. (1964), 'Ruskin's philosophy' (delivered in 1919), in A. Donagan (ed.), *Essays in the Philosophy of Art by R. G. Collingwood* (Bloomington: Indiana University Press), pp. 5–41.

Copeland, R. and Cohen, M. (eds) (1983), *What Is Dance?* (Oxford: Oxford University Press).

Copeland, R. (1990), 'In defence of formalism: the politics of disinterestedness', *Dance Theatre Journal* vol. 7, no. 4 (February) pp. 4–7, 37.

Croce, A. (1978), *Afterimages* (London: A. & C. Black).

Curl, G. (1983), 'R. K. Elliott's "As-If" and the Experience of Art', in M. Ross (ed.), *The Arts: A Way of Knowing* (Oxford: Pergamon), pp. 85–100.

Danto, A. (1968), *What Philosophy Is* (New York: Harper & Row).

Danto, A. (1981), *The Transfiguration of the Commonplace* (Cambridge, Mass: Harvard University Press).

Danto, A. (1986), *The Philosophical Disenfrachisement of Art* (New York: Columbia University Press).

Davidson, D. (1969), 'How is weakness of the will possible?', in J. Feinberg (ed.), *Moral Concepts* (Oxford: Oxford University Press), pp. 93–113.

Davies, S. (1987), 'Authenticity in musical performance', *British Journal of Aesthetics*, vol. 27, no. 1 (Winter), pp. 39–50.

De Man, P. (1979), *Allegories of Reading* (New Haven Conn.: Yale University Press).

Dickie, G. (1974), *Art and the Aesthetic* (Ithaca, NY: Cornell University Press).
Dickie, G. (1984), *The Art Circle* (New York: Haven Publications).
Dickenson, J. (1974), *Proprioceptive Control of Human Movement* (London: Lepus Books).
Diffey, T. J. (1969), 'The Republic of Art', *British Journal of Aesthetics*, vol. 9, no. 2, pp. 145–56. [Also available as Chapter Two of Diffey, T. J. (1991), *The Republic of Art and Other Essays* (New York: Peter Lang)].
Diffey, T. J. (1977), 'Review of R. Scruton *Art and Imagination*', *Mind*, vol. 86 (January), pp. 151–4.
Diffey, T. J. (1985), *Tolstoy's 'What Is Art?'* (London: Croom Helm).
Dilman, I. (1975), *Matter and Mind* (London: Macmillan).
Dummett, M. (1975), 'What is a theory of meaning?', in S. Guttenplan (ed.), *Mind and Language* (Oxford: Clarendon Press), pp. 97–138.
Dummett, M. (1978), *Truth and Other Enigmas* (London: Duckworth).
Durrell, Lawrence (1968), *Alexandria Quartet* (London: Faber).
Durrell, Lawrence (1970), *The Revolt of Aphrodite* (London: Faber).

Eagleton, T. (1976), *Marxism and Literary Criticism* (London: Methuen).
Eisner, E. (1974), 'Examining some myths in art education', *Student Art Education*, vol. 15, no. 3, pp. 7–16.
Elliott, R. K. (1973), 'Imagination in the experience of art', in G. Vesey (ed.), *Philosophy and the Arts (Royal Institute of Philosophy Lectures Vol. 6 1971/2* (London: Macmillan), pp. 88–105.
Elliott, R. K. (1978), 'Aesthetic theory and the experience of art', in J. Margolis (ed.), *Philosophy Looks at the Arts* (Second Edition) (Philadelphia: Temple University Press), pp. 45–57.

Feyerabend, P. K. (1978), *Science in a Free Society* (London: Verso/New Left Books).
Feyerabend, P. K. (1987), *Farewell to Reason* (London: Verso/New Left Books).
Fischer, E. (1963), *The Necessity of Art* (trans. A. Bostock) (Harmondsworth: Penguin).
Foster, S. L. (1986), *Reading Dancing* (Berkeley: University of California Press).
Fowles, John (1977), 'Revised Foreword' to *The Magus* (London: Jonathan Cape).
Fried, M. (1974), 'Two sculptures by Anthony Caro', in R. Whelan, *Anthony Caro* (Harmondsworth: Penguin), pp. 95–101.
Fried, M. (1977), 'Art and objecthood', in G. Dickie and R. Sclafani (eds), *Aesthetics: A Critical Anthology* (New York: St Martin's Press), pp. 438–60.
Fuller, P. (1980), *Beyond the Crisis in Art* (London: Writers and Readers Publishing Cooperative).
Fuller, P. (1988a) *Seeing Through Berger* (London and Lexington, Ky: The Claridge Press).
Fuller, P. (1988b), *Theoria: Art and the Absence of Grace* (London: Chatto & Windus).

Gibson, J. J. (1978), *The Senses Considered as Perceptual Systems* (London: George Allen & Unwin).
Gibson, R. (1984), *Structuralism and Education* (Sevenoaks: Hodder & Stoughton).

Gibson, R. (1986), *Critical Theory and Education* (Sevenoaks: Hodder & Stoughton).
Giddens, A. (1979), *Central Problems in Social Theory* (London: Macmillan).
Giddens, A. (1984), *The Constitution of Society* (Cambridge: Polity Press).
Giddens, A. (1987), *Social Theory and Modern Sociology* (Cambridge: Polity Press).
Goodman, N. (1968), *Languages of Art* (Indianapolis: Bobbs-Merrill).
Goodman, N. (1978), *Ways of Worldmaking* (Hassocks: Harvester).
Ground, I. (1989), *Art or Bunk?* (Bristol: Bristol Classical Press).
Guyer, P. (1979), *Kant and the Claims of Taste* (Cambridge, Mass: Harvard University Press).

Hacker, P. M. S. (1976), 'Locke and the meaning of colour words', in G. Vesey (ed.), *Impressions of Empiricism (Royal Institute of Philosophy Lectures*, vol. 9 1974/5) (London: Macmillan), pp. 23–46.
Hacker, P. M. S. (1986), *Insight and Illusion* (Revised Edition) (Oxford: Oxford University Press).
Hacker, P. M. S. (1987), *Appearance and Reality* (Oxford: Blackwell).
Hacker, P. M. S. (1990) *Wittgenstein: Meaning and Mind* (Oxford: Blackwell).
Hamby, C. (1984), 'Dance and the dancer', *British Journal of Aesthetics*, vol. 4, no. 1 (Winter), pp. 339–46.
Hanna, J. L. (1979), *To Dance is Human* (Austin: University of Texas Press).
Hanna, J. L. (1983), *The Performer–Audience Connection* (Austin: University of Texas Press).
H'Doubler, M. (1940), *Dance: A Creative Art Experience* (Madison: University of Wisconsin Press).
Hilmy, S. (1987), *The Later Wittgenstein* (Oxford: Blackwell).
Hirsch, E. D. (1967), *Validity in Interpretation* (New Haven Conn: Yale University Press).
Hirst, P. H. (1989), 'The concepts of physical education and dance education: a reply', in G. Curl (ed.), *Collected Conference Papers in Dance*, vol. 4 (London: National Association of Teachers in Further and Higher Education), pp. 38–43.
Hirst, P. H. and Peters, R. S. (1970), *The Logic of Education* (London: Routledge & Kegan Paul).
Holland, A. (1984), 'On what makes an epistemology evolutionary', *Proceedings of the Aristotelian Society Supplementary*, vol. 58, pp. 117–92.

Kaeppler, A. (1985), 'Structured movement systems in Tonga', in P. Spencer (ed.), *Society and the Dance* (Cambridge: Cambridge University Press), pp. 92–118.
Kant, I. (1952), *The Critique of Judgement* (trans. J. C. Meredith) (Oxford: Clarendon Press).
Kealiinohomoku, J. W. (1983), 'An anthropologist looks at ballet as a form of ethnic dance', in R. Copeland and M. Cohen (eds) *What Is Dance?* (Oxford: Oxford University Press), pp. 533–49.
Kenny, A. (1963), *Action, Emotion and the Will* (London: Routledge & Kegan Paul).
Kenny, A. (1973), *Wittgenstein* (London: Allen Lane).
Kenny, A. (1984), *The Legacy of Wittgenstein* (Oxford: Blackwell).

Kivy, P. (1975), 'What makes aesthetic terms aesthetic?', *Philosophy and Phenomenological Research*, vol. 36, pp. 197–211.

Kivy, P. (1978), 'The point of it all: an answer to Professor Hyde', *Philosophy and Phenomenological Research*, vol. 39, pp. 131–4.

Kivy, P. (1983), 'Platonism: a kind of defence', *Grazer Philosophische Studien*, vol. 19, pp. 109–20.

Kivy, P. (1987), 'Platonism in music: another kind of defence', *American Philosophical Quarterly*, vol. 24, no. 3 (July), pp. 245–52.

Kivy, P. (1988), 'Live performances and dead composers', in J. Dancy, J. M. E. Moravcsik and C. C. W. Taylor (eds), *Human Agency: Language, Duty and Value* (Stanford, Calif: Stanford University Press), pp. 237–57.

Kuhn, T. S. (1969), *The Structure of Scientific Revolutions* (Second Edition) (Chicago: University of Chicago Press).

Kuhn, T. S. (1976), 'Theory-change as structure-change: comments on the Sneed formalism', *Erkenntnis*, vol. 10, pp. 179–99.

Kuhn, T. S. (1977), *The Essential Tension* (Chicago: University of Chicago Press).

Laing, D. (1978), *The Marxist Theory of Art* (Hassocks: Harvester).

Lange, R. (1975), *The Nature of Dance* (Plymouth: Macdonald & Evans).

Lawler, L. B. (1964), *The Dance in Ancient Greece* (London: A. & C. Black).

Levin, D. M. (1983), 'Balanchine's formalism', in R. Copeland and M. Cohen (eds), *What Is Dance?* (Oxford: Oxford University Press), pp. 123–44.

Levinson, J. (1980), 'What a musical work is', *Journal of Philosophy*, vol. 77, pp. 5–27.

Lyons, J. (1970), *Chomsky* (London: Fontana).

Machlis, J. (1961), *Introduction to Contemporary Music* (London: J. M. Dent).

Malcolm, N. (1966), *Ludwig Wittgenstein: A Memoir* (Oxford: Oxford University Press).

Marcuse, H. (1978), *The Aesthetic Dimension* (London: Macmillan).

Margolis, J. (1984), 'The autographic nature of dance', in M. Sheets-Johnstone (ed.), *Illuminating Dance: Philosophical Explorations* (Cranbury, NJ: Associated University Presses), pp. 70–84.

Marx, K. (1973), *Grundrisse* (trans. M. Nicholaus) (Harmondsworth: Penguin).

Marx, K. and Engels, F. ([1846] 1970), *The German Ideology* (London: Lawrence & Wishart).

McDonagh, D. (1970), *The Rise and Fall and Rise of Modern Dance* (New York: New American Library).

McDonagh, D. (1973), *Martha Graham: A Biography* (New York: Praeger).

McFee, G. (1977), *Philosophy and Human Movement: Chelsea Papers in Human Movement* (Eastbourne: East Sussex College of Higher Education).

McFee, G. (1978), *Much of Jackson Pollock is Vivid Wallpaper* (Washington, DC: University Press of America).

McFee, G. (1980a), 'The fraudulent in art', *British Journal of Aesthetics*, vol. 20, no. 3 (Summer), pp. 215–28.

McFee, G. (1980b), 'The historicity of art', *Journal of Aesthetics and Art Criticism*, vol. 38, no. 3, pp. 307–24.

McFee, G. (1982), 'Psychology, aesthetics and Richard Wollheim', *Philosophical Inquiry*, vol. 4, no. 2 (Spring), pp. 99–109.

McFee, G. (1983), 'The notion of action: some second thoughts on determinism', *Momentum*, vol. 8, no. 2, pp. 12–18.

McFee, G. (1984), 'Wisdom on aesthetics: superstructure and substructure', in I. Dilman (ed.), *Philosophy and Life: Essays on John Wisdom* (The Hague: Martinus Nijhoff), pp. 83–122.

McFee, G. (1985), 'Wollheim and the institutional theory of art', *The Philosophical Quarterly*, vol. 35, no. 139 (April), pp. 179–85.

McFee, G. (1986), '"Goal of the Month": fact or fiction?', *Leisure Studies*, vol. 5, no. 2 (May), pp. 159–74.

McFee, G. (1989a), 'The concept of dance education', in G. Curl (ed.), *Collected Conference Papers in Dance*, vol. 4 (London: National Association of Teachers in Further and Higher Education), pp. 15–37.

McFee, G. (1989b). 'The logic of appreciation in the Republic of Art', *British Journal of Aesthetics*, vol. 29, no. 3 (Summer), pp. 230–8.

McFee, G. (1990), 'Davies' replies: a response', in *Grazer Philosophische Studien*, vol. 38, pp. 177–84.

McFee, G. (1991), 'Wittgenstein: understanding and "intuitive awareness"', in *Wittgenstein: Towards a Reevaluation (Proceedings of the 14th International Wittgenstein Symposium, 1989) Part Two* (Vienna: Holder-Pichler-Temsky), pp. 37–46.

McFee, G. (forthcoming), 'Critical reasoning', *Journal of Comparative Literature and Aesthetics*.

McGuinness, B. (1988), *Wittgenstein: a Life*, vol. 1 (London: Duckworth).

McTaggart, J. McT. E. (1934), *Philosophical Studies* (London: Edward Arnold).

Middleton, J. (1985), 'The dance among the Lugbara of Uganda', in P. Spencer (ed.), *Society and the Dance* (Cambridge: Cambridge University Press), pp. 165–82.

Mill, J. S. [1873] (1964), *Autobiography of John Stuart Mill* (New York: New American Library).

Mothersill, M. (1975), 'Review of Stanley Cavell's *Must We Mean What We Say?*, *The World Viewed*, *The Senses of Walden*', *Journal of Philosophy*, vol. 72, no. 2 (January), pp. 27–48.

Nagel, T. (1979), *Mortal Questions* (Cambridge: Cambridge University Press).

Nagel, T. (1986), *The View From Nowhere* (Oxford: Oxford University Press).

Nagel, T. (1987), *What Does It All Mean?* (Oxford: Oxford University Press).

O'Connor, D. J. (1971), *Free Will* (London: Macmillan).

O'Hear, A. (1984), 'On what makes an epistemology evolutionary', *Proceedings of the Aristotelian Society Supplementary*, vol. 58, pp. 193–217.

Orwell, George [1945] (1968), 'Revenge is sour', in *The Collected Essays, Journalism and Letters of George Orwell*, vol. 4 (New York: Harcourt, Brace & World).

Osborne, H. (1982), 'Expressiveness in the arts', *Journal of Aesthetics and Art Criticism*, vol. 40, no. 1 (Winter), pp. 19–26.

Parry, J. (1976), 'The kinaesthetic sense', *Research Papers in Physical Education*, vol. 3, pp. 15–18.

Passmore, J. (1968), *A Hundred Years of Philosophy* (Harmondsworth: Penguin).

BIBLIOGRAPHY

Pater, W. (1974), *Selected Writings of Walter Pater* Harold Bloom (ed.) (New York: New American Library).
Perry, J. (ed.) (1975), *Personal Identity* (Berkeley: University of California Press).
Phillips, D. Z. (1973), 'Allegiance and change in morality: a study in contrasts', in G. Vesey (ed.), *Philosophy and the Arts (Royal Institute of Philosophy Lectures,* Vol. 6 1971/2) (London: Macmillan), pp. 47–66.
Plato (1970), *The Laws* (trans. T. H. Saunders) (Harmondsworth: Penguin).
Polanyi, M. (1973), *Personal Knowledge* (London: Routledge & Kegan Paul).
Pole, D. (1983), *Aesthetics: Form and Emotion* (London: Duckworth).
Preston-Dunlop, V. (1963), *A Handbook for Modern Educational Dance* (Plymouth: Macdonald & Evans).
Putnam, H. (1982), *Reason, Truth and History* (Cambridge: Cambridge University Press).
Putnam, H. (1987), *The Many Faces of Realism* (La Salle, Ill: Open Court).
Putnam, H. (1990), *Realism With a Human Face* (Cambridge, Mass: Harvard University Press).

Quinton, A. (1963), 'Tragedy', in M. Levich (ed.), *Aesthetics and the Philosophy of Criticism,* (New York: Random House), pp. 185–203.
Quirey, B. (1976), *May I Have the Pleasure?* (London: BBC Publications).

Ravel, S. (1981), *Metacriticism* (Atlanta: University of Georgia Press).
Redfern, B. (1979), 'The child as creator, performer, spectator', in *Dance and the Child: Keynote Addresses and Philosophy Papers* (Canadian Association of Health, Physical Education and Recreation), pp. 3–24.
Redfern, B. (1983), *Dance, Art and Aesthetics* (London: Dance Books).
Redfern, B. (1986), *Questions in Aesthetic Education* (London: George Allen & Unwin).
Redpath, T. (1990), *Ludwig Wittgenstein: a Student's Memoir* (London: Duckworth).
Rhees, R. (1969), *Without Answers* (London: Routledge & Kegan Paul).
Rhees, R. (ed.) (1984), *Recollections of Wittgenstein* (Oxford: Oxford University Press).
Robinson, I. (1973), *The Decline of English* (Cambridge: Cambridge University Press).
Rorty, R. (1979), *Philosophy and the Mirror of Nature* (Princeton, NJ: Princeton University Press).
Rosen, C. (1975), *Schoenberg* (London: Fontana).
Rundle, B. (1979), *Grammar in Philosophy* (Oxford: Clarendon Press).
Russell, B. (1919), *Introduction to Mathematic Philosophy* (London: George Allen & Unwin).
Russell, B. (1921), *The Analysis of Mind* (London: George Allen & Unwin).
Russell, J. (1981), *The Meanings of Modern Art* (London: Thames & Hudson).

Sachs, C. (1937), *World History of the Dance* (trans. B. Schoenberg) (London: George Allen & Unwin).
Savile, A. (1972), 'The place of intention in the concept of art', in H. Osborne (ed.), *Aesthetics* (Oxford: Oxford University Press), pp. 158–76.
Savile, A. (1982), *The Test of Time* (Oxford: Clarendon Press).

Savile, A. (1986), 'Imagination and pictorial understanding', *Proceedings of the Aristotelian Society Supplementary*, vol. 40, pp. 19–44.
Saw, R. (1972), *Aesthetics: an Introduction* (London: Macmillan).
Schneewind, J. B. (ed.) (1968), *Mill (A Collection of Critical Essays)* (London: Macmillan).
Scruton, R. (1974), *Art and Imagination* (London: Methuen).
Scruton, R. (1981), *The Politics of Culture* (Manchester: Carcanet Press).
Scruton, R. (1983), *The Aesthetic Understanding* (Manchester: Carcanet Press).
Scruton, R. (1989), 'Analytic philosophy and the meaning of music', in R. Shusterman (ed.), *Analytic Aesthetics* (Oxford: Blackwell), pp. 85–96.
Searle, J. (1984), *Minds, Brains and Science* (London: BBC Publications).
Sharpe, R. A. (1979), 'Type, token, interpretation and performance', *Mind*, vol. 86, pp. 437–40.
Shaw, P. (1981), *Logic and Its Limits* (London: Pan Books).
Shoemaker, S. (1963), *Self-Knowledge and Self-Identity* (Ithaca, NY: Cornell University Press).
Shusterman, R. (1978), 'The anomalous nature of literature', *British Journal of Aesthetics*, vol. 18, no. 4 (Autumn), pp. 317–29.
Shusterman, R. (1981), 'Evaluative reasoning in criticism', *Ratio*, vol. 23, pp. 141–57.
Shusterman, R. (1984), *The Object of Literary Criticism* (Amsterdam: Rodopi).
Shusterman, R. (ed.) (1989), *Analytic Aesthetics* (Oxford: Blackwell).
Siegel, M. (1972), *At the Vanishing Point* (New York: Saturday Review Press).
Siegel, M. (1977), *Watching the Dance Go By* (Boston, Mass.: Houghton Mifflin).
Siegel, M. (1979), *The Shapes of Change* (Boston Mass.: Houghton Mifflin).
Sirridge, M. and Armelagos, A. (1977), 'The in's and out's of dance: expression as an aspect of style', *Journal of Aesthetics and Art Criticism*, vol. 36, pp. 15–24.
Sparshott, F. (1963), *The Structure of Aesthetics* (London: Routledge & Kegan Paul).
Sparshott, F. (1988), *Off The Ground* (Princeton, NJ: Princeton University Press).
Spencer, P. (ed.) (1985), *Society and the Dance* (Cambridge: Cambridge University Press).
Stebbing, L. S. (1937), *Philosophy and the Physicists* (Harmondsworth: Penguin).
Strawson, P. F. (1974), *Freedom and Resentment* (London: Methuen).

Thompson, E. P. (1978), *The Poverty of Theory* (London: Merlin Press).
Thornton, M. (1989), *Do We Have Free Will?* (Bristol: Bristol Classical Press).
Tolstoy, L. [1895] (1930), *What Is Art?* (trans. A. Maude) (Oxford: Oxford University Press).
Toulmin, S. E. (1972), *Human Understanding* vol. 1 (Oxford: Clarendon Press).
Toulmin, S. E. (1976), *Knowing and Acting* (West Drayton: Collier Macmillan).
Travis, C. (1981), *The True and the False* (Amsterdam: John Benjamins).
Travis, C. (1984), 'Are belief ascriptions opaque?', *Proceedings of the Aristotelian Society 1984–5*, vol. 85, pp. 73–100.
Travis, C. (1989), *The Uses of Sense* (Oxford: Clarendon Press).

Urmson, J. O. (1976), 'The performing arts', in H. D. Lewis (ed.), *Contemporary British Philosophy* (4th Series) (London: George Allen & Unwin), pp. 239–52.
Urmson, J. O. (1988), *Aristotle's Ethics* (Oxford: Blackwell).

Van Inwagen, P. (1983), *An Essay on Free Will* (Oxford: Clarendon Press).
Von Wright, G. H. (1982), *Wittgenstein* (Oxford: Blackwell).

Wallace, G. (1987), 'Art forgeries and inherent value', *British Journal of Aesthetics*, vol. 27, no. 4 (Autumn), pp. 358–62.
Walton, K. (1978), 'Categories of art' in J. Margolis (ed.), *Philosophy Looks at the Arts (Second Edition)* (Philadelphia: Temple University Press), pp. 88–114.
Waterman, R. (1962), 'The role of dance in human society', in B. J. Wooten (ed.), *Focus on Dance II: an Inter-disciplinary Search for Meaning in Movement* (Washington, DC: American Association for Health, Physical Education and Recreation), pp. 47–55.
Weigel, J. (1965), *Lawrence Durrell* (New York: Twayne Publishers).
Wiggins, D. (1980), *Sameness and Substance* (Oxford: Blackwell).
Wiggins, D. (1987), *Needs, Values, Truth* (Oxford: Blackwell).
Wiggins, D. (1990), 'Moral cognitivism, moral relativism and motivating beliefs', *Proceedings of the Aristotelian Society 1990–91*, pp. 61–87.
Wilkerson, T. E. (1974), *Minds, Brains and People* (Oxford: Clarendon Press).
Williams, D. (1976/7), 'Review of Lange *The Nature of Dance*', *Dance Research Journal*, vol. 8, no. 1, pp. 42–4.
Williams, R. (1965), *The Long Revolution* (London: Chatto & Windus).
Williams, R. (1974), *Television: Technology and Cultural Form* (London: Fontana).
Williams, R. (1980), *Problems in Materialism and Culture* (London: Verso/New Left Books).
Wimsatt, W. K. and Beardsley, M. (1978), 'The intentional fallacy', in J. Margolis (ed.), *Philosophy Looks at the Arts (Second Edition)* (Philadelphia: Temple University Press), pp. 293–306.
Winch, P. (1958), *The Idea of a Social Science* (London: Routledge & Kegan Paul).
Winch, P. (1973), *Ethics and Action* (London: Routledge & Kegan Paul).
Winch, P. (1987), *Trying to Make Sense* (Oxford: Blackwell).
Winterbourne, A. T. (1981), 'Objectivity in science and aesthetics', *British Journal of Aesthetics*, vol. 21, no. 3 (Summer), pp. 253–60.
Wisdom, J. (1953), *Philosophy and Psycho-Analysis* (Oxford: Blackwell).
Wisdom, J. (1965), *Paradox and Discovery* (Oxford: Blackwell).
Wittgenstein, L. (1953), *Philosophical Investigations* (trans. G. E. M. Anscombe) (Oxford: Blackwell).
Wittgenstein, L. (1958), *The Blue and Brown Books* (Oxford: Blackwell).
Wittgenstein, L. (1969), *On Certainty* (trans. D. Paul and G. E. M. Anscombe) (Oxford: Blackwell).
Wittgenstein, L. (1974), *Philosophical Grammar* (trans. A. Kenny) (Oxford: Blackwell).
Wittgenstein, L. (1975), *Lectures on the Foundations of Mathematics 1939* (Cora Diamond ed.) (Hassocks: Harvester).
Wolff, J. (1983), *Aesthetics and the Sociology of Art* (London: George Allen & Unwin).
Wollheim, R. (1971), 'Philosophy and the arts', in B. Magee (ed.), *Modern British Philosophy*, (London: Secker & Warburg), pp. 178–90.
Wollheim, R. (1973), *On Art and the Mind* (London: Allen Lane).
Wollheim, R. (1978), 'Are the criteria of identity that hold for a work of art in the different arts aesthetically relevant?', *Ratio*, vol. 20, no. 1 (June) pp. 29–48.

Wollheim, R. (1979), 'Pictorial style: two views', in B. Lang (ed.), *The Concept of Style* (Philadelphia: University of Pennsylvania Press), pp. 128–45.

Wollheim, R. (1980a), *Art and Its Objects* (Second Edition) (Cambridge: Cambridge University Press).

Wollheim, R. (1980b), 'The institutional theory of art', in Wollheim (1980a), pp. 157–66.

Wollheim, R. (1980c), 'Criticism as retrieval', in Wollheim (1980a), pp. 185–204.

Wollheim, R. (1980d), 'Seeing-as, seeing-in and pictorial representation', in Wollheim (1980a), pp. 205–26.

Wollheim, R. (1983), 'Art, interpretation and perception', *Kant oder Hegel: Proceedings of the Stuttgart Conference 1982*, (Stuttgart: Kleet-Cotta), pp. 549–59.

Wollheim, R. (1984), *The Thread of Life* (Cambridge: Cambridge University Press).

Wollheim, R. (1985), 'On the question: "why painting is an art"', in *Aesthetics (Proceedings of the 8th International Wittgenstein Symposium, 1983) Part One* (Vienna: Holder-Pichler-Temsky), pp. 101–6.

Wollheim, R. (1986), 'Imagination and pictorial understanding', *Proceedings of the Aristotelian Society Supplementary*, vol. 40, pp. 45–60.

Wollheim, R. (1987), *Painting as an Art* (London: Thames & Hudson).

Woltersdorff, N. (1981), *Works and Worlds of Art* (Oxford: Clarendon Press).

Yalden-Thomson, D. C. (1974), 'The Virginia Lectures', in R. Bambrough (ed.), *Wisdom: Twelve Essays* (Oxford: Blackwell), pp. 62–77.

√ Youngerman, S. (1974), 'Curt Sachs and his heritage: a critical review of *World History of the Dance* with a survey of recent studies that perpetuate his ideas', *CORD News*, vol. 6, pp. 6–19.

Ziff, P. (1981), 'About the appreciation of dance', in G. Fancher and G. Myers (eds), *Philosophical Essays on Dance* (New York: American Dance Festival), pp. 69–94.

Index

339

7798